THE BRAIN, BIOCHEMISTRY, AND BEHAVIOR

Arnold O. Beckman, Founder and Chairman of the Board,
Beckman Instruments, Inc.

THE BRAIN, BIOCHEMISTRY, AND BEHAVIOR

Proceedings of the Sixth Arnold O. Beckman
Conference in Clinical Chemistry

Edited by
Robert L. Habig

With a foreword by
H. Keith H. Brodie

Executive Editor
Virginia S. Marcum

The American Association for Clinical Chemistry
1725 K Street, NW
Washington, DC 20006

Previous Proceedings of Arnold O. Beckman Conferences in Clinical Chemistry, published by the American Association for Clinical Chemistry:

1, Clinician and Chemist: The Relation of the Laboratory to the Physician
2, The Clinical Biochemistry of Cancer
3, Aging—Its Chemistry
4, Human Nutrition: Clinical and Biochemical Aspects
5, Genetic Disease: Diagnosis and Treatment

Library of Congress Cataloging in Publication Data

Arnold O. Beckman Conference in Clinical Chemistry
  (6th : 1983 : Tarpon Springs, Fla.)
  The brain, biochemistry, and behavior.

  Bibliography: p.
  Includes index.
  1. Psychology, Pathological—Physiological aspects—
Congresses.   2. Neuropsychopharmacology—Congresses.
3. Brain chemistry—Congresses.   I. Habig, Robert L.,
1940–   .   II. American Association for Clinical
Chemistry.   III. Title.   [DNLM: 1. Brain—Drug effects—
Congresses.   2. Mental disorders—Drug therapy—
Congresses.   3. Behavior—Drug effects—Congresses.
W3 AR719 6th 1983b / WM 402 A761 1983b]

RC455.4.B5A75   1983   616.89'18   83–14057
ISBN 0–915274–22–1

Contents

Foreword

The Arnold O. Beckman Conferences have brought outstanding investigators together in the service of reviewing new knowledge generated at the interface of clinical chemistry and clinical medicine. The sixth Arnold O. Beckman Conference, like its predecessors, proved to be an outstanding success in framing the relevance of clinical chemistry to psychiatry. Indeed, over the past decade, no specialty of medicine has been more affected by developments in basic science and clinical chemistry than has psychiatry.

This volume, containing the papers presented at the sixth Arnold O. Beckman Conference, provides the reader a broad overview of the exciting developments in biochemical substrates of mental illness. The first several chapters highlight the prevalence of mental illness, noting that approximately 15% of our population suffer from some diagnosable mental disorder. The remainder of the volume focuses on specific clinical chemical determinations utilized by psychiatrists in their diagnosis and treatment of mental illness.

Specific laboratory tests such as the dexamethasone suppression test and the evaluation of the functioning of the thyroid axis, both used internationally in diagnosing depression, are described. Other clinical chemistry determinations are useful to the clinician in maximizing therapeutic efficacy related to the administration of drugs. Measurements of blood concentrations of tricyclic antidepressants, lithium, and some neuroleptic drugs are shown to be increasingly useful in patient management.

The role of clinical chemistry in helping neuropharmacologists understand the biological substrates of the disease process seen in mental illness is also described in this volume. Special chapters relate the neuropeptides, and dopamine- and other catecholamine-receptors in human brain, to specific disorders of affect and cognition.

vii

One cannot help but conclude after a thorough reading of this volume that within the past five years, a major role for clinical chemistry has emerged in the diagnosis and treatment of mental illness. Further, this role will be enhanced as new knowledge is generated concerning the biological abnormalities associated with mental illness and in the monitoring of pharmacotherapies used by the psychiatrist. To peruse the chapters of this volume is to explore the exciting generation of new knowledge concerning the scientific underpinnings of clinical psychiatry today.

H. Keith H. Brodie, M.D.

James B. Duke Professor of Psychiatry and Law
Chancellor, Duke University

Preface

This volume contains the proceedings of the Sixth Arnold O. Beckman Conference in Clinical Chemistry, held at the Innisbrook Conference Center, Tarpon Springs, Florida, in January, 1983. Arnold O. Beckman Conferences are sponsored by the American Association for Clinical Chemistry, and are generously supported by a personal yearly gift from Dr. Beckman, who is founder and Chairman of the Board of Beckman Instruments Company. Designed to bring together clinical laboratory scientists and physicians to discuss items of mutual interest in a particular field of clinical medicine, the conferences are intended to present the most current information available in a field of mutual interest to clinicians and clinical laboratories.

One of the significant features of a limited registration conference is that all of the attendees and speakers regularly attend all of the scientific sessions. For the attendees, hearing experts in the selected area present their most recent information is perhaps the major reason for attending the conference. However, the sometimes vigorous interaction among the speakers during the question-and-answer sessions can provide some of the most memorable moments. For that reason, the question-and-answer sessions that followed each group of speakers are also published as part of these proceedings.

The topic "The Brain, Biochemistry, and Behavior" was chosen as a reflection of the Program Committee's goal to assemble clinicians, basic scientists, and clinical laboratorians to discuss the effects that advances in each of these areas have upon each other. Attendees at the Conference were treated to three days of excellent presentations, stimulating question-and-answer sessions, and the ever-present informal, unstructured interaction that occurs outside of the lecture hall. The Conference, and thus this book, was organized in a number of sessions that the Program Committee felt would lead the attendee and thus the reader through the subjects in an appropriate fashion. The initial session was an overview of the effect of mental illness on society. Subsequent sessions dealt with endocrine function, current drug therapy, and receptor studies. Speakers in the final session discussed the interface between the laboratory and the clinician.

The credit for the success of such a conference must go to the Program Committee—Paul Orsulak, Mark Linnoila, and Keith Brodie—for their considerable efforts. All I had to do as Chairman was get them together and take notes. The assistance of Drs. Orsulak and Linnoila in enlisting many of the excellent speakers for the program is especially appreciated. The very professional assistance from the AACC national office staff must be recognized, especially the early help from Ms. Michele Tuttle and later the assistance of Ms. Deborah Woodcock.

I am grateful to Duke University for the time and encouragement for the planning of the Conference and the editing of these proceedings. Special notes of gratitude go to Ms. Brenda Howell and Ms. Deborah Brann for their many hours of secretarial assistance throughout the preparations for the Conference, typing the abstracts, and editing the manuscripts.

The Association continues to appreciate the generous support of Dr. Beckman for this Conference series. His personal interest and his attendance at the Conference are an inspiration to everyone. The Conference and these proceedings will, with his help, have a positive effect on laboratory medicine and on health care in general.

Robert L. Habig

Conference Participants

(1, speaker; 2, co-author; 3, session moderator)

Bernard Carroll, M.D.[1]
Chairman, Dept. of Psychiatry
University of Michigan
Ann Arbor, MI 48109

Jonathan O. Cole, M.D.[1,2]
Chief, Psychopharmacology Program
McLean Hospital
Belmont, MA 02146

Ian Creese, Ph.D.[1]
Dept. of Neurosciences
School of Medicine
University of California at San Diego
La Jolla, CA 92093

Ronald R. Fieve, M.D.[1]
Dept. of Clinical Psychiatry
Columbia College of Physicians and Surgeons
Medical Director, Foundation for Depression and
   Manic Depression, Inc.
Chief, Psychiatric Research, and
Head, Dept. of Lithium Studies
New York State Psychiatric Institute
New York, NY 10032

Robert L. Habig, Ph.D.[3]
Associate Director
Duke Hospital Laboratories
Durham, NC 27710

Anders Hedberg, Ph.D.[2]
Dept. of Pharmacology
University of Pennsylvania Medical School
Philadelphia, PA 19104

Peter Jatlow, M.D.[1]
Dept. of Laboratory Medicine
Yale University School of Medicine
New Haven, CT 06510

Harvey Karten, M.D.[1]
Depts. of Psychiatry, Neurobiology, and Anatomy
SUNY-Stony Brook
Stony Brook, NY 11790

Donald F. Klein, M.D.[1]
Research Director
New York State Psychiatric Institute
New York, NY 10032·

Gerald L. Klerman, M.D.[1]
Director, Psychiatric Epidemiology
Harvard Medical School and School of Public Health
and Psychiatry Service
Massachusetts General Hospital
Boston, MA 02114

Perry B. Molinoff, M.D.[1]
Dept. of Pharmacology
University of Pennsylvania
Philadelphia, PA 19104

Richard T. O'Kell, M.D.[3]
St. Luke's Hospital
Kansas City, MO 64111

Paul J. Orsulak, Ph.D.[2,3]
Dept. of Psychiatry and Pathology
Southwestern Medical School
Dallas, TX 75216

William Potter, M.D.[1]
National Institute of Mental Health
Bethesda, MD 20205

Arthur J. Prange, Jr., M.D.[1]
Dept. of Psychiatry
University of North Carolina
Chapel Hill, NC 27514

Fredric M. Quitkin, M.D.[2]
Dept. of Psychiatry
College of Physicians and Surgeons
Columbia University
New York, NY 10032

Alan Rosenbaum, M.D.[1,2]
Henry Ford Hospital
Detroit, MI 48202

Alan F. Schatzberg, M.D.[1,2]
Dept. of Psychiatry
Harvard Medical School at McLean Hospital
Belmont, MA 02146

Joseph J. Schildkraut, M.D.[1]
Dept. of Psychiatry
Harvard Medical School
Director, Neuropsychopharmacology Lab.
Massachusetts Mental Health Center
Director, Psychiatric Chem. Lab.
New England Deaconess Hospital
Boston, MA 02115

Attendees

Jagan N. Ahuja
SmithKline Instruments
Sunnyvale, CA 94086

Renato D. Alarcon
Univ. Hosp.
Birmingham, AL 35294

William L. Allan
Houston, TX 77024

Seymour W. Applebaum
Kew Gardens, NY 11415

Peter Banks
Clinical Chemistry News
Washington, DC 20006

Annette C. Barnes
Bartow, FL 33830

Faouzia Barouche
Dept. of Lithium Studies
New York State Psychiatric
    Institute
New York, NY 10032

John R. Bateman
Austin State Hosp.
Austin, TX 78751

Max Berenbom
Menorah Medical Center
Kansas City, MO 64110

Harriet Berg
St. Paul-Ramsey Medical Center
St. Paul, MN 55101

Jeff Berlant
Novato, CA 94948

Edward W. Bermes, Jr.
Loyola Univ. Medical Center
Maywood, IL 60546

Paige K. Besch
Department of Ob/Gyn
Baylor College of Medicine
Houston, TX 77030

David H. Beyer
Beaumont, TX 77701

Bernard Billon
Div. Clinical Biochemistry
Centre Hosp. Univ. de Sherbrooke
Sherbrooke, Quebec, Canada
J1H5N4

Bruce Bower
Psychiatric News
Washington, DC 20005

Lemuel J. Bowie
Div. Clinical Biochemistry
Evanston Hosp.
Evanston, IL 60201

Robert B. Brainard
Raleigh, NC 27612

Stephen S. Brockway
Pensacola, FL 32504

Lester Burke
Homewood, IL 60430

Carl A. Burtis
Oak Ridge National Lab.
Oak Ridge, TN 37830

Robert W. Bush
Bartholomew County Hosp.
Columbus, IN 47201

Roger R. Calam
St. John Hosp., Pathology
Detroit, MI 48236

Mary Cantonis
Abbott Laboratories
Diagnostics Div.
North Chicago, IL 60064

Kate Casano
International Medical News
  Group
Rockville, MD 20852

Andrew William Caswell
Psychiatric Diagnostic
  Laboratories of America, Inc.
Summit, NJ 07901

John C. Cate, IV
Kingsport, TN 37660

Leslie Champlin
APA Reports
Washington, DC 20005

Albert L. Chasson
Rex Hosp.
Raleigh, NC 27607

Mary H. Cheng
Children's Hosp. of Los Angeles
Clinical Lab.
Los Angeles, CA 90027

Anna Ciulla
Newark, DE 19711

Richard K. Cole
St. Petersburg, FL 33701

Rex B. Conn
Emory Univ. Hosp. Labs.
Atlanta, GA 30322

Victoria S. Conn
Emory Univ. Hosp. Clinical Labs.
Atlanta, GA 30322

James A. Demetriou
Bio-Science Laboratories
Van Nuys, CA 91405

Virginia P. Cook
Clinical Chemistry
Wesley Medical Center
Wichita, KS 67214

Gretchen DeWitt
Sunrise Assoc.
Williamsville, NY 14221

Debra C. DiGiacomandrea
Lawrence Allen Cosimano
SmithKline Clinical Lab.
Miami, FL 33183

St. Petersburg *Evening Independent*
St. Petersburg, FL 33731

Juliet C. Diller
Steven Cothers
Syva Co.
Palo Alto, CA 94301

New York, NY 10280

James C. Dohnal
Evanston Hosp.
Deborah M. Crean
Plantation, FL 33317

Dept. of Pathology
Evanston, IL 60201

Catherine P. Crowl
Palo Alto, CA 94303

Kay Dowgun
Serial Publications
W.B. Saunders Co.
Philadelphia, PA 19105

Jane A. Cyran
Towaco, NJ 07082

Jerry Dowlny
Wauwatosa, WI 53226

Earl Damude
Canadian Clinical Lab.
Toronto, Ontario, Canada
M5W1A7

Susan H. Dugan
American Medical Labs., Inc.
Fairfax, VA 22030

David C. De Jong
St. Francis Hosp. of Wichita, Inc.
Wichita, KS 67201

Neil H. Edison
North Miami, FL 33181

xvi

Lacy Edmundson
Dallas, TX 75230

Claire B. Elliott
Baptist Medical Center
Birmingham, AL 35213

Howard C. Elliott
Baptist Medical Center
Birmingham, AL 35213

Joseph R. Elliott
St. Luke's Hosp.
Dept. of Pathology
Kansas City, MO 64111

Victor S. Fang
The Univ. of Chicago
Chicago, IL 60637

Barbara Fitzgerald
Norton Psychiatric
Louisville, KY 40232

Martin Fleisher
Memorial Sloan-Kettering
New York, NY 10021

Michael W. Fowler
Oklahoma Christian College
Edmond, OK 73034

Albert D. Fraser
Victoria General Hosp.
Div. Clinical Chemistry
Halifax, Nova Scotia
Canada B3H1V8

Helen Free
Elkhart, IN 46514

Al Free
Elkhart, IN 46514

Herbert A. Fritsche
M.D. Anderson Hosp.
Dept. of Lab. Medicine
Houston, TX 77030

Nancy Gaby
Bowman Gray School of Medicine
Winston-Salem, NC 27103

Arun K. Garg
Royal Columbian Hosp.
New Westminster, B.C.
Canada V3L3W7

Patricia E. Garrett
Lahey Clinic Medical Center
Dept. of Lab. Medicine
Burlington, MA 01805

Barbara Gau
Burroughs Wellcome Co.
Research Triangle Park, NC 27709

Fred George
Enterprise, AL 36330

Benjamin Gerson
N. E. Deaconess Hosp.
Lab. of Pathology
Boston, MA 02215

Jack G. Gilbey
Porter-Starke Services, Inc.
Valparaiso, IN 46383

Bill Haden
Beckman Instruments, Inc.
Carlsbad, CA 92008

Morris Gold
Woodbury, NY 11797

Duane Q. Hagen
St. Louis, MO 63141

Janice Goldman
Sinai Hosp. of Detroit
Dept. of Lab. Medicine
Detroit, MI 48235

Ellen Hale
USA Today
Washington, DC 20006

Norris Hansell
Champaign, IL 61820

Marina H. Gonzalez
Miami, FL 33184

Susana Alicia Hassan
Washington, DC 20036

Harold J. Grady
Baptist Hosp.
Kansas City, MO 64131

Alan H. Hayden
Pittsford, NY 14534

Stanley Grand
Westbury, NY 11590

Gary Hemphill
Metropolitan Medical Center
Dept. of Pathology
Minneapolis, MN 55404

Paul J. Green
Pathology Dept.
Thomas Jefferson Univ.
Philadelphia, PA 19107

Noel Hermele
Springfield, MA 01103

R. N. Gupta
St. Joseph's Hosp.
Dept. of Lab. Medicine
Hamilton, Ontario
Canada L8N1Y4

Luis A. Herrero
Clearwater Psychiatric Assoc.
Clearwater, FL 33516

Penny C. Hickman
Beaumont Neurological Center
Beaumont, TX 77701

Jocelyn M. Hicks
Children's Hosp. National
    Medical Center
Clinical Lab.
Washington, DC 20010

Tom Hill
Medical Post
Lighthouse Point, FL 33064

Earle W. Holmes
Loyola Univ. Med. Center
Maywood, IL 60153

Delsie Horne
Mercy Hosp.
Portsmouth, OH 45662

Jonathan Horowitz
Waban, MA 02168

Myer G. Horowitz
Jewish Hosp.
Cincinnati, OH 45229

Hsiang-Yun Hu
Abbott Laboratories
North Chicago, IL 60064

Richard W. Hubbard
Loma Linda Univ. Medical Center
Redlands, CA 92373

Richard M. Iammarino
West Virginia Univ. Hosp.
Clinical Lab.
Morgantown, WV 26506

V. T. Innanen
Div. of Clinical Chemistry
Women's College Hosp.
Toronto, Ontario, Canada
MSS1B2

Gloria Jean Jackson
Abbott Laboratories
Mental Health Diagnostics
North Chicago, IL 60064

Anna P. Jaklitsch
Syva Co.
Palo Alto, CA 94303

Albert W. Jekelis
UMDNJ-Rutgers Community
    Mental Health Center
Clinical Lab.
Piscataway, NJ 08854

George F. Johnson
Dept. of Pathology
Univ. of Iowa
Iowa City, IA 52242

Peter Johnson
Mayo Clinic
Rochester, MN 55901

Francois B. Jolicoeur
Univ. Medical School
Dept. of Psychiatry
Sherbrooke, Quebec, Canada
J1H5N4

Tina Joramo
Great Falls, MT 59403

Stephen E. Kahn
Loyola Univ. Medical Center
Clinical Chemistry
Maywood, IL 60153

Gordon F. Kapke
Orlando Regional Medical Center
Orlando, FL 32806

Raymond E. Karcher
William Beaumont Hosp.
Royal Oak, MI 48072

Betty Karron
Allentown, PA 18103–3091

Joan Keenan
Medical Center Hosp.
Largo, FL 33540

Joseph H. Keffer
St. Francis Hosp.
Miami Beach, FL 33141

John T. Kelly
Dept. of Family Practice
Minneapolis, MN 55455

Fraser Kent
Miami Magazine
Miami, FL 33129

David W. Kinniburgh
Univ. of Utah Medical Center
Clinical Chemistry Lab.
Salt Lake City, UT 84132

J. Y. Kiyasu
Roosevelt Hosp.
Pathology Dept.
New York, NY 10019

Harold Klein
Brooklyn, NY 11217

David D. Koch
Middleton, WI 53562

Mary Ann Langrall
Clifton, NJ 07013

Harrison M. Langrall
Clifton, NJ 07013

Hal G. Lankford
Omaha, NB 68112

Dennis E. Leavelle
Mayo Clinic
Rochester, MN 55905

Samuel Levin
Wilmette, IL 60091

Arnold L. Lieber
Miami, FL 33137

Cheng I. Lin
Syva Co.
Palo Alto, CA 94303–0847

James S. Lo
St. Catharines
Ontario, Canada 12M6L4

Paula M. S. Lopez
Williamsville, NY 14221

Charles A. Loshon
Hartford Hosp.
Clinical Chemistry Lab.
Hartford, CT 06115

P. A. Luhan
East Lyme, CT 06333

Cathy M. Macek
JAMA Medical News
Durham, NC 27707

Virginia S. Marcum
Clinical Chemistry
Winston Salem, NC 27103

D. M. Martin
Psychiatric Diagnostic Labs. of
  America, Inc.
Summit, NJ 07980

Howard L. Masco
New Port Richey, FL 33552

Charles P. Maurizi
Medical Center of Central Georgia
Macon, GA 31208

Mohammed Mazharuddin
Wayne County General Hosp.
Research Dept.
Wayne, MI 48184

Thomas McClane
Lakeland, FL 33803

Robert C. McComb
Hartford Hosp.
Hartford, CT 06115

Samuel Meites
Childrens Hosp.
Clinical Chemistry Lab.
Columbus, OH 43205

Robert S. Melville
Garrett Park, MD 20766

Brenda Michniewig
Clearwater, FL 33515

Fernando J. Milanes
Miami, FL 33173

Janice L. Miller
West Palm Beach, FL 33409

Diane V. Mohr
Waltham, MA 02154

Thomas P. Moyer
Dept. of Lab. Medicine
Mayo Clinic
Rochester, MN 55901

A. A. Mylroie
Chicago State Univ.
Chicago, IL 60628

John D. Nagle
International Clinical Labs.
  Northeast
Randolph, MA 02368

Karen L. Nickel
Bio-Science Laboratories
Van Nuys, CA 91405

Eileen Nickoloff
Squibb Institute for Medical
  Research
Princeton, NJ 08540

Stephen Noel
New Port Richey, FL 33552

Carroll Oakley
New Paltz, NY 12561

Raphael J. Osheroff
Alexandria, VA 22304

David G. Ostrow
Biologist Psychiatry Program
VA Lakeside Medical Center
Chicago, IL 60611

Nicholas M. Papadopoulos
Clinical Chemistry, NIH
Bethesda, MD 20817

Mark Petricevic
Fairview General Hosp.
Scott Research Lab.
Cleveland, OH 44111

William T. Pope
Dept. of Pathology
Medical Center of Central Georgia
Macon, GA 31208

Larry H. Porter
Burroughs Wellcome Co.
Research Triangle Park, NC 27709

William H. Porter
Dept. of Pathology
Univ. of Kentucky Medical Center
Lexington, KY 40536

Marcel Pouliot
Hospital du Sacrement
Clinical Chemistry Dept.
Quebec City, Quebec
Canada G1S4L8

Pauline Powers
Univ. Medical Service Assoc., Inc.
College of Medicine
Dept. of Psychiatry
Tampa, FL 33612

Vidmantas A. Raisys
Harborview Medical Center
Dept. of Lab. Medicine
Seattle, WA 98104

C. Ray Ratliff
Bio Analytics
Palm City, FL 33490

Lester Rauer
Philadelphia, PA 19124

Marilyn Rhuey Rautio
Boca Raton Community Hosp.
Boca Raton, FL 33432

Nadja N. Rehak
Bethesda, MD 20817

Donald W. Renn
FMC Corporation
Rockland, MA 94841

Randall S. Riggs
Providence Medical Center
Clinical Lab.
Seattle, WA 98124

Ruick Rolland
Atlanta, GA 30307

Robert B. Rombauer
Becton Dickinson & Co.
Paramus, NJ 07652

Burton J. Rosenberg
Burroughs Wellcome Co.
The Wellcome Research Lab.
Research Triangle Park, NC 27709

Stephen O. Rushing
Webster, TX 77598

Jean P. Safdy
Ames Div., Miles Labs.
Elkhart, IN 45615

James C. Sams
Scottsville, VA 24590

Michael B. Schiffman
Becton Dickinson & Co.
Paramus, NJ 07652

Joyce A. Schoenheimer
Radix Organization, Inc.
New York, NY 10021

Michael Sheehan
Good Samaritan Hosp.
Portland, OR 97210

Susan Shellabarger
Mead CompuChem
Research Triangle Park, NC 27709

Charlotte E. Shideler
Wesley Medical Center
Dept. of Lab. Medicine
Wichita, KS 67214

Clarence Shub
Mayo Clinic
Rochester, MN 55905

Antonina Sidorowicz
Northampton, MA 01060

Tillman L. Simmons
North Charlston, SC 29405

Albert C. Smith
VA Medical Center, Lab. Service
Gainesville, FL 32602

Catherine Smith
Abbott Laboratories
North Chicago, IL 60064

S. J. Soldin
Hosp. for Sick Children
Dept. of Biochemistry
Toronto, Ontario, Canada
M5G1X8

Elizabeth B. Solow
Indiana Univ. Medical Center
Indianapolis, IN 46223

Adrian Sondheimer
New York, NY 10023

Debra Kaplan Sondheimer
New York, NY 10023

Donald K. Soules
Oakwood Hosp. Lab.
Dearborn, MI 48124

A. Michael Spiekerman
Scott and White Hosp. and Clinic
Temple, TX 76508

Nena Spirit
Livingston, NJ 07039

Linda Stanley
Diagnostic Medicine
Oradell, NJ 07649

Loren Steffen
St. Peter Hosp.
Olympia, WA 98506

Jo Sterling
Winter Haven Hosp.
Clinical Lab.
Winter Haven, FL 33880

James C. Sternberg
Beckman Instruments, Inc.
Healthcare Group Research
Brea, CA 92621

Ed Valentine
Abbott Laboratories
North Chicago, IL 60064

John Vasiliades
Dept. of Pathology
Creighton Univ.
Omaha, NB 68131

Richard F. Straw
Eskaton-American River Hosp.
Carmichael, CA 95608

Lilla S. Sun
Beckman Instruments
Brea, CA 92621

Z. H. Verjee
Hosp. for Sick Children
Dept. of Biochemistry
Toronto, Ontario, Canada
M5G1X8

Jerry J. Thoma
Southbend Medical Foundation
Dept. of Toxicology
Southbend, IN 46601

Bill Vorkink
Fairbanks Memorial Hosp.
Fairbanks, AK 99701

Stephan G. Thompson
Ames Div., Miles Labs.
Elkhart, IN 46515

Alexander S. Vujan
Venice, FL 33595

Mary K. Walker
Edward Hines Jr. VA Hosp.
Hines, IL 60141

Lance Trexler
Medical Psychology
Indianapolis, IN 46219

Marc Walter
Waterbury Hosp.
Waterbury, CT 06721

Diana S. Trundle
Morton F. Plant Hosp. Lab.
Clearwater, FL 32317

Robert J. Walton
Oakwood Hosp.
Pathology Dept.
Dearborn, MI 48124

Richard T. Tulley
Earl K. Long Memorial Hosp.
Baton Rouge, LA 70815

Judy M. Walton
Oakwood Hosp.
Chemical Lab.
Dearborn, MI 48124

John C. Waraska
Waters Associates, Inc.
Milford, MA 01757

Donald L. Warkentin
Overlook Hosp.
Ambler, PA 19002

Myron M. Warshaw
Northwest Pathologist, Ltd.
Arlington Heights, IL 60005

John M. Waud
Port Huron Hosp.
Port Huron, MI 48060

Emma Weinel
Medical Technology
Milwaukee Psychiatric Hosp.
Wauwatosa, WI 53213

Richard H. Weisler
Raleigh, NC 27609

David J. Wells
Loyola Univ. Medical Center
Maywood, IL 60153

Robert M. White
Charlotte, NC 28211

George H. Wien
Wien Laboratories, Inc.
Succasunna, NJ 07876

Franklin C. Wong
Dept. of Pathology
Chicago Medical School
Univ. of Health Science
North Chicago, IL 60064

Geoffrey Zeldes
E. R. Squibb & Sons, Inc.
Princeton, NJ 08540

Gary A. Zimmerman
Seattle Univ.
Seattle, WA 98122

Ben Zinser
Beckman Instruments, Inc.
Fullerton, CA 92634

THE BRAIN,
BIOCHEMISTRY,
AND BEHAVIOR

The Prevalence and Impact of Mental Illness on Society

Gerald L. Klerman

Mental illness is a major public health and social problem in the United States and other industrial and urban societies, approximately 15% of the U.S. population having a diagnosable mental disorder in any one year. Suicide and related problems of violent death and homicide are among the leading causes of death in this country, particularly for young men and especially members of minority groups—blacks, Hispanics, and native Americans. Use of tranquilizing drugs, particularly the anti-anxiety drugs related to the benzodiazepines, involves approximately 10 to 15% of the adult population.

Of total health-care costs—more than $240 billion in 1982 (almost 10% of the gross national product)—expenses for mental health and related problems of alcoholism and drug abuse account for about 15% of dollar expenditures. Expenses for operating mental health facilities, particularly mental hospitals and community mental health centers, are among the major expenditures of state governments. In the majority of states, the largest group of public service employees is the workers in mental health facilities. These quantitative indices are paralleled by widespread public interest in topics of personality, psychotherapy, depression, and mental illness, as evidenced in the mass communications media.

Here I will review recently available knowledge about the scope of mental illness and the patterns of utilization of mental health facilities, and will assess the impact of mental illness on American society.

Scope of the Problem

In 1955, approximately 600 000 individuals were hospitalized in public mental hospitals, representing a 10% increase per decade

3

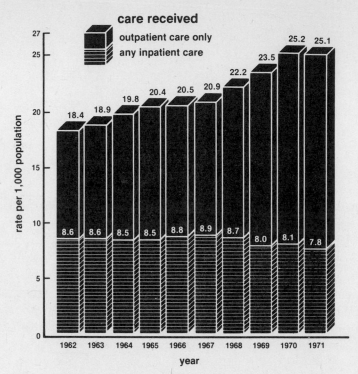

Fig. 1. Annual rate per 1000 population of persons receiving psychiatric services by locus of care

(since 1900) in the number of resident patients in public hospitals. This growth became a matter of public concern in the early 1950s, so much so that in 1955 the U.S. Congress created a Joint Commission on Mental Health and Mental Illness to assess the situation. Alarm was expressed that if the rate of increase in hospitalization evident in the 1940s and the early 1950s were to continue, by 1980 one million persons would reside in public mental hospitals. The cost of constructing facilities in which to house them would have been $2 billion (in 1950 dollars), in addition to the monies required for staffing, maintenance, and treatment.

As is well known, the situation changed dramatically in 1955 and there has been a steady decline in the mental health hospital census (Figure 1). The focus of attention shifted from the public mental hospital to other types of facilities for treatment of the mentally ill, mainly due to expansion of outpatient usage of mental health services (Figure 2). Between 1955 and 1980, there has

4

subjects in an appropriate fashion. The initial session was an over-view of the effect of mental illness on society. Subsequent sessions dealt with endocrine function, current drug therapy, and receptor studies. Speakers in the final session discussed the interface be-tween the laboratory and the clinician.

The credit for the success of such a conference must go to the Program Committee—Paul Orsulak, Mark Linnoila, and Keith Brodie—for their considerable efforts. All I had to do as Chairman was get them together and take notes. The assistance of Drs. Orsulak and Linnoila in enlisting many of the excellent speakers for the program is especially appreciated. The very professional assistance from the AACC national office staff must be recognized, especially the early help from Ms. Michele Tuttle and later the assistance of Ms. Deborah Woodcock.

I am grateful to Duke University for the time and encourage-ment for the planning of the Conference and the editing of these proceedings. Special notes of gratitude go to Ms. Brenda Howell and Ms. Deborah Brann for their many hours of secretarial assis-tance throughout the preparations for the Conference, typing the abstracts, and editing the manuscripts.

The Association continues to appreciate the generous support of Dr. Beckman for this Conference series. His personal interest and his attendance at the Conference are an inspiration to every-one. The Conference and these proceedings will, with his help, have a positive effect on laboratory medicine and on health care in general.

Robert L. Habig

Preface

This volume contains the proceedings of the Sixth Arnold O. Beckman Conference in Clinical Chemistry, held at the Innisbrook Conference Center, Tarpon Springs, Florida, in January, 1983. Arnold O. Beckman Conferences are sponsored by the American Association for Clinical Chemistry, and are generously supported by a personal yearly gift from Dr. Beckman, who is founder and Chairman of the Board of Beckman Instruments Company. Designed to bring together clinical laboratory scientists and physicians to discuss items of mutual interest in a particular field of clinical medicine, the conferences are intended to present the most current information available in a field of mutual interest to clinicians and clinical laboratories.

One of the significant features of a limited registration conference is that all of the attendees and speakers regularly attend all of the scientific sessions. For the attendees, hearing experts in the selected area present their most recent information is perhaps the major reason for attending the conference. However, the sometimes vigorous interaction among the speakers during the question-and-answer sessions can provide some of the most memorable moments. For that reason, the question-and-answer sessions that followed each group of speakers are also published as part of these proceedings.

The topic "The Brain, Biochemistry, and Behavior" was chosen as a reflection of the Program Committee's goal to assemble clinicians, basic scientists, and clinical laboratorians to discuss the effects that advances in each of these areas have upon each other. Attendees at the Conference were treated to three days of excellent presentations, stimulating question-and-answer sessions, and the ever-present informal, unstructured interaction that occurs outside of the lecture hall. The Conference, and thus this book, was organized in a number of sessions that the Program Committee felt would lead the attendee and thus the reader through the

Conference Participants

(1, speaker; 2, co-author; 3, session moderator)

Bernard Carroll, M.D.[1]
Chairman, Dept. of Psychiatry
University of Michigan
Ann Arbor, MI 48109

Jonathan O. Cole, M.D.[1,2]
Chief, Psychopharmacology Program
McLean Hospital
Belmont, MA 02146

Ian Creese, Ph.D.[1]
Dept. of Neurosciences
School of Medicine
University of California at San Diego
La Jolla, CA 92093

Ronald R. Fieve, M.D.[1]
Dept. of Clinical Psychiatry
Columbia College of Physicians and Surgeons
Medical Director, Foundation for Depression and
    Manic Depression, Inc.
Chief, Psychiatric Research, and
Head, Dept. of Lithium Studies
New York State Psychiatric Institute
New York, NY 10032

Robert L. Habig, Ph.D.[3]
Associate Director
Duke Hospital Laboratories
Durham, NC 27710

Anders Hedberg, Ph.D.[2]
Dept. of Pharmacology
University of Pennsylvania Medical School
Philadelphia, PA 19104

Peter Jatlow, M.D.[1]
Dept. of Laboratory Medicine
Yale University School of Medicine
New Haven, CT 06510

Harvey Karten, M.D.[1]
Depts. of Psychiatry, Neurobiology, and Anatomy
SUNY-Stony Brook
Stony Brook, NY 11790

Donald F. Klein, M.D.[1]
Research Director
New York State Psychiatric Institute
New York, NY 10032

Gerald L. Klerman, M.D.[1]
Director, Psychiatric Epidemiology
Harvard Medical School and School of Public Health
and Psychiatry Service
Massachusetts General Hospital
Boston, MA 02114

Perry B. Molinoff, M.D.[1]
Dept. of Pharmacology
University of Pennsylvania
Philadelphia, PA 19104

Richard T. O'Kell, M.D.[3]
St. Luke's Hospital
Kansas City, MO 64111

Paul J. Orsulak, Ph.D.[2,3]
Dept. of Psychiatry and Pathology
Southwestern Medical School
Dallas, TX 75216

William Potter, M.D.[1]
National Institute of Mental Health
Bethesda, MD 20205

Arthur J. Prange, Jr., M.D.[1]
Dept. of Psychiatry
University of North Carolina
Chapel Hill, NC 27514

Fredric M. Quitkin, M.D.[2]
Dept. of Psychiatry
College of Physicians and Surgeons
Columbia University
New York, NY 10032

Alan Rosenbaum, M.D.[1,2]
Henry Ford Hospital
Detroit, MI 48202

Alan F. Schatzberg, M.D.[1,2]
Dept. of Psychiatry
Harvard Medical School at McLean Hospital
Belmont, MA 02146

Joseph J. Schildkraut, M.D.[1]
Dept. of Psychiatry
Harvard Medical School
Director, Neuropsychopharmacology Lab.
Massachusetts Mental Health Center
Director, Psychiatric Chem. Lab.
New England Deaconess Hospital
Boston, MA 02115

Attendees

Jagan N. Ahuja
SmithKline Instruments
Sunnyvale, CA 94086

Renato D. Alarcon
Univ. Hosp.
Birmingham, AL 35294

William L. Allan
Houston, TX 77024

Seymour W. Applebaum
Kew Gardens, NY 11415

Peter Banks
Clinical Chemistry News
Washington, DC 20006

Annette C. Barnes
Bartow, FL 33830

Faouzia Barouche
Dept. of Lithium Studies
New York State Psychiatric
  Institute
New York, NY 10032

John R. Bateman
Austin State Hosp.
Austin, TX 78751

Max Berenbom
Menorah Medical Center
Kansas City, MO 64110

Harriet Berg
St. Paul-Ramsey Medical Center
St. Paul, MN 55101

Jeff Berlant
Novato, CA 94948

Edward W. Bermes, Jr.
Loyola Univ. Medical Center
Maywood, IL 60546

Paige K. Besch
Department of Ob/Gyn
Baylor College of Medicine
Houston, TX 77030

David H. Beyer
Beaumont, TX 77701

Bernard Billon
Div. Clinical Biochemistry
Centre Hosp. Univ. de Sherbrooke
Sherbrooke, Quebec, Canada
J1H5N4

Bruce Bower
Psychiatric News
Washington, DC 20005

Lemuel J. Bowie
Div. Clinical Biochemistry
Evanston Hosp.
Evanston, IL 60201

Robert B. Brainard
Raleigh, NC 27612

Stephen S. Brockway
Pensacola, FL 32504

Lester Burke
Homewood, IL 60430

Carl A. Burtis
Oak Ridge National Lab.
Oak Ridge, TN 37830

Robert W. Bush
Bartholomew County Hosp.
Columbus, IN 47201

Roger R. Calam
St. John Hosp., Pathology
Detroit, MI 48236

Mary Cantonis
Abbott Laboratories
Diagnostics Div.
North Chicago, IL 60064

Kate Casano
International Medical News
   Group
Rockville, MD 20852

Andrew William Caswell
Psychiatric Diagnostic
   Laboratories of America, Inc.
Summit, NJ 07901

John C. Cate, IV
Kingsport, TN 37660

Leslie Champlin
APA Reports
Washington, DC 20005

Albert L. Chasson
Rex Hosp.
Raleigh, NC 27607

Mary H. Cheng
Children's Hosp. of Los Angeles
Clinical Lab.
Los Angeles, CA 90027

Anna Ciulla
Newark, DE 19711

Richard K. Cole
St. Petersburg, FL 33701

Rex B. Conn
Emory Univ. Hosp. Labs.
Atlanta, GA 30322

Victoria S. Conn
Emory Univ. Hosp. Clinical Labs.
Atlanta, GA 30322

James A. Demetriou
Bio-Science Laboratories
Van Nuys, CA 91405

Virginia P. Cook
Clinical Chemistry
Wesley Medical Center
Wichita, KS 67214

Gretchen DeWitt
Sunrise Assoc.
Williamsville, NY 14221

Debra C. DiGiacomandrea
St. Petersburg *Evening Independent*
St. Petersburg, FL 33731

Lawrence Allen Cosimano
SmithKline Clinical Lab.
Miami, FL 33183

Juliet C. Diller
New York, NY 10280

Steven Cothers
Syva Co.
Palo Alto, CA 94301

James C. Dohnal
Evanston Hosp.
Dept. of Pathology
Evanston, IL 60201

Deborah M. Crean
Plantation, FL 33317

Catherine P. Crowl
Palo Alto, CA 94303

Kay Dowgun
Serial Publications
W.B. Saunders Co.
Philadelphia, PA 19105

Jane A. Cyran
Towaco, NJ 07082

Jerry Dowlny
Wauwatosa, WI 53226

Earl Damude
Canadian Clinical Lab.
Toronto, Ontario, Canada
M5W1A7

Susan H. Dugan
American Medical Labs., Inc.
Fairfax, VA 22030

David C. De Jong
St. Francis Hosp. of Wichita, Inc.
Wichita, KS 67201

Neil H. Edison
North Miami, FL 33181

Lacy Edmundson
Dallas, TX 75230

Claire B. Elliott
Baptist Medical Center
Birmingham, AL 35213

Howard C. Elliott
Baptist Medical Center
Birmingham, AL 35213

Joseph R. Elliott
St. Luke's Hosp.
Dept. of Pathology
Kansas City, MO 64111

Victor S. Fang
The Univ. of Chicago
Chicago, IL 60637

Barbara Fitzgerald
Norton Psychiatric
Louisville, KY 40232

Martin Fleisher
Memorial Sloan-Kettering
New York, NY 10021

Michael W. Fowler
Oklahoma Christian College
Edmond, OK 73034

Albert D. Fraser
Victoria General Hosp.
Div. Clinical Chemistry
Halifax, Nova Scotia
Canada B3H1V8

Helen Free
Elkhart, IN 46514

Al Free
Elkhart, IN 46514

Herbert A. Fritsche
M.D. Anderson Hosp.
Dept. of Lab. Medicine
Houston, TX 77030

Nancy Gaby
Bowman Gray School of Medicine
Winston-Salem, NC 27103

Arun K. Garg
Royal Columbian Hosp.
New Westminster, B.C.
Canada V3L3W7

Patricia E. Garrett
Lahey Clinic Medical Center
Dept. of Lab. Medicine
Burlington, MA 01805

Barbara Gau
Burroughs Wellcome Co.
Research Triangle Park, NC 27709

Fred George
Enterprise, AL 36330

Benjamin Gerson
N. E. Deaconess Hosp.
Lab. of Pathology
Boston, MA 02215

Jack G. Gilbey
Porter-Starke Services, Inc.
Valparaiso, IN 46383

Bill Haden
Beckman Instruments, Inc.
Carlsbad, CA 92008

Morris Gold
Woodbury, NY 11797

Duane Q. Hagen
St. Louis, MO 63141

Janice Goldman
Sinai Hosp. of Detroit
Dept. of Lab. Medicine
Detroit, MI 48235

Ellen Hale
USA Today
Washington, DC 20006

Norris Hansell
Champaign, IL 61820

Marina H. Gonzalez
Miami, FL 33184

Susana Alicia Hassan
Washington, DC 20036

Harold J. Grady
Baptist Hosp.
Kansas City, MO 64131

Alan H. Hayden
Pittsford, NY 14534

Stanley Grand
Westbury, NY 11590

Gary Hemphill
Metropolitan Medical Center
Dept. of Pathology
Minneapolis, MN 55404

Paul J. Green
Pathology Dept.
Thomas Jefferson Univ.
Philadelphia, PA 19107

Noel Hermele
Springfield, MA 01103

R. N. Gupta
St. Joseph's Hosp.
Dept. of Lab. Medicine
Hamilton, Ontario
Canada L8N1Y4

Luis A. Herrero
Clearwater Psychiatric Assoc.
Clearwater, FL 33516

Penny C. Hickman
Beaumont Neurological Center
Beaumont, TX 77701

Jocelyn M. Hicks
Children's Hosp. National
    Medical Center
Clinical Lab.
Washington, DC 20010

Tom Hill
Medical Post
Lighthouse Point, FL 33064

Earle W. Holmes
Loyola Univ. Med. Center
Maywood, IL 60153

Delsie Horne
Mercy Hosp.
Portsmouth, OH 45662

Jonathan Horowitz
Waban, MA 02168

Myer G. Horowitz
Jewish Hosp.
Cincinnati, OH 45229

Hsiang-Yun Hu
Abbott Laboratories
North Chicago, IL 60064

Richard W. Hubbard
Loma Linda Univ. Medical Center
Redlands, CA 92373

Richard M. Iammarino
West Virginia Univ. Hosp.
Clinical Lab.
Morgantown, WV 26506

V. T. Innanen
Div. of Clinical Chemistry
Women's College Hosp.
Toronto, Ontario, Canada
MSS1B2

Gloria Jean Jackson
Abbott Laboratories
Mental Health Diagnostics
North Chicago, IL 60064

Anna P. Jaklitsch
Syva Co.
Palo Alto, CA 94303

Albert W. Jekelis
UMDNJ-Rutgers Community
    Mental Health Center
Clinical Lab.
Piscataway, NJ 08854

George F. Johnson
Dept. of Pathology
Univ. of Iowa
Iowa City, IA 52242

Peter Johnson
Mayo Clinic
Rochester, MN 55901

Francois B. Jolicoeur
Univ. Medical School
Dept. of Psychiatry
Sherbrooke, Quebec, Canada
J1H5N4

Tina Joramo
Great Falls, MT 59403

Stephen E. Kahn
Loyola Univ. Medical Center
Clinical Chemistry
Maywood, IL 60153

Gordon F. Kapke
Orlando Regional Medical Center
Orlando, FL 32806

Raymond E. Karcher
William Beaumont Hosp.
Royal Oak, MI 48072

Betty Karron
Allentown, PA 18103–3091

Joan Keenan
Medical Center Hosp.
Largo, FL 33540

Joseph H. Keffer
St. Francis Hosp.
Miami Beach, FL 33141

John T. Kelly
Dept. of Family Practice
Minneapolis, MN 55455

Fraser Kent
Miami Magazine
Miami, FL 33129

David W. Kinniburgh
Univ. of Utah Medical Center
Clinical Chemistry Lab.
Salt Lake City, UT 84132

J. Y. Kiyasu
Roosevelt Hosp.
Pathology Dept.
New York, NY 10019

Harold Klein
Brooklyn, NY 11217

David D. Koch
Middleton, WI 53562

Mary Ann Langrall
Clifton, NJ 07013

Harrison M. Langrall
Clifton, NJ 07013

Hal G. Lankford
Omaha, NB 68112

Dennis E. Leavelle
Mayo Clinic
Rochester, MN 55905

Samuel Levin
Wilmette, IL 60091

Arnold L. Lieber
Miami, FL 33137

Cheng I. Lin
Syva Co.
Palo Alto, CA 94303–0847

James S. Lo
St. Catharines
Ontario, Canada 12M6L4

Paula M. S. Lopez
Williamsville, NY 14221

Charles A. Loshon
Hartford Hosp.
Clinical Chemistry Lab.
Hartford, CT 06115

P. A. Luhan
East Lyme, CT 06333

Cathy M. Macek
JAMA Medical News
Durham, NC 27707

Virginia S. Marcum
Clinical Chemistry
Winston Salem, NC 27103

D. M. Martin
Psychiatric Diagnostic Labs. of
America, Inc.
Summit, NJ 07980

Howard L. Masco
New Port Richey, FL 33552

Charles P. Maurizi
Medical Center of Central Georgia
Macon, GA 31208

Mohammed Mazharuddin
Wayne County General Hosp.
Research Dept.
Wayne, MI 48184

Thomas McClane
Lakeland, FL 33803

Robert C. McComb
Hartford Hosp.
Hartford, CT 06115

Samuel Meites
Childrens Hosp.
Clinical Chemistry Lab.
Columbus, OH 43205

Robert S. Melville
Garrett Park, MD 20766

Brenda Michniewig
Clearwater, FL 33515

Fernando J. Milanes
Miami, FL 33173

Janice L. Miller
West Palm Beach, FL 33409

Diane V. Mohr
Waltham, MA 02154

Thomas P. Moyer
Dept. of Lab. Medicine
Mayo Clinic
Rochester, MN 55901

A. A. Mylroie
Chicago State Univ.
Chicago, IL 60628

John D. Nagle
International Clinical Labs.
  Northeast
Randolph, MA 02368

Karen L. Nickel
Bio-Science Laboratories
Van Nuys, CA 91405

Eileen Nickoloff
Squibb Institute for Medical
  Research
Princeton, NJ 08540

Stephen Noel
New Port Richey, FL 33552

Carroll Oakley
New Paltz, NY 12561

Raphael J. Osheroff
Alexandria, VA 22304

David G. Ostrow
Biologist Psychiatry Program
VA Lakeside Medical Center
Chicago, IL 60611

Nicholas M. Papadopoulos
Clinical Chemistry, NIH
Bethesda, MD 20817

Mark Petricevic
Fairview General Hosp.
Scott Research Lab.
Cleveland, OH 44111

William T. Pope
Dept. of Pathology
Medical Center of Central Georgia
Macon, GA 31208

Larry H. Porter
Burroughs Wellcome Co.
Research Triangle Park, NC 27709

William H. Porter
Dept. of Pathology
Univ. of Kentucky Medical Center
Lexington, KY 40536

xxii

Marcel Pouliot
Hospital du Sacrement
Clinical Chemistry Dept.
Quebec City, Quebec
Canada G1S4L8

Pauline Powers
Univ. Medical Service Assoc., Inc.
College of Medicine
Dept. of Psychiatry
Tampa, FL 33612

Vidmantas A. Raisys
Harborview Medical Center
Dept. of Lab. Medicine
Seattle, WA 98104

C. Ray Ratliff
Bio Analytics
Palm City, FL 33490

Lester Rauer
Philadelphia, PA 19124

Marilyn Rhuey Rautio
Boca Raton Community Hosp.
Boca Raton, FL 33432

Nadja N. Rehak
Bethesda, MD 20817

Donald W. Renn
FMC Corporation
Rockland, MA 94841

Randall S. Riggs
Providence Medical Center
Clinical Lab.
Seattle, WA 98124

Ruick Rolland
Atlanta, GA 30307

Robert B. Rombauer
Becton Dickinson & Co.
Paramus, NJ 07652

Burton J. Rosenberg
Burroughs Wellcome Co.
The Wellcome Research Lab.
Research Triangle Park, NC 27709

Stephen O. Rushing
Webster, TX 77598

Jean P. Safdy
Ames Div., Miles Labs.
Elkhart, IN 45615

James C. Sams
Scottsville, VA 24590

Michael B. Schiffman
Becton Dickinson & Co.
Paramus, NJ 07652

Joyce A. Schoenheimer
Radix Organization, Inc.
New York, NY 10021

Michael Sheehan
Good Samaritan Hosp.
Portland, OR 97210

Elizabeth B. Solow
Indiana Univ. Medical Center
Indianapolis, IN 46223

Susan Shellabarger
Mead CompuChem
Research Triangle Park, NC 27709

Adrian Sondheimer
New York, NY 10023

Charlotte E. Shideler
Wesley Medical Center
Dept. of Lab. Medicine
Wichita, KS 67214

Debra Kaplan Sondheimer
New York, NY 10023

Donald K. Soules
Oakwood Hosp. Lab.
Dearborn, MI 48124

Clarence Shub
Mayo Clinic
Rochester, MN 55905

A. Michael Spiekerman
Scott and White Hosp. and Clinic
Temple, TX 76508

Antonina Sidorowicz
Northampton, MA 01060

Tillman L. Simmons
North Charlston, SC 29405

Nena Spirit
Livingston, NJ 07039

Albert C. Smith
VA Medical Center, Lab. Service
Gainesville, FL 32602

Linda Stanley
Diagnostic Medicine
Oradell, NJ 07649

Catherine Smith
Abbott Laboratories
North Chicago, IL 60064

Loren Steffen
St. Peter Hosp.
Olympia, WA 98506

S. J. Soldin
Hosp. for Sick Children
Dept. of Biochemistry
Toronto, Ontario, Canada
M5G1X8

Jo Sterling
Winter Haven Hosp.
Clinical Lab.
Winter Haven, FL 33880

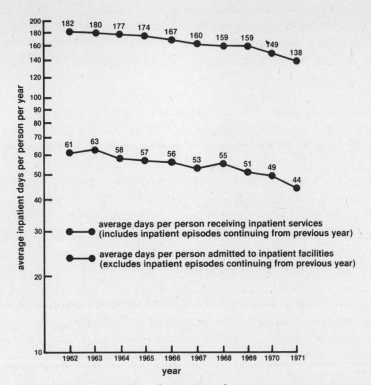

Fig. 2. Average number of inpatient days per person per year

been an almost eightfold increase in utilization of professional mental health services. The 1955 figure cited earlier represents only about 1% of the U.S. population.

Epidemiologic Data

This eightfold increase in utilization of mental health facilities should not be interpreted as a eightfold increase in incidence or prevalence of mental illness. The current available epidemiologic data indicate that the prevalence of mental illness, particularly the psychotic and more severe forms, appears to have remained fairly constant over the past 150 years, adjusted for the changing age distribution of the population. However, the willingness of the public to utilize mental health services has changed.

Nevertheless, questions arise as to what is the true magnitude of psychiatric problems in the population in general and what are the appropriate conditions under which psychiatry and mental health services should be used. These are two different questions. The first is a question as to fact, namely, the extent to which there are, by some objective criteria, mental illnesses of various sorts in the population. The second question is one of value and social policy, namely, what is legitimate and appropriate as to the use of psychiatry and other mental health services.

Psychiatry emerged in the mid-19th century as a medical specialty. Psychotherapy began as a medical health procedure. Freud, Prince, and others in the late 19th century and early 20th century who began writing about psychotherapy regarded it as a medical treatment for hysteria, neurasthenia, and other neuropsychiatric conditions. The root word "therapy" indicates treatment, implying treatment of some condition that is implicitly regarded as "illness," "sickness," "disease," or "pathology."

I propose approaching the issues of legitimacy of psychiatry from an epidemiologic point of view—inquiring as to which segments of the population would meet alternative criteria of appropriateness for mental health services, including the use of drugs and psychotherapies. Psychiatric services are actually used and are potentially legitimate for the following three populations (Figure 3):

1. A "core" group of people with definable mental disorder—about 15% of the population, or approximately 30–35 million individuals.

2. Individuals who cope with various adverse life events and who experience distressing emotional symptoms but not necessarily a definable and diagnosable mental illness—approximately 50 million persons per year.

3. Individuals with problems of living who have the desire to enhance their personal happiness and satisfaction—this size of group is potentially unlimited.

The Core Group: Patients with Diagnosable Mental Disorders

The President's Commission on Mental Health, appointed by President Carter in 1977, highlighted the need for relating the use of mental health services to data on the prevalence of mental disorders. Psychiatric epidemiology, a relatively new branch of mental health research for investigating how mental disorders are distributed in the population, reflects recent developments in diagnosis, genetics, psychopharmacology, neurobiology, and

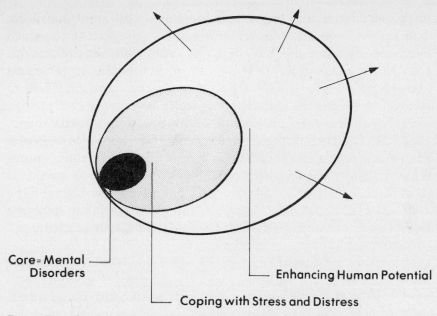

Core = Mental Disorders

Enhancing Human Potential

Coping with Stress and Distress

Fig. 3. Boundaries between mental illness and mental health

particularly psychopathology *(1, 2)*. Epidemiological investigations study the frequency with which various groups (according to age, ethnic background, education, urbanization of the place of residence, and social class) seek psychiatric treatment, and the kind of treatment they seek.

Regier et al. *(3)* summarized available epidemiological data and recent mental health service research findings to estimate the percent of the population with a mental disorder and the proportion utilizing various types of specialized mental health services and general medical treatment. They concluded that at least 15% of the U.S. population is affected by some mental disorder in one year. In addition to that 15% (about 32 million persons in 1975), there is a substantial proportion, probably another 15%, who have symptoms of anxiety, stress, and distress related to problems of living. Many of these persons use the mental health or general health-care system for coping and consolation.

Three disorders predominate in this 15% incidence of mental disorders: depression and affective disorders, alcoholism and related problems, and anxiety states. There is some overlap in these

7

categories, especially between alcoholism and depression (4). Schizophrenia, the disorder that results in the greatest degree of institutionalization and consumes the most public resources and attention (owing to its early age of onset, chronic nature, and high social disability), has a prevalence of about 1%. Another significant finding (3) is that the majority of the 15% of persons with mental disorders are seen in the health-care system. However, only one-fifth of these were served in the specialized mental health-care sector; three-fifths were identified in the general medical-care sector, and one-fifth remained untreated.

Table 1. **Estimated Prevalence of Selected Alcohol, Drug, and Mental Disorders**

Disorders, by age category	Prevalence, % (rate per 100 persons)
Children (under 18)	8–10
Adults (18–65)	10–15
Depression and affective disorders	4.5–8
Anxiety, phobia, and other neuroses	4–7
Alcoholism and alcohol problems	2.5–8
Drug dependence	0.5–1
Schizophrenia	0.5–1
Aged (over 65)	10

Subsequent to the Report of the President's Commission, the National Institute of Mental Health has supported a large-scale epidemiologic project called the Epidemiologic Catchment Area Project. Grants have been given to five universities to study large community samples, 3000 subjects each, in the metropolitan areas of New Haven, St. Louis, Baltimore, and Los Angeles and in the rural area surrounding Durham, NC. In addition, oversampling of persons in institutions and of individuals over age 65 is being undertaken, in which a newly developed structured interview, the Diagnostic Interview Schedule, is being used. The preliminary results of these studies, presented at the 1982 Meeting of the American Public Health Association in Montreal, Canada, confirmed that about 15% of the population has a diagnosable mental disorder, the most prevalent forms of which are alcoholism and various forms of depression, with schizophrenia and other major functional psychoses affecting about 1% of the population.

As additional findings from this important study emerge, we will gain further information not only about the prevalence of mental disorders but also about their incidence and about important risk factors such as age, sex, social class, and life stress.

For the "core" group, those with a definable mental illness, there is little at issue as to the legitimacy of psychiatric treatment. Policy makers, mental health professionals, and the public at large agree that treatment is appropriate for individuals who suffer from disorders diagnosable by the criteria of the American Psychiatric Association Diagnostic Statistical Manual III (DSM-III) or the World Health Organization International Classification of Diseases. Although there is still some lingering debate around the "myth" of mental illness or the validity of some diagnostic categories, a controversy from the 1960s, there is an increasing acceptance of the concept of multiple mental disorders that can be reliably diagnosed operationally by the type of criteria embodied in the DSM-III (2). Epidemiologic evidence from Scandinavia, The United Kingdom (1), and North America indicates that about 15 to 20% of the population have such illnesses and that the majority of these illnesses are nonpsychotic, involving anxiety, depressive states, and alcoholism (2, 3).

For patients in this large core group, the policy issue is not legitimacy or appropriateness of treatment but evidence for safety or efficacy. The use of psychotherapy for these individuals is within the health model of treatment for disorders that render patients distressed and potentially disabled and at a higher risk for various forms of mortality and medical morbidity.

Persons Coping with Stress

One of the major advances in mental health research since World War II has been a growing recognition of the role of adverse life events and other stressors as precipitants of changes in the health states of an individual, including mental health. Individuals experiencing stressful life events suffer health problems in three stages: immediately after the stress, during the period of adjustment, and later. During the period of adjustment in coping with life events emotional symptoms such as depression, anxiety, and tension increase and are associated with bodily changes in sleep, appetite, level of activity, and sexual performance. Moreover, people coping with these stressful events make greater use of the

9

health-care system and increase their use of alcohol, tobacco, and various sedatives. Anti-anxiety drugs such as Valium (diazepam), Librium (chlordiazepoxide), and other benzodiazepines are often used by persons attempting to cope with these stressful events (5).

In the United States there may be as many as 50 million people a year who cope with various forms of adverse life events (Table 2). Treatment is appropriate in these circumstances to help reduce distress during the period of coping and adaptation and to help prevent the development of overt psychiatric or medical illnesses.

Table 2. **Epidemiology of Life Stress**

Stressful life event	Estimated millions of persons affected annually	
	Directly	Indirectly
Death	1.5	4
Divorce	3	6
Retirement	10	20
Unemployment	7	20
Chronic medical illness	10	20

The use of psychotherapy and of drug treatments to assist people who are coping with life stress can thus be justified both as direct treatment and to offset the likelihood of developing adverse health consequences, as has been increasingly documented.

Persons Seeking Enhancement of Their Personal Potential

Since the Korean War numerous psychotherapies proposing the enhancement of personal potential have been crystallized in the fields of humanistic psychology and the "human potential movement." This is the group that presents the most problems from the viewpoint of public policy.

Most of the proponents of humanistic psychology and of the human potential movement explicity reject the health model. Such leaders of the field as Maslow (6) and Rogers (7) criticize the model as emphasizing symptoms and the negative aspects of personality rather than enhancing human potential. From their point of view, the legitimacy of psychotherapy is *not* as a health intervention but for enhancement of human potential and promotion of personal satisfaction. Within this definition, there is no limit to the number of persons for whom some form of psychotherapy might be appropriate. Few among us have not wished to be more productive and sexually attractive, have a better memory, play better tennis, lose weight, or delay the onset of aging. The promise of psychotherapy is that it will do all these things without any adverse side affects. The social issues included in the use of psychotherapy for these goals are similar to those that arise with use of drugs for the enhancement of performance by athletes, the use of stimulant drugs by college students preparing for examinations or by football players getting "psyched up" for Sunday afternoon, the use of LSD and other hallucinogens for expansion of consciousness, or the use of cocaine or cannabis derivatives by musicians and other artists.

Changes in Utilization of Mental Health Services, 1955–1980

As mentioned previously, the critical year for understanding the revolutionary changes in psychiatry and the mental health system is 1955. In that year, nearly 600 000 patients were in public mental hospitals, the main facility for treatment of mental illness. There were very few private hospitals, which were mainly for wealthy and upper-middle-class people, and fewer than 10 000 psychiatrists and other professionals were in private practice. Only a small number of outpatient clinics and child-guidance centers augmented private practitioners in providing ambulatory treatment.

In 1955, the situation changed dramatically: for the first time in over a century, the census of public mental hospitals showed a decline instead of an increase. Since then, the mental health system has experienced a major shift—from almost total reliance on a system of involuntary incarceration in public institutions to a more voluntary pluralistic system.

Until the 1950s, the delivery of mental health services was almost exclusively monopolized by large public institutions. Now, not only has the primary locus of treatment shifted dramatically from institutional to community settings but also there has been

11

radical reapportioning of services among the different types of psychiatric facilities (8).

Current trends toward pluralism, diversity, and de-institutionalization in mental health care are in sharp contrast to the centralization, isolation, and institutionalization that characterized the first half of this century. These changes are primarily the result of new forms of technology—both pharmacological and psychological—coupled with increasing support by the federal government. However, despite effective new treatments and the emergence of progressive alternatives to institutional care, many patients became "better," but not "well."

Two major developments revolutionized the treatment of severe mental illness. The first was the introduction in the 1950s of the phenothiazines. These new drugs contributed to the effective treatment and symptomatic management of many severely psychotic patients. They also led to briefer hospitalizations and to increased percentages of patients discharged from the hospitals.

Moreover, new psychosocial methods of treatment had begun to emerge prior to the introduction of the phenothiazines. In the 1940s, the philosophical attitudes of the hospital keepers began to change in response to criticisms of their institutions. Efforts at internal hospital reform included avoiding seclusion and restraint, implementing open-door policies, improving internal power relations, and breaking down administrative and other barriers between the hospital and the community.

Psychosocial reform and reconstruction efforts quickly affected mental health professions and were symbolized in theory and research as "social psychiatry" and in practice as the "therapeutic community." Major efforts at therapeutic reform were first initiated in Britain but were rapidly extended to the United States, where they escalated during the 1950s and 1960s. These reforms were crystallized in the ideal of the therapeutic community, which coupled the belief in the human potential for change with techniques of group dynamics to improve interpersonal communication and behavior.

In the early to mid-1960s, the social psychiatrist reformers were joined by civil libertarians, conservative budget advisors, and the federal government in support of de-institutionalization policies in state and local mental health programs. Although their theoretical rationales differed dramatically, these diverse groups developed a short-lived consensus on matters of mental health care. Lawyers argued that institutions deprived patients not only of their health, but also of their civil rights. Conservative budget advisors, pressured by strong economic forces, eagerly joined the push toward de-institutionalization because it provided an opportunity to shift the burden of financing from the state to the national level. Federal efforts to address the management of mental illness culminated in 1963, when a series of programs was established to stimulate and support community services as alternatives to institutional care.

The Dramatic Decline of Institutional Care

Statistical data from the past quarter-century reflect not only the shift in locus of care from public mental hospitals to community, but also changes in the distribution of care provided by the various types of inpatient facilities (Figure 4). The most dramatic change in mental health care has been the sharp decline in the number of public mental-hospital residents from 559 000 in 1955 to fewer than 200 000 in 1975, a 65% decrease (9).

As the population of institutions decreased, outpatient treatment facilities in the community increased. Currently the largest area of growth in mental health care is in outpatient and ambulatory facilities of all kinds—free-standing outpatient services as well as those affiliated with psychiatric and general hospitals, public and private facilities. To illustrate, in 1955 inpatient services accounted for 77% of the episodes of care, while 23% were handled in outpatient settings; by 1975, that trend had reversed (10) (Figure 5).

When the absolute numbers are converted to number of patient-care episodes per 100 000 population, the diverging trends between inpatient and outpatient care become even more evident. The rate for inpatients has remained relatively stable, at about 800 episodes per 100 000 population. In contrast, utilization of outpatient services has increased significantly, from about 1100 per 100 000 population in 1955 to around 2000 in 1971 to 8000 in 1980.

The downward population trend in mental institutions is attributed largely to a decrease in average duration of hospitalization (Figure 6). Unpublished data from the National Institute of Mental Health indicate that between 1971 and 1975 there was a 41%

13

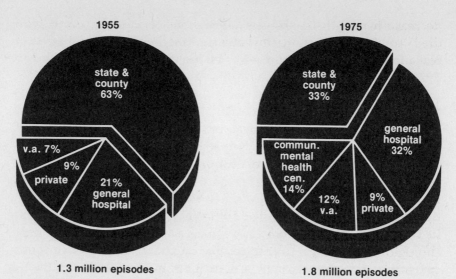

1955

state &
county
63%

v.a. 7%

9%
private

21%
general
hospital

1.3 million episodes

1975

state &
county
33%

general
hospital
32%

commun.
mental
health
cen.
14%

12%
v.a.

9%
private

1.8 million episodes

Fig. 4. Percent distribution of inpatient care episodes by type of psychiatric facility, 1955 and 1975

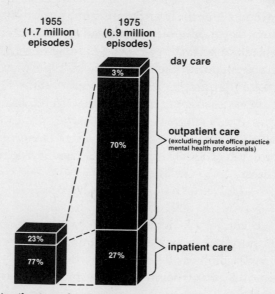

1955
(1.7 million
episodes)

1975
(6.9 million
episodes)

day care

3%

outpatient care
(excluding private office practice
mental health professionals)

70%

23%

77%

27%

inpatient care

Fig. 5. Percent distribution of patient care episodes in U.S. mental health facilities by modality, 1955 and 1975

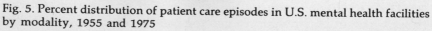

Figures for outpatient care exclude care by mental health professionals in private office practice

14

decrease in length of stay for admissions (excluding those who died) to state and county psychiatric hospitals, the median stay for admissions decreasing from 44 days in 1971 to 26 days in 1975.

The Problems of De-Institutionalization

The combined result of these trends has been the movement of treatment out of the mental hospital and into the community (Figure 7). Mental health institutions have undergone a steady reduction in resident populations and a radical puncturing of their delivery systems (11). However, just as there are critics of institutionalization, so too there are critics of de-institutionalization and its concomitants. Some believe that the pharmacological and psychological technology that originally facilitated the shift in locus of treatment has now become too extreme and represents an unacceptable degree of behavior control.

The quality of care received by patients released from institutions to community facilities is another area of concern. Notwithstanding, patients may have a positive response to a new location, even if professionals consider it inferior to the hospital setting.

The creation of community mental health facilities has introduced its own set of problems: unrealistic expectations of their capabilities, lack of sufficient funding to achieve their goals, development of an uncoordinated network of community resources, and inadequate planning for patient release, referral, and follow-up. Problems can arise when patients are discharged from institutions into crowded, substandard, or inappropriate facilities. On the other hand, many other mentally ill persons enter, re-enter, or remain in public institutions when they could be treated in the community.

Use of Pharmacologic Agents

It is important to recognize the rapid growth of the use of drugs and other biological treatments. Beginning in 1952–1955, several new and effective psychopharmacologic agents became available in North America. The first of these were the antipsychotics, particularly chlorpromazine and other drugs useful in the treatment of psychoses and major mental illnesses such as schizo-

15

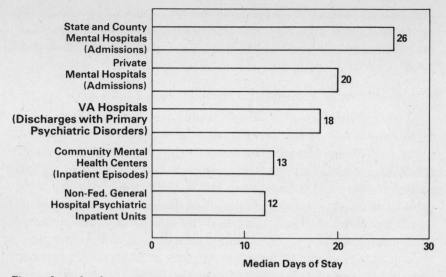

Fig. 6. Length of stay in mental health inpatient settings, 1975

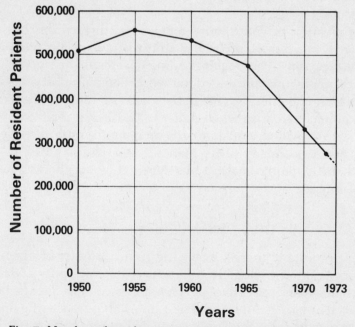

Fig. 7. Number of resident patients at year's end in state and county mental hospitals

16

phrenia and manic depressive illness. Meprobamate (marketed as Miltown and Equanil) was the first of the anti-anxiety drugs or minor tranquilizers. In the 1960s Valium and Librium and a large number of their derivatives were introduced.

The extent of the use of these drugs has caused considerable controversy. In any given year, between 10 and 12% of the general population receives a prescription for some psychoactive drug, most often an anti-anxiety agent. Antidepressants and the anti-psychotic drugs valuable in treating hospitalized patients and patients with serious mental illnesses represent only a small fraction of the total prescriptions.

As will be discussed, not all patients who receive psychopharmacologic agents have a diagnosable mental illness. Many of them have symptoms of anxiety, depression, tension, and insomnia associated with medical illnesses such as arthritis, cardiovascular disease, or gastrointestinal disease; many others are also experiencing symptoms in response to life stress.

Changes between 1964 and 1977 in the absolute number of prescriptions for psychotherapeutic drugs are shown in Figure 8. The increase in prescriptions for anti-anxiety drugs, which far exceed those for other classes of psychoactive drugs, is the most striking trend, and the one most discussed. Prescriptions for anti-anxiety drugs increased rapidly from 1964 to peak at more than 100 million in 1973. Although this number has plateaued and even decreased slightly to 90 million prescriptions in 1977, usage remains high by any criterion.

Changes in prescriptions of other classes of psychotherapeutic drugs have been of relatively less magnitude. The use of stimulants, mainly amphetamines, has decreased dramatically since the early 1970s, mainly because of an awareness of their adverse effects and evidence for their limited efficacy in the treatment of obesity or depression. The use of antidepressants has risen very slowly, not at all commensurate with the epidemiological evidence as to the prevalence of depression. Prescriptions for hypnotics and sedatives, particularly the barbiturates, have declined, mainly because of public concern about adverse effects and the availability of more effective and safer nonbarbiturate hypnotics. Prescriptions for antipsychotics, the drugs used primarily in treating schizophrenia, have remained relatively stable at about 15 million annually after a slight increase during the early 1970s.

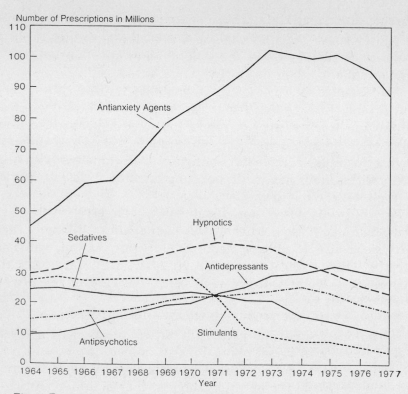

Fig. 8. Prescriptions for psychotherapeutic drugs filled in U.S. drugstores, 1964–1977

These data regarding psychotherapeutic drugs are derived from several national surveys (5, 12), in which about 10% of the adult population reported using prescriptions for minor tranquilizers during the year preceding the interview. Most (85%) of these prescriptions are written by nonpsychiatric physicians.

The extent of drug use having been documented, let us examine its relation to life stress, emotional symptoms, and demographic characteristics such as age and sex. Mellinger et al. (12), who obtained data on psychic distress (from a short version of the Hopkins symptom checklist) and on life crises (from a short version of the Holmes–Rahe social-readjustment rating scale), found that almost all patients taking psychotherapeutic drugs were manifestly symptomatic. The stereotype of the bored, suburban housewife popping Valium is not true. Psychotherapeutic drug use (primarily of minor tranquilizers) was strongly related to level of psychic distress and life crisis. For example, in the high-distress group, 30% had used psychotherapeutic drugs during the past year, as compared with 8% of those classified as experiencing low distress.

Another way to interpret these figures is to note that 30% of the highly distressed persons used psychotherapeutic drugs, whereas 70% did not. This 70% may be interpreted as the prevalence of untreated individuals. Opponents of psychotherapeutic drug use see the 30% usage rate as too high, whereas advocates see it as too low.

Mellinger et al. *(12)* also noted a striking sex-related difference in psychotherapeutic drug use: women use these drugs about twice as frequently as men. One determinant of this difference may be that women go to physicians more often than men do and thus are more likely to be prescribed drugs. Similarly, at all specified levels of life stress, as measured by the Holmes–Rahe technique used in the study, women reported more symptoms than men did. When combined ratings on psychic distress and life crises were calculated, the disparity between the sexes in amount of psychotherapeutic drug use increased.

The interaction between selected independent variables—sex, age, and psychic distress—and the dependent variables of psychotherapeutic drug and alcohol use is complex. Although use of psychotherapeutic drugs increased with age in both men (more dramatically) and women with high distress, as age increased the sex-related difference in drug use diminished; however, men of all ages used far more alcohol than did women. Balter, from the group of Mellinger et al. *(12)*, has recently reported preliminary results from a further nationwide survey conducted in the late 1970s that confirm the earlier findings described above. The use of psychoactive drugs is still high, and the individuals who use these drugs are experiencing life stress and associated psychic distress. There is some evidence of a decline in the mid-1970s in prescriptions for minor tranquilizers, after publicity and congressional hearings about the possible dangers of dependence and over-prescription. Nevertheless, these drugs continue to be widely used, particularly by general physicians and the family practitioners, for whom the minor tranquilizers are the "first line" of treatment decisions for almost all forms of nonpsychotic mental illness.

Although public opinion is not clear-cut about the moral and social implications of using these drugs, in nationwide surveys of the patients who are taking these drugs approximately 77% report receiving symptomatic benefit and consider them a major way of coping with stresses of life and medical illnesses. Moreover, a substantial minority of patients who are taking these drugs have chronic medical illnesses such as hypertension, arthritis, and other disorders.

As new drugs become available, particularly for better treatment of alcoholism and for combating the memory loss of dementia, we can probably expect further increases in the use of psychopharmacologic agents.

The Expanding Use of the Psychotherapies

The preceding section has documented the shifts in patterns of utilization of mental health services, particularly the use of outpatient institutions. Parallel with these changes has been a tremendous expansion of ambulatory services, especially in the outpatient ambulatory sector, including the use of psychotropic drugs and psychotherapy. Psychiatrists now represent only about one-quarter of all outpatient contacts.

Another index is the increasing reimbursement of nonpsychiatric practitioners by various third-party payments. In current estimates of ambulatory mental health benefits provided by third-party payment, particularly Blue Cross–Blue Shield, only about 50% goes to the psychiatrist, the remainder going to psychologists, social workers, and other practitioners, depending on the state of licensure and certification.

The Growth of the Psychotherapies

The field of psychotherapy now has more definition, more specifiable application, and more predictable results than it has ever had. A profusion of new psychotherapeutic schools and new techniques continues to increase. The scientific procedures for evaluating the efficacy of psychotherapeutic outcomes are also improving, so that it is increasingly possible to cite evidence about the psychotherapies and potentially to disseminate this evidence to the professions and to the public.

New treatment techniques have been invented, debated, taught, and practiced; multiple professions have become involved in the

20

practice of psychotherapy; the number of practitioners has increased; the number of schools, institutes, and training programs for teaching people to practice psychotherapy has multiplied; accordingly, public attention to psychotherapy has increased immensely.

The amount of money spent on psychotherapy has also increased tremendously. Extrapolating only from the conservative estimates by the Group for the Advancement of Psychiatry *(13)*, the direct cost of psychotherapy in the U.S. exceeds $1 billion per year, "an order of magnitude comparable to that of the pharmacotherapy industry."

It is difficult to catalogue neatly all the different activities that can be included as psychotherapy. There is no universally accepted terminology covering the many kinds of psychological treatment used for emotional problems, alcoholism, drug abuse, development disabilities, and other mental health problems. The vast majority of treatments, however, consist chiefly of some types of face-to-face exchanges between a professional administering the treatment (the psychotherapist) and the person who receives it (the patient or client).

The largest class of psychotherapies are those that involve more or less exclusively verbal dialogues. The class includes virtually all treatments that go under the title of counseling, case work, insight therapy (including most forms of psychoanalysis), client-centered or nondirective therapy, psychiatric or psychological interviews or consultations, encounter groups, humanistic or existential therapy, rational–emotive therapy, transactional analysis, and most forms of group psychotherapy and behavior therapy.

A second class of psychotherapeutic activity also uses verbal interactions as the main technique of treatment, but in more dramatic or unusual forms than that of conventional conversation, and often combined with specific behavioral methods of rehearsal or with altered states of consciousness. This category includes psychodrama, gestalt therapy, desensitization, implosive therapy, behavior shaping or operant conditioning, and hypnosis.

A third class of treatments makes active use of chemical or physical manipulation of the body. Included here are aversion therapies, biofeedback, bioenergetic therapy, and rolfing. One form of aversion therapy involves the treatment of alcoholism by emetic agents.

The above classes do not include all the named forms of psychotherapies, of which 200 or more "brand names" may exist *(14)*. They do, however, represent most kinds of psychological treatment used by psychiatrists, psychologists, social workers, nurses, counselors, and other professionals who claim expertise in this domain. Because there is no single term that adequately covers the field, I shall use the term "psychotherapy" to refer to treatment methods and classes otherwise called "mental treatment," "psychological treatment," and "therapy."

Increasing Numbers and Types of Mental Health Practitioners

Accompanying the proliferation of new psychotherapies has been a parallel expansion in the number of practitioners. In 1955, soon after the Korean War but before the development of the community mental health centers and the expansion of social programs as part of the "War on Poverty" and "Great Society" era, there were only about 10 000 psychiatrists, half of whom were in clinical practice or private practice. A small number of clinical psychologists were in private practice, and there were even fewer social workers. Over the ensuing 25 years the number and types of practitioners of psychotherapy have increased greatly. I would estimate there are now about 100 000 psychotherapy practitioners, who include the following:

Psychiatrists. There are about 33 000 psychiatrists, of whom probably two-thirds (between 20 000 and 25 000) do some sort of private or institutional practice of psychotherapy.

Psychologists. Of about 55 000 psychologists, approximately one-half are clinical psychologists; school psychologists and consulting psychologists would total another 30 000.

Psychiatric social workers. About 70 000 persons have a master's degree in psychiatric social work; of this group, probably about one-quarter—about 20 000—are involved in some form of private practice.

In addition, there are an increasing number of psychiatric nurses with master's degrees, marriage and family counselors, and pastoral counselors and clergymen who have taken formal training in counseling or psychotherapy.

What is characteristic of the recent trend is a growth not only in the absolute number of practitioners of psychotherapy but also in the diversity of their professional backgrounds. Whereas at the end of World War II psychotherapy was dominated by the psychiatrists, and the psychiatrists by the psychoanalyst, today the psychiatrist in general and psychoanalysts in particular are in the minority.

Prospects for the Future

The past 25 years have witnessed several important trends in mental health care: a decline in the resident census in public mental health hospitals, an increase in outpatient treatment and facilities, relative stability in the number of hospitalization episodes per 100 000 population, and briefer duration of hospitalization. The combined results of these trends is increased pluralism, diversity, and de-institutionalization in mental health care. The changes are primarily the consequence of the success of psychopharmacologic agents, new forms of psychotherapy, changing attitudes of the public, and increased financial support by the federal government.

During the same 25 years, there have been significant advances in the scientific status of psychiatry. Research in genetics, psychopathology, and psychopharmacology has contributed to a better empirical and experimental basis for the diagnosis and treatment of psychiatric disorders. Moreover, advances in social science and epidemiology have provided better data as to the scope of the problem and the magnitude of mental illness.

The significant changes I have reviewed here, particularly those in the utilization of mental health services, including psychiatry, will have to be interpreted in the context of a broadening definition of the scope of psychiatry. The marked expansion in utilization of mental health services does not indicate an increase in the incidence or prevalence of mental illness; on the contrary, available evidence indicates that the prevalence of mental illness has remained fairly constant in North America over recent decades. Rather, what has changed is the attitude of the public towards regarding mental illness as treatable and the willingness of more segments of the population with emotional and psychological problems to seek professional help from psychiatrists and other mental health professionals. Nonetheless, even with this tremendous expansion, only a minority of individuals with any form of mental illness are treated for that condition by a mental health professional.

The Changing Federal Role

Federal efforts to reform the delivery of mental health services were initiated in the 1950s when Congress established the Joint Commission on Mental Illness and Health. The resulting report and its recommendations led to President Kennedy's landmark 1963 address to Congress on mental illness and mental retardation. The passage in 1963 of the Mental Retardation Facilities and Community Mental Health Centers Construction Act established guidelines and promised federal funding for community facilities to treat mentally ill patients. This legislation marked a dramatic shift in treatment ideology and radically changed the locus of mental health care.

The goal of caring for and treating the mentally ill in community facilities rather than in mental institutions has been endorsed over the years by four Presidents and the Congress, and the federal role in mental health has grown substantially. The amount and types of financial assistance the federal government provides, and the requirements, standards, and restrictions imposed, as well as the policies of federal agencies, have significantly influenced both the progress and problems encountered in de-institutionalization.

One important role of the federal government has been to provide funds for mental health services, and not (except for the Department of Defense and Veteran's Administration hospitals) to run them. Most of the federal health dollar is used to provide health insurance—including Medicaid and Medicare—and to fund community mental health centers. These efforts have radically changed the structure of the delivery system toward pluralism by increasing the number of treatment alternatives available to patients.

Furthermore, the portion of federal funds devoted to support of research has enormously benefited psychiatric patients, by leading to the two major technologic advances directly responsible for the shift away from institutional and toward community care. Psychopharmacology is most visible, but advances in psychosocial treatment techniques have also been significant. Together, these technological achievements have contributed to shorter hospital stays, the control of psychoses, and advances in community care and treatment of mental health problems.

With the Reagan administration, major changes have been initi-

24

ated. The funding of community programs by federal dollars is about to cease and what federal monies will be appropriated will be administered through the states via the new program of block grants. The full impact of these changes in federal policy is unclear, but the public support of community mental health programs will probably diminish.

The Evolving Pluralistic System

As increasing numbers of patients have been given, via their health insurance, more options regarding the type of facility in which they can receive treatment, the system is becoming increasingly pluralistic. No longer is the mental health system a state-owned and state-operated monopoly. The availability of more individual practitioners, nonprofit hospitals, and volunteer agencies has greatly increased the number of treatment alternatives. The voucher system, in the form of health insurance, has given patients and their families increasing freedom. The care and treatment of mentally ill people in the community has become an alternative to institutional care, but with uncertain financing and lack of community facilities, the progress made could falter in the 1980s.

The Social Context

The tremendous expansion of mental health care, particularly with drugs and psychotherapy, has taken place in an era of rising economic well-being and increasing education of the population. The growth of values around individualism, self-determination, and self-fulfillment, and the increasing legitimization of the search for personal happiness, including artistic and creative expression, increased sexual freedom, and greater mobility, have also occurred during this period.

Within the context of these larger historical changes, the health care system must increasingly cope with periods of stress and distress. The traditional social supports for buttressing people against life stress have been the family, the church, and the immediate neighborhood. All these are increasingly less available to modern men and women as they cope with the demands for personal happiness and the ethic of self-fulfillment. In this context, mental health services—psychiatry, psychotherapy, and psychopharmacology—are rational, modern promises of individual ful-

25

fillment that reinforce the general tendency toward personalism.

In the interval of a mere quarter-century, our country has witnessed the introduction of psychotherapeutic drugs, their use as potent agents to ameliorate severe mental disorders, and their widespread use to relieve symptoms of distress. The consequences have been both far-reaching and controversial. Drug therapies have transformed the entire system of mental health services, enabling it to shift its locus from the institution to the community, thereby radically restructuring mental health care facilities. Drug therapies are now also widely used in the general health-care system, where they are frequently prescribed for relief of psychic distress. Although many points remain controversial, there is no doubt that new technologies and increased availability of mental health services have improved the treatment of mental disorders and enhanced our lives, emotional comfort, and ability to cope with life's vicissitudes. The increased use of Valium and Librium heralds this new trend toward alleviation of distressing symptoms via the medical profession. The Declaration of Independence did not promise the absence of anxiety, guilt, and insomnia, but rather spoke for life, liberty, and the pursuit of happiness. The change in definition for utilization of health-care services will most likely promote an increase in mental health care through the medical care system.

The urban industrial society of today with its secular orientation and geographic mobility relies less on social supports of family, church, and neighbors and more on the health-care system. Geographic mobility means that fewer friends and family are called upon for support when individuals find themselves lonely, disabled, or distressed. In a time when religion and social supports are lacking, people turn increasingly to what is available, namely, the health-care system. It is effective and specialized and, most important, it has a financial base of support—the insurance system. In addition to prolonging life, the health-care system maintains and expands the size and quality of life of the population through reduction of mortality and morbidity, maintains an effective labor force by reducing disability due to illness, and promotes cohesion by regulating social control. This last function includes not only the extreme case of the use of psychiatry for the control of political dissidents in the Soviet Union but also the incarceration of socially disruptive and handicapped individuals, as has been

26

the practice in the United States. In some societies the health system serves as a socializing force for the acculturation of new population groups, as in the case of Israel. Increasingly in the United States and other industrialized societies the health system provides a way to help individuals and families cope with distress and life tensions and their personal performance and happiness.

With the expansion of mental health services has come the inclusion of neurotic distress, including anxiety and depression, as legitimate objects for psychiatric attention or for services to be provided by other members of the health-care system. These developments provide a quasi-experimental case for defining the limits of the extent to which health and illness are socially defined and the extent to which the health-care system is called upon to deal with the quality of life as well as its prolongation.

Summary

Recent epidemiologic studies indicate that about 12–18% of the population have some diagnosable mental disorder in a given year (point prevalence). The prevalence of mental disorder does not seem to have changed much in the past century, although there may be changes in incidence and in the pattern both in children and in the elderly. What has changed drastically are the patterns of utilization, leading to an increasing percentage of those with mental illness seeking help in the general health-care system and in the mental health system in particular. Nevertheless, only about one-quarter of persons with diagnosable disorders are treated in the specialty system. The patterns of utilization have been affected by changing social attitudes, particularly more education, affluence, secularization away from religion and the church, and emphasis on individual attainment and personal satisfaction. The economic support for treatment of mental illness will depend on the changing balance of responsibility among federal, state, and nongovernmental sources of funding.

References

1. Robins L. Psychiatric epidemiology. *Arch Gen Psychiatry* **35**, 697–702 (1978).
2. Weissman MM, Klerman GL. Epidemiology of mental disorders. *Arch Gen Psychiatry* **35**, 705–712 (1978).

3. Regier DA, Goldberg ID, Taube CA. The de facto U.S. mental health services system. *Arch Gen Psychiatry* **35**, 685–693 (1978).
4. Pottenger M, McKernon J, Patrie LE, et al. The frequency and persistence of depressive symptoms in the alcohol abuser. *J Nerv Ment Dis* **166**, 562–570 (1978).
5. Ulenhuth EH, Balter MB, Lipman RS. Minor tranquilizers; clinical correlates of use in an urban population. *Arch Gen Psychiatry* **35**, 650–655 (1978).
6. Maslow AH. *Motivation and Personality,* Harper & Row, New York, NY, 1954.
7. Rogers CR, Dymond RF, Eds. *Psychotherapy and Personality Change,* University of Chicago Press, Chicago, IL, 1954.
8. Klerman GL. Better but not well: Social and ethical issues in the deinstitutionalization of the mentally ill. *Schizophr Bull* **3**, 617–631 (1977).
9. Kramer M. Psychiatric services and the changing institutional scene, 1950–1985. National Institute of Mental Health, Rockville, MD, 1977.
10. Taube CA, Redlick RW. Provisional data on patient care episodes in mental health facilities, 1975. Statistical Note 139, National Institute of Mental Health, Rockville, MD, 1977.
11. Greenblatt M, Glazier E. The phasing out of mental hospitals in the United States. *Am J Psychiatry* **132**, 1135–1140 (1975).
12. Mellinger GD, Balter MB, Manheimer DI, et al. Psychic distress, life crises and use of psychotherapeutic medication. *Arch Gen Psychiatry* **35**, 1045–1052 (1978).
13. Group for the Advancement of Psychiatry. *Pharmacotherapy and Psychotherapy: Paradoxes, Problems and Progress,* **9,** Author Publishers, New York, NY, 1975, pp 261–431.
14. Parloff MB. Shopping for the right therapy. *Saturday Rev* **3**, 14–20 (1976).

Clinical Diagnosis and Classification
of Affective Disorders

Alan F. Schatzberg

The recent proliferation of effective treatments for patients with mood disorders has generated considerable interest in diagnosis and classification. What 20 years ago was a limited armamentarium of treatments for depression (electroconvulsive therapy and monoamine oxidase inhibitors) has now been enlarged to include not only tricyclic antidepressants, but also a host of second-generation drugs (including tetracyclics) that are effective in treating depressed patients. Similarly, the introduction of lithium carbonate in the late 1960s, the first effective preventative treatment for manic episodes in bipolar manic-depressive patients, has now been complimented by increasing use of carbamazepine and sodium valproate to treat patients with cycling manic-depressive illness. Because these somatic agents are currently available, it is imperative that clinicians have a thorough working knowledge of diagnosis. Clinicians must be able to recognize not only classic forms of psychiatric disorders but also atypical subtypes that may respond to routine treatment. For these reasons, effort has been expended toward refining the diagnosis of patients with mood disorders.

Accurate diagnosis is also extremely important in investigating etiologic factors: the underlying biology, genetics, etc. For example, only after agreement has emerged as to the diagnostic criteria of bipolar depression can investigators study underlying pathophysiological processes. Further, comparing classic and atypical types of a particular disorder may lead to defining biological characteristics that are common to both or that differentiate between them. This can then lead to a more elaborate classification that includes not only signs and symptoms but biological measures as well. In psychiatry, diagnosis/classification is no longer an academic exercise but rather an evolving process that also serves as the foundation for both current practice and research. Here I will review key aspects regarding the diagnosis and classification of patients with affective or mood disorders. After reviewing major themes in the literature of the previous 60 years, I will outline what direction I think classification may take.

Many investigators have proposed classification systems; taken together, the systems overlap greatly, although they also display some specific differences. Recent years have seen attempts to integrate these disparate systems into more universal systems. All the while, work continues on improving classification and will continue until the key features of specific disorders have been defined. The St. Louis group *(1)* has emphasized five key components in defining syndromes: symptomatology of the illness, exclusion of the other disorders, genetic inheritance patterns, laboratory studies, and outcome. Because these factors have yet to be precisely determined for many mood disorders, current research represents only an approach to the goal of a unified classification system.

Affective or mood disorders include depressive conditions, in which the patient presents with a predominantly lowered mood and a constellation of vegetative or somatic symptoms, and manic or elated conditions, which present with rather different symptoms (e.g., decreased need for sleep, increased energy, etc.). Some manic patients may also suffer from depression, concomitantly or alternating with manic episodes. A review of the literature suggests "depression" consists of a group of disorders that can be discriminated among on the basis of biological or clinical characteristics. The manic syndromes have tended to be viewed as more homogeneous, although here, too, this is not entirely clearcut.

Depressive Disorders

Classification systems for depressive disorders have often emphasized dichotomies for making comparisons. However, these distinctions have been defined uniquely by almost every investigator, the result often being confusion. To understand the classification of depressive illnesses, let us review the key terms (i.e., the key dichotomous categories) that enter into many systems. These dichotomies (listed in Table 1) include: *(a)* endogenous and autonomous vs nonendogenous, exogenous, and reactive; *(b)* psychotic vs neurotic; *(c)* unipolar vs bipolar; *(d)* primary vs secondary; and *(e)* the more recent biological dichotomies, including low vs high 3-methoxy-4-hydroxyphenylglycol (MHPG) excretion, and dexamethasone suppression vs nonsuppression.

In his pioneer work, Kraepelin *(2, 3)* separated dementia praecox from manic-depressive psychosis primarily on the basis of outcome. More specifically, manic-depressive illness generally had a better prognosis than did dementia praecox, which was often marked by a chronically deteriorating course. Kraepelin further

---

Table 1. **Dichotomous Classifications of Depressive Disorders**

Endogenous/autonomous vs exogenous, reactive, nonendogenous, and neurotic
Psychotic vs neurotic
Unipolar vs bipolar
Primary vs secondary
Recent applications of biological findings:
  Dexamethasone suppression vs nonsuppression
  Low MHPG vs high MHPG
  Shortened REM latency vs normal REM latency

REM, rapid eye movement.

---

divided the depressive disorders (under manic-depressive illness) into classic (which appear to be similar to endogenous) and exogenous types; these differed in the degree to which the patients reacted to environmental stimuli. Since Kraepelin, investigators have defined endogenous and nonendogenous syndromes in various ways. A complete description of this debate can be found elsewhere *(4, 5)*; however, I will review key aspects of this endogenous/nonendogenous dichotomy because endogenous depression represents a major syndrome for clinicians and researchers.

Endogenous vs nonendogenous. Although endogenous depression has been variously described, there is considerable agreement regarding its morphology. The current emphasis is on a clustering of signs and symptoms, most notably anergia (lack of energy), psychomotor retardation (feeling slowed down in movement or concentration), sleep disturbance, loss of appetite, diurnal variation in mood (classically, feeling worse in the morning and better at night), suicidal ideation, anhedonia or lack of pleasure, guilt, and worthlessness.

The earliest investigators used the term endogenous/nonendogenous dichotomy more loosely. Kraepelin implied an endogenous/nonendogenous dichotomy but used somewhat different terms. Lange *(6)*, working in Germany, followed up on Kraepelin's pioneer work, dividing manic-depressive illness into three major groups: a classic nonprecipitated disorder (endogenous), psychogenic melancholia (exogenous), and an intermediate group. He attempted to separate these syndromes on several counts, including symptoms, family history, and reactivity of syndrome. Endogenous depression in Lange's system was not caused by external events, and the symptoms were not influenced by environmental changes (i.e., did not improve when hearing good news). Thus, endogenous for Lange meant nonprecipitated and nonchanging (autonomous). Specific symptoms included constipation, psychomotor retardation, and weight loss, and the syndrome was also characterized by a positive family history for similar disorders. For Lange, persons with exogenous depressions tended to have reactive symptoms, an absence of vegetative signs, a tendency to blame their environment, and family history syndromes of other disorders, including schizophrenia, epilepsy, or "constitutional psychopathy." Specific symptoms that characterized exogenous syndromes were often harder to define, and nonendogenous syndromes were precipitated by environmental stimuli.

Thus, in Lange's work, a variety of dimensions were linked together, precipitation vs nonprecipitation, specific biologic symptoms vs the absence of biologic symptoms, and active (changing in response to environmental stimuli) vs autonomous (nonchanging). These various dimensions do not overlap completely, such that rigidly defining syndromes on the basis of more than one of them has often led to confusion in classification. For example, if one defined syndromes on the basis of symptoms (e.g., presence or absence of vegetative symptoms) and one also stated that endogenous syndromes were nonprecipitated, how did one diagnose a patient who had a persistent endogenous syndrome that had been preceded by an important life stress? More recent classifications, such as the *Diagnostic and Statistical Manual of Mental Disorders,* 3rd edition (DSM III) *(7)*, have defined syndromes primarily on the basis of symptoms, with "qualifiers" to describe precipitation and other dimensions. These will be elaborated later.

The confusion that began with Lange was exacerbated by later researchers, who would variously define or emphasize these distinct dimensions. In the end, endogenous depressions came to be defined as one or more of the following: *(a)* a syndrome with specific signs and symptoms; *(b)* a nonprecipitated disorder occurring secondary to biological factors; *(c)* a disorder that is nonreactive, i.e., does not change with the environment. Nonendogenous disorders have been characterized as being: *(a)* precipitated by various environmental stresses; *(b)* reactive or changing in symptoms; *(c)* having a constellation of various signs and symptoms that include anxiety, obsession, histrionic behavior, self-pitying behavior, whining, frequent tearfulness, and the absence of vegetative symptomatology. Currently, most workers emphasize presenting signs and symptoms in defining these syndromes.

Psychotic vs neurotic.   Another related dichotomy has been the psychotic/nonpsychotic or psychotic/neurotic dichotomy. In short, this is another area of confusion that has recently been clarified in the DSM III. Early on, Kraepelin used the term psychotic to describe manic-depressive illness because he felt that the illness was severe enough to often result in suicide. Thus the term did not indicate merely a break with reality but rather severity, and many workers prior to DSM III used the term in this way, particularly in the DSM II *(8)* (see below). Psychotic depressive disorders tended to have characteristics of endogenous symptoms, although exceptions were possible because the two represented different dimensions (severity vs type of symptoms). DSM III has incorporated psychotic/nonpsychotic as descriptions of, but not criteria for, major categories of depression. "Psychotic" in DSM III is used to indicate a break with reality.

Unipolar vs bipolar.   Unipolar vs bipolar is the third clinical dichotomy that has been commonly used over the years. Kraepelin subsumed under manic-depressive many types of disorders, including those with and without histories of mania. He included a variety of anxiety disorders and endogenous and nonendogenous depressive syndromes in an effort to separate these disorders from dementia praecox, which had a more ominous prognosis. Over the years, investigators found that depressive illnesses were more complex and devoted much effort into subclassifying depressive disorders. Major examples are the work of Leonhard *(9)* and Perris *(10)* to differentiate unipolar and bipolar disorders. These investigators in the late 1950s and 1960s noted that patients with bipolar depressions (i.e., those who had a history of mania or hypomania) could be distinguished from unipolar patients (those without a history of mania or hypomania) on the basis of family history and course. Whereas bipolar patients had frequent episodes of mania or hypomania, unipolar patients, by definition, did not. Moreover, bipolar patients tended to have relatives who showed bipolar illnesses, whereas unipolar patients had much lower incidences of bipolar illness in their families. This distinction has great implications for treatment and management.

Primary vs secondary. A fourth dichotomy, primary vs secondary, has been used to discriminate between patients whose depression occurred after the presentation of another disorder (e.g., the "secondary" depression of the previously alcoholic or character-disorder patient) and those whose depressions occurred de novo—"primary." This distinction has been somewhat less in vogue in recent years, greater emphasis now being placed on presenting signs and symptoms than on previous history.

Other dichotomies. Interestingly, dichotomous reasoning or approach to classification has found its way into biological studies, as evidenced in several major foci of research. One example has been the emphasis on discriminating between depressed patients with low or high concentrations of urinary MHPG *(11)*; another has been the dichotomous characterization of dexamethasone suppression vs nonsuppression *(12)*. This type of approach in part reflects the statistical methods used to analyze data and the difficulties of generating large enough samples of patients to allow for more subtle analyses of biological data. More recent evidence by our group *(13–15)* suggests that a dichotomous method of analyzing data may be less advantageous than previously thought, because depressive illnesses consist of several heterogenous subtypes.

DSM I–III

The Diagnostic and Statistical Manuals of Mental Disorders of the American Psychiatric Association (DSM I–III) have been the official classifications for the practice of psychiatry in the United States. DSM I was promulgated in 1952 *(16)*, DSM II in 1968, and DSM III in 1980. The differences between DSM II and DSM III are important, in that they highlight controversial and confusing aspects of classification and point to the evolving nature of classification in psychiatry.

DSM II

The DSM II classification of mood disorders was confusing and included many of the paradoxes alluded to above. In this system (see Table 2), schizophrenia and major affective disorders were

---

Table 2. **DSM II Classification of Affective Disorders**

Psychoses not attributed to physical conditions
    Schizophrenia
        Schizoaffective type
    Major affective disorders
        Involutional melancholia
        Manic-depressive illness
            Manic type
            Depressed type
            Circular type
        Other psychotic disorders
        Psychotic depressive reaction
Neuroses
    Depressive neurosis
Personality disorders
    Cyclothymic

---

listed under the rubric, "psychosis not attributed to physical conditions." Thus, by definition, major affective disorders were psychotic even if the patient did not show evidence of disorganized thinking—e.g., delusions or hallucinations. Psychosis in this sense indicated that these illnesses were severe. A similar use was seen in the DSM II designation of organic brain syndromes as being psychotic—i.e., severe and nonreversible.

In DSM II, involutional melancholia, manic-depressive illness, and psychotic depressive reaction all fell under major affective disorders. Involutional melancholia syndrome, emphasized by Kraepelin and others, described a severe endogenous depressive syndrome in the elderly, generally occurring at the climacterium, and characterized by severe agitation, paranoia, and guilty and nihilistic delusions (e.g., a belief that one's food was being poisoned, because one was bad or had caused harm to others). The syndrome is no longer listed in DSM III because it is now believed to be a variant of severe endogenous depression or major depression, which may also occur in younger patients.

Manic-depressive illness included the manic, depressed, and circular types. Although no strict symptom criteria were provided for any of these syndromes, the depressed phase of manic-depressive was characterized by classic endogenous or vegetative symptomatology, as described above. However, there were problems in diagnosing patients as having this syndrome. For example, for a patient to be defined as having DSM II manic-depressive illness (depressed phase), the episode had to have been unprecipitated and severe. Moreover, the patient did not have to have a previous history of mania or hypomania to be called manic-depressive. Thus, an endogenous syndrome was defined by symptoms and nonprecipitation, and patients whom we would term "major" or "unipolar" today would be called manic-depressive even though they had shown no previous history of mania or hypomania. This led to obvious confusion. Further, the patient was a priori labeled psychotic even though he or she often had shown no signs of a thought disorder.

Patients whose severe endogenous-like syndromes (as defined by vegetative symptoms) had been preceded by an important life event were classified as having a psychotic depressive reaction. However, this was also confusing. For example, a patient who had a precipitated, severe depression would be labeled as having psychotic depressive reaction even if he had a previous history of mania or hypomania. In short, manic-depressive was used less to describe a bipolar diathesis (i.e., alternating mania or hypomania with depressive episodes) than to define a nonprecipitated and severe syndrome. Obviously, the work of Perris *(10)* and Leonhard *(9)*, who pointed to differences in genetic and outcome factors between unipolar and bipolar patients, had not been included in this system.

The neurotic depressive disorders were milder and generally precipitated. A patient with a milder depressive syndrome that had not been precipitated was difficult to place. Obviously then, the DSM II resulted in considerable confusion among practitioners who were attempting to diagnose their patients precisely.

DSM III

Many of these confusing features have been clarified in the current DSM III classification of depressive disorders, which attempts to unify various systems and is an outgrowth of the Research Diagnostic Criteria originally proposed by Feighner et al. *(1)*. DSM III provides specific diagnostic criteria (in almost checklist form) for making diagnoses; its classification of affective disorders is outlined in Table 3. Major affective disorders include: *(a)* bipolar disorders, which can be divided into depressed, manic, and circular subtypes, and *(b)* major depression—a unipolar depression closely similar to an endogenous type of depressive disorder. Symptom criteria are identical for both bipolar and major depressive disorders. A more pronounced form of major depression is termed "major depression with melancholia."

Table 3. **DSM III Classification of Affective Disorders**

Major affective disorders
  Bipolar disorder
  Major depression
Other specific affective disorders
  Cyclothymic disorder
  Dysthymic disorder (depressive neurosis)
Atypical affective disorder
  Atypical bipolar disorder
  Atypical depression
Schizoaffective disorder
Situational disorder with depressed mood

"Dysthymic disorder" is a milder, more chronic form of illness and bears greater similarity to the nonendogenous syndromes described by others. The "cyclothymic" personality presents with alternating mild periods of elation and depression and may be viewed as a form of bipolar disorder. Last is the "situational reaction with depressed mood," an acute depressive reaction to a precipitant that may have accompanying limited vegetative symptomatology, but not sufficiently chronic or severe to be considered dysthymic disorder or major depression.

The criteria for mania include the presence of elevated, expansive, or irritable mood and three of the following: *(a)* increased activity, *(b)* grandiosity, *(c)* decreased need for sleep, *(d)* flight of ideas, *(e)* pressured speech, *(f)* distractibility, *(g)* spending sprees and other potentially damaging behavior. The syndrome classically has been described as lasting three to six months. Less common than major depression, the incidence of bipolar disorders is estimated as approximately 1%. Patients with this disorder often alternate between mania or hypomania and periods of depression.

Previously, many patients with bipolar disorder were often diagnosed as schizophrenic, the result of a misidentification of certain psychotic symptoms that also occur in mania. Many patients with frank mania demonstrate paranoia and disorganized cognitive functioning, often in the later stages of an episode. During such periods, their symptoms may be difficult to distinguish from those of schizophrenic psychosis. In a detailed review of the literature regarding this important discrimination several years ago *(17)*, the authors noted that what others had called "good prognosis schizophrenia" often represented a form of bipolar disorder that had been misdiagnosed or mislabeled. They argued that the psychotic symptoms of a so-called schizophrenic patient often failed to discriminate between patients with schizophrenia and those with bipolar disorders. Rather, premorbid functioning, course, the previous presence of pronounced affective symptoms, and a positive family history for depression and mania are more effective discriminants between these disorders. The importance of this discrimination cannot be overemphasized now that lithium carbonate is an effective treatment for many patients with manic-depressive illness; many patients who had been previously diagnosed as schizophrenic have, in fact, turned out to respond to lithium carbonate.

The depression of the manic-depressive illness is similar to that seen in the patients with major depression. To fulfill DSM III criteria, a patient must have dysphoric mood or loss of pleasure and four of the following: *(a)* appetite and weight disturbance, *(b)* insomnia or hypersomnia, *(c)* psychomotor agitation or retardation, *(d)* loss of interest or pleasure, *(e)* decreased energy or increased fatigue, *(f)* guilt or worthlessness, *(g)* decreased ability to concentrate, *(h)* suicidal ideation, etc. Although many patients with major depression show psychomotor retardation in conjunction with both anxiety and agitation, this may be more common in the elderly. The incidence of major depression is estimated as approximately 5%.

Unfortunately, the criteria for this disorder—requiring only four symptoms—may be too broad. However, patients who have a pervasive depressed mood (distinctly different from the previous premorbid functioning) and significant weight loss, excessive guilt, severe psychomotor retardation, early morning awakening, and diurnal variation are diagnosed as "major depression with melancholia," a label that appears more closely akin to a severe endogenous depression. The DSM III also allows for other subtyping of major depression. For one, the significance of preceding psychosocial stressors is rated. Further, the presence of psychotic features that are mood congruent (i.e., are commensurate with a pervasive lowering of mood) is indicated by the term "major depression with psychotic features." This depressive psychosis is often akin to that described for involutional patients (delusions of nihilism, guilt, or self-deprecation) but is not limited to the elderly. Hence, "involutional melancholia" no longer appears, although I believe further research in this area is required. One difficult diagnostic area revolves around depressed patients with paranoid, but not self-deprecatory, delusions. In some systems these patients may be subsumed under schizoaffective disorder; many such patients, however, may have a major depression with less typical features.

The dysthymic disorder or depressive neurosis is more chronic. Depression dominates over a one- to two-year period with little in the way of symptom-free intervals. The syndrome is distinguished from major depression by having less in the way of somatic symptoms; to diagnose a patient as dysthymic, therefore, one must first rule out major depression. The incidence of this disorder, which is less responsive to somatic therapy than is major depression, is approximately 5%.

Cyclothymic individuals have mild cycles that do not meet criteria for bipolar disorder. Their fluctuations of mood need not be attendant on external precipitants. The relationship of this disorder to bipolar manic-depressive illness requires further study. However, the experience of Akiskal (18) suggests that cyclothymics may in fact be a subgroup of bipolar patients, an area of great interest that also requires further research.

Patients with situational disorders with depressed mood have less in the way of vegetative symptomatology than their major depressed counterparts, and their illnesses are better delineated than are the dysthymics'. Psychotherapy can be extremely helpful with such reactions.

Schizoaffective disorder is reserved for patients who do not meet criteria for major depression with psychotic features, bipolar disorder, or schizophrenia. Many of these patients may, in fact, have a form of psychotic depression.

Table 4. **Common Medical Causes of Depression**

Hyperthyroidism and hypothyroidism
Hyperadrenalism and adrenal insufficiency
Chronic hepatitis
Collagen disorders (e.g., systemic lupus erythematosus)
Cerebral insults
Parkinsonism
Carcinoma of head of pancreas
Drug-induced depressions (e.g., due to reserpine or α-methyldopa)

Medical Causes of Depression

Many patients who present to primary care and other physicians with complaints of depression and lack of energy actually suffer from a medical or neurological disorder. Clinicians must first evaluate the medical and neurological condition of their patients and rule out other possible contributing disorders before making a DSM III diagnosis. Common medical causes of depressive-type syndromes are listed in Table 4; they include thyroid abnormalities (hypo- and hyperthyroidism), Cushing's disease, Addison's disease, chronic hepatitis, carcinoma (particularly that of the head of the pancreas), infectious mononucleosis (and other similar infections), antihypertensive agents (particularly reserpine and α-methyldopa), and cerebral vascular insults. The latter may produce depression with considerable vegetative symptomatology as well as positive results for dexamethasone suppression tests (19, 20).

One of the most difficult differential diagnoses is that between the dementia of Alzheimer's disease and the pseudodementia of depression in the elderly. Because depressed patients may present with profound psychomotor retardation, to the point that their ability to concentrate and to remember is limited, they may appear demented. Advances in neuroradiological, neuropsychological, and neuropsychiatric techniques have not increased substantially our ability to discriminate between dementia and pseudodementia, although clinical signs and symptoms may help to distinguish between the two. Wells *(21)* suggests that patients with pseudodementia tend to show positive previous histories and family histories of depression. Such patients and their families are often able to pinpoint the development of their decreased performance and are upset by it. When given neuropsychological tests, these patients will often show anergia with a decreased interest in performing and an avoidance of test taking.

In contrast, demented patients tend to show a rather more insidious onset and shallower mood changes. A history of depression may be less common than in pseudodementia. They demonstrate near-misses on tests. In contrast to the pseudodemented patient, they tend not to avoid tests and they are generally less aware of their own deficits.

Still, the clinician often faces a difficult differential diagnosis. Because the pseudodemented patient will often respond to antidepressants or electroconvulsive therapy, some advocate that a trial of one or the other is in order in any case of doubt *(22)*. To them, the "upside gain" far outweighs the "downside risk" of leaving a patient untreated and perhaps chronically ill.

Other Syndromes

Various types of depressions not really clearly defined in the DSM III have been described by a number of investigators—for example, the diagnosis of hysteroid or reactive dysphoria, as described by Klein *(23)*. This can be a chronic and pervasive illness, in which the individual reacts to interpersonal loss by demonstrating dysphoric depressive symptoms, including anxiety and self-destructive behavior. Klein has argued that such patients are highly responsive to monoamine oxidase inhibitors and has hypothesized that a possible disorder involving phenylethylamine (a neurotransmitter) may be involved in the underlying pathophysiology. He and others have also used the term "atypical depression," to indicate the lack of vegetative symptomatology, a sometimes chronic and more pervasive course, considerable anxiety, reversed diurnal variation, irritability, and personality problems.

These syndromes are very similar to the diagnosis of "borderline personality disorder," as used by many clinicians. In DSM III this diagnosis is rather more restrictive than that used in general clinical practice. By the DSM III criteria, such patients have a chronic and pervasive disorder characterized by micro-psychotic episodes, poor work history, self-destructive activity, irritability and anger, a variety of acting-out behaviors (including self-mutilation, alcohol abuse, and drug abuse), and the absence of vegetative symptomatology. As used more widely by clinicians, the diagnosis of borderline personality disorder is applied loosely to many patients with hysteroid dysphoria or atypical depression. The possible biology of borderline personality disorder requires further elaboration.

Genetic and Biological Classifications

In recent years, the ability to discriminate among disorders on the basis of symptoms, course, and treatment response has led to considerable research into the underlying biological processes that might differentiate among them. Such research offers the opportunity and the hope that, in the future, classification systems might include various biological and genetic criteria to classify the depressive disorders.

Pioneering in the use of genetics to classify depressive illnesses, Winokur has over the years refined his system *(24, 25)*. In brief, Winokur divides primary affective disorders into bipolar and unipolar illnesses. Unipolar depression in particular may be further divided along genetic patterns into depressive spectrum disorder (family history of alcoholism and psychopathy but less than a history of primary depression), sporadic depressive disorder (no pronounced family history of depression or other illnesses), and familial pure depressive disorder (family history of depression alone).

In recent years, the dexamethasone suppression test has been

Table 5. Possible DSM IV Classification for Affective Disorders

Major affective disorders
  Bipolar disorder
    Manic
    Depressed
    Cyclic
      Rapid cycling disorder
      Bipolar, nonrapid cyclic
Major depressive disorder
  Type I[a]
  Type II[a]
  Type III[a]
  Type IV, psychotic
Dysthymic disorder
  Type I, drug responsive
  Type II, responsive to psychotherapy
Cyclothymic disorder
  Type A: less severe type of bipolar disorder, positive response to lithium
  Personality disorder
Other disorders

[a] Defined by symptoms, clusters of biological measures, genetic patterns, and response to treatment.

used to validate this system (see the chapters by Drs. Carroll and Rosenbaum in this book for a description of the test). Schlesser et al. *(26, 27)* and Coryell et al. *(28)* have reported a high incidence of nonsuppression in unipolar patients with familial pure depressive disease, and significantly lower incidences of nonsuppression in depressive spectrum and sporadic depressive diseases. Whether, in fact, nonsuppression or suppression patterns in this test may also correlate with other subtypes of depression will require further elaboration.

Other biological measures have also been used to discriminate among some types of depressive illnesses. Of particular note has been the use of urinary MHPG to discriminate among various depressive illnesses. One major hypothesis proposed by Maas in 1975 *(11)* assumed two types of depression: one was characterized by low urinary concentrations of MHPG, which was believed to reflect a disorder involving low-norepinephrine activity, the other (a high-MHPG syndrome) represented normal norepinephrine activity but abnormal or decreased serotonin activity. This hypothesis has undergone considerable modification over the years. Recently, our group has proposed that there are perhaps three unipolar subtypes that can be differentiated on the basis of concentrations of urinary MHPG *(14)*.

Although further research obviously is needed in this area, these data all point to the possibility that over the next few years a combined classification system involving such measures as dexamethasone suppression test results, urinary concentrations of catecholamines, and other biological determinants, coupled with signs and symptoms and genetic data, may serve as the basis for a future (DSM IV) classification of affective disorders. It is hoped this would lead to systems more closely akin to those seen in other medical specialties. A possible classification system is highlighted in Table 5. In DSM IV the biological and clinical characteristics could also be combined with responses to treatments, to provide the clinician with a practical classification system. Such a system would represent the outcome of the great efforts expended over the past 50+ years in the investigation of the diagnosis, biology, and treatment of depressed patients.

References

1. Feighner JP, Robins E, Guze SB, et al. Diagnostic criteria for use in psychiatric research. *Arch Gen Psychiatry* **26,** 57–63 (1972).
2. Kraepelin E. *Lectures on Clinical Psychiatry.* William Wood, New York, NY, 1904.
3. Kraepelin E. *Manic-Depressive Insanity and Paranoia,* translated by M. Barclay, E & S Livingstone, Edinburgh, 1921.
4. Schatzberg AF. Classification of depressive disorders. In *Depression: Biology, Psychodynamics, and Treatment,* JO Cole, AF Schatzberg, SH Frazier, Eds., Plenum Press, New York, NY, 1978, pp 13–40.
5. Kendell RE. The classification of depressions: A review of contemporary confusion. *Br J Psychiatry* **129,** 15–28 (1976).
6. Lange J. Über melancholie. *Z Gesamte Neurol Psychiatr* **101,** 293–319 (1926).
7. American Psychiatric Association. *Diagnostic and Statistical Manual of Mental Disorders,* 3rd ed., Washington, DC, 1980.
8. American Psychiatric Association. *Diagnostic and Statistical Manual of Mental Disorders,* 2nd ed., Washington, DC, 1968.
9. Leonhard K. *Aufteilung der Endogenen Psychosen,* Akademie Verlag, Berlin, 1959.
10. Perris C. A survey of bipolar and unipolar recurrent depressive psychoses. *Acta Psychiatr Scand,* Suppl, 194 (1966).

11. Maas JW. Biogenic amines and depression: Biochemical and pharmacological separation of two types of depression. *Arch Gen Psychiatry* **32**, 1356–1361 (1975).
12. Carroll BJ, Feinberg M, Greden JF, et al. A specific laboratory test for melancholia. *Arch Gen Psychiatry* **38**, 15–22 (1981).
13. Schatzberg AF, Rosenbaum AH, Orsulak PJ, et al. Toward a biochemical classification of depressive disorders III. Pretreatment urinary MHPG levels as predictors of response to treatment with maprotiline. *Psychopharmacology* **75**, 34–38 (1981).
14. Schatzberg AF, Orsulak PJ, Rosenbaum AH. Toward a biochemical classification of depressive disorders V. Heterogeneity of unipolar depressions. *Am J Psychiatry* **139**, 471–475 (1982).
15. Schatzberg AF, Rothschild AJ, Stahl JB, et al. The dexamethasone suppression test: Identification of subtypes of depression. *Am J Psychiatry* **140**, 88–91 (1983).
16. American Psychiatric Association. *Diagnostic and Statistical Manual of Mental Disorders,* 1st ed., Washington, DC, 1952.
17. Pope HG, Lipinski J. Diagnosis in schizophrenia and manic depressive illness: A reassessment of the specificity of "schizophrenic" symptoms in the light of current research. *Arch Gen Psychiatry* **35**, 811–828 (1978).
18. Akiskal H. Cyclothymic disorders. In *The Affective Disorders,* J Davis, J Maas, Eds., American Psychiatric Press, Washington, DC, 1983.
19. Finkelstein S, Benowitz LD, Baldessarini RJ, et al. Mood, vegetative disturbance, and dexamethasone suppression test after stroke. *Ann Neurol* **12**, 463–468 (1982).
20. Ross D, Rush AJ. Diagnosis and neuroanatomical correlates of depression in brain-damaged patients. *Arch Gen Psychiatry* **38**, 1344–1354 (1981).
21. Wells CE. The differential diagnosis of psychiatric disorders in the elderly. In *Psychopathology in the Aged,* JO Cole, JE Barrett, Eds., Raven Press, New York, NY, 1980, pp 19–31.
22. Janowsky DS. Pseudodementia in the elderly: Differential diagnosis and treatment. *J Clin Psychiatry* **43** (Suppl), 19–25 (1982).
23. Klein DF. Endogenomorphic depression. *Arch Gen Psychiatry* **31**, 447–454 (1974).
24. Winokur G, Belhan D, von Valkenburg V, et al. Is a familial definition of depression both feasible and valid? *J Nerv Ment Dis* **166**, 764–768 (1978).
25. Winokur G. Familial (genetic) subtypes of pure depressive disease. *Am J Psychiatry* **136**, 911–913 (1979).
26. Schlesser MA, Winokur G, Sherman BM. Genetic subtypes of unipolar primary depressive illness distinguished by hypothalamic–pituitary–adrenal axis activity. *Lancet* **i**, 739–741 (1979).

27. Schlesser MA, Winokur G, Sherman BM. Hypothalamic–pituitary–adrenal axis activity in depressive illness. *Arch Gen Psychiatry* **37**, 737–743 (1980).
28. Coryell W, Gaffney G, Burkhardt PE. The dexamethasone suppression test and familial subtypes of depression—a naturalistic replication. *Biol Psychiatry* **17**, 33–40 (1982).

Toward a Biochemical Classification of Depressive Disorders, and the Emerging Field of Psychiatric Chemistry

Joseph J. Schildkraut, Alan F. Schatzberg, Paul J. Orsulak, Alan H. Rosenbaum, and Jonathan O. Cole

The search for possible biological abnormalities in the depressive disorders received a major stimulus in the late 1950s when it was first established that specific pharmacological agents were effective in the treatment of certain types of depressive disorders. Early neuropharmacological findings led to the formulation of the catecholamine hypothesis of affective disorders, which has proved to be of considerable heuristic value to research in this field (1). The biological heterogeneity of depressive disorders was discussed in an early review of the catecholamine hypothesis of affective disorders (1), and it was noted that various alterations in catecholamine metabolism might be of importance in the pathophysiology of certain types of depressions.

From the outset this focus on catecholamine metabolism was considered at best an oversimplification of an extremely complex biological state, which undoubtedly involved abnormalities in many other neurotransmitter or neuromodulator systems, as well as endocrine changes and other biochemical abnormalities. Nonetheless, the possibility that different subgroups of patients with depressive disorders might be characterized by differences in the metabolism of norepinephrine and the physiology of noradrenergic neuronal systems, including alterations in noradrenergic receptor sensitivity, was suggested more than 15 years ago (1). Since that time, studies by our research group (2–8), as well as by other investigators, have provided data supporting this possibility; this literature has been reviewed recently (9).

During the past decade, considerable attention was focused on the possibility that depressive disorders could be dichotomized into "noradrenergic" or "serotonergic" depressions on the basis of pretreatment biochemical data and differential responses to various tricyclic antidepressant drugs (10). However, this notion—which was based, in part, on the presumed differences in effects of various tricyclic antidepressant drugs on the inhibition of norepinephrine and serotonin uptake—no longer seems tenable in the light of more recent findings from studies of depressed patients (6, 9, 11), as well as more recent data concerning the complex neuropharmacological effects of antidepressant drugs (12–14). In this context, an early review of the catecholamine hypothesis of affective disorders specifically cautioned against attempts to separate depressions on the basis of simple dichotomies, and emphasized the broad clinical and biological heterogeneity of these disorders (1).

For many years, our collaborative research group has been engaged in a series of studies designed to elucidate aspects of the biochemical pathophysiology of the depressive disorders. The long-term goal of this research program is to develop a classification of depressive disorders based, in part, on the biochemical differences between different types of depressions. A major focus of our research has been on the use of measurements of catecholamine metabolism as clinical aids in classifying the depressive disorders on the basis of differences in underlying biochemical pathophysiology, and as predictors of responses to specific antidepressant drugs.

Here we review and summarize selected aspects of our collaborative research program, in the context of research performed by other investigators. In particular, we shall emphasize the impact of such research on the emerging field of psychiatric chemistry.

Utility of Measuring MHPG in Urine

In the Pathophysiology and Classification of Depressive Disorders

Since the late 1960s 3-methoxy-4-hydroxyphenylglycol (MHPG)[1] has been recognized as a major metabolite of norepi-

---

[1] Abbreviations used: MHPG, 3-methoxy-4-hydroxyphenylglycol; VMA, vanillylmandelic acid; MAO, monoamine oxidase.

nephrine originating in the brain (15–17). Although urinary MHPG may also derive in part from the peripheral sympathetic nervous system, so that the fraction of urinary MHPG deriving from norepinephrine originating in the brain remains uncertain (18–20), it is generally recognized that the concentration of MHPG in urine might nonetheless be of value in exploring the pathophysiology of depressions and in defining subgroups of depressive disorders.

For example, in longitudinal studies of patients with naturally occurring or amphetamine-induced bipolar manic-depressive episodes, many studies show that amounts of urinary MHPG excreted in 24 h were lower during periods of depression and higher during periods of mania or hypomania than during periods of remission (21–28). All depressed patients, however, do not excrete comparably low amounts of MHPG (29, 30). Consequently, many investigators have explored the possibility that urinary concentrations of MHPG as well as other catecholamine metabolites might provide a biochemical basis for differentiating among the depressive disorders.

Ten years ago, our group initially reported that excretion of urinary MHPG was significantly lower in bipolar manic-depressive depressions than in patients with unipolar, nonendogenous, chronic characterological depressions (31, 32). This finding of decreased urinary MHPG in patients with bipolar manic-depressive depressions, as well as in patients with schizoaffective depressions (in the absence of a history of chronic asocial, eccentric, or bizarre behavior), has been confirmed by several other laboratories (2, 6, 33–39). In contrast, there were no differences in concentrations of urinary vanillylmandelic acid (VMA) between patients with bipolar manic-depressive depressions and those with unipolar depressions (2, 6). This is important because reports that circulating MHPG might be converted to VMA (19, 20) have raised questions concerning the specific value of urinary MHPG (e.g., in contrast to VMA) as an index of norepinephrine metabolism in the brain or as a biochemical marker in studies of depressed patients (40).

In various studies of patients with unipolar depressions, low (41–44), normal (35, 37, 38), or high (45) values for urinary MHPG excretion have been reported. Diagnostic heterogeneity may account for these discrepancies: early findings from our laboratory (2), which revealed a wide range of urinary MHPG values in patients with unipolar depressive disorders, have been confirmed and extended in our more recent investigations.

In our early series of 16 patients with unipolar endogenous depressions, the mean amount of urinary MHPG excreted was 1950 μg/24 h (2); in a subsequent study of an enlarged sample (6), 26 of 50 patients with unipolar depressions had urinary MHPG values >1950 μg/24 h, while only three of 20 patients with bipolar manic-depressive or schizoaffective depressions had MHPG values >1950 μg/24 h (chi square = 6.61; $p < 0.025$). A scatter plot of MHPG values in this series of depressed patients revealed a natural break in MHPG results around 2500 μg/24 h, suggesting the possible existence of a subgroup of unipolar depressions with MHPG excretion >2500 μg/24 h. For example, in this series, 17 of 50 patients with unipolar depressions had urinary MHPG >2500 μg/24 h, while only one of the 20 patients with bipolar manic-depressive or schizoaffective depressions had MHPG >2500 μg/24 h (chi square = 4.9; $p < 0.05$).

Thus, the data from this series of patients with unipolar depressive disorders further substantiated the biochemical heterogeneity of unipolar depressions, demonstrating that some patients excrete low amounts of MHPG (similar to values seen in the bipolar manic-depressive or schizoaffective depressions), while others excrete large quantities (sometimes higher than control values), and still others have MHPG values in an intermediate range. We stress, however, that urinary excretion of MHPG in most depressed patients falls within the broad range of values observed in normal control subjects $(6, 46)$. Thus, although results for urinary MHPG may help to differentiate among subtypes of depressive disorders once a clinical diagnosis of depression has been made, the quantity of urinary MHPG excreted cannot be used to make a diagnosis of depression per se.

Supporting these findings, a histogram of the distribution of urinary MHPG values in a series of 102 patients with unipolar major depressive disorders revealed a clustering of patients whose urinary excretion of MHPG exceeded 2500 μg/24 h, in addition to clusters at lower MHPG values (Figure 1). As shown in Table 1, the existence of a biologically meaningful subgroup of unipolar depressions with very high excretion of urinary MHPG is also supported by the findings of a study of patients with very severe unipolar depressions (8), in which there was a subgroup of patients

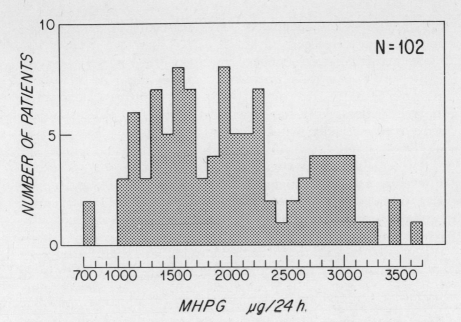

Fig. 1. Distribution of urinary MHPG excretion values in patients with unipolar major depressive disorders

Table 1. **Excretion of Urinary Free Cortisol by Depressed Patients with High Pretreatment Excretion of MHPG**

Group	N	Cortisol, mean ± SEM, µg/24 h
Depressed		
MHPG > 2500 µg/24 h	7	335 ± 33[a,b]
MHPG ≤ 2500 µg/24 h	17	137 ± 16[a]
Controls	22	66 ± 4

[a] $p < 0.001$, compared with controls.
[b] $p < 0.001$, compared with depressed patients with MHPG ≤ 2500 µg/24 h. Source: 8.

with very high excretion of urinary MHPG (>2500 µg/24 h) who also had very high excretion of urinary free cortisol (>200 µg/24 h). To rule out the possibility that the high values for urinary free cortisol and urinary MHPG observed in this series of severely depressed patients might be secondary to anxiety, excretion of urinary MHPG and urinary free cortisol was studied in patients with moderate to severe anxiety states; markedly increased excretion of urinary free cortisol (>200 $\mu g/24$ h) was not observed. However, the very high values for urinary free cortisol observed in the series of severely depressed patients might be related to the severity of the depression, in that preliminary data from a study of patients with less severe depressions revealed few patients with markedly increased excretion of urinary free cortisol (47).

One possibility that might explain our finding of a subgroup of severely depressed patients with high urinary MHPG and markedly increased urinary free cortisol is that, in these patients, increased excretion of MHPG and urinary free cortisol may occur as a secondary response to an increase in cholinergic activity. This possibility is consistent with the hypothesis that central cholinergic factors may play a role in the etiology of the depressive disorders (48–50) and is particularly intriguing in view of the following findings of other investigators:

1. Physostigmine, an anticholinesterase, and other pharmacological agents that increase brain cholinergic activity exacerbate depressive symptoms in depressed patients (48, 51) and induce depressive symptoms in normal controls (52).

2. Physostigmine produces an increase in plasma concentrations of cortisol in normal controls (52).

3. Physostigmine can overcome dexamethasone suppression of the hypothalamic–pituitary–adrenal–cortical axis in normal subjects, thereby mimicking the abnormal escape from dexamethasone suppression seen in some depressed patients who show cortisol hypersecretion (53).

4. Physostigmine produces an increase of MHPG in cerebrospinal fluid in normal subjects (54).

Thus, the marked increases of urinary free cortisol that we observe in some patients with severe unipolar depressive disorders could result from an increase in cholinergic activity, and the increased urinary MHPG in these patients could represent a secondary noradrenergic response to such cholinergic hyperactivity. These findings suggest that the anticholinergic effects of certain antidepressants may contribute to their antidepressant effects in some depressed patients with high pretreatment excretion of urinary MHPG. Noteworthy in this regard are recent preliminary reports on the antidepressant effects of certain anticholinergic drugs (55, 56).

As a Predictor of Differential Responses to Antidepressant Drugs

Studies from several laboratories indicate that pretreatment values for urinary excretion of MHPG may aid in predicting responses to certain tricyclic and tetracyclic antidepressant drugs. Specifically, depressed patients with "low" pretreatment values for urinary MHPG respond more favorably to treatment with imipramine (5, 11, 30, 57–60), desipramine (30), nortriptyline (61), or maprotiline (4, 60, 62) than do patients with "high" MHPG excretion. In contrast, some studies (57, 59, 62–64) have found that depressed patients with "high" pretreatment excretion of urinary MHPG respond more favorably to treatment with amitriptyline than do patients with lower MHPG excretion, but this has not been observed in all studies (11, 65–67, and M. Roffman, personal communication). Further research will clearly be required to account for these differences in findings. Nevertheless, the findings of these studies do point to differences between amitriptyline and imipramine: "low" pretreatment values for urinary MHPG have been shown in many studies to predict more favorable responses to treatment with imipramine, whereas this has not been found in any of the studies of amitriptyline.

Our recently published prospective studies have confirmed that patients who excrete relatively little urinary MHPG ($\leq$1950 μg/ 24 h) respond more favorably to treatment with imipramine or maprotiline than do patients who excrete more MHPG (4, 5). Because our findings (described above) suggested that there may be at least three subtypes of unipolar depressive disorders that could be discriminated on the basis of differences in pretreatment values for urinary MHPG (6), we combined the data from these two studies of the pretreatment rate of excretion of MHPG as a predictor of responses to imipramine and maprotiline, to provide us enough patients to compare treatment responses in these three subtypes.

Although further studies in a larger series of patients will be required for confirmation, our findings (Table 2) suggest that depressed patients with very high excretion of MHPG (>2500 μg/

Table 2. **Distributions of Favorable Responses to Maprotiline or Imipramine Treatment after Four Weeks**

MHPG, $\mu g/24$ h	Favorable antidepressant response[a]	
	Yes	No
≤1950	17	8
1951–2500	1	13
>2500	5	8

[a] Defined as a decrease in the Hamilton Depression Rating Scale ≥60% from baseline value. The differences in response of the three MHPG groups to treatment is significant (chi square = 13.7, $p < 0.005$).

24 h) may be more responsive to treatment with imipramine or maprotiline than are patients with intermediate MHPG excretion (1951–2500 $\mu g/24$ h); neither group, however, is as responsive to these drugs as are patients with low pretreatment excretion of urinary MHPG (≤1950 $\mu g/24$ h). Moreover, as described in a recently published paper (4), we observed that patients with low pretreatment urinary MHPG responded rapidly to relatively low doses of maprotiline, whereas those patients with more MHPG excretion who did respond to maprotiline required significantly higher doses and longer periods of drug administration.

The complex effects on noradrenergic, dopaminergic, and other neurotransmitter systems, including alterations in various indices of presynaptic and postsynaptic receptor functions, that are observed after chronic administration of various antidepressant drugs (68–70) suggest that empirical trials will be required to assess the value of urinary MHPG excretion, or any other biochemical measure, as clinically useful predictors of responses to a specific antidepressant drug. For example, patients with normal or high urinary excretion of MHPG who show suppression of cortisol in response to dexamethasone have been reported to respond favorably to treatment with mianserin, whereas patients with low urinary MHPG excretion, whose cortisol secretion is not suppressed by dexamethasone, do not respond to mianserin (71).

Summary of Studies of Urinary MHPG

In summary, several studies have shown that patients with bipolar manic-depressive depressions have lower mean urinary excretion of MHPG than do patients with unipolar depressions or control subjects. Moreover, our recent studies substantiate the biochemical heterogeneity of the unipolar depressive disorders, and suggest that there may be at least three subtypes of unipolar depressions that can be discriminated on the basis of differences in urinary excretion of MHPG. Subtype I, with low pretreatment urinary MHPG, may have low norepinephrine output as a result of a decrease in norepinephrine synthesis, a decrease in its release from noradrenergic neurons, or both. In contrast, Subtype II, with intermediate values for urinary MHPG, may have normal norepinephrine output but abnormalities in other biochemical systems. And Subtype III, with high urinary excretion of MHPG, may have a high norepinephrine output in response to alterations in noradrenergic receptors, an increase in cholinergic activity, or both, as described above. Further studies will be required to confirm these findings; to explore their therapeutic implications; and to explore the many possible pathophysiological abnormalities that may be associated with these subtypes of unipolar depressive disorders.

D-Type Equation

Several years ago, by applying stepwise multivariate discriminant function analysis to data on urinary catecholamines and metabolites, we generated an empirically derived equation that provided an even more precise discrimination between bipolar manic-depressive and unipolar nonendogenous chronic characterological depressions than did urinary MHPG alone *(3)*. This discrimination equation for computing the Depression-type (D-type) score was of the form:

$$\text{D-type score} = C_1(\text{MHPG}) - C_2(\text{VMA}) + C_3(\text{NE}) - C_4(\text{NMN} + \text{MN})/\text{VMA} + C_0$$

where NE = norepinephrine, NMN = normetanephrine, MN = metanephrine, and C_{0-4} = the constant and various coefficients.

In generating this equation a scale was established so that low scores were related to patients with bipolar manic-depressive depressions, and high scores were related to unipolar nonendogenous depressions. Preliminary validation of this equation was then obtained in a sample of patients whose data had not been used to derive the equation *(3)*. We have recently determined D-type scores in an additional series of more than 80 depressed patients— classified according to diagnostic criteria previously used in our research *(2, 3)*—whose data were not used in the original derivation of this equation (i.e., in selecting the terms and determining the coefficients and constant) or in its preliminary validation.

In the light of our finding that patients with unipolar depressive disorders appear to be biochemically heterogeneous with respect to urinary MHPG, we were particularly interested in the distribution of D-type scores in the newly studied patients with "unipolar" depressions (diagnosed on the basis of clinical histories and presenting signs and symptoms). The D-type scores, computed with the original D-type equation with the previously derived coefficients and constant, segregated these newly studied unipolar depressions into two widely separated groupings, one with D-type scores <0.5—i.e., in the range of values similar to that previously observed in bipolar manic-depressive depressions *(3)*—and another with considerably higher D-type scores.

Relatively few patients with typical bipolar manic-depressive depressions could be included in our recent studies because most patients with this diagnosis now receive maintenance lithium treatment and we could not ethically discontinue this treatment to study such patients biochemically. However, many of the patients in this newly studied series had depressive disorders that could not be assigned unambiguously to one of the diagnostic categories in our classification system, usually because of clinical features suggesting the possibility of a bipolar disorder, or a schizophrenia-related disorder. In this series of 37 patients with diagnostically unclassifiable depressive disorders, we were particularly interested in exploring the hypothesis that patients with low D-type scores would show clinical features suggestive of a bipolar disorder even though the clinical diagnosis of a definite bipolar disorder could not be made in these patients. In support of this hypothesis we found that, of the eight diagnostically unclassifiable depressed patients with the lowest D-type scores, seven met the criteria for at least a probable bipolar disorder, both in our classification system and according to the Research Diagnostic Criteria *(77)*. In contrast, of the 29 remaining patients with diagnostically unclassifiable depressions, only seven showed comparable evidence for bipolarity (chi square $= 8.2$; $p < 0.01$).

On the basis of earlier findings we had hypothesized that low D-type scores in patients with so-called "unipolar" depressions might aid in identifying those patients having latent bipolar disorders even before the first clinical episode of mania or hypomania. In a recent pilot follow-up study of a subset of the sample of depressed patients who participated in our collaborative research program over the past seven years, our findings suggest that D-type scores <0.5 can identify patients at risk for developing manic episodes, even in the absence of a prior clinical history suggestive of a bipolar disorder.

Although the D-type equation was generated mathematically to provide the best least-squares fit of the data, and the terms were not selected by the investigators, the inclusion of VMA as well as other urinary catecholamines and metabolites (of peripheral origin) in this empirically derived equation may be correcting for that fraction of urinary MHPG that comes from peripheral sources rather than from the brain *(3)*. Moreover, several years ago, we suggested that the fourth term—i.e., the ratio (NMN + MN)/VMA—might be inversely related to monoamine oxidase (MAO) activity, normetanephrine and metanephrine being convertible to VMA by deamination *(3)*. Indeed, such an inverse correlation has recently been documented between this ratio and platelet MAO activity in a series of 90 patients in whom we obtained concurrent measurements ($r = - 0.29; p < 0.005$). Besides confirming that this fourth term of the D-type equation is related to platelet MAO activity, this correlation (although modest) also suggests that measurement of platelet MAO activity may provide functionally relevant information with respect to monoamine metabolism, in that it relates in a logical way to a ratio of nondeaminated and deaminated urinary catecholamine metabolites.

The Emerging Field of Psychiatric Chemistry

We have already reached a point where the clinical laboratory can be used in psychiatry as it is in other fields of medicine, both to assist the physician in making more specific diagnoses and to aid the physician in prescribing more effectively. Recognizing this, the Harvard Medical School Department of Psychiatry and Department of Pathology at the New England Deaconess Hospital established in 1977 a Psychiatric Chemistry Laboratory as a model academic laboratory facility for the integration and translation of biochemical research into clinical psychiatric practice. In addition to providing specialized clinical laboratory tests for use in psychiatry, an explicit aim of the Psychiatric Chemistry Laboratory has been to provide education and consultative services to assist physicians in using and interpreting these tests *(73)*.

One may now draw an analogy between the depressions and certain other medical disorders, e.g., pneumonias, that are diagnosed on the basis of clinical data. In the case of pneumonias, the physician makes a diagnosis on the basis of history and physical examination (including a chest roentgenogram). Having made the diagnosis, sputum cultures can then be obtained to help determine the specific type of pneumonia and the specific antibiotic or other form of treatment that may be most effective. Similarly, in the case of depressions, the physician diagnoses depression on the basis of clinical history and examinations of physical and mental status. Having made the diagnosis of depression, a physician can then use specialized clinical laboratory tests to obtain further information to assist in determining the type of depression the patient has and the forms of treatment most likely to be effective.

Although the biochemical tests we have today do not necessarily enable physicians to select a clinically effective treatment on the first trial, the use of these clinical laboratory tests can increase the probability of their doing so. Considering the time it takes for antidepressant drugs to exert their clinical effects, even a small increase in the percentage of patients who receive an effective drug on the first clinical trial of treatment would represent a major advance in the treatment of patients with depressive disorders.

This work was supported in part by grant no. MH15413 from the National Institute of Mental Health. We thank Mrs. Gladys Rege for her assistance in the preparation of this paper.

References

1. Schildkraut JJ. The catecholamine hypothesis of affective disorders: A review of supporting evidence. *Am J Psychiatry* **122,** 509–522 (1965).
2. Schildkraut JJ, Orsulak PJ, Schatzberg AF, et al. Toward a biochemical classification of depressive disorders I: Differences in urinary

MHPG and other catecholamine metabolites in clinically defined subtypes of depressions. *Arch Gen Psychiatry* **35**, 1427–1433 (1978).

3. Schildkraut JJ, Orsulak PJ, LaBrie RA, et al. Toward a biochemical classification of depressive disorders II: Application of multivariate discriminant function analysis to data on urinary catecholamines and metabolites. *Arch Gen Psychiatry* **35**, 1436–1439 (1978).

4. Schatzberg AF, Rosenbaum AH, Orsulak PJ, et al. Toward a biochemical classification of depressive disorders III. Pretreatment of urinary MHPG levels as predictors of response to treatment with maprotiline. *Psychopharmacology* **75**, 34–38 (1981).

5. Schatzberg AF, Orsulak PJ, Rosenbaum AH, et al. Toward a biochemical classification of depressive disorders IV: Pretreatment urinary MHPG levels as predictors of antidepressant response to imipramine. *Commun Psychopharmacol* **4**, 441–445 (1980–1981).

6. Schatzberg AF, Orsulak PJ, Rosenbaum AH, et al. Toward a biochemical classification of depressive disorders V: Heterogeneity of unipolar depressions. *Am J Psychiatry* **139**, 471–475 (1982).

7. Gudeman JE, Schatzberg AF, Samson JA, et al. Toward a biochemical classification of depressive disorders VI. Platelet MAO activity and clinical symptoms in depressed patients. *Am J Psychiatry* **139**, 630–633 (1982).

8. Rosenbaum AH, Maruta T, Schatzberg AF, et al. Toward a biochemical classification of depressive disorders VII. Urinary free cortisol and urinary MHPG in depressions. *Am J Psychiatry* **140**, 314–318 (1983).

9. Schildkraut JJ, Schatzberg AF, Mooney JJ, Orsulak PJ. Depressive disorders and the emerging field of psychiatric chemistry. In *Psychiatry Update: The American Psychiatric Association Annual Review,* **2.** L Grinspoon, Ed., American Psychiatric Press, Inc., Washington, DC, 1983, pp 457–471, 538–542.

10. Maas JW. Biogenic amines and depression: Biochemical and pharmacological separation of two types of depression. *Arch Gen Psychiatry* **32**, 1357–1361 (1975).

11. Maas JW, Kocsis JH, Bowden CL, et al. Pretreatment neurotransmitter metabolites and response to imipramine or amitriptyline treatment. *Psychol Med* **12**, 37–43 (1982).

12. Charney DS, Menkes DB, Heninger GR. Receptor sensitivity and the mechanisms of action of antidepressant treatment. *Arch Gen Psychiatry* **38**, 1160–1180 (1981).

13. Baldessarini RJ. Overview of recent advances in antidepressant pharmacology: Part II. *McLean Hosp J* **7**, 1–27 (1982).

14. Richelson E. Pharmacology of antidepressants in use in the United States. *J Clin Psychol* **43** (11, Sec. 2), 4–11 (1982).

15. Maas JW, Landis DH. *In vivo* studies of metabolism of norepinephrine in central nervous system. *J Pharmacol Exp Ther* **163**, 147–162 (1968).
16. Schanberg SM, Breese GR, Schildkraut JJ, et al. 3-Methoxy-4-hydroxyphenylglycol sulfate in brain and cerebrospinal fluid. *Biochem Pharmacol* **17**, 2006–2008 (1968).
17. Schanberg SM, Schildkraut JJ, Breese GR, Kopin IJ. Metabolism of normetanephrine-H^3 in rat brain—identification of conjugated 3-methoxy-4-hydroxyphenylglycol as major metabolite. *Biochem Pharmacol* **17**, 247–254 (1968).
18. Maas JW, Hattox SE, Greene NM, Landis DH. 3-Methoxy-4-hydroxyphenethyleneglycol production by human brain *in vivo*. *Science* **205**, 1025–1027 (1979).
19. Blombery PA, Kopin IJ, Gordon EK, et al. Conversion of MHPG to vanillylmandelic acid. *Arch Gen Psychiatry* **37**, 1095–1098 (1980).
20. Mardh G, Sjoquist B, Anggard E. Norepinephrine metabolism in man using deuterium labelling: The conversion of 4-hydroxy-3-methoxyphenylglycol to 4-hydroxy-3-methoxymandelic acid. *J Neurochem* **36**, 1181–1185 (1981).
21. Greenspan K, Schildkraut JJ, Gordon EK, et al. Catecholamine metabolism in affective disorders III. MHPG and other catecholamine metabolites in patients treated with lithium carbonate. *J Psychiatr Res* **7**, 171–183 (1970).
22. Schildkraut JJ, Watson R, Draskoczy PR, Hartmann E. Amphetamine withdrawal: Depression and MHPG excretion. *Lancet* **ii**, 485–486 (1971).
23. Schildkraut JJ, Keeler BA, Rogers MP, Draskoczy PR. Catecholamine metabolism in affective disorders: A longitudinal study of a patient treated with amitriptyline and ECT. *Psychosom Med* **34**, 470 (1972). Plus erratum: *Psychosom Med* **35**, 274 (1973).
24. Watson R, Hartmann E, Schildkraut JJ. Amphetamine withdrawal: Affective state, sleep patterns and MHPG excretion. *Am J Psychiatry* **129**, 263–269 (1972).
25. Bond PA, Jenner FA, Sampson GA. Daily variations of the urine content of 3-methoxy-4-hydroxyphenylglycol in two manic-depressive patients. *Psychol Med* **2**, 81–85 (1972).
26. Bond PA, Dimitrakoudi M, Howlett DR, Jenner FA. Urinary excretion of the sulfate and glucuronide of 3-methoxy-4-hydroxyphenylethyleneglycol in a manic-depressive patient. *Psychol Med* **5**, 279–285 (1975).
27. DeLeon-Jones FD, Maas JW, Dekirmenjian H, Fawcett JA. Urinary catecholamine metabolites during behavioral changes in a patient with manic-depressive cycles. *Science* **179**, 300–302 (1973).
28. Post RM, Stoddard FJ, Gillin C, et al. Alterations in motor activity,

sleep and biochemistry in a cycling manic-depressive patient. *Arch Gen Psychiatry* **34**, 470–477 (1977).

29. Maas JW, Fawcett JA, Dekirmenjian H. 3-Methoxy-4-hydroxyphe-nylglycol (MHPG) excretion in depressive states. *Arch Gen Psychiatry* **19**, 129–134 (1968).

30. Maas JW, Fawcett JA, Dekirmenjian H. Catecholamine metabolism, depressive illness and drug response. *Arch Gen Psychiatry* **26**, 252–262 (1972).

31. Schildkraut JJ, Keeler BA, Grab EL, et al. MHPG excretion and clinical classification in depressive disorders. *Lancet* **i**, 1251–1252 (1973).

32. Schildkraut JJ, Keeler BA, Papousek M, Hartmann E. MHPG excretion in depressive disorders: Relation to clinical subtypes and desynchronized sleep. *Science* **181**, 762–764 (1973).

33. Maas JW, Dekirmenjian H, DeLeon-Jones F. The identification of depressed patients who have a disorder of norepinephrine metabolism and/or disposition. In *Frontiers in Catecholamine Research—Third International Catecholamine Symposium,* E Usdin, S Snyder, Eds., Pergamon Press, New York, NY, 1973, pp 1091–1096.

34. DeLeon-Jones F, Maas JW, Dekirmenjian H, Sanchez J. Diagnostic subgroups of affective disorders and their urinary excretion of catecholamine metabolites. *Am J Psychiatry* **132**, 1141–1148 (1975).

35. Goodwin FK, Post RM. Studies of amine metabolites in affective illness and in schizophrenia: A comparative analysis. In *Biology of Major Psychoses,* DX Freedman, Ed., Raven Press, New York, NY, 1975, pp 299–332.

36. Garfinkel PE, Warsh JJ, Stancer HC, Godse DD. CNS monoamine metabolism in bipolar affective disorders. *Arch Gen Psychiatry* **34**, 735–739 (1977).

37. Goodwin FK, Potter WZ. Norepinephrine metabolite studies in affective illness. In *Catecholamines: Basic and Clinical Frontiers,* **2**, E Usdin, I Kopin, J Barchas, Eds., Pergamon Press, New York, NY, 1979, pp 1863–1865.

38. Beckmann H, Goodwin FK. Urinary MHPG in subgroups of depressed patients and normal controls. *Neuropsychobiology* **6**, 91–100 (1980).

39. Edwards DJ, Spiker DG, Neil JF, et al. MHPG excretion in depression. *Psychiatry Res* **2**, 295–305 (1980).

40. Linnoila M, Karoum F, Potter WZ. High correlation of norepinephrine and its major metabolite excretion rates. *Arch Gen Psychiatry* **39**, 521–523 (1982).

41. Maas JW. Clinical and biochemical heterogeneity of depressive disorders. *Ann Intern Med* **88**, 556–663 (1978).

42. DeLeon-Jones FD, Maas JW, Dekirmenjian H, Sanchez J. Diagnostic

subgroups of affective disorders and their urinary excretion of cate-cholamine metabolites. *Am J Psychiatry* **132,** 1141–1148 (1975).

43. Taube SS, Kirstein LS, Sweeney DR, et al. Urinary 3-methoxy-4-hydroxyphenylglycol and psychiatric diagnosis. *Am J Psychiatry* **135,** 78–82 (1978).

44. Casper RC, Davis JM, Pandey GN, et al. Neuroendocrine and amine studies in affective illness. *Psychoneuroendocrinology* **2,** 105–113 (1977).

45. Garfinkel PE, Warsh JJ, Stancer HC. Depression: New evidence in support of biological differentiation. *Am J Psychiatry* **136,** 535–539 (1979).

46. Hollister LE, Davis KL, Overall JE, Anderson T. Excretion of MHPG in normal subjects. Implications for biological classification of affective disorders. *Arch Gen Psychiatry* **35,** 1410–1415 (1978).

47. Rosenbaum AH, Maruta T, Schatzberg AF, et al. Urinary free cortisol and MHPG levels in anxious patients and normal controls. Presented at Society of Biological Psychiatry Annual Meeting, New Orleans, May 1981.

48. Janowsky DS, El-Yousef M, Davis JM, Sekerke HJ. A cholinergic–adrenergic hypothesis of mania and depression. *Lancet* **ii,** 632–635 (1972).

49. Sitaram N, Gillin JC. Development and use of pharmacological probes of the CNS in man: Evidence of cholinergic abnormality in primary affective illness. *Biol Psychiatry* **15,** 925–955 (1980).

50. Risch SC, Kalin NH, Janowsky DS. Cholinergic challenges in affective illness: Behavioral and neuroendocrine correlates. *J Clin Psychopharmacol* **1,** 186–192 (1981).

51. Garver DL, Davis JM. Biogenic amine hypothesis of affective disorders. *Life Sci* **24,** 383–394 (1979).

52. Risch SC, Cohen RM, Janowsky DS, et al. Mood and behavioral effects of physostigmine on humans are accompanied by elevations in plasma β-endorphin and cortisol. *Science* **209,** 1545–1546 (1980).

53. Carroll BJ, Greden JF, Haskett R, et al. Neurotransmitter studies of neuroendocrine pathology in depression. *Acta Psychiatr Scand* **61** (Suppl 80), 183–199 (1980).

54. Davis KL, Hollister LE, Goodwin FK, Gordon EK. Neurotransmitter metabolites in cerebrospinal fluid of man following physostigmine. *Life Sci* **21,** 933–936 (1977).

55. Kasper S, Moises HW, Beckmann H. The anticholinergic biperiden in depressive disorders. *Pharmakopsychiatr Neuro-Psychopharmakol* **14,** 195–198 (1981).

56. Jimerson DC, Nurnberger JI, Simmons S, Gershon ES. Anticholinergic treatment for depression. In *Syllabus and Scientific Proceedings,* 135th

Annual Meeting, American Psychiatric Association, 1982, pp 218–219.

57. Beckmann H, Goodwin FK. Antidepressant response to tricyclics and urinary MHPG in unipolar patients. *Arch Gen Psychiatry* **32**, 17–21 (1975).

58. Steinbook RM, Jacobson AF, Weiss BL, Goldstein BJ. Amoxapine, imipramine, and placebo: A double-blind study with pre-therapy urinary 3-methoxy-4-hydroxyphenylglycol levels. *Curr Ther Res* **26**, 490–496 (1979).

59. Cobbin DM, Requin-Blow B, Williams LR, Williams WO. Urinary MHPG levels and tricyclic antidepressant drug selection. *Arch Gen Psychiatry* **36**, 1111–1115 (1979).

60. Rosenbaum AH, Schatzberg A, Maruta T, et al. MHPG as a predictor of antidepressant response to imipramine and maprotiline. *Am J Psychiatry* **137**, 1090–1092 (1980).

61. Hollister LE, Davis KL, Berger PA. Subtypes of depression based on excretion of MHPG and response to nortriptyline. *Arch Gen Psychiatry* **37**, 1107–1110 (1980).

62. Gaertner HJ, Kreuter F, Scharek G, et al. Do urinary MHPG and plasma drug levels correlate with response to amitriptyline therapy? *Psychopharmacology* **76**, 236–239 (1982).

63. Schildkraut JJ. Norepinephrine metabolites as biochemical criteria for classifying depressive disorders and predicting responses to treatment. Preliminary findings. *Am J Psychiatry* **130**, 696–699 (1973).

64. Modai I, Apter A, Golomb M, Wijsenbeek H. Response to amitriptyline and urinary MHPG in bipolar depressive patients. *Neuropsychobiology* **5**, 181–184 (1979).

65. Sacchetti E, Allaria E, Negri F, et al. 3-Methoxy-4-hydroxyphenylglycol and primary depression: Clinical and pharmacological considerations. *Biol Psychiatry* **14**, 473–484 (1979).

66. Coppen A, Ramo Rao VA, Ruthven CRJ, et al. Urinary 4-hydroxy-3-methoxyphenylglycol is not a predictor for clinical response to amitriptyline in depressive illness. *Psychopharmacology* **64**, 95–97 (1979).

67. Spiker DG, Edwards D, Hanin I, et al. Urinary MHPG and clinical response to amitriptyline in depressed patients. *Am J Psychiatry* **137**, 1183–1187 (1980).

68. Sulser F, Vetulani J, Mobley PK. Mode of action of antidepressant drugs. *Biochem Pharmacol* **27**, 257–261 (1978).

69. Charney DS, Menkes DB, Heninger GR. Receptor sensitivity and the mechanisms of action of antidepressant treatment. *Arch Gen Psychiatry* **38**, 1160–1180 (1981).

70. Waldmeier PC. Noradrenergic transmission in depression: Under-

or overfunction. *Pharmakopsychiatr Neuro-Psychopharmakol* **14,** 3–9 (1981).

71. Cobbin DM, Cairncross KD, Jurd S, et al. Urinary MHPG levels and the dexamethasone test predict clinical response to the antidepressant drug mianserin. *Neuroendocrinol Lett* **3,** 133–138 (1981).
72. Spitzer RL, Endicott J, Robins E. Research diagnostic criteria. Rationale and reliability. *Arch Gen Psychiatry* **35,** 773–782 (1978).
73. Schildkraut JJ, Orsulak PJ, Copeland BE, Legg MA. Clinical Laboratory Tests in Depressions and Schizophrenias—Offered by the Psychiatric Chemistry Laboratory in Cooperation with the New England Deaconess Hospital, Department of Pathology. New England Deaconess Hospital, Boston, MA, 1978.

Discussion—Session I

QUESTION: Some patients, particularly schizophrenics, seem less prone to physical illnesses like cancer or rheumatoid arthritis. Do you have any explanation for that?

DR. KLERMAN: I don't think that situation is completely established. For a while there was concern that patients treated with reserpine or even phenothiazines might have an increase in breast cancer, particularly since these drugs increase prolactin activity. However, we don't really know enough to make any definite statements. In a previous era there was a high death rate among mental patients, probably from suicide, poor nutrition, and infectious disease. I am not convinced that the follow-up studies are sufficiently good yet for me to make any clear response to your question.

Q: Is there any correlation between the incidence of attention-deficit disorders and a history of mania?

DR. SCHATZBERG: I have not seen any good studies on such a relationship. One of the problems is a question of definition. For example, some hyperactive children will grow up to present mood problems. Perhaps we may find that the offspring of patients with manic-depressive illness will have some type of hyperactivity or perhaps a related illness.

DR. KLERMAN: The best studies are prospective studies of children initially diagnosed with attention-deficit disorder, some of whom are in their twenties now. Many of these children become what might be called delinquent or have difficulty adjusting to society in their adolescent years. Such children don't seem to have a higher rate of bipolar mania than others. Some seem to be at risk for difficulty when they reach late adolescence and young adulthood, but mania does not appear to be their most serious or most frequent abnormality.

Q: What is the apparent role of acetylcholine and serotonin in depression?

DR. SCHILDKRAUT: Many neurochemical substances are involved in the pathophysiology of depressive disorders. A good body of data suggest that acetylcholinergic systems are involved; fairly good data suggest that the indoleamine system—serotonin—is involved, and we presented evidence today for the involvement of the catecholaminergic systems. But after running through the various known aminergic systems in the brain, I like to talk about the whole host of other systems—not catecholamines and indoleamines, but what I call the "unknownamines."

I believe there is far more to be learned about the brain and its neurochemistry than we have yet encountered. With the depressions, like the pneumonias, we may find broad-ranging categories of disorders with various specific subtypes. The progress we are making in the biological classification of depressions today might be analogous to distinguishing the bacterial pneumonias from the viral pneumonias from the noninfectious pneumonias. Perhaps that is the kind of distinction the three groups of values for MHPG excretion might represent. Within those three categories, many different, specific disorders are perhaps yet to be distinguished. By distinguishing these disorders, we will eventually be able to develop treatments that are much more specific for the individual types of depressions.

Q: Are anorexia nervosa and bulimia manifestations of unipolar depression?

DR. SCHATZBERG: Bulimics have a reasonably high incidence of dexamethasone nonsuppression. Further, these patients tend to have a relatively high incidence of family histories of affective disorder,[1,2] and recent studies show that they respond to tricyclic antidepressants.[3] The question is, do they have a form of major depression? In fact, a lot of them probably do; however, a lot of the bulimia patients who are nonsuppressives have considerable depressive symptomatology and high Hamilton Depression Rating Scale scores.

What we might be describing is a shift in the expression of depression. That is, these patients have a fair number of vegetative

---

[1] Hudson JI, Laffer PS, Pope HG. Bulimia related to affective disorder by family history and response to the dexamethasone suppression test. *Am J Psychiatry* **139**, 685–687 (1982).

[2] Hudson JI, Pope HG, Jonas JM, et al. Family history study of anorexia nervosa and bulimia. *Br J Psychiatry* **142**, 133–138 (1983).

[3] Pope HG, Hudson JI. Treatment of bulimia with antidepressants. *Psychopharmacology* (in press).

symptoms, but instead of having the usual anorexia, or perhaps for some social or even biological reason, they show binge-eating as a way of dealing with or expressing their appetite problems. Whether, in fact, patients who have bulimia or binge-eating without depressive symptomatology do have a depressive disorder is an intriguing question.

Anorexia nervosa is also probably a heterogeneous group of disorders. Some of these patients look depressed and respond to antidepressants; some of them are really quite psychotic and have, perhaps, schizophrenic disorders, which thus require some other treatment; and some have a mixture of other kinds of symptoms. In some of these cases we are probably dealing with a symptom rather than a specific illness. We may need to define the subtypes of the illness. In this area we are probably several years behind where we are in diagnosing and classifying depressive disorders.

Q: What is the risk of withholding drugs from patients during a biochemical evaluation of their condition?

DR. SCHILDKRAUT: This question is analogous to what was asked about antibiotics when I was in medical school. Could you withhold treatment with antibiotics until you got cultures and learned what organism you were going to treat? Withholding antidepressant drugs until one gets these kinds of biochemical tests is, in the long range, to the patient's benefit. After all, most of these antidepressant drugs take up to six weeks to act. If the small wait at first from doing such biochemical studies helps to increase the likelihood of the clinician's picking the right drug in the first clinical trial, the wait is quite justified.

Q: Do you recommend measurement of the catecholamine metabolites in "routine clinical laboratories"?

DR. SCHILDKRAUT: As with any biochemical test, several things must be considered. One has to have the capability to do the test and to maintain quality control on the test. And the laboratory doing this sort of work has to do it in sufficient volume with sufficient quality-control data built in, so that the test is not just being done sporadically.

Second, the laboratory must be able at this early stage to provide consultation and education about these tests because we are dealing with an area that is relatively new to psychiatrists, just as it is new to clinical chemists.

All too often, the psychiatrist who is notified that biochemical tests are available will simply write out the requisition slips to ask for all of them, have the results sent back to him, and then call the lab and say, "Okay, here are the numbers, what should I do?" Well, one of the possible answers to that "what should I do" may be that you should not have ordered the tests in the first place.

Finally, maybe the patient should be given a much more extensive clinical evaluation before one can make sense of the tests.

A laboratory has to be in a position to provide education and consultative services at this stage of the game because the psychiatrists and the general physicians don't yet know what to make of these test results.

Dr. KLERMAN: I do not think the problem in using these tests is that our professional colleagues are insufficiently informed. Rather, I think that, because the tests of using the D-type score and catecholamine metabolites have not been sufficiently validated, they are not ready for clinical use. They should be restricted to investigational purposes, and I would urge they not be used in settings other than research settings. The tests are promising and suggestive, but a suggestion is not sufficient, in my opinion, to recommend them for use other than in research settings, where there are well-defined protocols. In the absence of a protocol, their use is very premature.

Q: Is the early detection of the bipolar manic-depressive disorder, by using the D-type score, of benefit to the patient?

Dr. SCHILDKRAUT: Certainly one of the practical values of this is to know when you are dealing with a depressed patient who has a low D-type score if you want to start that patient on an antidepressant. I generally recommend that one use antidepressants rather cautiously in these patients, with slow dose increases, and with close and frequent monitoring of the patient's clinical condition, so that he or she does not develop a florid manic episode during the treatment, which can happen with antidepressant drugs. Therefore, I believe that knowing a patient's D-type score does have some benefit at the present. It is too early to tell, however, just what the full applicability of these D-type scores is going to be in early identification of patients with bipolar disorders.

The Dexamethasone Suppression Test for Depression

Bernard J. Carroll

The overnight dexamethasone suppression test (DST) was developed originally as a screening test for patients with Cushing's disease. When hypersecretion of cortisol was identified in patients with severe depression, the DST was studied in this population also. Since the late 1960s many reports confirm that depressed patients have abnormal DST results. Recent studies have focused on standardization of the test in psychiatric use and on its possible clinical applications. An obvious application of this index of biologic disturbance may be to improve our recognition of patients with endogenous depression (melancholia) who require somatic antidepressant treatments. As Nelson and Charney *(1)* recently emphasize, "The nature of major depressive illness, most often discussed in the literature as endogenous, is a depressive state which once developed is autonomous, is associated with alteration in neurophysiology, and requires biological intervention."

DST Procedure and Laboratory Assay

In the recommended procedure *(2)* for the DST in psychiatric practice, the patient takes a 1-mg tablet of dexamethasone at 2300 hours. The next day, blood samples for determination of plasma cortisol are drawn at 1600 and 2300 hours. For convenience, only the 1600-hours sample is obtained from outpatients. An increase in the plasma concentration of cortisol in *either* blood sample signifies an abnormal (positive) test result. The cutoff for normal plasma concentrations of cortisol is 50 μg/L with the competitive protein binding assay used in my laboratory. Strictly speaking, this assay measures total plasma corticoids *(3)* rather than "plasma cortisol" alone.

When other protein binding or radioimmunoassay methods of measuring plasma cortisol are used, special care is needed to ensure that the assay has good precision and accuracy in the low range of plasma cortisol concentrations. Recently concern has arisen about the wide variation among routine (nonspecialized) laboratories in the accuracy of plasma cortisol assays, especially at low concentrations, around 50 μg/L (4). The need to correct this potential source of error cannot be stressed too strongly.

The antibodies in commercial radioimmunoassay reagent kits are not uniformly specific for cortisol, so different cutoff values will result. With highly specific antibodies the cutoff value may be as low as 35, 40, or 45 μg/L (5–7). With other radioimmunoassays the cutoff value may be as high as 100 μg/L (8). Each laboratory should, therefore, standardize its own assay procedure and, ideally, should define its own cutoff value based on a local study of normal subjects.

Clinical chemists should keep in mind that the typical assay for cortisol in hospital laboratories is *not* designed to provide maximum precision and accuracy in the low range of cortisol values. This goal can readily be achieved, however, by modifying the assay system. In my laboratory, for example, we have modified the competitive protein binding procedure to yield a sensitivity intermediate between the micro- and ultramicro-assay procedures originally described by Murphy (3). This is accomplished by increasing the dilution of the pooled human plasma reagent (the source of corticosteroid-binding globulin) from 20- to 50-fold (from 5% to 2% plasma). This adjustment shifts the sensitivity of the assay to the left, so that most values in the range of 50 μg/L fall on the steepest portion of the binding curve. For the first assay of every sample, we use duplicate aliquots of the ethanolic extracts of patient's plasma. The standards (run in triplicate) are 0, 0.5, 1, 2, 4, 10, 15, and 20 ng of cortisol per tube. We also use magnesium silicate (Florisil) rather than fuller's earth as the adsorbent. Quality-control plasma pool samples at low, intermediate, and high concentrations are always included. Coefficients of variation should be <5% (intra-assay) and <10% (inter-assay).

When the first reported value is <30 or >70 μg/L, that value is reported. When the first value is between these limits, the sample is re-assayed with three different-volume aliquots of the ethanolic extract of plasma, to provide at least two separate and duplicate estimates on the steep portion of the binding curve. The mean of these four values is reported. Although this double-checking is often redundant, it improves the precision of assay of borderline-abnormal samples.

With the above procedure, the sensitivity (true-positive rate) of the DST for melancholia is about 65% and the specificity (true-negative rate) is about 95% (2). With the outpatient protocol (only one blood sample), the sensitivity will be about 50%. On the basis of these results, an abnormal DST result will carry a high diagnostic confidence (predictive value) for melancholia; a negative test result, however, will not rule out the diagnosis of melancholia. This point must be clearly understood by clinicians who use the test.

Exclusion Criteria

Valid DST results will not be obtained if any of the technical exclusion factors below are present. Certain drugs will interfere with the test, as will a number of medical and metabolic conditions. Aside from drug considerations, the basic principle to remember is that *patients should be medically healthy and physiologically stable when the test is performed.*

Several anticonvulsant and sedative–hypnotic drugs cause false-positive DST results by accelerating the rate of metabolism of dexamethasone: phenytoin (Dilantin), barbiturates, meprobamate (Miltown), glutethimide (Doriden), methyprylon (Noludar), methaqualone (Quaalude), and carbamazepine (Tegretol). These drugs may need to be discontinued for as long as three weeks before a valid DST result can be obtained. Obviously, valid results cannot be obtained for epileptic patients who cannot be withdrawn from their anticonvulsant drugs.

Any major medical condition can be associated with false-positive tests, including uncontrolled cardiac failure or hypertension, renal failure, disseminated cancer, and infections. Recent major trauma or surgery, fever, nausea, dehydration, and temporal lobe disease should also be excluded. Endocrine conditions such as high-dosage estrogen treatment, pregnancy, Cushing's disease, and unstable diabetes mellitus can cause false-positive test results. Severe weight loss (malnutrition, rigid dieting, anorexia nervosa) also causes spuriously positive results, especially if body weight is less than ideal weight. False-positive results have been noted also in patients withdrawing from recent heavy alcohol use and in those currently abusing alcohol (alcohol-induced pseudo-Cushing's disease). We recently observed escape of plasma cortisol from dexamethasone suppression in a normal volunteer subject who had a vasovagal episode with fainting.

False-negative results will be found in association with hypopituitarism, Addison's disease, long-term synthetic steroid therapy, indomethacin (9), high-dosage cyproheptadine treatment, and possibly high-dosage benzodiazepine treatment. The commonly used psychotropic drugs such as lithium, tricyclic antidepressants, monoamine oxidase inhibitors, neuroleptic drugs, and chloral hydrate, however, do *not* cause false-positive DST results. Whether, and how often, they can cause false-negative results is still being evaluated.

To avoid the effects of prolonged steroid administration, the DST should not be given more often than every five to seven days. From a clinical perspective, more than weekly testing would seldom be appropriate.

What Does an Abnormal DST Result Tell the Clinician?

Provided the technical issues mentioned above are controlled, what does an abnormal DST result tell the clinician? Endocrinologically, it indicates disinhibited function of the limbic system–hypothalamopituitary–adrenal axis. The origin of this functional disturbance is thought to be in the limbic system of the brain, which ultimately regulates neuroendocrine function. The same regions of the brain also regulate emotions and affective states (10).

The most conservative position at present is that the abnormal DST gives the clinician *indirect* evidence of disturbed function of the limbic system in melancholic patients. The neuroendocrine disturbance may be regarded as a "limbic system noise" phenomenon. The lack of absolute sensitivity of the DST may then be more readily understood, as may the fact that in some patients the test is intermittently positive (11).

Some comparisons from clinical neurology may be helpful at this point. The sensitivity of the routine electroencephalogram (EEG) for adult-onset epilepsy is about 70%. Like the DST in depression, the EEG in epilepsy is only an indirect index of the underlying pathologic process *(12)*. Indeed, the best way to regard the DST in depression may be to view it as *the neuroendocrine equivalent of an EEG of the limbic system.* Clinicians experienced in the care of patients with complex partial seizures (temporal lobe epilepsy) also know that depth electrode recordings in this condition may be intermittently abnormal.

Despite its status as an indirect marker of disturbed limbic system function, the DST can give the clinician useful information. The diagnostic utility of the test comes from its temporal association with episodes of melancholia and from its specificity. This face validity is supported by several other lines of evidence for its predictive validity and construct validity *(10, 11)*.

Relation to Diagnostic Subtypes of Depression

We are all familiar with several current schemes for the diagnosis and classification of depression by clinical features *(13–15)*. All of these are provisional conventions, which enable different centers to describe their depressed patients with some reliability, but their validity has not been established *(1)*. The broad category termed "major depressive disorder" in the recent Third Edition of the Diagnostic and Statistical Manual (DSM III) of the American Psychiatric Association *(15)* is very heterogeneous; the "melancholia" subtype of DSM III also has been criticized by several groups *(1, 16)*. Any proposed clinical classification will need to be validated by studies of family history, natural history, treatment response, and biological markers. The DST might serve as one such marker, along with others *(17)*. Eventually, these markers may help us to improve or choose among the various clinical classifications. In time, new definitions of depressive subtypes may emerge that give the laboratory markers diagnostic weight along with the traditional clinical features. Historically, the same process has occurred in many other areas of medicine.

Results of the DST are often abnormal in melancholic patients, as this term is used in my investigative unit *(2, 16, 18)*. By contrast, patients with equally severe but nonendogenous depression have normal DST results *(2, 16)*. Other groups report abnormal DST results in primary depression but not in secondary depression *(19, 20)*. There is disagreement on this point. Our own results

73

suggest that the rate of abnormal DST results for patients with secondary depression depends on the proportion of melancholic patients in this group (10). Current studies with DSM III (15) or the Research Diagnostic Criteria (RDC) (14) suggest that, by these conventions, the DST does not distinguish between melancholia and nonendogenous depression (20–22). It remains to be seen whether this represents a problem for the DST or for the DSM III and RDC [or for the elastic way these criteria are used in actual practice (23)]. The entire field has reached an interesting dialectic phase, as we go through the iterative process of testing the DST first as a dependent variable, and then as an independent variable, in relation to the clinical diagnostic categories of depression.

Variance in the Independent Variables

The key issue to keep in mind as this debate continues is that significant and sometimes alarming variance is known to exist in the clinical diagnoses that are now used as the independent variables. For example, even in careful research studies, the coefficient of diagnostic concordance [Cohen's kappa (24)] is seldom greater than about 0.55 to 0.65 for diagnoses of endogenous depression (25, 26). In more routine clinical settings the diagnostic reliability is likely to be even less secure, and kappa values of about 0.4 would be expected. The effect of this variance in the independent variable (diagnostic unreliability) on the apparent performance of a laboratory test can easily be computed (Table 1). Even when the diagnostic reliability is acceptable by current clinical standards (kappa 0.50), the apparent performance of a quite good test will be weaker than its true performance. The apparent loss of specificity is particularly serious. If the clinical diagnoses are less secure, then the apparent test performance will be even more affected. If the agreement among diagnosticians is only 65% (kappa 0.30), then the apparent sensitivity will be only 49% and the apparent specificity will drop to 69%.

These considerations raise sobering problems of epistemology and methodology for the development and validation of diagnostic tests. So long as the clinical diagnoses (independent variables) within a given center are themselves insecure, and so long as there is known variability among clinical centers in the accurate

74

Table 1. **Effect of Diagnostic Error on the Apparent Performance of a Laboratory Test**

	Actual	*Apparent*
Sensitivity, %	70	55
Specificity, %	90	75
Predictive value (abnormal result), %	88	69

The apparent sensitivity, specificity, and positive predictive value of a laboratory test are seriously impaired, even when the clinical diagnostic assessments are only moderately unreliable. The calculations above are based on a test with a true sensitivity of 70% and a true specificity of 90%, used in a group of patients for whom the diagnostic reliability (Cohen's kappa) is 0.50, which requires 75% overall diagnostic agreement between two physicians. The calculations assume a standardized 50% prevalence rate for the index diagnosis *(27).*

use of diagnostic criteria, then apparently discrepant reports from different programs must be interpreted with caution. For example, the apparently poor specificity of the DST in the NIMH Collaborative Study of the Psychobiology of Depression *(22)* could readily be attributed to diagnostic reliability problems in the study, which involved multiple psychiatrists at six different centers.

Clinical Applications

The DST is *not* recommended as a screening test for all psychiatric patients, but should be used in clinical contexts where it may help to resolve a specific question *(10, 11).* As with all laboratory tests, if the DST is used in a population where the prevalence of the index disorder (melancholia) is low, then the predictive value of an abnormal test result will be greatly reduced *(17, 18).* Further, among melancholic patients, abnormal DST results occur in close relationship to episodes of depression, but usually not in the euthymic intervals. Thus the DST is not useful as a trait marker of subjects predisposed to develop melancholia.

The clinical applications discussed below are supported by positive reports, usually from more than one center. However, larger-scale and better-designed studies are still needed to document the clinical utility of the test in these areas. Certainly, use of the DST by general clinicians must be regarded as *optional* at the present time.

Confirmation or Support of a Clinical Diagnosis

The DST can be useful in confirming a diagnosis of melancholia, even if the clinician is confident of the diagnosis. Such confirmatory use of laboratory tests by other medical specialties is routine, because the laboratory measures can provide a degree of objectivity that is impossible to achieve with clinical methods alone.

In patients with less certain or disputed diagnoses, the finding of an abnormal DST result may contribute strongly to the final assessment, especially when there is clinical disagreement about the importance of apparent psychogenic precipitants. Despite the new diagnostic criteria that de-emphasize precipitants, many clinicians still have difficulty making the diagnosis of melancholia when clear precipitants are thought to be present.

Some patients are more willing to accept the diagnosis, to form a treatment alliance, and to comply with antidepressant drug treatment when their DST results are abnormal. For other patients, the knowledge of abnormal laboratory findings helps them resist the pressure of guilty and self-deprecatory ideas about their illness. Still others will interpret the test results in a negative, pessimistic way. All patients, therefore, need careful explanation, education, and support by the physician when reviewing the results of the test. The *psychological meaning* of the test result to the patient needs to be addressed and can be used to advantage by the physician in the treatment relationship.

Selection of Treatment

Depressed patients with abnormal DST results will require somatic antidepressant treatment in addition to whatever psychotherapeutic and supportive measures are thought necessary; in my experience, these patients will not respond to psychotherapy alone. So far, there is no good evidence that abnormal DST results predict response to any particular antidepressant of the tricyclic or the monoamine oxidase inhibitor classes. When indicated on clinical grounds, electroconvulsive therapy should be given.

Monitoring Response to Treatment

As patients improve with treatment, their DST responses gradually approach normal values *(29, 30)*. When the test results convert to normal before significant clinical change is evident, this is usually a good prognostic sign that the patient will eventually respond *(29, 30)*. Some patients improve clinically but their test results remain abnormal; such patients frequently have an early relapse if the treatment is stopped *(31, 32)*. On the other hand, it has *not* been established that normalization of the DST result is in itself a sufficient indication to stop active somatic antidepressant treatment.

This application of the test in monitoring the response to treatment is another reason for obtaining a DST during the evaluation of depressed patients.

Prediction of New Episodes

In rapidly cycling bipolar patients the DST results become abnormal one to three days before the onset of the depressive phase *(33)*. In the only study performed to date of a patient with the more usual episodic course, the test results became abnormal three weeks before the recurrence of a depressive episode. If this pattern is confirmed by further studies, then the DST might be used to anticipate new episodes of depression in selected patients.

Intermittently abnormal test results have recently been reported for patients maintained on long-term preventive treatment with lithium carbonate (A. Coppen, personal communication, 1982); the abnormal test results did not necessarily precede relapses in these patients. If confirmed, this observation tells us several important things about the DST in depressives and about the action of lithium. For example, it suggests that these patients developed recurrent disturbance of limbic system function that, without the lithium treatment, would have led to relapses. This is consistent with the clinical course of patients who are withdrawn from preventive treatment with lithium: they revert to the same frequency of episodes as before the lithium was given. Second, Dr. Coppen's observation suggests that lithium acts to suppress the clinical manifestation of the recurrent pathology in the limbic system at a site "below" the primary lesion. For these reasons, abnormal DST results in longitudinal monitoring of patients taking preventive lithium carbonate may *not* necessarily indicate an imminent relapse.

Suicide Alert

At least two groups *(34, 35)* report that nearly all melancholic patients who committed suicide had abnormal DST results. The test might thus alert clinicians to the risk of suicide in melancholic patients. The test would *not* be useful for other patients at high risk of suicide, such as alcoholics and schizophrenics, because these patients have normal DST results.

77

Among melancholic patients, abnormal DST results will most likely be observed in association with other established clinical risk factors for suicide (active suicidal ideas, previous suicide attempts, delusional depression, hopelessness, and so forth). When these clinical risk factors are present, then the clinical staff should be even further alerted by the finding of an abnormal test result. In no way, however, should their alertness be diminished by a normal test result if the patient appears clinically at risk to attempt suicide.

Special Diagnostic Problems

As noted earlier, the best-established diagnostic use of the DST is in the differentiation between melancholic and nonendogenous depression, especially when the importance of psychogenic precipitants is unclear or disputed. Several other difficult diagnostic problems frequently arise in clinical practice, however, for which objective laboratory markers like the DST might be very useful.

Catatonic patients. Preliminary reports suggest that abnormal DST results occur in mute and catatonic depressives but not in catatonic schizophrenic patients (see *11*). Such patients must be adequately hydrated when tested. Indeed, as I emphasized long ago *(36)*, an important principle for all psychotic patients is that the test should not be given within the first two days after admission to the hospital. Such patients often have been living in chaotic circumstances before admission, and they are frequently ketotic and dehydrated when first seen. They should receive adequate nutritional supplements and rehydration before one attempts to obtain a valid DST result.

Geriatric depressive pseudodementia. If the correct diagnostic distinction is not made between true dementia and depressive pseudodementia in elderly patients, many treatable cases will be missed. Some preliminary reports suggest that the DST can help with this differential diagnosis *(37, 38)*, but further systematic studies of demented patients are needed before this application of the DST is accepted. In two recent studies of patients with senile dementia of the Alzheimer type, DST results were abnormal in almost 50% *(39, 40)*. The clinical significance and mechanism of this neuroendocrine disturbance in demented patients should be pursued for the possibility that it may help us understand the mechanism in depressed patients.

Pseudodementia presents diagnostic problems mainly when there is apparent dementia of recent onset. The two studies of Alzheimer-type dementia cited above involved patients with long-standing disease. A standard diagnostic principle of geriatric medicine is to carefully exclude a treatable cause of recent-onset dementia. Depression is one of the most common such causes. I recommend, therefore, that we look very carefully for a treatable depression whenever a patient with apparent dementia of recent onset has an abnormal DST result. The case reports mentioned above *(37, 38)* confirm the value of this approach for some patients.

Depression in adolescents. Many clinicians fail to recognize and diagnose episodes of melancholia in adolescent patients. Although the diagnosis can usually be made if the right questions are asked, the diagnostic "set" of the clinician is often the limiting factor. Some depressed adolescents, however, present with unusual clinical features, which obscure the affective disorder. They may be diagnosed initially as having a schizophreniform disorder, but are later reclassified as affective disorder on follow-up. Their DST results are consistent with affective disorder from the beginning *(41).* Other adolescent patients with more typical melancholia have abnormal DST results with the same frequency as adult melancholic patients *(2, 42).*

Depression in childhood. The existence of syndromal depressions in prepubertal children is gradually being recognized. As with adolescents, however, most clinicians still do not consider the diagnosis in dysphoric children. In one recent report a 0.5-mg dose DST was studied in children, ages 6–12 years. The sensitivity and specificity of this procedure for prepubertal melancholia were similar to the values reported for the 1-mg dose DST in adults *(43).*

"Masked depression." Some depressed patients present a prominent somatic focus of complaint and do not discuss their mood disturbance. When the clinician also fails to ask about the patient's mood and related features, a case of "masked depression" is created. A recent study of patients referred to a chronic pain clinic revealed a significant group with clinical depression, abnormal DST results, abnormal sleep EEG features, and good responses to amitriptyline *(44).*

Complicated depression. When patients with another chronic psychiatric disorder (such as borderline personality disorder) develop

79

a superimposed episode of melancholia, the clinician often fails to recognize the new condition and to treat it effectively. Such patients, with two distinct but interacting disorders, are among the most difficult melancholic patients to treat. The character disorder will often cause serious unreliability in the assessment of specific melancholic features.

Two studies in patients with borderline personality disorder and depressed mood have confirmed that many such patients do have abnormal DST results (45, 46). In principle, concurrent treatment with antidepressant drugs (tricyclics or monoamine oxidase inhibitors) should supplement the psychotherapeutic management of these patients. Controlled trials of this matter are needed.

Summary

The DST is a practical laboratory test that can be used in outpatient or inpatient settings. The required laboratory technology is available at most hospitals. No subjective, behavioral, or metabolic side effects occur with the single-dose administration of dexamethasone, and the test is well tolerated by patients. The test is not affected by most of the usual psychotropic drugs and no special dietary precautions are needed. The recommended procedure for inpatients yields good sensitivity (67%) and high specificity (96%).

Like many laboratory tests, the DST will be most useful if there is a moderate probability that the disorder being considered (melancholia) is actually present (17, 27). If the prevalence of melancholia in the population tested is at least 35%, then the predictive value (diagnostic confidence) of an abnormal test result will be at least 90%. If the prevalence is very low, however, then the predictive value also will be much lower. Thus, the DST is not suitable for screening unselected patients, but should be used when the clinician thinks it might help to answer a specific diagnostic question.

Several clinical applications of the DST are being developed, as outlined above, and new potential uses are being considered. For example, data from the McLean Hospital group (47) suggest that, depending on the clinical context, the test results may be of value not only for distinguishing melancholic from other depressed states but also for the frequently difficult differential diagnosis of mania from schizophrenia. All these proposed uses of the test need further study, however, as the procedure moves out of investigative units into other clinical settings. As the test becomes more widely used, it will be important to remember that physicians treat patients, not laboratory results, and that the results of the test should always be interpreted in their clinical context. Provided that the principles of requesting and interpreting the test are observed as discussed above, the DST has real potential for aiding clinicians in the diagnosis and management of patients. Given the known unreliability of clinical diagnoses, we can expect that the laboratory test result will at times cause clinicians to reevaluate their patients and to recognize treatable depressions that were previously overlooked.

References

1. Nelson JC, Charney DS. The symptoms of major depressive illness. *Am J Psychiatry* **138,** 1–13 (1981).
2. Carroll BJ, Feinberg M, Greden JF, et al. A specific laboratory test for the diagnosis of melancholia. Standardization, validation and clinical utility. *Arch Gen Psychiatry* **38,** 15–22 (1981).
3. Murphy BEP. Some studies of the protein-binding of steroids and their application to the routine micro and ultramicro measurement of various steroids in body fluids by competitive protein-binding radioassay. *J Clin Endocrinol Metab* **27,** 973–990 (1967).
4. Meltzer HY, Fang VS. Cortisol determination and the dexamethasone suppression test. *Arch Gen Psychiatry* **40,** 501–505 (1983).
5. Rubin RT, Poland RE, Blodgett ALN, et al. Endocrine responses to perturbation tests in primary endogenous depression. In *Biological Psychiatry,* C Perris, G Struwe, B Jansson, Eds., Elsevier, Amsterdam, 1981, pp 1239–1243.
6. Rush AJ, Giles D, Roffwarg HP, et al. Sleep EEG and dexamethasone suppression test findings in outpatients with unipolar major depressive disorders. *Biol Psychiatry* **17,** 327–341 (1982).
7. Wilens TE, Arana GW, Baldessarini RJ, et al. Comparison of solid-phase radioimmunoassay and competitive protein binding method for post-dexamethasone cortisol levels in psychiatric patients. *Psychiatry Res* **8,** 199–206 (1983).
8. Aggernaes H, Kirkegaard C, Krog-Meyer I, et al. Dexamethasone suppression test and TRH test in endogenous depression. *Acta Psychiatr Scand* **67,** 258–264 (1983).

9. Mathe AA. False normal dexamethasone suppression test and in-domethacin. *Lancet* **ii**, 714 (1982).

10. Carroll BJ. The dexamethasone suppression test for melancholia. *Br J Psychiatry* **140**, 292–304 (1982).

11. Carroll BJ. Clinical applications of the dexamethasone suppression test for endogenous depression. *Pharmacopsychiatria* **15**, 19–25 (1982).

12. Walton JN, Ed. *Brain's Diseases of the Nervous System,* 8th ed., Oxford University Press, Oxford, 1977.

13. Feighner JP, Robins E, Guze SB, et al. Diagnostic criteria for use in psychiatric research. *Arch Gen Psychiatry* **26**, 57–63 (1972).

14. Spitzer RL, Endicott J, Robins E. *Research Diagnostic Criteria for a Selected Group of Functional Disorders,* 3rd ed., New York State Psychiatric Institute, New York, NY, 1977.

15. *Diagnostic and Statistical Manual of Mental Disorders,* 3rd ed., American Psychiatric Association, Washington, DC, 1980.

16. Carroll BJ, Feinberg M, Greden JF, et al. Diagnosis of endogenous depression: Comparison of clinical, research and neuroendocrine criteria. *J Affective Disorders* **2**, 177–194 (1980).

17. Carroll BJ. Implications of biological research for the diagnosis of depression. In *New Advances in the Diagnosis and Treatment of Depressive Illness,* J Mendlewicz, Ed., Elsevier, Amsterdam, 1980, pp 85–107.

18. Feinberg M, Carroll BJ. Separation of subtypes of depression using discriminant analysis. *Br J Psychiatry* **140**, 384–391 (1982).

19. Schlesser MA, Winokur G, Sherman BM. Hypothalamic–pituitary–adrenal axis activity in depressive illness. *Arch Gen Psychiatry* **37**, 737–743 (1980).

20. Coryell W, Gaffney G, Burkhardt MS. DSM III and the primary–secondary distinction: A comparison of concurrent validity by means of the dexamethasone suppression test. *Am J Psychiatry* **139**, 120–122 (1982).

21. Meltzer HY, Fang VS, Tricou BJ, et al. Effect of dexamethasone on plasma prolactin and cortisol levels in psychiatric patients. *Am J Psychiatry* **139**, 763–768 (1982).

22. Stokes P, Stoll P, Maas J, et al. Dexamethasone suppression test: Clinical utility. History, physiology, clinical utility: An overview. *Am Psych Assoc Syllabus Sci Proc,* Abstract 35A, 100 (1983).

23. Carroll BJ. Problems of paradigm, definition and method in depression. In *The Origins of Depression: Current Concepts and Approaches,* J Angst, Ed., Springer Verlag, Berlin, in press, 1983.

24. Fleiss JL. *Statistical Methods for Rates and Proportions,* 2nd ed., Wiley, New York, NY, 1981.

25. Helzer JE, Clayton PJ, Pambakian R, et al. Reliability of psychiatric diagnosis. II. The test-retest reliability of diagnostic classification.

Arch Gen Psychiatry **34**, 136–141 (1977).

26. Spitzer RL, Endicott J, Robins E. Research diagnostic criteria. Rationale and reliability. *Arch Gen Psychiatry* **35**, 773–782 (1978).

27. Galen RS, Gambino SR. *Beyond Normality: The Predictive Value and Efficiency of Medical Diagnoses,* Wiley, New York, NY, 1975.

28. Carroll BJ. Use of the dexamethasone suppression test in depression. *J Clin Psychiatry* **43** (II, Sec. 2), 44–48 (1982).

29. Albala AA, Greden JF, Tarika J, et al. Changes in serial dexamethasone suppression tests among unipolar depressives receiving electroconvulsive treatment. *Biol Psychiatry* **16**, 551–560 (1981).

30. Greden JF, Gardner R, King D, et al. Dexamethasone suppression tests in antidepressant treatment of melancholia. *Arch Gen Psychiatry* **40**, 493–500 (1983).

31. Greden JF, Albala AA, Haskett RF, et al. Normalization of dexamethasone suppression tests: A probable index of recovery among endogenous depressives. *Biol Psychiatry* **15**, 449–458 (1980).

32. Holsboer F, Liebl R, Hofschuster E. Repeated dexamethasone suppression test during depressive illness: Normalization of test result compared with clinical improvement. *J Affective Disorders* **4**, 93–101 (1982).

33. Greden JF, DeVigne JP, Albala AA, et al. Serial dexamethasone suppression tests among rapid cycling bipolar patients. *Biol Psychiatry* **17**, 455–462 (1982).

34. Carroll BJ, Greden JF, Feinberg M. Suicide, neuroendocrine dysfunction and CSF 5-HIAA concentrations in depression. In *Recent Advances in Neuropsychopharmacology,* B Angrist, Ed., Pergamon, Oxford, 1981, pp 307–313.

35. Coryell W, Schlesser MA. Suicide and the dexamethasone suppression test in unipolar depression. *Am J Psychiatry* **138**, 1120–1121 (1981).

36. Carroll BJ, Curtis GC, Mendels J. Neuroendocrine regulation in depression. II. Discrimination of depressed from non-depressed patients. *Arch Gen Psychiatry* **33**, 1051–1058 (1976).

37. Rudorfer MV, Clayton PJ. Depression, dementia and dexamethasone suppression. *Am J Psychiatry* **138**, 701 (1981).

38. McAllister TW, Ferrell RB, Price TRP, et al. The dexamethasone suppression test in two patients with severe depressive pseudodementia. *Am J Psychiatry* **139**, 479–481 (1982).

39. Spar JE, Gerner R. Does the dexamethasone suppression test distinguish dementia from depression? *Am J Psychiatry* **139**, 238–240 (1982).

40. Raskind M, Pesking E, Rivard F, et al. Dexamethasone suppression test and cortisol circadian rhythm in primary degenerative dementia. *Am J Psychiatry* **139**, 1468–1471 (1982).

41. Targum SD. Neuroendocrine dysfunction in schizophreniform disorder: Correlation with six-month clinical outcome. *Am J Psychiatry* **140,** 309–313 (1983).
42. Crumley FE, Clerenger J, Steinfink D, et al. Preliminary report on the dexamethasone suppression test for psychiatrically disturbed adolescents. *Am J Psychiatry* **139,** 1062–1064 (1982).
43. Poznanski EO, Carroll BJ, Banegas MC, et al. The dexamethasone suppression test in prepubertal depressed children. *Am J Psychiatry* **139,** 321–324 (1982).
44. Blumer D, Zorick F, Heilbronn M, et al. Biological markers for depression in chronic pain. *J Nerv Ment Dis* **170,** 425–428 (1982).
45. Carroll BJ, Greden JF, Feinberg M, et al. Neuroendocrine evaluation of depression in borderline patients. *Psychiatr Clin North Am* **4,** 89–99 (1981).
46. Extein I, Pottash AL, Gold M. Neuroendocrine tests in depressed borderlines. American Psychiatric Association, 134th Annual Meeting, 1981.
47. Arana GW, Barreira PJ, Wilens T, et al. Clinical studies of the dexamethasone suppression test in psychotic illnesses. *Am Coll Neuropsychopharmacol Abstr* **21,** 79 (1982).

The Role of the Thyroid Axis in Affective Disorders

Arthur J. Prange, Jr.

The affective disorders, mania and depression, are related to the hypothalamic–pituitary–thyroid (HPT)[1] axis in a variety of ways (1, 2). In this brief review I will emphasize only two: the use of a thyroid hormone to accelerate or enhance the response to a standard antidepressant treatment, and a fault within the HPT axis characteristic of a large minority of depressed patients.

An Outline of the HPT Axis

Thyroliberin (thyrotropin-releasing hormone, TRH), the first so-called hypothalamic hypophysiotropic hormone to be discovered (3, 4), is secreted from cells in the median eminence of the hypothalamus into the portal venous system. When it reaches the anterior pituitary gland, it binds to membrane receptors and induces the release of thyrotropin (thyroid-stimulating hormone, TSH) (5). Lactotrops and somatotrops, which secrete prolactin and growth hormone, respectively, also bind thyroliberin (6). Thyrotropin, released by thyroliberin into the general circulation, binds to thyroid cells, causing an increase in the release and synthesis of the thyroid hormones thyroxin (T_4) and L-triiodothyronine (T_3). These hormones have widespread metabolic effects: increased oxygen consumption, heat production, and protein synthesis. They also exert feedback actions at the pituitary and hypothalamus, and directly affect the function of the nervous system (7). In blood, thyroid hormones are mostly bound to proteins, mainly globulins and albumins (8).

---

[1] Abbreviations used: HPT, hypothalamus–pituitary–thyroid; T_4, thyroxin; T_3, triiodothyronine; TCA, tricyclic antidepressant.

85

Thyroid status can be regulated at the hypothalamus and pituitary, but there are other sites as well. In iodine deprivation, the thyroid gland synthesizes and secretes relatively more T_3 than T_4 (8), thereby producing a molecule that is several times more potent (per mole) while using fewer iodine atoms. Peripheral tissues also influence thyroid status. Because about half of T_4 found in blood is de-iodinated by peripheral tissues to T_3, the major source of T_3 is T_4 rather than direct thyroid secretion (9). Although the major function of T_4 is as a precursor for the more active T_3, T_4 itself has intrinsic metabolic effects (8, 9). In another peripheral process that influences thyroid status, T_4 is converted not only to T_3, but also to "reverse" T_3 (10); the former, 3,3',5-L-triiodothyronine, is metabolically potent, whereas reverse T_3, 3,3',5'-L-triiodothyronine, is metabolically inert. The ratio of these substances varies in certain conditions (10).

The Therapeutic Use of T_3 in Depression

In early work my coworkers and I noted that both in a patient (11) and in mice (12), imipramine, a standard tricyclic antidepressant (TCA) drug, appeared more toxic in the presence of gross hyperthyroidism. If interactions between the drug and excess thyroid hormone were manifested as enhanced toxicity, then, we reasoned, interactions between the drug and small amounts of the hormone might be manifested as enhanced therapeutic benefit. Two aspects of this hypothesis have been tested.

Accelerated responses to TCAs. The first clinical possibility we examined was the idea that T_3 might accelerate the response to a TCA in drug-naive patients (patients previously untreated with the drug). In four studies to test this concept (1, 13–15), we examined 60 patients, 40 women and 20 men, all suffering from primary depression. Unipolar–bipolar distinctions were not made systematically in this early work, but in retrospect it is clear that at least 75% of patients had unipolar depression, i.e., had not had mania as well. We did distinguish, however, between patients with psychomotor retardation and those who lacked it. The study populations were as follows: Study 1, psychomotor-retarded women; Study 2, nonretarded women; Study 3, psychomotor-retarded men; Study 4, nonretarded men. Patients proven to be euthyroid by the usual historical, physical, and biochemical criteria were then randomly assigned to either of two treatment groups. Severity of depression was evaluated three times per week by patients and by raters who were ignorant of the patients' treatment. In all four studies treatment regimens were as follows:

	Imipramine, days 1–28	T_3, days 4–28
Imipramine + placebo	150 mg orally	Placebo
Imipramine + T_3	150 mg orally	25 μg orally

Results are summarized in Table 1. Women, whether with psychomotor retardation or not, showed faster overall improvement if they were also receiving T_3; nearly all aspects of the depression syndrome were benefitted by T_3 and none was worsened (data not shown). In men, on the other hand, T_3 failed to hasten improvement. Drug toxicity was slight in all four studies and appeared to be unaffected by the hormone, suggesting that concentrations of the drug in blood had not been increased. Additional information on this point is given below.

Feighner et al. *(16)*, attempting to replicate our findings, gave depressed patients more imipramine (200 mg daily), with T_3 (25 μg daily) for a shorter time (10 days). They found only a trend for T_3-treated patients to improve more rapidly than placebo-treated patients. In interpreting their findings, we have argued *(17)* that, for reasons of dosage, patient selection, design, and statistical analysis, the risk of a false-negative finding was exaggerated.

Wheatley *(18)* studied 52 depressed outpatients in a 21-day, double-blind procedure. Patients received one of three treatments: amitriptyline (100 mg in all groups) plus 40 μg of T_3 daily; amitriptyline plus 20 μg of T_3 daily; and amitriptyline plus placebo daily. The two groups of patients treated with amitriptyline plus T_3 improved faster and had lower scores for severity of depression at the end of the study than the group of patients who received amitriptyline plus placebo. For several aspects of depression the larger dose of T_3 was superior to the smaller. As in our studies, women profited from the hormone more than men did. Within the treatment group of amitriptyline plus 20 μg of T_3, patients with low thyroid indices responded better than patients with high indices, suggesting some pre-existing, though covert, thyroid fault. Because side effects were equally distributed among the groups, Wheatley attributed them solely to the amitriptyline.

87

Table 1. Responses of Depressed Patients: Imipramine Plus Placebo vs Imipramine Plus T₃

Study	Depression subtype	Treatment[a]	n	Mean Ham D scores by days[b]												
				0	2	5	7	9	12	14	16	19	21	23	26	28
1, F	Retarded	IMI + P	10	25	25	22	19	21	21	18	16	14	14	13	12	11
		IMI + T₃	10	25	23	15	12	9	9	8	7	7	6	4	5	5
2, F	Not retarded	IMI + P	10	25	25	22	19	16	14	11	12	9	9	6	7	6
		IMI + T₃	10	25	23	13	7	7	7	6	4	5	5	4	3	3
3, M	Retarded	IMI + P	7	22	19	13	14	10	10	9	8	7	6	7	6	5
		IMI + T₃	6	24	19	11	7	7	7	6	5	5	6	5	6	3
4, M	Not retarded	IMI + P	3	25	19	12	7	8	9	6	10	8	13	9	10	9
		IMI + T₃	4	25	18	12	10	10	8	8	8	9	7	7	11	9
Total F		IMI + P	20	25	25	22	19	18	17	15	14	12	11	10	10	9
		IMI + T₃	20	25	23	14	10	8	8	7	6	6	5	4	4	4
Total M		IMI + P	10	25	19	11	12	9	9	8	9	7	7	7	7	7
		IMI + T₃	10	23	21	14	8	8	8	8	6	7	7	7	9	7

[a] Imipramine (IMI) was started on day 1. L-Triiodothyronine (T₃) or placebo (P) was started on day 4. Measures of variance and statistical analysis are given in the source publications (1, 13–15).
[b] Ham D, Hamilton Rating Scale for Depression.

Coppen et al. *(19)* performed a double-blind study of 30 hospitalized patients with severe unipolar depression. Patients were assigned to one of four treatments: L-tryptophan (6 g daily); imipramine (150 mg daily); and each of these agents combined with T_3 (25 μg daily) for the first 14 days of the study. The thyroid hormone did not influence the response to the amino acid, but it markedly enhanced the therapeutic response to imipramine. Once again, this effect was limited to women, all of whom, rather unusually, were completely free of depression at the end of the study at four weeks. Side effects appeared to be diminished by T_3, but this may merely have reflected enhanced efficacy. One should recall that some items that appear on a depression inventory (headache, for example) will inevitably appear on an inventory of side effects.

Converting TCA failure to success. The second clinical possibility to attract attention regarding T_3 was the idea that the hormone might convert TCA "failures" to "successes." Interest stemmed from the fact that, although most depressed patients show a favorable response of some degree to TCA treatment, about 20 to 25% fail to achieve full remission *(20)*. Five single-blind studies, involving a total of 136 patients, have addressed this question *(21–25)*. Depressed patients in various subcategories of the syndrome have received various TCAs and various doses of T_3 (50 μg orally per day or less). Remarkably, in each study, two-thirds to three-fourths of TCA failures were rapidly converted to successes by the use of T_3. The question arises, of course, whether the addition of T_3 to a TCA regimen accomplishes something that could not be accomplished simply by increasing TCA dosage. Banki *(22)* offered evidence on this point by studying 96 TCA failures. For some he added T_3 to the TCA regimen, of whom 39 of 52 promptly improved; for some he increased the dosage of TCA, of whom 10 of 44 improved. In a similar study *(23)* he found respective improvement rates of 23/33 and 4/16.

Recently Goodwin et al. *(26)* reported a double-blind study in which eight of 12 failures were rapidly converted to successes. In these studies, as in the single-blind studies, and as in our own anecdotal experience, among TCA failures the men appeared to profit from the addition of T_3 as often as the women. In some TCA failures who later responded to T_3, serum concentrations of TCA had been in the range that is usually therapeutic.

T_3 as an antidepressant. Early in our work the question arose whether T_3 alone has antidepressant value. To assess this, to attempt to confirm our original findings, and to explore the useful dosage range of T_3 to be used as an adjunct to a TCA, we studied 27 women with primary depression, who were randomly assigned to one of three regimens of oral medication *(1, 13)*.

| | | | T_3, μg | | |
Group	n	Imipramine, mg^a	Days 3–4	Days 5–6	Days 7–11
A: Fixed imipramine	10	150	0	0	0
B: Increasing T_3	8	0	25	50	62.5
C: Fixed imipramine + increasing T_3	9	150	25	50	62.5

[a] Days 1–28.

A zero indicates that the patients received a placebo. Assessment by raters ignorant of treatments revealed that Groups B and C, who received increasing T_3, improved rapidly. Mean scores (Hamilton Rating Scale for Depression) for the three groups on Day 5 were as follows; Group A, 23; Group B, 15; Group C, 13. However, by Day 12 scores in Groups B and C had increased, the nature of symptoms suggesting that this worsening was due to the high dose of T_3 (62.5 μg), which had been stopped only on Day 11 and presumably was still active. Group A patients showed throughout the trial the slow, steady response characteristic of treatment with imipramine. From these results we concluded as follows: when not excessive (as shown in other work), T_3 accelerates the therapeutic action of imipramine; T_3 doses > 50 μg per day are excessive in most patients whether or not they are receiving imipramine; and T_3 alone may have antidepressant action, but this may be limited by toxicity. In fact, the question has not yet been answered whether T_3 alone in daily doses of 50 μg, or even 25 μg, would exert an antidepressant effect comparable with that of a TCA.

Mechanisms. Despite uncertainty about the value and limitations of T_3 alone, the case seems well established that T_3 as an adjunct to a TCA regimen will accelerate the antidepressant response of women. In men as well as in women, T_3 will convert most TCA failures to successes. The question arises, of course, as to how these events occur. Several studies in animals pertaining to TCA–T_3 interactions (12, 27–33) are reviewed in detail elsewhere (1). Of special interest in the present context is the finding that, although it grossly affects the clinical response to imipramine, T_3 appears not to affect the disposition of the drug (27). Garbutt et al. (33) showed that T_3 has no effect on blood concentrations of imipramine or its metabolite, desmethylimipramine, in patients and no clear effect on the actions of these agents on electrocardiographic measurements. These findings are consistent with the regular observation that as much as 50 μg of T_3 per day does not increase the toxicity of a standard TCA regimen.

Among all studies there is consensus that in drug-naive patients T_3 is useful as an adjunct only in women, whereas in TCA failures it is useful in both sexes. The most parsimonious explanation is that drug-naive men show a more rapid response to TCA than women, as appears to be the case (1), and thus have less to gain from adjunctive T_3. But this explanation only raises another question: Why do men show more rapid TCA responses? Just as this question is currently moot, so is it difficult to decide whether with adjunctive T_3 one is treating some occult disorder of the HPT axis or is applying some pharmacologic principle. The smallness of the dose of T_3 militates for the former view.

The state of the organism clearly does play a role in TCA response. Whybrow et al. (34) showed that, the greater the evidence of spontaneous thyroid activation in depressed patients, the quicker their subsequent response to imipramine. Thus administration of T_3 to depressed patients may accomplish only what the organism might later in most cases accomplish spontaneously, i.e., a tendency toward remission and a readiness to respond to treatment.

A Response Fault within the HPT Axis

As noted above, thyroliberin is the hypothalamic tripeptide that prompts the release of thyrotropin from the anterior pituitary. When synthetic thyroliberin became available for human injection, our group applied it to the study of depressed patients. To 10 women with the unipolar form of the disorder we gave 0.5 mg intravenously, a very high dose, and found that two showed a virtually null thyrotropin response, while a third showed only a marginal response (35). The usual cause for such low pituitary response is excess negative-feedback inhibition by thyroid hormones, as in hyperthyroidism. However, these women were euthyroid by historical, physical, and biochemical criteria.

In the past decade, more than 40 studies, involving more than 1000 depressed patients, have addressed the response of thyrotropin to thyroliberin. These data have been the subject of a recent comprehensive review (36).

Nearly all workers have reported that at least some of their depressed patients have blunted thyrotropin responses to thyroliberin, but this statement, of course, requires a definition of blunting. Although we have proposed a standard technique (36), many variations have been used, which makes generalizations difficult. Nevertheless, if controls are studied by one's own technique and if a blunted response is defined as an increase of thyrotropin over baseline values that is less than ever seen in controls, then about 25% of patients with primary depression show blunted responses in the absence of a currently recognized endocrinological explanation.

Among mental patients, is a blunted thyrotropin response to thyroliberin limited to depression? Mania has not been adequately studied and controversy exists. Gold et al. (37) found blunting in a high proportion of patients, but other authors have not, or have found only trends in the mean responses of groups of manic patients (38). Schizophrenic patients appear not to show blunting (39). In anorexia nervosa thyrotropin responses after thyroliberin are of normal magnitude but often delayed (40–43).

From the above it would seem that thyrotropin blunting is fairly specific to depression. However, there is an important exception. In tests with alcoholic patients (44–46), whether they were in alcoholic withdrawal or in postwithdrawal, or had in fact been abstinent for two years or longer, the men showed about the same frequency of blunting as did depressed patients. Whether this endocrine link between alcoholism and depression is related somehow to apparent genetic links (47) is uncertain.

If blunting of thyrotropin release after injection of thyroliberin seems reasonably specific to depression and alcoholism, in what way is it informative? The answer to this question depends in some measure on the resolution of a prior issue, the question of whether a blunted thyrotropin response is a trait marker or a state marker. Loosen and I *(36)* included this issue in our review, and reported that in five studies of depressed patients the blunted responses changed to normal responses with clinical remission, in five studies the blunted responses usually persisted, and in three studies the blunted responses sometimes normalized and sometimes persisted. Thus, a blunted response in a given individual may be a state marker but, on the other hand, may be a trait marker. If a blunted response were always a state marker, one could readily share the enthusiasm of Kirkegaard et al. *(48)* in using recovery of the endocrine response to predict not only a salutary outcome to standard antidepressant treatment but also a clinical remission that is less likely than otherwise to end in early relapse. If, on the other hand, a blunted response were always a trait marker, this might prove extremely useful in identifying high-risk subjects and in sorting out relationships between depression and alcoholism. Apparently, however, the state–trait issue must be clarified in each patient before it is of practical clinical use. Moreover, because of the complexity of regulation of pituitary responses, derangement in any of several physiological mechanisms could lead to the final common abnormality of a blunted thyrotropin response.

The significance of a blunted thyrotropin response is not entirely obscure, however. Of numerous factors that could plausibly contribute to it, in depression, at least, several seem not to: increasing age, prior drug intake, severe illness, and increasing concentrations of thyroid hormones and cortisol. Moreover, the distribution of blunted thyrotropin response between the primary and secondary forms of depression and between the unipolar and bipolar forms is uncertain. There is some reason to think that the longer depressive illness lasts, the more probable is thyrotropin blunting *(36)*.

The neurochemical determination of a blunted thyrotropin response has also been explored. Apparently, when the pituitary secretion of a substance is deficient, then either the pituitary contains less of that substance, in this case thyrotropin, or the pituitary is somehow less able to secrete whatever amount it contains. As regards decreased secretory capacity, one thinks first of increased negative feedback, as would occur from thyroid hormones or from cortisol, but these hormones generally do not account

93

for thyrotropin blunting in depression. The concentration of cortisol, to be sure, is often increased in depression but is only poorly correlated with thyrotropin blunting *(36)*. Within the pituitary, dopamine, the classical effect of which is to damp the secretion of prolactin, damps the thyrotropin response to thyroliberin *(49)*. Because thyroliberin prompts the release of prolactin as well as of thyrotropin, one would expect that a dopamine-induced blunted thyrotropin response to thyroliberin would be accompanied by a blunted prolactin response. This, however, seems not to be the case. After injection of thyroliberin the two events are only poorly correlated *(36)*.

It has also been suggested that a blunted thyrotropin response may be caused by hypersecretion of thyroliberin, which when chronic would cause down-regulation of receptors on pituitary thyrotrops. Chronic administration of thyroliberin in normals obliterates the normal diurnal rhythm of thyrotropin secretion *(50)*; depressed patients show a disturbance in this rhythm *(51, 52)*, suggesting the presence of thyrotropin hypersecretion. Disturbances in brain biogenic activity could account for thyroliberin hypersecretion—either increased norepinephrine activity, which stimulates thyroliberin-secreting cells, or less serotonin activity, which inhibits them *(53, 54)*. In depression, decreased norepinephrine activity has often been suggested, though increased activity has been posited recently *(55)*. The existence of less serotonin activity in some depressed patients is a venerable formulation *(56, 57)*; nevertheless, neuroendocrine events are so complexly regulated that the proposed use of a defect in any one of them to support existence of a putative fault in brain neurotransmission must be approached with caution.

Conclusions

In other places *(1, 2)* the attempt has been made to develop schemes that would accommodate the variety of relationships between the HPT axis and the affective disorders, especially depression. These concepts center around the fact that thyroid hormones penetrate the brain and the idea that within the brain they influence the sensitivity of receptors on neurons subserving pathways that, when disordered, account for the symptoms of mania and depression. Such schemes would account for the observation that

94

depression is common in hypothyroidism and would accommodate the idea that a shift toward hypothyroidism, even within the range of normal, would increase vulnerability to depression. The schemes would suggest that even when the HPT axis is not causally involved in depression, it might become involved, once depression has occurred, as a means of compensation. If the HPT axis *is* invoked as restitution, then a thyroid hormone used as a supplement to standard treatment might hasten recovery—as is the case. If HPT restitution is grossly delayed or inadequate, then adding a thyroid hormone to a standard regimen might convert therapeutic failures to successes. If the HPT axis sometimes plays a role in cause and often becomes invoked as restitution, then disturbances of the HPT axis should be more frequent in a population of depressed patients than in populations of other mental disorders or in a normal population—as also seems to be the case. Additional studies, especially clinical studies extended over time, are needed to clarify these and related issues.

References

1. Prange AJ Jr, Wilson IC, Breese GR, Lipton MA. Hormonal alteration of imipramine response: A review. In *Hormones, Behavior, and Psychopathology*, EJ Sachar, Ed., Raven Press, New York, NY, 1976, pp 41–67.
2. Whybrow PC, Prange AJ Jr. Perspectives: A hypothesis of thyroid–catecholamine-receptor interaction. *Arch Gen Psychiatry* **38**, 106–113 (1981).
3. Guillemin R. Peptides in the brain: The new endocrinology of the neuron. *Science* **202**, 390–402 (1978).
4. Schally AV. Aspects to hypothalamic regulation of the pituitary gland. *Science* **202**, 18–28 (1978).
5. Grant G, Vale W, Guillemin R. Interactions of thyrotropin-releasing factor with membrane receptors of pituitary cells. *Biochem Biophys Res Commun* **46**, 28–34 (1972).
6. Dannies PS, Gautuik KM, Tashjjian AH Jr. A possible role of cyclic AMP in mediating the effects of thyrotropin-releasing hormone on prolactin release and on prolactin and growth hormone synthesis in pituitary cells in culture. *Endocrinology* **98**, 1147–1159 (1976).
7. Balasz R, Kovacs S, Teichgraben P, et al. Biochemical effects of thyroid deficiency on the developing brain. *J Neurochem* **15**, 1335–1349 (1968).

8. Robbins J, Rall JE, Groden P. The thyroid and iodine metabolism. In *Duncan's Disease of Metabolism.* **III.** *Endocrinology,* PK Bondy, LE Rosenberg, Eds., W.B. Saunders & Co., Philadelphia, PA, 1974, pp 1009–1104.

9. Ingbar SH, Woeber KA. The thyroid gland. In *Textbook of Endocrinology,* 5th ed., RH Williams, Ed., W.B. Saunders & Co., Philadelphia, PA, 1974, pp 117–247.

10. Chopra IJ, Sack J, Fisher DA. Reverse T3 in the fetus and newborn. In *Perinatal Thyroid Physiology and Disease,* DA Fisher, GN Burrow, Eds., Raven Press, New York, NY, 1975, pp 33–40; discussion, p 48.

11. Prange AJ Jr. Paroxysmal auricular tachycardia apparently resulting from combined thyroid–imipramine treatment. *Am J Psychiatry* **119,** 994–995 (1963).

12. Prange AJ Jr, Lipton MA. Enhancement of imipramine mortality in hyperthyroid mice. *Nature (London)* **196,** 588–589 (1962).

13. Prange AJ Jr. Therapeutic and theoretical implications of imipramine–hormone interactions in depressive disorders. In *Proceedings of the V World Congress of Psychiatry* **274,** Amsterdam, Excerpta Medica, 1971, pp 1023–1031.

14. Prange AJ Jr, Wilson IC, Rabon AM, et al. Enhancement of imipramine antidepressant activity by thyroid hormone. *Am J Psychiatry* **126,** 457–469 (1969).

15. Wilson IC, Prange AJ Jr, McClane TK, et al. Thyroid–hormone enhancement of imipramine in nonretarded depression. *N Engl J Med* **282,** 1063–1967 (1970).

16. Feighner JP, King LJ, Schuckit MA, et al. Hormonal potentiation of imipramine and ECT in primary depression. *Am J Psychiatry* **128,** 1230–1238 (1972).

17. Prange AJ Jr. Discussion of paper by Feighner, et al. *Am J Psychiatry* **128,** 55–58 (1972).

18. Wheatley D. Potentiation of amitriptyline by thyroid hormone. *Arch Gen Psychiatry* **26,** 229–233 (1972).

19. Coppen A, Whybrow PC, Noguera R, et al. The comparative antidepressant value of L-tryptophan and imipramine with and without attempted potentiation by liothyronine. *Arch Gen Psychiatry* **26,** 234–241 (1972).

20. Klein DF, Davis JM. *Diagnosis and Drug Treatment of Psychiatric Disorders.* Williams and Wilkins Co., Baltimore, MD, 1969.

21. Earle BV. Thyroid hormone and tricyclic antidepressants in resistant depressions. *Am J Psychiatry* **126,** 1667–1669 (1970).

22. Banki CM. Trijodthyronin alkalmazasa a depressio kezeleseben. (Triiodothyronine in the treatment of depression.) *Orvosi Hetilap* **116,** 2543–2547 (1975).

23. Banki CM. Cerebrospinal fluid amine metabolites after combined amitriptyline–triiodothyronine treatment of depressed women. *Eur J Clin Pharmacol* **11**, 311–315 (1977).
24. Tsutsui S, Yamazaki Y, Namba T, et al. Combined therapy of T3 and antidepressants in depression. *J Int Med Res* **7**, 138–146 (1979).
25. Ogura C, Okuma T, Shimoyama N, et al. Combined thyroid (triiodothyronine) tricyclic antidepressant treatment in depressive states. *Seishin Igaku* **15**, 527–536 (1973).
26. Goodwin FK, Prange AJ Jr, Post RM, et al. L-Triiodothyronine converts tricyclic antidepressant non-responders to responders. *Am J Psychiatry* **139**, 34–38 (1982).
27. Breese GR, Traylor TD, Prange AJ Jr. The effect of triiodothyronine on the disposition and actions of imipramine. *Psychopharmacologia* **25**, 101–111 (1972).
28. Prange AJ Jr, Lipton MA, Love GN. Diminution of imipramine mortality in hypothyroid mice. *Nature (London)* **197**, 1212–1213 (1963).
29. Prange AJ Jr, Lipton MA, Love GN. The effect of altered thyroid status on desmethylimipramine mortality in mice. *Nature (London)* **204**, 1204–1205 (1964).
30. Avni J, Edelstein EL, Khazan N, et al. Comparative study of imipramine, amitriptyline and their desmethyl analogues in the hypothyroid rat. *Psychopharmacologia* **10**, 426–430 (1967).
31. Breese GR, Prange AJ Jr, Lipton MA. Pharmacological studies of thyroid–imipramine interactions in animals. In *The Thyroid Axis, Drugs, and Behavior,* AJ Prange Jr, Ed., Raven Press, New York, NY, 1974, pp 29–48.
32. Prange AJ Jr, Bakewell WE. Effects of imipramine and respirine on body size and organ size in euthyroid and hyperthyroid growing rats. *J Pharmacol Exp Ther* **151**, 409–412 (1966).
33. Garbutt J, Malekpour B, Brunswick D, et al. Effects of triiodothyronine on drug levels and cardiac function in depressed patients treated with imipramine. *Am J Psychiatry* **136**, 980–982 (1979).
34. Whybrow PC, Coppen A, Prange AJ Jr, et al. Thyroid function and the response to liothyronine in depression. *Arch Gen Psychiatry* **26**, 242–245 (1972).
35. Prange AJ Jr, Wilson IC, Lara PP, et al. Effects of thyrotropin releasing hormone in depression. *Lancet* **ii**, 999–1002 (1972).
36. Loosen PT, Prange AJ Jr. Serum thyrotropin response to thyrotropin-releasing hormone in psychiatric patients: A review. *Am J Psychiatry* **139**, 405–416 (1982).
37. Gold MS, Pottash ALC, Extein I, et al. The TRH test in the diagnosis of major and minor depression. *Psychoneuroendocrinology* **6**, 159–169 (1981).

38. Takahashi S, Kondo H, Yoshimura M, et al. Thyrotropin responses to TRH in depressive illness: Relation to clinical subtypes and prolonged duration of depressive episode. *Folia Psychiatr Neurol Jpn* **28,** 355–365 (1974).

39. Prange AJ Jr, Loosen PT, Wilson IC, et al. Behavioral and endocrine responses of schizophrenic patients to TRH (Protirelin). *Arch Gen Psychiatry* **36,** 1086–1093 (1979).

40. Miyai K, Toshihide Y, Azukizawa M, et al. Serum thyroid hormones and thyrotropin in anorexia nervosa. *J Clin Endocrinol Metab* **40,** 334–338 (1975).

41. Aro A, Lamberg BA, Pelkonen R. Hypothalamic dysfunction in anorexia nervosa. *Acta Endocrinol Suppl* **199,** 202 (1975).

42. Croxson MS, Ibbertson HK. Low serum triiodothyronine (T3) and hypothyroidism in anorexia nervosa. *J Clin Endocrinol Metab* **44,** 167–174 (1977).

43. Jeuniewic N, Brown GM, Garfinkel PE, et al. Hypothalamic function as related to body weight and body fat in anorexia nervosa. *Psychosom Med* **40,** 187–198 (1978).

44. Loosen PT, Prange AJ Jr, Wilson IC. TRH (Protirelin) in depressed alcoholic men: Behavioral changes and endocrine responses. *Arch Gen Psychiatry* **36,** 1086–1093 (1979).

45. Loosen PT, Prange AJ Jr. TRH in psychiatric patients. *N Engl J Med* **303,** 224–225 (1980).

46. Loosen PT, Prange AJ Jr. TRH in alcoholic men: Endocrine responses. *Psychosom Med* **41,** 584–585 (1979).

47. Winokur G, Cadoret R, Dorzab J, et al. Depressive disease—a genetic study. *Arch Gen Psychiatry* **24,** 135–144 (1971).

48. Kirkegaard C, Norlem N, Lauridsen UB, et al. Protirelin stimulation test and thyroid function during treatment of depression. *Arch Gen Psychiatry* **32,** 1115–1118 (1975).

49. Burrow GN, May PB, Spaulding SW, et al. TRH and dopamine interaction affecting pituitary hormone secretion. *J Clin Endocrinol Metab* **45,** 65–72 (1977).

50. Spencer CA, Greenstadt MA, Wheeler WS, et al. The influence of long term low dose thyrotropin releasing hormone infusions on serum thyrotropin and prolactin concentrations in man. *J Clin Endocrinol Metab* **51,** 771–775 (1980).

51. Golstein J, van Cauter E, Linkowski P, et al. TSH nyctohemeral pattern in primary depression: Differences between unipolar and bipolar women. *Life Sci* **27,** 1695–1703 (1980).

52. Weeke A, Weeke J. Disturbed circadian variation of serum thyrotropin in patients with endogenous depression. *Acta Psychiatr Scand* **57,** 281–289 (1978).

53. Martin JB, Reichlin S, Brown GM. *Clinical Neuroendocrinology*, F.A. Davis Co., Philadelphia, PA, 1977.
54. Reichlin S. Neuroendocrinology. In *Textbook of Endocrinology* (see ref. *9*), pp 588–645.
55. Maas JW. Neurotransmitters and depression. *Trends Neurosci* **2**, 306–309 (1979).
56. Prange AJ Jr, Wilson IC, Lynn CW, et al. L-Tryptophan in mania: Contribution to a permissive hypothesis of affective disorders. *Arch Gen Psychiatry* **5**, 56–62 (1974).
57. Coppen A, Prange AJ Jr, Whybrow PC, et al. Abnormalities of indoleamines in affective disorders. *Arch Gen Psychiatry* **26**, 474–478 (1972).

Discussion—Session II

QUESTION: Please comment on the 40% of depressed patients who do not exhibit dexamethasone suppression. What other potential neurochemical or pituitary–adrenal axis abnormalities might be present?

DR. CARROLL: The issue really is, are the 40% of patients with normal dexamethasone suppression test (DST) results a different subgroup who look clinically like the ones who have the neuroendocrine disturbance? My feeling is that we should be very conservative in our interpretations. I believe the remaining 40% really do have the same disease as the 60-odd percent who show abnormal results. It is more likely that we have a somewhat overly sensitive test than that we have two radically distinct groups of patients. For example, I talked about the DST as a kind of neuroendocrine equivalent of a limbic system electroencephalogram (EEG) recording. For cases of adult-onset epilepsy, the sensitivity of the scalp EEG recording in that clinical population is about 70%. That does not mean the other 30% do not have epilepsy—of course they do. Rather, the EEG in neurology and the DST in psychiatry are somewhat insensitive and certainly quite indirect ways of assessing the function of brain regions that are responsible for the clinical disorders.

The second answer to this question is to use the DST with other endocrine procedures, such as the thyroliberin test Dr. Prange just talked about. The potential certainly exists for using these two tests, and perhaps others being developed, in parallel or in series, to help us maximize the rate of positive laboratory identification of the melancholic group.

Q: Have you observed nonsuppression at 1600 hours, after administration of 1 mg of dexamethasone, with suppression at the 2300-hours sample? Could late absorption of dexamethasone be involved?

DR. CARROLL: We certainly have observed it, which is one reason for recommending more than one blood-sampling time. Keep in mind that you are doing single-point sampling against a fluctuating profile of episodic secretion of cortisol. Any one blood sample may be drawn right at the trough between two secretory episodes—in which case, even though secretion of adrenal steroids has resumed, there may appear to be suppression. This is essentially a statistical matter, and is one reason for drawing at least two samples from the patients you have available in the hospital.

Q: In the thyroliberin studies, thyrotropin is released; then, in response to the thyrotropin, triiodothyronine (T_3) and thyroxin (T_4) are released from the thyroid gland. Could it have been the T_3 or T_4 that caused the apparent therapeutic effect?

DR. PRANGE: What happens is that in almost everybody—normals, endocrine patients, depressed patients, almost everybody except patients with anorexia nervosa—the maximum thyrotropin response to thyroliberin occurs about 30 min after intravenous administration. The tremendous increase in thyrotropin that reaches the thyroid gland prompts a slight increase in T_3 and T_4. Interestingly, the T_3 response precedes the T_4 response, and this is unexplained. Under usual circumstances, the gland secretes mostly T_4, and T_3 comes mainly from peripheral de-iodinization of T_4. In any case, the amounts of the two hormones secreted by the thyroid gland after a dose of thyroliberin that is supramaximum for thyrotropin release are not great. In early studies they were undetected. This is one reason to think that release of thyroid hormones does not account for the behavioral effects seen after thyroliberin administration. Another reason is that we have observed that a single dose of a thyroid hormone given to a depressed patient has no behavioral effect.

Q: Is there a difference between results after electroconvulsive treatment and after tricyclic antidepressants, and what is the relationship between recovery, DST results, and clinical outcome?

DR. CARROLL: The relationship is that as patients improve, no matter what the method of treatment, or even if it is a spontaneous recovery, there generally is improvement in the DST results, at the same time or shortly before clinical improvement by the patient is apparent. There does not seem to be any systematic difference in the lag time between the two events, whether from shock or drugs—or from spontaneous improvement, for that matter. But, clearly, the change in the DST results in patients who are receiving drugs is not simply a direct effect of the drugs themselves. The evidence for this is that when these patients fail to respond to drug treatment, despite documented adequate concentrations of drugs in the plasma, the test results remain abnormal.

Q: Is there any diagnostic value in extremely low concentrations of cortisol relative to mania?

DR.CARROLL: I don't think that means very much at all; we have simply taken a categorical approach and set a cutoff value; below that, statistically speaking, we have to say the test result is normal. Some people like to talk about borderline abnormal values in the range of 35 to 50 μg/L; maybe we will eventually reach that degree of sophistication, but there is not much evidence for doing it yet.

Regarding the manic patients, bipolar subjects will frequently show the DST disturbance when they are in a depressed phase; in a manic phase, they generally have, to our surprise, quite normal DST results—unless they are about to switch into their next depression, in which case the DST results may go abnormal for several days before the switch. If they are in the mixed state, the Kraepelinian mixed manic-depressive state, where they show features of both depression and mania simultaneously, then their DST results will be abnormal.

Q: In the studies where T_3 potentiated the antidepressant action of imipramine, how do you know that the imipramine–T_3 groups, as compared with the imipramine–placebo groups, didn't just have higher blood concentrations of imipramine?

DR. PRANGE: During the time our early studies were done, there were no generally available methods for determination of tricyclic drug concentrations, though there was the concept that after a fixed dose of a tricyclic different individuals had quite different drug concentrations in their blood. Given this variability, could that account for our findings? I doubt it very much. In any clinical trial there is variability in the study population in many parameters. The main reason for random assignment of patients to treatment groups is to distribute inequality between groups in any of these parameters. Relying on the laws of chance, in the present case one has to think that there is virtually no chance that most of the women randomly assigned to receive imipramine and T_3 were also those who were so constituted as to achieve high concentrations of imipramine on a schedule of fixed administration.

There is another aspect to the question, though, and that is whether T_3 alters the blood concentrations of imipramine. In our early studies we guessed that this had not happened, because the higher drug concentrations would cause increased side effects whereas, in fact, the incidence of side effects was about equal between treatment groups. Our guess turned out to be correct. Breese and his colleagues *(Psychopharmacologia* **25:** 101–111, 1972) performed one or another endocrine manipulation including manipulation of thyroid state, and gave animals various doses of imipramine. Then they studied the metabolism of imipramine and its disposition in various tissues and found that none of the endocrine manipulations had much effect. Finally, Garbutt et al. *(Am J Psychiatry* **136:** 980–982, 1979) provided more direct evidence. They put depressed women on standard doses of imipramine and at intervals measured the concentrations of imipramine and its metabolite desmethylimipramine. Then they added T_3 to see if it affected either parameter. In their study T_3 had no effect on the concentrations of imipramine or desmethylimipramine or on their ratio.

Tricyclic Antidepressants—
How to Maximize Therapeutic Response

William Z. Potter

Over the last decade, physicians showed impressive progress in the clinical utilization of the tricyclic antidepressants (TCAs). This value judgment is based not on direct studies but rather on the shared clinical experience of practitioners and investigators. We believe that therapeutic advances explain the almost universal difficulty that current clinical investigators are experiencing in trying to recruit the classic depressed patients in whom the most definitive TCA-response studies were performed; that is, because most such patients are now receiving TCA therapy, it is difficult to find untreated patients to provide reliable baseline values. Carefully done trials in well-defined populations show that the rate of response to TCA treatment in nondelusional depression is in the 80–90% range when plasma concentrations of drug are controlled (17, 24). However, in the many studies that show a poor response rate no matter what the concentration of TCA, the apparent discrepancies can be explained on the basis of patient selection.

Importance of Diagnosis and Patient Selection

Many readily available reviews now summarize the relationship of TCA concentration to psychiatric outcome (3, 5, 20, 32, 42). Specific findings are discussed below; the point here is, when depressions are broken down into subcategories such as endogenous and nonendogenous, investigators find a relationship between TCA concentration and patient's response in the former but not the latter (30, 39). There is an often-discussed difference between the repeatedly positive results of Kragh-Sorenson et al. (24, 25), who studied endogenously depressed patients treated

104

with nortriptyline, and the negative results of Burrows et al. *(12, 14)*, who studied a clinically heterogeneous population. This latter group included "patients with personality problems, others with important environmental problems, bereaved patients, patients with sexual problems and, in addition, some whose depression appeared to have no precipitating cause." Obviously, very wide criteria were used in the latter studies.

To quote from Marie Åsberg *(5)*, a leading Scandinavian investigator in the field:

> Both types of criteria, the narrow and the wide, are equally legitimate, and the choice between them will depend on the aim of the particular study. If an investigator is oriented towards basic research and intends to study pharmacokinetic and pharmacodynamic properties of a drug, he will probably prefer to work with a highly selected patient group, where the likelihood of a positive treatment response is maximal. The ideal patient for this type of research is the previously untreated, physically healthy, middle-aged patient, with a not too long history of a typical endogenous depression.
>
> All practicing psychiatrists in countries with a developed mental health care system will know that this type of depressed patient is the exception rather than the rule. In clinical practice, TCAs are often prescribed to patients who are old, physically ill, who take a number of different drugs for diverse ailments, and whose diagnostic status is far from clear. A researcher who is interested in cost-benefit aspects of large scale plasma level monitoring will presumably wish to study these patients as well. But it would be equally erroneous to conclude from the first type of study that drug monitoring is useful for all depressives, as it would be to conclude from a negative finding in the second type of study that it is not good for anyone.

These methodological caveats direct our attention to the specific population in whom we are trying to achieve maximum TCA response rates. In what follows, a clear distinction will be made as to whether recommendations result from studies of what are generally called endogenous depressions (as discussed earlier by Dr. Schatzberg) or from those in less-well-defined groups. The practical consequences of over-generalizing recommendations to the entire population of patients complaining of depression is enormous, the prevalence rates in the general population ranging from an average of 0.5–0.6% for endogenous bipolar depression, through 3–4% for all nonbipolars, to 15–20% for "depressive symptoms." In the U.S. alone, therefore, we are discussing whether results from a group of studies can be generalized to about 1 million individuals or to 10 million or more.

Because others here will address the issue of whether patients have subtypes of depression (Dr. Klein) and show differential rates of response to (e.g.) TCAs, monoamine oxidase inhibition, and lithium (Dr. Fieve), I will only briefly review the NIMH clinical recommendations for treatment with TCAs. These recommendations are based on features associated with good antidepressant response, which are easily recognized as consistent with a diagnosis of endogenous depression, even without monitoring the concentration of the drug (Table 1). Predictors of poor TCA response

---

Table 1. **Clinical Features Associated with TCA Response**

Good TCA response
  Decreased appetite, weight loss
  Early morning awakening
  Diurnal variation
  Decreased reactivity to environment
  Psychomotor retardation or agitation
  Decrease in functional capacity
  Prior history of affective illness
  Family history of drug response

Poor TCA response
  Increased appetite, weight gain
  Increased sleep
  Phobic features
  High level of anxiety
  Obsessive–compulsive features

---

are those features found in so-called "atypical" depressions, which can be further subdivided as will be discussed by Dr. Klein.

Once diagnostic issues are settled, there are generally three possibilities:

1. The patient will respond to a dose of TCA that produces an adequate concentration of the drug in plasma.

2. The patient will not respond to any dose of TCA.

3. The patient would respond, but other factors (e.g., side effects) prevent use of adequate dose of TCA.

Some have also suggested that biochemical subtypes may have

differential responses to more or less potent inhibitors of norepi-nephrine or serotonin uptake (for a review, see *19*); but, as already mentioned, high response rates are frequently reported for any TCA when clinical factors and blood concentrations are controlled *(17, 24, 48)*. Thus, although investigators agree that a few patients are true nonresponders (the second possibility above), no consistent recommendation emerges on how to identify this population except by the already discussed clinical features. As regards the third possibility, more progress has been made. Many of the TCA drug actions that fall under the general heading of "side effects" and may interfere with the clinical use of TCAs are more easily quantifiable than is the degree of clinical improvement. It is frequently possible to establish direct relationships between the plasma concentration of drugs and their effects. Thus, control of pharmacokinetic variance may be particularly useful in reducing side effects.

After briefly reviewing the general principles necessary for evaluating the relevance of pharmacokinetics in the clinical use of the TCAs, I will discuss examples of what additional recommendations can be made on the basis of existing knowledge.

Pharmacokinetic Variance among TCAs

The major determinant of interindividual pharmacokinetic differences is drug metabolism. Other processes that affect concentration of a drug in plasma include absorption, distribution, and renal clearance, which are relatively stable in an otherwise healthy population of depressed patients. Certain conditions associated with systematic changes in one of these processes, such as decreased renal clearance in the aged, will be identified and discussed later. The importance of drug metabolism for TCAs is highlighted by the demonstration that only about 1% of these drugs is usually excreted unchanged in the urine. Because of variations in metabolism, a fixed dose of a standard TCA administered to a group of patients will typically produce an interindividual range of concentrations that varies by a factor of 10 *(2, 39)*.

The relevance of this variation to effect is based on the fundamental pharmacological principle that drug action is directly proportional to its *free* (unbound) concentration at the site of action. In the treatment of chronic states such as depression or hyperten-

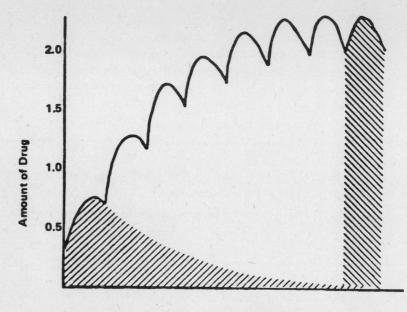

Time (hours)

Fig. 1. Accumulation of drug after repeated oral administration of a fixed dose at a dosing interval of two-thirds of the elimination half-life

For example, a drug with an 18-h half-life, minimum for most TCAs, administered every 12 h will require seven dosing intervals (84 h) or 3.67 half-lives [84 h/(18 h/half-life)] to reach steady-state. The area under the plasma concentration-time curve after the first dose (shaded area, *left*) is equal to the area under the curve during subsequent dosing intervals (shaded area, *right*). (See *32*)

sion, this can be logically extended to a principle that the effect of the drug should be proportional to its mean *steady-state free* concentration. (Steady-state is, by definition, the condition in which the amount of drug entering the system is equivalent to the amount being eliminated.) As shown in Figure 1, it may take considerable time to achieve steady-state, depending on the half-life of elimination of a drug. As a rule of thumb, given fixed dosing, 95% of a steady-state concentration is obtained after five biologic half-lives of the drug. More detailed presentations of these basic pharmacokinetics are readily available *(16, 55)*.

These well-established basics are worth remembering when considering TCA concentration/response curves. A sigmoidal relationship can frequently be established between the $\log_{10}$ concentration and some response (Figure 2). Ideally, a TCA would have

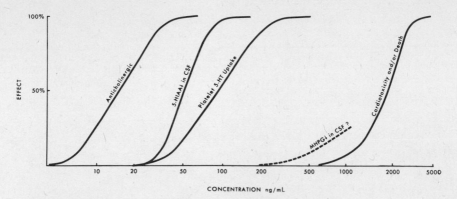

Fig. 2. Concentration dependency of amitriptyline effects

5-HIAA, 5-hydroxyindoleacetic acid; 5-HT, 5-hydroxytryptamine; CSF, cerebro-spinal fluid; MHPG, 3-methoxy-4-hydroxyphenylglycol

a single action, for which a safe concentration producing maximal effect could be identified. The empirical practice of increasing doses to achieve increased response rate is based on this approach. There are, however, two problems with this: first, the assumption that the response curve after achieving maximum effect is flat; second, the fact that most antidepressants have multiple effects, many of which are significant within the concentration range usually obtained with therapeutic doses of drugs (Figure 2).

The first problem has been most extensively explored with nortriptyline, which clearly is less effective as an antidepressant when higher concentrations are achieved (for a review, see 6). This phenomenon of a relatively narrow concentration range associated with good clinical response has been called a "therapeutic window." Recent demonstrations that chronic treatment with nortriptyline also produces high concentrations of an active hydroxy metabolite (10-OH-nortriptyline) (8, 23) have raised the possibility that it is either the hydroxy metabolite or the sum of nortriptyline plus the hydroxy metabolite that truly defines the therapeutic window (see below). Interestingly, nortriptyline is the only antidepressant for which an upper therapeutic limit of concentration has been convincingly demonstrated.

The second problem is best illustrated by looking at a series of likely concentration/response curves for another TCA, desipramine. As shown in Figure 3, within the 50–300 ng/mL (50–300 μg/L) range of concentrations likely to be obtained with standard

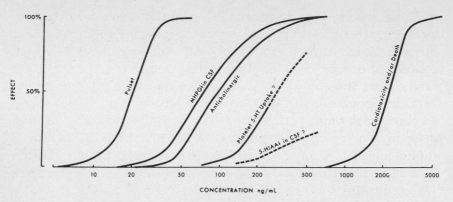

Fig. 3. Concentration dependency of desipramine effects

Abbreviations as in Fig. 2

doses, many related effects are possible. For instance, one may have almost maximum effects on noradrenergic parameters, as evidenced by decreases of 3-methoxy-4-hydroxyphenylglycol (MHPG) in cerebrospinal fluid, with minimal effects on serotonergic parameters such as platelet serotonin uptake, if one maintains concentrations in the 100 ng/mL range *(1)*. The principle here is that, with multiple-action drugs such as the TCAs, there is a high probability that side effects will occur at concentrations close to, overlapping with, or even less than therapeutic ones. For example, as discussed in detail later, for amitriptyline the maximum anticholinergic effects may occur at concentrations considerably lower than those required for therapeutic action (Figure 2). Moreover, unless plasma concentrations of the drug are monitored, they may fall outside of the therapeutic range of drug concentration while producing clear "effects." Again, with amitriptyline, a patient complaining of a very dry mouth may tempt the clinician to reduce the dose, where what is really needed is a dose increase not likely to worsen an already maximal anticholinergic effect.

A final important feature of response curves, which I refer to just in passing, is that a drug's effect is related to its *free* (unbound) concentration (for a review, see *45*). In most studies of TCAs methodological difficulties have prevented the determination of free drug concentrations; moreover, there is considerable disagreement concerning the absolute concentration of free drug, even in those reports that do attempt to quantify unbound drug (for a review, see *32*). Although variations in protein binding of TCAs do occur, such as increases during inflammatory states in which concentrations of α_1-acid glycoprotein increase *(31)*, these are rarely great and contribute far less than do variations in metabolism. In populations from whom it has been possible to obtain cerebrospinal fluid, perhaps the best available measure of free drug in the central nervous system *(7, 37)*, investigators have found high ($r > 0.90$) correlations between total plasma (bound + free) and cerebrospinal fluid concentrations of antidepressants *(35)*, indicating that the plasma concentration of a drug is usually an accurate index of its relative free concentration and should be appropriate for establishing concentration/response relationships.

Interestingly, large changes in binding are most relevant for the interpretation of unusual values for plasma concentration. The simple relationship best descriptive of the behavior of extensively metabolized basic lipophilic drugs is:

$$C_{ss} = dose/pCl_{int}$$

where C_{ss} = steady-state concentration of drug in plasma
p = fraction of "free" (unbound) drug in plasma
Cl_{int} = intrinsic clearance, which refers to the ability of the liver to remove a drug by all pathways in the absence of any blood flow limitations

Hence an increase in α_1-acid glycoprotein secondary to an acute inflammatory condition (e.g., pneumonia) would *decrease* the free fraction and produce a reciprocal *increase* in the total C_{ss}. The actual free drug concentration ($C_{ss} \times p$), however, would remain the same: free drug at steady-state = pC_{ss} = dose/Cl_{int}. Thus free drug concentration is simply a function of the dose and the intrinsic clearance. This demonstrates that it is the interindividual variation in metabolism that is actually responsible for interindividual variation in free drug concentration. Variations in binding would be irrelevant except that one is usually attempting to interpret the total C_{ss} as a measure of free drug. Fortunately, as mentioned above, in most cases this total concentration is a good relative index of the concentration of free drug. These perhaps counterintuitive relationships are explored in detail elsewhere *(56)*.

Table 2. **Reported Anticholinergic Activity of TCAs Given in Acute or Chronic Treatment**

Effect	Amitriptyline	Desipramine	Ref.
	% change		
Acute treatment[a]			
Salivary flow decrease	55 (50)	20 (50)	10
	60 (50)	10 (50)	50
	60 (50)		49
	32 (50)	0 (50)	4
	>80 (150)		38
Pupil diameter	0 (50)	+10 (50)	50
Pilocarpine miosis	−25 (50)	−3[b] (50)	50
Chronic treatment[a]			
Salivary flow decrease	>80 (~120)	<43 (<120),	9
		>44 (>120)	44
Pupil diameter		19/23[c] (80)	46
Pilocarpine miosis		0/15 (80)	46
Tyramine mydriasis		−60/−60 (80)	46
Phenylephrine mydriasis		−30/−45 (80)	46

[a] Nos. in parentheses indicate TCA dose; mg/day for acute, ng/mL for chronic treatment.
[b] Difference not significant.
[c] After one week/three weeks of treatment.

Side Effects and Pharmacokinetics

Typically, side effects presumably related to blockade of the cholinergic or noradrenergic receptors are the most frequent restrictors of the use of TCAs in otherwise appropriate patients. Studies now available that provide quantitative measures of relative anticholinergic activity focus on salivary flow or pilocarpine-induced miosis (Table 2). As Table 2 shows, amitriptyline is a far more potent inhibitor of salivary flow than is desipramine. This is consistent with the preclinical findings that tertiary tricyclics such as amitriptyline, imipramine, and chlorimipramine (Figure 4) are more potent blockers of muscarinic receptors than are their secondary amine forms (Table 3).

Studies in patients and volunteers reinforce the findings on salivary flow. Desipramine both acutely and chronically increases resting pupil diameter, which could occur either through cholinergic blockade or tonic adrenergic stimulation. The latter appears to be the case because desipramine does not block miosis produced by the cholinergic agonist pilocarpine, whereas amitriptyline does

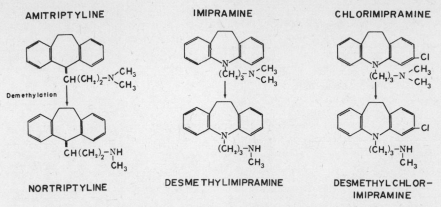

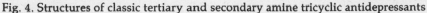

Fig. 4. Structures of classic tertiary and secondary amine tricyclic antidepressants

(Table 2, ref. *50*). Moreover, amitriptyline, a potent anti-muscarinic, does not by itself produce miosis. Studies involving chronic administration of desipramine indicate that the absolute extent of pilocarpine-induced miosis is actually increased rather than blocked, presumably as a function of increased pupil diameter (Table 2). Tyramine- or phenylephrine-induced mydriasis, however, is blocked by chronic treatment with desipramine to produce concentrations in the 80 ng/mL range, suggesting that postsynaptic alpha blockade is significant, at least in this tissue.

There is considerable confusion in the literature regarding the cardiovascular effects of TCAs. Table 4 summarizes those effects

Table 3. **Interactions of TCAs with Receptors in Rat Brain**

	Relative potency of receptors[a]			
	α-Adrenergic (^{3}H-WB-4101)	Muscarinic (^{3}H-QNB)	Histaminergic (^{3}H-mepyram)	Serotonergic (^{3}H-d-LSD)
Secondary amine tricyclics				
Nortriptyline	++	++	++	+++
Desipramine	++	+	+	++
Tertiary amine tricyclics				
Amitriptyline	++++	++++	++++	++++
Imipramine	+++	+++	++	++
Chlorimipramine	+++	+++	++	++

[a] Estimates of relative potencies (++++ = most potent), as measured with tritiated labels, drawn from references *21, 29, 40, 41, 52.*

Table 4. **Cardiovascular Effects of TCAs**

Blood pressure
  Tertiary amine TCAs worsen hypotension in 10–20% of patients
  Secondary amine TCAs slightly increase blood pressure
Electrocardiographic changes
  All TCAs increase heart rate, secondary > tertiary
  QRS and QT_c prolonged at TCA concentration > 1000 ng/mL
  Overdose can produce fatal arrhythmias, whereas therapeutic range shows
    antiarrhythmic activity
Hemodynamics
  Slight decrease in cardiac output, especially from tertiary amine TCAs; these
    drugs are tolerated, however, in patients in treated heart failure

for which there is some consensus. Increased blood pressure after doses of secondary amine TCAs is documented for desipramine in volunteers (43) and nortriptyline in patients (15). There are various opinions concerning the severity of any of these side effects (for reviews, see 11 and 13) except in patients with substantial pre-existing orthostatic hypotension (18, 25, 51) or, obviously, in patients after overdose. One of the most recent and careful studies reveals TCAs to be surprisingly well-tolerated in patients with cardiac disease (54).

Clinically insignificant but real electrocardiogram changes such as prolongation of the PR, QRS, and QTc intervals occur after TCA administration but are only weakly correlated with plasma concentrations of TCAs in the therapeutic range (53). If concentrations seen after overdose are included, the correlation with significant and potentially dangerous prolongation of these intervals is fairly robust ($r = 0.75$, $p < 0.01$) (47).

Finally, in terms of the usually minor side effect of increased pulse rate, effects may be maximal at low drug concentrations in plasma, at least for the most potent norepinephrine-uptake inhibitor, desipramine. At steady-state, desipramine at 30 ng/mL produces the same sustained pulse increases in young adult volunteers as it does at 60 ng/mL (43). Pulse increases in older patients are much less marked, even at much higher concentrations (53). In light of the potency of desipramine as an uptake inhibitor and its relative lack of anticholinergic activity, we suggest a concentration/response curve for pulse increase as shown in Figure 3, which may reflect the results of increased intrasynaptic norepi-

114

nephrine acting on cardiac beta receptors (27). The usual teaching is that pulse increases are secondary to the anticholinergic properties of TCAs (11), although there is no real experimental evidence for such a conclusion.

Careful clinical investigation with pharmacokinetic monitoring is causing us to reassess clinical lore concerning the side effects of TCAs. In the absence of heart block and significant pre-existing orthostatic hypertension, any TCA would appear to be relatively safe in standard doses. Secondary amines are helpful in avoiding orthostatic hypotension in susceptible individuals (25, 43). Patients receiving tertiary TCA compounds can be reassured that increasing the dose is unlikely to worsen any annoying anticholinergic side effects; conversely, reducing the doses of secondary TCAs may completely eliminate or avoid this problem. Further refinements should permit us to make more definite recommendations about specific antidepressants and the concentrations at which they produce side effects. Nonetheless, there may still be rare individuals in whom more severe effects such as urinary retention will prevent TCA use. There are no data to indicate whether judicious selection of a TCA with one spectrum of receptor-interaction potencies at a controlled concentration in plasma will avoid even this latter type of side effect.

One unusual problem may arise during conscientious monitoring of TCA concentrations in a patient who is generally considered at risk—i.e., an elderly individual with concomitant, not necessarily cardiovascular, illness for which he or she might be receiving medications. If total TCA concentrations are high, in the 1000 ng/mL range, and the patient is doing well and does *not* have a significantly prolonged QRS interval, should the dose of TCA be reduced? In terms of pharmacokinetic principles, this might be one of those cases where plasma protein binding of TCAs has increased, as might occur in patients with rheumatoid arthritis who have increased α_1-acid glycoprotein. Under these conditions, despite the high total concentration, the effective free TCA may be no different from that for far lower total concentrations in patients with normal protein binding. The answer, therefore, depends on understanding several variables. Obviously, to make the interpretation of pharmacokinetics relevant to the production of maximum therapeutic response, one must consider the individual case.

Plasma Concentrations of and Response to Antidepressants

Given an understanding of pharmacokinetic principles, the extensive range of metabolism of TCAs, and critical reviews of studies relating concentration to antidepressant effect in endogenous depression *(3, 6, 20, 32, 42)*, certain indications for obtaining measures of such relationships can be recommended (Table 5). Although new investigations are under way and preliminary reports have been published, it is still too soon to set therapeutic ranges

---

Table 5. **Indications for Measuring Concentrations of TCAs in Plasma**

I. Compliance	Requires repeated sampling, results from single-dose prediction, or urinary measurements to interpret.
II. Failure to respond	May have very low concentration despite compliance.
III. Exaggerated responses	High concentrations on low doses, expected in slow hydroxylators ($<5\%$ of population).
IV. High risk and polypharmacy	Patients with some types of cardiovascular disease or on drugs that affect TCA metabolism, especially neuroleptics.
V. Maximized response	Defined for only two TCAs: Nortriptyline—aim for 50–150 ng/mL range; often need to *reduce* dose; keep *below* 150 ng/mL. Imipramine—required combined concentration with metabolite, desipramine, in 200–250 ng/mL range; usually *increase* dose; no defined upper limit.

---

for amitriptyline, chlorimipramine, and desipramine for treating endogenous depressions. Moreover, given the current difficulty in finding appropriate patient populations, definitive studies may never be possible, so that only rough guidelines may emerge, drawn from the experiences of many centers and laboratories. Thus, items I and III in Table 5 require special comment.

A single plasma sample is not sufficient to assess compliance (Table 5, Item I); we must know what concentration to expect if the patient took the medication within a certain period before the test, because the same dose produces such variable concentrations at steady-state. If repeated samples, taken days apart but at the same interval since the last previous dose, yield the same value, then we know that the subject is at least taking the drug at fixed times before the testing; but we do not really know whether the patient is at his or her own steady-state for the *prescribed* dose. The only way to know for sure would be to give a single fixed dose at a known time, obtain some measure of the area under the curve for plasma concentration vs time, and predict the expected steady-state value *(2, 33)*. If the patient's concentration of drug is outside of this predicted range for the appropriate dose, then there is not true compliance, or else some other intervening variable such as altered binding or drug metabolism has come into play.

Item III in Table 5, "exaggerated responses," refers to the increasing evidence that about 5% of a Caucasian population will be very slow metabolizers of TCAs, particularly as regards aromatic ring hydroxylation *(26, 28, 35)*. Because a few people will thus achieve therapeutic concentrations of the drug on low doses, there is a substantial risk of giving too much TCA, at least in the case of nortriptyline, for which an upper therapeutic limit has been relatively well established.

Another curious aspect to this issue of interpretation of plasma concentrations involves metabolism via the hydroxylation pathway. None of the reviewed reports included measurements of the pharmacologically and clinically active hydroxy metabolites of the TCAs *(8, 34, 35, 36)*. At the time these studies were done, the TCA hydroxy metabolites were thought either to lack any potency for inhibiting monoamine re-uptake or not to cross the blood–brain barrier in clinically significant quantities. Subsequently, however, it has been shown that the major TCAs are hydroxylated before excretion (Figure 5), and substantial steady-state amounts of the free hydroxylated forms exist both in plasma and cerebrospinal fluid *(8, 35, 36)*, thus contributing to the clinical effects of the TCAs.

Fortunately, in otherwise healthy depressed patients, there is a 0.70 correlation between parent TCA and hydroxy-TCA concentrations, so that measurement of parent TCAs may suffice as an overall indicator of the relative amounts of the total active compounds *(35)*. This may not be the case, however, in the small

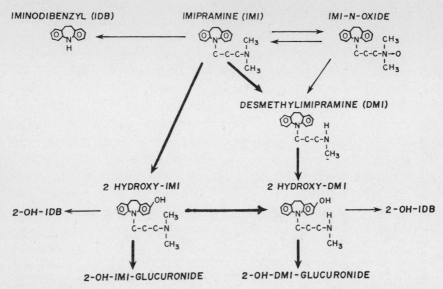

Fig. 5. Known metabolic pathways for the major tricyclic antidepressant, imipramine, in humans

Similar pathways have been shown for amitriptyline and chlorimipramine

percentage of the Caucasian population (5–9%) who have a genetically determined relatively deficient capability to hydroxylate debrisoquine *(26)*. TCA hydroxylation may also be deficient, in which case the concentration of the parent TCA will not accurately indicate the concentration of the hydroxy metabolite. Moreover, the clinical suggestion of an increased sensitivity of the elderly to both the therapeutic and side effects of TCAs, which so far has been corroborated only in open studies with a small number of patients, may be elucidated in future studies in which both the TCAs and their hydroxy metabolites are quantified.

In unselected measurements of OH-nortriptyline in patients who were not necessarily at steady-state, OH concentrations apparently increased with age *(8)*. We have shown *(22)* that similar increases of OH-desipramine in the elderly can be explained on the basis of the known decrease of renal function with aging, the renal clearance of OH-desipramine decreasing as the plasma concentration increases. There are, however, no changes in the plasma concentrations of parent drug desipramine in these elderly subjects (Figure 6).

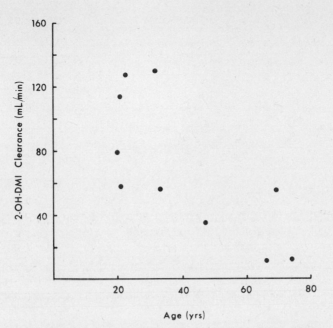

Fig. 6. Renal clearance of 2-hydroxydesipramine (2-OH-DMI) vs age

Source: *22*

Conclusions

A thorough clinical evaluation remains the most important tool for identifying most of the patients who are likely to respond to standard doses of TCAs. Advances in our understanding of the multiple side effects of TCAs increase the possibility that an adequate dose of TCA can be attained. There remains, however, a substantial number of patients—as many as 20%—whose clinical profile predicts they would respond but who fail to do so. In this population, the monitoring of TCA concentrations can be an important therapeutic tool: failure of response owing to poor compliance or extremely rapid or slow metabolism, or limitation of dose secondary to fears of cardiovascular side effects or drug interactions, can be addressed and rectified.

In the future, TCA concentrations and those of their active hydroxy metabolites may also prove of clinical relevance in subpopulations such as the elderly. One of the most important outcomes of the systematic study of the pharmacokinetics and pharmacodynamics of TCAs may be the impetus provided for developing new effective compounds that are less complex in their metabolism and actions. For the present, however, TCAs remain by far the most important class of antidepressant drugs; their proper use will continue to have great impact on the treatment of major depressive disorders for many years to come.

References

1. Åberg-Wistedt A, Jostell KG, Ross SD, Westerlund D. Effects of zimelidine and desipramine on serotonin and noradrenaline uptake mechanisms in relation to plasma concentrations and to therapeutic effects during treatment of depression. *Psychopharmacology* **74**, 297–305 (1981).
2. Alexanderson B. Pharmacokinetics of nortriptyline in man after single and multiple oral doses: The predictability of steady-state plasma concentrations from single-dose plasma-level data. *Eur J Clin Pharmacol* **4**, 82–91 (1972).
3. Amsterdam J, Brunswick D, Mendels J. The clinical application of tricyclic antidepressants and pharmacokinetics and plasma levels. *Am J Psychiatry* **137**, 653–662 (1981).
4. Arnold SE, Kahn RJ, Faldetta LL, et al. Tricyclic antidepressants and peripheral anticholinergic activity. *Psychopharmacology* **74**, 325–328 (1981).
5. Åsberg M. On the clinical importance of plasma concentrations of tricyclic antidepressant drugs: A review of evidence. In *Clinical Pharmacology in Psychiatry*, E Usdin, Ed., Elsevier North Holland, New York, NY, 1981, pp 301–310.
6. Åsberg M, Sjoqvist F. On the role of plasma level monitoring of tricyclic antidepressants in clinical practice. *Commun Psychopharmacol* **2**, 381–391 (1978).
7. Bertilsson L, Braithwaite R, Tybring G, et al. Plasma protein binding of desmethylchlorimipramine studied with various techniques. *Clin Pharmacol Ther* **26**, 265–271 (1979).
8. Bertilsson L, Mellstrom B, Sjoqvist F. Pronounced inhibition of noradrenaline uptake by 10-hydroxy-metabolites of nortriptyline. *Life Sci* **25**, 1285–1292 (1979).
9. Bertram U, Kragh-Sorensen P, Rafaelsen OJ, Larsen NE. Saliva secretion following long-term antidepressant treatment with nortriptyline controlled by plasma levels. *Scand J Dent Res* **87**, 58–64 (1979).
10. Blackwell B, Stefopoulos A, Enders P, et al. Anticholinergic activity of two tricyclic antidepressants. *Am J Psychiatry* **135**, 722–724 (1978).

11. Burgess CD. Effects of antidepressants on cardiac function. *Acta Psychiatr Scand* **63** (Suppl 290), 370–379 (1981).
12. Burrows GD, Davies B, Scoggins BA. Plasma concentration of nortriptyline and clinical response in depressive illness. *Lancet* **ii**, 619–623 (1972).
13. Burrows GD, Norman T, Hughes I. Cardiovascular effects of antidepressants. In *Clinical Pharmacology in Psychiatry*, E Usdin et al., Eds., Macmillan Press, London, 1981, pp 319–341.
14. Burrows GD, Scoggins BA, Turecek LR, Davies M. Plasma nortriptyline and clinical response. *Clin Pharmacol Ther* **16**, 639–644 (1974).
15. Freyschuss U, Sjoqvist F, Tuck D, Åsberg M. Circulatory effects in man of nortriptyline, a tricyclic antidepressant drug. *Pharmacol Clin* **2**, 68–71 (1970).
16. Gibaldi M, Perrier D. *Pharmacokinetics*, Marcel Dekker, Inc., New York, NY, 1975.
17. Glassman AH, Perel JM, Shostak M, et al. Clinical implications of imipramine plasma levels for depressive illness. *Arch Gen Psychiatry* **34**, 197–204 (1977).
18. Glassman AH, Bigger JT Jr, Giardina EV, et al. Clinical characteristics of imipramine-induced orthostatic hypotension. *Lancet* **ii**, 468–472 (1979).
19. Goodwin FK, Cowdry RW, Webster MH. Predictions of drug response in the affective disorders: Toward an integrated approach. In *Psychopharmacology—A Generation of Progress*, MA Lipton et al., Eds., Raven Press, New York, NY, 1978, pp 1277–1288.
20. Gram LF. Plasma level monitoring of tricyclic antidepressant therapy. *Clin Pharmacokinet* **2**, 237–251 (1977).
21. Hall H, Ogren SO. Effects of antidepressant drugs on different receptors in the brain. *Eur J Pharmacol* **30**, 381–391 (1981).
22. Kitanaka I, Zavadil AP III, Cutler NR, Potter WZ. Altered hydroxydesipramine concentrations in the elderly. *Clin Pharmacol Ther* (1981).
23. Kragh-Sorensen P, Borga O, Garle M, et al. Effect of simultaneous treatment with low doses of perphenazine on plasma and urine concentrations of nortriptyline and 10-hydroxynortriptyline. *Eur J Clin Pharmacol* **11**, 479–483 (1977).
24. Kragh-Sorensen P, Hansen CE, Brastrup PC, Hvidberg EF. Self-inhibiting action of nortriptyline's antidepressive effect at high plasma levels. *Psychopharmacologia* **45**, 305–316 (1976).
25. Kragh-Sorensen P, Kristensen CB, Pedersen OL, et al. Antidepressant treatment with imipramine and nortriptyline in elderly patients. In *Clinical Pharmacology in Psychiatry, op cit* (ref *13*), pp 351–357.
26. Mahgoub A, Idle JR, Pringe LG, et al. Polymorphic hydroxylation of debrisoquine in man. *Lancet* **ii**, 584–586 (1977).

27. McDevitt DG. Measurement by non-invasive methods of beta-adrenoceptor activity in man. In *Advances in Pharmacology and Therapeutics* (Proc 7th Int Cong Pharmacol), JP Tillement, Ed., Pergamon Press, Oxford, 1979, pp 77–87.

28. Mellstrom B, Bertilsson L, Sawe J, et al. E- and Z-10-hydroxylation of nortriptyline: Relationship to polymorphic debrisoquine hydroxylation. *Clin Pharmacol Ther* **30**, 189–193 (1981).

29. Ogren SO, Ross SB, Holm AC, Baumann L. Re-evaluation of the indoleamine hypothesis of depression. Evidence for a reduction of functional activity of central 5-HT systems by antidepressant drugs. *J Neural Transm* **46**, 85–103 (1979).

30. Olivier-Martin R, Marzin D, Buschenschutz E, et al. Concentrations plasmatiques de l'imipramine et de la desmethylimipramine et effet anti-depresseur au cours d'un traitement controlé. *Psychopharmacologia* **41**, 187–195 (1975).

31. Piafsky KM, Borga O. Plasma protein binding of basic drugs. II. Importance of α_1-acid glycoprotein for interindividual variation. *Clin Pharmacol Ther* **22**, 545–549 (1977).

32. Potter WZ, Bertilsson L, Sjoqvist F. Clinical pharmacokinetics and psychotropic drugs—fundamental and practical aspects. In *The Handbook of Biological Psychiatry*, Part **VI**, *Practical Applications of Psychotropic Drugs and Other Biological Treatments*. HM Van Praag, O Rafaelson, M Lader, A Sachar, Eds., Marcel Dekker, Inc., New York, NY, 1981, pp 71–134.

33. Potter WZ, Zavidil AP, Kopin IJ, Goodwin FK. Single-dose kinetics predict steady-state concentrations of imipramine and desipramine. *Arch Gen Psychiatry* **37**, 314–320 (1980).

34. Potter WZ, Calil HM, Manian AA, et al. Hydroxylated metabolites of tricyclic antidepressants: Preclinical assessment of activity. *Biol Psychiatry* **14**, 601–613 (1979).

35. Potter WZ, Calil HM, Sutfin T, et al. Active metabolites of imipramine and desipramine in man. *Clin Pharmacol Ther* **31**, 393–401 (1982).

36. Potter WZ, Calil HM, Zavadil AP III, et al. Steady-state concentrations of hydroxylated metabolites of tricyclic antidepressants in patients: Relationship to clinical effect. *Psychopharmacol Bull* **16(2)**, 32–34 (1980).

37. Potter WZ, Muscettola G, Goodwin FK. Binding of imipramine to plasma protein and to brain tissue: Relationship to CSF tricyclic levels in man. *Psychopharmacology* **63**, 187–192 (1979).

38. Rafaelsen OM, Clemmesen L, Lund H, et al. Comparison of peripheral anticholinergic effects of antidepressants: Dry mouth. *Acta Psychiatr Scand* **63** (Suppl 290), 364–369 (1981).

39. Reisby N, Gram LF, Beck P, et al. Imipramine: Clinical effects and pharmacokinetics. *Psychopharmacology* **54**, 263–272 (1977).
40. Richelson E. Tricyclic antidepressants block H_1 receptor cells of mouse neuroblastoma cells. *Nature (London)* **274**, 176–177 (1978).
41. Richelson E. Tricyclic antidepressants and neurotransmitter receptors. *Psychiatr Ann* **9**, 186–195 (1979).
42. Risch SC, Huey LY, Janowsky DS. Plasma levels of tricyclic antidepressants and clinical efficacy: Review of the literature, Parts I and II. *J Clin Psychiatry* **40**, 4–16, 58–69 (1979).
43. Ross RJ, Zavadil AP, Calil HM, et al. The effects of desmethylimipramine on norepinephrine, pulse and blood pressure in volunteers. *Clin Pharmacol Ther* **33**, 429–437 (1983).
44. Rudorfer MV, Young RC. Anticholinergic effects and plasma desipramine levels. *Clin Pharmacol Ther* **28**, 703–706 (1980).
45. Sellers EM, Abel JG, Romach MK, et al. Sources of variation in binding of psychotherapeutic drugs to plasma proteins. In *Clinical Pharmacology in Psychiatry, op cit* (ref *5*), pp 199–212.
46. Shur E, Checkley S. Pupil studies in depressed patients: An investigation of the mechanism of action of desipramine. *Br J Psychiatry* **140**, 181–184 (1982).
47. Spiker DB, Weiss AN, Chang SS, et al. Tricyclic antidepressant overdose: Clinical presentation and plasma levels. *Clin Pharmacol Ther* **18**, 539–546 (1975).
48. Stewart JW, Quitkin F, Fyer A, Klein DF. Efficacy of desmethylimipramine in endogenomorphically depressed patients. *Psychopharmacol Bull* **16**(3), 52–54 (1980).
49. Swift CG, Hawthorne JM, Clarke P, Stevenson IH. Cardiovascular, sedative, and anticholinergic effects of amitriptyline and zimelidine in young and elderly patients. *Acta Psychiatr Scand* **63** (Suppl 290), 425–432 (1981).
50. Szabadi E, Gaszner P, Bradshaw C. Effects of amitriptyline and desipramine on cholinergic and adrenergic responses in the human iris. *Br J Psychiatry* **137**, 433–439 (1980).
51. Thayssen P, Bjerre M, Kragh-Sorensen P, et al. Cardiovascular effects of imipramine and nortriptyline in elderly patients. *Psychopharmacology* **74**, 360–364 (1981).
52. U'Prichard DC, Greenberg DA, Sheehan PP, Snyders SH. Tricyclic antidepressants: Therapeutic properties and affinity for alpha-adrenergic receptor binding sites in the brain. *Science* **199**, 197–198 (1978).
53. Veith RC, Friedel RO, Bloom V, Bielski R. Electrocardiogram changes and plasma desipramine levels during treatment of depression. *Clin Pharmacol Ther* **27**, 796–802 (1980).

54. Veith RC, Raskind MA, Caldwell JH, et al. Cardiovascular effects of tricyclic antidepressants in depressed patients with chronic heart disease. *N Engl J Med* **306**, 954–959 (1982).
55. Wagner JG. *Biopharmaceutics and Relevant Pharmacokinetics*. Drug Intelligence Publ, Hamilton, IL, 1971.
56. Wilkinson GR, Shand DG. A physiological approach to hepatic drug clearance. *Clin Pharmacol Ther* **18**, 377–390 (1975).

Effectiveness of Monoamine Oxidase Inhibitors: A Review

Frederic M. Quitkin and Donald F. Klein

In the 25 years since the first reports suggested that monoamine oxidase (MAO)[1] inhibitors had antidepressant properties, extensive controversy has arisen regarding their use: first, because of occasional associated hypertensive crises, and second, because of questions of their efficacy as compared with the tricyclic antidepressants (TCAs). In fact, as recently as five years ago, clinical lore suggested that MAO inhibitors should be used only in depressed patients who were refractory to other treatment methods.

In 1979, in our first review of MAO inhibitors, we suggested they were underutilized. During the past four years there has indeed been increased interest in these agents. Here we will review the salient features of our earlier paper, emphasize work published on the clinical utility of MAO inhibitors appearing since 1979, and present preliminary findings on our ongoing studies.[2]

The issue of toxicity has been extensively reviewed elsewhere (1, 2) and therefore will not be considered in detail here. Once paroxysmal hypertension was related to the ingestion of tyramine or other pressor agents, the risk of this complication could be greatly reduced through modification of drug intake and diet.

However, recent reports, and our own work, suggest that MAO inhibitors have several less serious but distinctly distressing side effects that seriously complicate the prescription of these drugs.

---

[1] Abbreviations used: MAO, monoamine oxidase (EC 1.4.3.4); TCA, tricyclic antidepressant; DSM-II, -III, Diagnostic Statistical Manual, second and third editions, respectively; DI, diagnostic index; PEA, phenylethylamine; 5-HTP, 5-hydroxytryptophan.

[2] This presentation is a revision and expansion of a paper published previously: Quitkin F, Rifkin A, Klein DF. Monoamine oxidase inhibitors: A review of antidepressant effectiveness. *Arch Gen Psychiatry* **36**, 749–760 (1979). Permission has been granted by the *Archives* for reproduction of portions of that paper.

These side effects, which have not been emphasized, include sexual dysfunction, increased appetite with weight gain, and sleeplessness; they are interesting because they may be a clue in determining how the MAO inhibitors produce benefits.

Function and Metabolism of Monoamine Oxidase

The enzyme monoamine oxidase [EC 1.4.3.4; amine:oxygen oxidoreductase (deaminating) (flavin-containing)] is widely distributed in the brain and many other organs; much indirect evidence suggests that more than one form of the enzyme exists (3, 4). MAO catalyzes the oxidative deamination of tyramine, norepinephrine, dopamine, serotonin, and other biogenic amines to pharmacologically inactive acidic derivatives. Because some of these amines are hypothesized to regulate changes in mood, it is logical to suspect that alteration of MAO may also affect mood. In normal subjects, MAO inhibitors have received little study, but sedation and mild stimulation have been observed.

Various MAO inhibitor compounds (including several structurally unrelated to currently used agents) appear to have an antidepressant effect. Their only apparent shared characteristic is that they inhibit MAO. The antidepressant effect of MAO inhibitors has been a cornerstone of the monoamine theories of depression, which implicate serotonin, norepinephrine, or dopamine in the pathogenesis of depressive disorders.

Classification of MAO Inhibitors

The MAO inhibitors used in psychiatry can be divided into two main categories: hydrazines and nonhydrazines, each with roughly equal therapeutic effects. The utility of a third group, the selective inhibitors, has not been determined.

We will focus primarily on evidence for the efficacy of phenelzine sulfate (Nardil) and tranylcypromine sulfate (Parnate), the two most widely used and studied of the available MAO inhibitors, and representative of the two main groups mentioned.

Inhibitors of specific forms of MAO, MAO_A and MAO_B, will also be reviewed: in theory, specific MAO inhibitors should have fewer side effects if their concentrations are maintained within a specific range, because they selectively inhibit the metabolism of some but not other neurotransmitters. This may eventually provide a means of identifying which neurotransmitters are implicated in different depressive syndromes. Other MAO inhibitors of theoretical or historical interest will be briefly discussed. MAO inhibitors by type, brand name, and availability are listed in Table 1.

Table 1. **Monoamine Oxidase Inhibitors and Their Availability**

Generic name	Brand name	Status[a]
Hydrazines		
Iproniazid	Marsilid	Withdrawn.
Isocarboxazid	Marplan	Available in U.S. but not actively marketed.
Mebanazine	Actomol (U.K.)	Not available in U.S.
Nialamide	Niamid	Not available in U.S.
Phenelzine sulfate	Nardil	Available in U.S.
Pheniprazine	Catron	Withdrawn.
Nonhydrazines		
Pargyline hydrochloride	Eutonyl	Approved as an antihypertensive.
Tranylcypromine sulfate	Parnate	Available in U.S.
Selective MAO inhibitors		
Clorgyline (inhibits MAO$_A$)		Not available in U.S.
N-α-Dimethyl-N-(2-propinyl)-phenethylamine (inhibits MAO$_B$)	Deprenyl	Not available in U.S.

[a] As of March 1983.

Hydrazine derivatives.   The use of the first hydrazine MAO inhibitor, *iproniazid,* was often complicated by liver toxicity. Because free hydrazines are toxic, an attempt was made to increase drug potency and reduce liver toxicity by masking the hydrazine moiety with an acyl radical that would be subject to heterolytic cleavage at the target organ, thus leaving the free radical hydrazine. To improve the stereospecificity of drug action, an isoxyazolyl carbonyl group was introduced to allow ready cleavage and facilitate passage across the blood–brain barrier; thus *isocarboxazid* was synthesized. *Nialamide* was synthesized similarly, but the isopropyl substitute of iproniazid was replaced with a complex moiety. *Phe-*

nelzine has the simplest side chain of all the hydrazine MAO inhibitors.

Nonhydrazine derivatives. In an effort to find a more clinically useful amphetamine-like drug, Burger and Yost *(5)* synthesized the first nonhydrazine MAO inhibitor, *tranylcypromine,* by converting the isopropyl side chain of amphetamine to a cyclopropyl side chain. The drug was tested unsuccessfully as a nasal decongestant. Its MAO-inhibiting properties were discovered in the late 1950s by Maass and Nimmo *(6)* and by Tedeschi et al. *(7),* leading to its use as an antidepressant. Although it has never been clearly established, some believe that tranylcypromine maintains a more stimulating effect (to be differentiated from antidepressant effect) than phenelzine. *Pargyline,* the other major nonhydrazine MAO inhibitor, is approved for use in the United States as an antihypertensive only; it is a relatively selective inhibitor of MAO_B.

Selective MAO inhibitors. There appear to be at least two types of MAO, referred to as MAO_A and MAO_B. Type MAO_A has a greater propensity to deaminate certain substrates such as tyramine and serotonin, and MAO_B other substrates such as phenethylamine. Electrophoretic patterns also suggest that there are at least two types of MAO *(8).* Among the specific MAO inhibitors currently being studied, clorgyline is a relatively selective inhibitor of MAO_A, and N-α-dimethyl-N-(2-propinyl)-phenethylamine (Deprenyl; Hungary) is a selective inhibitor of MAO_B; both are investigational drugs only. Most MAO inhibitors decrease the amounts of intestinal MAO, allowing absorption of increased concentrations of sympathomimetics such as tyramine; this is believed to play a role in the pathogenesis of hypertensive crises. Because Deprenyl has little effect on intestinal MAO, the likelihood of hypertensive crises associated with its use may be less *(8).* Most of the clinically available MAO inhibitors are not specific and inhibit both types of MAO. The theoretical implications of selective inhibition will be discussed later.

Acetylator Status—Theoretical Relevance

Because one step in the metabolism of hydrazine derivatives is acetylation, there has been an interest in the relationship of "acetylator status" and therapeutic response to MAO inhibitors.

The rates of acetylation are genetically determined, with considerable interindividual variation *(9, 10)*. By determining what percentage of a weight-related oral dose of sulfamethazine is acetylated and excreted in the urine, patients can be divided into "fast" or "slow" acetylators; this, in turn, should predict their phenelzine acetylation rate. Differences in the rate at which phenelzine is metabolized might account for some of the variance in studies of efficacy of the drug *(11)*.

Marshall *(12)*, however, has questioned the relevance of phenelzine acetylation, noting that acetylation as a step in phenelzine metabolism has never been demonstrated. Although many hydrazine drugs undergo acetylation in the process of biotransformation, Marshall states that acetylphenelzine has never been found in humans or animals.

Tilstone et al. *(13)* presented indirect evidence that acetylphenelzine is produced when homogenates of rat and human liver are incubated with phenelzine in vitro. However, Sanders and Rawlins *(14)* suggest that this method does not directly identify acetylphenelzine, thus implying that direct evidence of the acetylation of phenelzine is still lacking. This interesting problem, which could explain why some patients do not respond to phenelzine, requires further study. The different rates of improvement of "fast" and "slow" acetylators in studies that classify patients in terms of this variable are discussed later.

MAO Inhibition and Therapeutic Effect—Theoretical Relevance

Because the MAO inhibitors have relatively complex functions in the central nervous system, there is no assurance that their antidepressant effects are necessarily related to inhibition of MAO. Establishment of a demonstrated relationship between percent of MAO inhibition and antidepressant effect would suggest a relevant mechanism.

Using depressed terminally ill patients, MacLean et al. *(15)* and Pare *(16)* demonstrated that the onset of therapeutic antidepressant effect correlates with brain MAO inhibition. With some MAO inhibitors, MAO inhibition takes place approximately two to three weeks after the onset of treatment, a period corresponding to the onset of therapeutic effect.

If MAO inhibition is the mechanism by which these drugs

exert their antidepressant effects, we should project at least a three- to four-week trial before anticipating clinical improvement. Obviously, direct assay of the inhibition of brain MAO is not feasible. A peripheral biological index of brain MAO inhibition might be a useful aid in individualizing dosages.

Platelet MAO inhibition. Ravaris et al. *(17),* studying inhibition of platelet MAO as an index of brain MAO inhibition, found that the mean degree of platelet MAO inhibition was 83.2% for patients treated with 60 mg of phenelzine per day and 58.6% for those treated with 30 mg per day; in a small pilot study, 45 mg of phenelzine per day induced a mean platelet MAO inhibition of 77% (range, 65% to 92%). They suggest that approximately 85% inhibition of brain MAO is needed before brain monoamines increase. However, the relationship or ratio of platelet MAO inhibition to brain MAO inhibition is unknown. If we assume that inhibition of MAO in the two sites is roughly parallel, then clearly daily doses of 30 mg of phenelzine are inadequate and 45 mg is probably only a marginally effective dose. That at least 60 mg of phenelzine per day is required to achieve 85% inhibition is consistent with the clinical studies we will discuss subsequently, which suggest that many patients require this dose to achieve a clinical effect. The details of the relationship of percent platelet MAO inhibition and clinical outcome will be presented later.

Diagnosis of Depression

The Diagnostic Statistical Manual II (DSM II) provided only general guidelines for making diagnoses. Because it presented no specific criteria but only descriptions, the clinician was forced to rely on his own interpretation of salient diagnostic features. Diagnosis thus became an idiosyncratic process, and many of the studies reviewed here were done before the recent interest in making the diagnostic process more consistent. Lack of specific criteria not only diminishes diagnostic reliability but also makes it difficult to understand what type of patient has been included in a study.

A useful format would be to examine the evidence suggesting that a drug or class of drugs is useful in a specific diagnostic entity. Because dysphoric symptoms clearly are seen in heterogeneous diagnostic groups, members of which probably have different responses to treatment, it is crucial to study discrete homogeneous groups to delineate which types of patients respond to specific drugs.

Unfortunately, there has been a virtual absence of clearly defined diagnostic criteria for the group of patients most likely to respond to MAO inhibitors, the "neurotic" or atypical depressive. Given these limitations, we will reproduce the authors' descriptions of the populations studied in the papers cited. Some of the descriptions antedate the important concept of utilizing specific inclusion and exclusion criteria, and readers will have to make their own judgments as to the nature of the sample studied.

Atypical Depression

As a brief orientation we will review some of the salient problems concerning the term "neurotic depression." The importance is that a group of patients referred to as "atypical depressive" may be those who specifically benefit from MAO inhibitors. Because of the overlap in groups described by some investigators as neurotic depressives and by others as atypical, we will discuss the historical and theoretical bases of these two terms together.

Historically, the term "neurotic" was used to distinguish patients with mild depressive symptoms from those with a "psychotic" form of affective illness. The neurotic–psychotic dichotomy in this context suggests that these terms are a measure of severity. However, this usage was inconsistent in DSM-II because all manic-depressive illnesses were considered psychotic, implying that neurotic forms of affective illness were categorically and qualitatively different. The term "neurotic depression" is now considered imprecise and obsolete and is not included in the DSM-III. "Dysthymic disorder" would encompass many of the patients formerly referred to as "neurotic depressives."

In many studies of MAO inhibitors in outpatients, the patients were categorized as neurotic depressives without a more specific definition of the nature of the sample studied. Some studies, on the other hand, gave specific entrance criteria, which we include in this review.

Johnstone and Marsh (18) and Mountjoy et al. (19) presented criteria for diagnosing "neurotic depression." Mountjoy et al. required persistent dysphoric mood and absence of features indicative of "unequivocal endogenous" depression. Evidence of un-

131

equivocal endogenous depression depended on the presence of psychotic symptoms (delusions, hallucinations, previous mania) or two or more vegetative signs (early morning awakening, marked diurnal variation, marked retardation, autonomous mood, and lack of precipitating event).

However, the pathognomonic features of endogenous depression have not been identified, and it is unclear whether any specific phenomenologic features always appear in endogenous depression. The specific exclusion criteria used by Mountjoy et al. are a distinct improvement over the previously used undefined criterion: mild severity. However, a patient could have a mild endogenous depression and still meet the criteria of Mountjoy et al. for "neurotic depression." Other psychiatric illness, such as schizophrenia and cerebral disease, also disqualified the patient.

Johnstone and Marsh's use of Carney's Neurotic/Endogenous Rating Scale probably resulted in a patient sample similar to that of Mountjoy et al. These attempts to make diagnostic criteria more specific were important methodological steps.

The term "atypical" is also poorly defined. Sargant (20, 21) was one of the first to suggest that such patients benefit from MAO inhibitors. He characterized these patients as having "hysterical types of depressive reaction, and some of them could just as well be diagnosed as anxiety states with depressive and hysterical features." They frequently did not benefit from electroconvulsive therapy. He further described this group as sometimes exhibiting irritability, hyperreactivity, increased emotionality, various degrees of depression, and sometimes phobic fears of going out into the street or traveling alone. Hyperphagia, hypersomnolence, reversed diurnal variation (symptoms worse in the evening), and waves of lethargy were seen in some of these patients. We believe that Sargant was combining several different diagnostic subtypes, including panic disorder (phobic anxious) and hysteroid dysphoric (22) patients.

We will use the term "atypical neurotic" to refer to patient samples that were not endogenous but were inadequately characterized; the term "atypical" will be used only if the investigators had made a specific attempt to select patients with atypical features such as reactive mood, reversed diurnal variation, hyperphagia, hypersomnolence, and rejection sensitivity.

Panic Disorder or Phobic Anxiety

In earlier work panic disorder was not differentiated from atypical depression; therefore, a distinctive definition of panic disorder is required. Patients with panic disorder experience recurrent spontaneous panic attacks, that is, feelings of sudden, extreme fear and terror accompanied by sympathetic nervous system discharge (23). Autonomic dysregulation, palpitations, dyspnea, sweating, dizziness, or dryness of mouth often occurs at the height of the panic.

These patients frequently develop phobic avoidance of situations in which the panic attacks have a propensity to occur or in which they may be blocked from access to help, such as subways, crowds, and tunnels. This syndrome is then often referred to as agoraphobia (22). Phobic anxiety is a term derived from the phobic anxiety depersonalization syndrome (24). We do not include the anticipatory anxiety of the simple phobic who is afraid of only specific objects such as spiders or knives.

Atypical Depression vs Phobic Anxiety

There is often a failure to distinguish between the panic disorder syndrome, which can occur without the symptoms associated with atypical depression such as overeating and oversleeping, and atypical depression. Hordern (25), in a discussion of atypical depression, stated that "such patients whose illnesses resemble the phobic-anxiety-depersonalization syndrome described by Roth exhibit a reversed diurnal variation of mood with fatigue, emotionality, initial insomnia and a tendency to blame others."

Initial insomnia, reversed diurnal variation, and increased emotionality are generally associated with atypical depression but not with phobic anxiety. We believe that Sargant and Hordern combined two separate syndromes: atypical depression and phobic anxiety. We suspect that the studies of phenelzine that purported to include patients with "mixed phobias" also included atypical depression.

The more recent studies of Robinson et al. (26) also appear to include a proportion of patients with panic disorder. This distinction is crucial if one wishes to identify patients who benefit from MAO inhibitors but not from TCAs, because patients with panic disorder clearly benefit from TCAs. If panic disorders are included with atypical depressives in a trial contrasting the efficacy of MAO inhibitors and TCAs, patients with panic disorder will benefit from TCAs and therefore will blur any specific roles for MAO inhibitors vs TCAs. Therefore, patients with panic disorder or agoraphobia should be excluded from such contrasts.

The picture is not simple, however, because some patients have clear-cut vegetative atypical features as well as spontaneous panic attacks and (or) phobias. Accordingly, there are three groups: pure panic with phobia; pure vegetative atypical; and a mixture of the two. In assessing the relative utility of TCAs and MAO inhibition, these groups of patients should be identified for appropriate within-group contrasts. We are currently conducting such a study.

Endogenous Depression

Most studies of the utility of MAO inhibitors in endogenous depression were done more than a decade ago. Few specified diagnostic criteria, except the British Medical Research Council study (27), in which patients were primary depressives who had one or more vegetative features.

Even today there is a lack of consensus concerning minimum criteria for diagnosing endogenous depressive disorder. There is little diagnostic disagreement for those patients who exhibit the full-blown syndrome, which includes a history of reasonable personal and social functioning; a highly stereotyped phasic shift with altered sleep, appetite, and sex drive; a pervasive loss of interest associated with inability to experience pleasure; difficulty concentrating; preoccupation with death; guilt; hopelessness; pessimism; lack of reactivity to environmental change; sadness; and withdrawal. This severe expression of the illness is usually associated with either psychomotor agitation or retardation, and mood-congruent delusions and hallucinations may occur.

However, probably not more than 10% of all those with marked depressive affect have the full range of endogenous depressive symptoms; the rest have various psychopathologic features in many combinations. There is little present agreement concerning pathognomonic features or the minimum criteria necessary to make the diagnoses. Given these limitations and the fact that most of the samples studied were poorly described, we have reproduced what diagnostic descriptive material was offered.

Evidence of Efficacy of MAO Inhibitors—
Criteria for Study Review

Many studies of MAO inhibitors involved outpatient "neurotic depressives." These patients develop symptoms in response to external events and tend to have high response rates to placebos. Consequently, the utility of any treatment is difficult to assess without placebo control. Therefore, we will emphasize studies contrasting the effects of the MAO inhibitors with those of placebos, rather than studies that have compared MAO inhibitors with other active treatments.

Wherever possible, we have tabulated the number and description of patients studied, study design, study length, drug dosage, concomitant medications, and major findings. Comments have also been included on ambiguities or design faults. Where details were unavailable, this has been indicated.

Table 2 is a summary of all placebo-controlled studies for testing the efficacy of phenelzine in neurotic or atypical depressives. Table 3 summarizes primarily studies of endogenous depressives treated with phenelzine. To avoid reducing this report to a series of abstracts, we will present the highlights of the studies in the text, and not repeat tabulated details.

Hydrazines

Phenelzine vs placebo in nonendogenous depressives. Phenelzine, the most extensively studied MAO inhibitor, is generally considered the most effective one, although clear evidence of this is lacking. Anecdotal evidence suggests that it has the added advantage of a lower incidence of associated hypertensive crises *(2, 25, 28)*.

Studies by Robinson et al. *(29)* and Ravaris et al. *(17)* support the utility of phenelzine in atypical-neurotic depressives. The samples consisted of nonsuicidal adult patients with "disabling depressive symptomatology," most of whom were referred by their family physicians and had not responded to treatment with TCAs or benzodiazepines. Patients were also characterized as being similar to Paykel's *(30)* group, selected by means of cluster analysis and referred to as "anxious depressives"; they were described as having "an admixture of anxiety and minor neurotic symptoms" such as fatigue, obsessional symptoms, and deperson-

(*text continues on page 142*)

Table 2. Phenelzine–Placebo Studies in Nonendogenous Depressives

Study	No. of patients	Patient description	Design
Hare et al., 1962 (36)	43	39 day-hospital, 4 inpatients; diagnoses: primary depressive illness; no attempt to distinguish endogenous and reactive types	Two-wk random crossover
Greenblatt et al., 1964 (37)	51	Neurotic depressives included as part of larger study; diagnostic criteria not specified	Eight-wk, double-blind collaborative study in three state hospitals
Lascalles, 1966 (35)	40	Patients had atypical facial pain; atypical depressive symptoms included difficulty falling asleep, fatigue, irritability, agitation "similar to West and Dally's atypicals," "lacked hysterical features"	Double-blind crossover
Tyrer et al., 1973 (40)	40	Primary diagnosis of agoraphobia; social phobias included fear of eating in public places, conversing with colleagues at work, etc.	Patients prospectively matched for type of phobia, depression rating, and overall severity
Robinson et al., 1973 (29)	87	Nonsuicidal outpatients with "disabling depressive symptoms"; patients similar to Paykel's anxious depressives (moderately depressed with anxiety and neurotic symptoms); similar to West and Dally's atypical depressives	Blind six-wk study

Dose and duration	Results	Comments
henelzine, 60 mg/day; dextroamphetamine, 10 mg/day; or lactose "5/7 or 7/7 days/ wk"; each patient took each drug for one of three-consecutive two-wk periods	Phenelzine better for agitation and anxiety	Conclusions limited by crossover design; effects of drug and time confounded; treatment period too short
andomly assigned to one of four treatments: (1) imipramine, 200–250 mg, (2) phenelzine, 60–75 mg, (3) isocarboxazid, 40–50 mg, (4) electroconvulsant treatment (minimum, nine treatments); later, "in 2nd yr," placebo group added	100% of neurotic depressives responded to phenelzine, but 83% to placebo	High improvement rate with placebo does not permit conclusions about effect of phenelzine
henelzine, 45 mg/day, vs placebo; each treatment phase lasted one month; patients rated on abbreviated Hamilton Scale	Each active drug period associated with significant decrease in depression and atypical facial pain; patients who received placebo first did not have reduction in depression; those switched to placebo (after phenelzine improvement) had increase in depression	Proper patient classification is unresolved: are they atypical depressives with "good premorbid" history, who have atypical pain as a secondary feature?
andomly assigned to drug or placebo: phenelzine, 45 mg/ day first mo; if not improved, 90 mg/day second mo; three patients received diazepam	32 patients completed study; eight dropouts due to side effects (six receiving phenelzine); for analysis limited to 14 matched pairs, phenelzine patients' overall assessment and improvement on secondary phobias significantly improved	Although patients began to improve earlier, statistically significant improvement not evident for two mo; no significant improvement in main phobia
henelzine, starting dose, 60 mg; range, 45–75 mg; mean, 58.5 mg; attempted to achieve 80% MAO inhibition; patients matched on "risk" factors and randomly assigned to drug or placebo; chlordiazepoxide prescribed if initial anxiety severe	Phenelzine patients better on 15/16 prospectively selected items; 11/16 were statistically significant, including total depression, anxiety, and psychiatrist blind ratings	11 drug and 16 placebo patients dropped out, usually due to intolerable symptoms (11 were hospitalized)

Table 2. *Continued*

Study	No. of patients	Patient description	Design
Johnstone and March, 1973 *(18)*	97	Outpatients who scored as neurotic on Carney's Neurotic/Endogenous Scale	Acetylator status determined with sulfamethazine; double blind crossover
Solyom et al., 1973 *(41)*	50	Mixed phobics; population not well described; not all agoraphobic	50 matched patients, three-mo study
Raskin et al., 1974 *(39)*	169	Neurotic depressives included as part of collaborative study; excluded those considered involutional, manic-depressive, psychotic, or schizophrenic; no other diagnostic criteria	Seven-wk, nine-hospital collaborative study
Ravaris et al., 1976 *(17)*	62	Patients similar to those in 1973 Robinson et al. study *(29)*; symptoms included depression, anxiety, fatigue, phobia, difficulty coping with work and family problems	Similar to 1973 study; patients matched on basis of depressive index derived from ratir scale that included atypical and endogenous items, age, and sex
Johnstone, 1976 *(43)*	30	Outpatients who scored as neurotic on Carney's Neurotic/Endogenous Scale	Acetylator status determined with sulfamethazine
Ballenger et al., 1977 *(42)*	78	Sample confined to agoraphobics; all had panic attacks	12-wk study
Mountjoy et al., 1977 *(19)*	117	44 had anxiety neurosis, 43 neurotic depression, 30 phobic neurosis; patients with endogenous features, obsessive neurosis, alcoholism, and schizophrenia excluded; operationalized criteria reported, those for neurotic depression described in text	Four-wk comparison

138

Dose and duration	Results	Comments
Three wk of phenelzine or placebo; patients taking active drug received 45 mg first wk, thereafter 90 mg/day	51 slow, 46 fast acetylators; data from 25 patients not used for various reasons, leaving 72; analysis appropriately confined to first three-wk period; only slow acetylators had statistically significant improvement with phenelzine	Authors suggest that previous variable results with MAO inhibitors may be due to failure to consider acetylator status
Randomly assigned to one of five treatments: (1) aversion relief, (2) systematic desensitization, (3) flooding, (4) phenelzine, 45 mg/day plus brief psychotherapy, (5) placebo plus brief psychotherapy	Phenelzine patients improved on several measures including anxiety, phobias, and social maladaptions; phenelzine patients had greater improvement than placebo patients on 5/7 measures	Distinguished from study by Tyrer et al. *(40)* in that main phobia improved; phenelzine group improved fastest; authors suggest combination of behavior therapy and drug
Comparison of phenelzine (45 mg), placebo, and diazepam (30 mg); medication taken for four wk and tapered off in fifth wk; patients reevaluated at seventh wk	75% of patients completed three wk, 39% seven wk; diazepam helped some anxious depressives; phenelzine had no beneficial effects	High dropout rate and relatively low phenelzine dose (45 mg/day was rarely exceeded) limit generalizability of this study
Phenelzine, 30 or 60 mg, or placebo for six wk	49 patients completed study; for 12/16 prospectively selected measures, 60-mg group better than placebo; 30-mg group not better than placebo; depressed mood improved with 60 mg	13 dropouts, eight in first two wk (not due to side effects); three terminated for poor response, one from each group, but should have been included in analysis
All patients received phenelzine, 30 mg three times a day for 21 days	13 slow and 17 fast acetylators; slow acetylators had greater improvement on several scales measuring mood	Although study did not have placebo group, the group prospectively selected as most likely to respond was considered most improved by blind rater
Randomly assigned to phenelzine (45 mg/day), imipramine (150 mg/day), or placebo for six wk; if unimproved, dose increased to phenelzine, 60 mg/day, or imipramine, 200 mg/day; all patients had group therapy	Patients treated with phenelzine and imipramine did statistically better on various measures at six and 12 wk than those receiving placebo; nonsignificant trend for phenelzine patients to do better than imipramine patients	On phobic disability, phenelzine patients were rated improved at six and 12 wk compared with placebo patients
Phenelzine, 45 mg/day first two wk, 75 mg/day last two wk; all patients received diazepam, mean dose, 18 mg/day in phenelzine group and 15.6 mg/day in placebo group; nitrazepam also given at bedtime	Depressives receiving phenelzine significantly better on global improvement and anxiety scales, phobics on social phobic scale	Significant differences demonstrated only when 34 dropouts, equally distributed between phenelzine and placebo groups, were excluded; fact that both groups received diazepam may have blurred differences in improvement

139

Table 3. **Phenelzine–Placebo Studies in Endogenous Depressives**

Study	No. of patients	Patient description	Design
Hutchinson and Smedberg, 1960 (47)	34	Recurrent endogenous depressives; all had previously undergone ECT; no other criteria reported	Comparison of two regimens
Agnew et al., 1961 (50)	11	All had depressive symptomatology (included schizophrenia and depressed "schizoid personality"); no specific criteria described	Three-wk double-blind study
Rees and Davies, 1961 (48)	21	13 endogenous depressives, four neurotics, and three with mixed features; no specific criteria reported	Double-blind, three-wk crossover
Greenblatt et al., 1964 (37)	281	All patients had severe depression, including schizophrenia and character disorders; no specific criteria reported; excluded organic brain syndrome, alcoholism	Eight-wk, double-blind collaborative study in three state hospitals
British Medical Research Council, 1965 (27)	269	Endogenous depressives, without recent somatic treatment; operationalized criteria but specific number of features required not specified	Four-wk, double-blind collaborative comparison
Schildkraut et al., 1965 (49)	17	Recurrent endogenous depressives, middle-aged, with vegetative signs; half had previous episodes treated with ECT	Three-wk, double-blind comparison
Raskin et al., 1974 (39)	325	Neurotic, psychotic, and schizophrenic patients with depression; specific criteria not reported; divided sample into subtypes: anxious, hostile, and withdrawn retarded depression	Seven-wk, nine-hospital collaborative study

ECT, electroconvulsant treatment.

Dose and duration	Results	Comments
Group A: two wk phenelzine then two wk placebo then two wk phenelzine; *group B:* two wk placebo then four wk phenelzine; dose, 45 mg/day	At six wk, group B had significantly greater improvement than group A on 5/14 items	Design minimized drug effects
Phenelzine, 15 mg three times a day	With phenelzine, two patients much improved, one slightly, one worse; with placebo, one patient worse, four no change; trend for phenelzine patients to be better	Small sample and heterogeneous sample limit conclusions
Phenelzine, 90 mg/day	With phenelzine, more patients rated as markedly improved; during first three-wk drug-placebo comparison, phenelzine patients had greater reduction in depression	
randomly assigned to one of four treatments: (1) imipramine, 200–250 mg, (2) phenelzine, 60–75 mg, (3) isocarboxazid, 40–50 mg, (4) ECT (minimum, nine treatments); later, "in second yr," placebo group added	For all diagnostic groups, 76% of ECT, 49% of imipramine, 50% of phenelzine, 46% of placebo, and 28% of isocarboxazid patients showed marked improvement	High placebo but relatively low phenelzine improvement rate; phenelzine not effective, but neither was imipramine; therefore, not sensitive test of phenelzine efficacy
imipramine, 200 mg; phenelzine, 60 mg; placebo; and ECT	ECT and imipramine patients did better than placebo and phenelzine patients; phenelzine patients no better than placebo patients	Council does not support use of phenelzine in endogenous depressives
phenelzine, 45–60 mg; imipramine, 100–200 mg; or placebo	No placebo patients improved; 5/6 improved with phenelzine and imipramine	Rate of improvement with phenelzine significantly better than with placebo
comparison of phenelzine (45 mg), placebo, and diazepam (30 mg); medication taken for four wk and tapered off in fifth wk; patient reevaluated at seventh wk	75% of patients completed three wk, 39% seven wk; diazepam helped some anxious depressives; phenelzine had no beneficial effects	High dropout rate and relatively low phenelzine dose (45 mg/day was rarely exceeded) limit generalizability of this study

alization. They are similar to the West and Dally *(31)* group of atypical depressives, who were characterized by phobic anxiety states and secondary depression; others had "anxiety hysteria" or were "inadequate." West and Dally do not define most of these terms; however, their patients appear to be characterized by good premorbid personality, with subsequent development of chronic anxiety, depression, overreactivity and fatigue, self-reproach, and poor response to electroconvulsive therapy. They lacked early morning awakening.

In the first study by Robinson et al. *(29)*, patients were withdrawn from previous medication and kept drug-free for at least five days. They were then randomized into two treatment groups, one given placebo and the other phenelzine at a starting dose of 60 mg/day: this was adjusted, depending on side effects, to between 45 and 75 mg/day. Of the 33 patients treated with phenelzine and 27 with placebo who completed the study, the phenelzine-treated patients had significantly greater improvement on all five composite ratings of total depression, total anxiety, somatic anxiety, hypochrondriasis-agitation, and psychomotor change, as well as a variety of individual measures of psychopathology.

The same group confirmed this work in a subsequent study *(17)* involving a similar design and patient sample. In both studies, the group means for baseline measures of pathologic illness were virtually identical. The second study *(17)* had three treatment groups: one given phenelzine at 60 mg/day; the second, phenelzine at 30 mg/day; and the other, placebo. The group treated with 60 mg of phenelzine per day demonstrated significantly greater improvement than the placebo group on virtually all measures of psychopathology, thus replicating the original study. The group treated with 30 mg of phenelzine did no better than the placebo group. Of the patients treated with 60 mg, 71% were definitely improved, but only 6% of the patients treated with 30 mg and 21% of the placebo patients were rated definitely improved.

Each patient was given a diagnostic index (DI) score *(32)*, derived from the 42 items used to rate depression: the 17 Hamilton Depression Scale items and 25 other items measuring aspects of the depressive syndrome. Items were assigned negative and positive weights so that patients at the endogenous pole would have a high positive score and those at the atypical pole a low or negative score. The five items given the highest positive weights were suicidal ideation, weight loss, depressed mood, agitation, and retardation. Psychic anxiety, somatic anxiety, initial insomnia, general somatic symptoms, and suicidal attempts (communicative) were the items given the five most negative weights.

The trend for patients with low or negative DI scores to have a higher rate of improvement with phenelzine than those with a higher DI score was not statistically significant (33). At each DI score apparently there was an approximately equal number of placebo responders. At the very lowest DI scores (only eight patients), the response rate to phenelzine was very high. It is unclear from the data presented whether specific clinical features characterized these eight patients. Across all other DI scores, the percentage of definitely improved patients was approximately equal. This suggests that there may be a small group of patients with low DI scores who are most likely to benefit from MAO inhibitors.

In a more recent publication, Robinson et al. (34) reported that by using scores from a depression scale interview (Standardized Depression Interview), they were able to identify with cluster analyses three patient groups that closely resembled three of the four groups described by Paykel (30). Preliminary analysis of these data (34) suggested that the best response to phenelzine occurred in the group with the fewest endogenous features.

Other placebo-controlled studies that demonstrated a therapeutic effect of phenelzine with atypical or neurotic depression were done by Lascalles (35) and Hare et al. (36). In the study by Greenblatt et al. (37), although 100% of the "psycho-neurotic" depressives improved with phenelzine, the drug was not found to be superior to placebo, which also was associated with a very high improvement rate (83%).

Mountjoy et al. (19) randomly assigned to phenelzine or placebo 44 anxious patients, 43 depressed patients, and 30 with phobic neurosis. Compared with patients receiving placebos, patients receiving phenelzine demonstrated significant improvement on a variety of scales; phobics improved on a phobic scale, and depressives improved on a self-rated anxiety and global improvement scale. However, anxiety neurotics treated with phenelzine actually had a significant increase in anxiety, probably because, we suspect, the phobic neurosis group included all phobic anxious patients.

143

Thus, patients with panic attacks were probably included in the phobic group and not in the anxiety neurosis group. It is our impression that antidepressants are useful only for the anxiety associated with panic attacks, which may explain the lack of utility of phenelzine in this group of anxiety neurotics (38). The increase in anxiety may have been the anxious patients' reaction to phenelzine-induced side effects such as orthostatic hypotension and the necessity to adhere to dietary limitations.

A large collaborative study by Raskin et al. (39) that included "neurotic depressives" did not demonstrate the superiority of phenelzine to placebo. The interpretation of this study is complicated by a high dropout rate, a low phenelzine dose (45 mg/day), and the difficulties inherent in a collaborative study involving nine hospitals.

Two studies involving samples of mixed phobics showed significantly greater overall improvement in patients receiving phenelzine (40, 41). In one, in addition to improvement in overall assessment, the phenelzine-treated group showed improvement in secondary but not primary phobia (40). In the other, the primary phobia was improved in patients treated with phenelzine (41).

In a study in which the sample was confined to agoraphobics with panic, patients treated with phenelzine or imipramine showed statistically better improvement than patients receiving placebo (42). Superior response to phenelzine over imipramine was insignificant.

As previously mentioned, interest has focused on the heterogeneity of acetylation rate, which may account for some patients responding and others not responding to phenelzine. Johnstone and Marsh (18) found that approximately half of their patients were slow acetylators and half were fast. However, because they did not fully present the data distribution, it is unclear whether the distribution of acetylation rate was bimodal or the sample was merely divided arbitrarily. The group studied was depressed patients who scored in the neurotic range on Carney's Neurotic/Endogenous Rating Scale. Utilizing a fixed dose schedule, which started at 45 mg of phenelzine per day and increased to 90 mg, they found significant drug–placebo differences in slow but not rapid acetylators. In addition, slow acetylators demonstrated greater improvement than fast acetylators at the end of three weeks.

These findings were later replicated by Johnstone (43) with a similar group of hospitalized patients. Although this study did not include a placebo group, a "blind" rater was able to detect greater improvement in those patients prospectively designated as most likely to respond to phenelzine. If phenelzine were inactive, it seems unlikely that this would have occurred unless one assumes slow acetylators are more likely to be placebo responders or have a benign course. Therefore, if acetylation rate is taken into account, phenelzine may be even more potent for a subset of depressives than is apparent from the treatment effect on a heterogeneous group.

However, preliminary data compiled by Robinson et al. (34) have not shown a clear-cut relationship between therapeutic outcome and acetylator status, although the correlation of the ratio of acetylated to free sulfapyridine to several measures of improvement suggested the possibility that "slow" acetylators improve more. Obviously, more work is needed.

In summary, nine studies involved a phenelzine–placebo contrast in neurotic or atypical depressives (17–19, 29, 35–37, 39, 43) and three studies (40–42) involved primarily phobic samples. In the study by Greenblatt et al. (37), the high placebo improvement rate (83%) makes phenelzine–placebo comparisons futile. Ten of the remaining 11 studies reported significantly more improvement for phenelzine than for placebo. Even if we disregard the three studies dealing with phobic patients, seven of eight studies demonstrate the superiority of phenelzine in atypical-neurotic depressives. We believe that demonstrating a significant effect of phenelzine in seven of eight (or 10 of 11) studies clearly demonstrates it to be a useful agent. That two groups of investigators confirmed their original findings in subsequent studies (17, 18, 29, 43) is also particularly impressive.

To put these studies of phenelzine in perspective, it may be useful to recall that Klein and Davis (22), in their review of the efficacy of TCAs, reported that TCAs were superior to placebo in 76% of the studies (48/63). Thus, the percentage of studies demonstrating the efficacy of phenelzine in samples of atypical-neurotic depressives is similar to the percentage of TCA studies showing efficacy in a more typical group of depressives. Klein and Davis found no study in which placebo was superior to TCA, and in this review of MAO inhibitor efficacy we have found only one clear exception. The anxiety neurotic subgroup studied by Mountjoy et al. *(19)* had less anxiety while receiving placebo than while receiving phenelzine. [In the study by Greenblatt et al. *(37),* depressives treated with isocarboxazid may have done worse than the placebo group, but the manner in which data are presented does not permit a definitive statement.] Therefore, significantly greater improvement with placebo than with an MAO inhibitor is rare. If one were dealing with an inactive substance, by chance alone placebo should be better than "drug" one in 20 times, and the converse should also be true. We think that there is no question that phenelzine is useful in this subgroup of depressives. However, this group needs to be better defined.

Phenelzine vs TCA vs placebo. It seems likely that unipolar depressive disorder consists of many different subtypes. If a subtype had a greater likelihood of responding to one class of antidepressants than another, this would suggest that it is a distinct syndrome, the pathophysiology of which differs from other subtypes. In light of prior studies contrasting TCAs and MAO inhibitors that found TCAs to be superior, a patient group that preferentially responded to MAO inhibitors would very likely be a distinct unipolar subgroup.

Raft et al. *(44)* contrasted the effects of phenelzine, amitriptyline, and placebo. Patients attending a pain clinic, who met Feighner criteria for definite primary depression, were selected if "they were judged to require antidepressant therapy." It is not clear whether the symptom pictures were predominantly endogenous or not. In addition, previous treatment, if any, is not discussed (a prior history of refractoriness to a TCA or to electroconvulsive therapy would alter the implications of the findings).

Despite these limitations, this study has interesting implications. Twenty-nine patients entered the study and 23 completed it. Ten received phenelzine, seven received amitriptyline, and six received placebo. Doses as great as 90 mg of phenelzine or 300 mg of amitriptyline per day were used during a six-week trial. In terms of mean Hamilton Depression Scale scores, phenelzine was superior to amitriptyline, and amitriptyline was superior to placebo. No statistical differences emerged until the fifth week, which suggests that these were not nonspecific treatment effects. In our experiences, differences between drug and placebo that emerge after several weeks of treatment are more likely to be a true drug-related effect.

Without knowing the previous treatment history, we do not know whether phenelzine was superior to TCA in a group refractory to prior treatment with TCA, or whether this was an untreated group with a unique pathophysiology who had increased likelihood of responding to MAO inhibitors. A more complete description of the sample would have been desirable.

A new generation of TCA vs MAO inhibitor trials has appeared in the past few years involving samples of patients who are primarily heterogeneous, nonendogenous outpatients (26, 45, 46). These trials have similar good design and were well-executed. The samples have included virtually all outpatients with depressive illness, with or without anxiety. Depressed patients with phobias and panic were included, but those with clear-cut endogenous depression were excluded.

In general, the results across these three trials are similar. Both TCAs and MAO inhibitors were effective agents in the populations studied, with little evidence that any subgroup, typology, or symptom cluster responded preferentially. We conclude from these studies that mild to moderately depressed patients constitute a heterogeneous group containing a definite portion of patients with a biological diathesis treatable with either TCAs or MAO inhibitors. The evidence is insufficient, however, to conclude whether there are subgroups who specifically benefit from one or the other kind of drug.

We have been studying a group of patients, referred to as atypical depressives, for whom we have developed the following set of specific inclusion and exclusion criteria:

1. Meets research diagnostic criteria for major, minor, or intermittent depression (23).

2. Maintains mood reactivity when depressed.

3. Shows two or more of the following: increased appetite or weight gain while depressed; oversleeping or spending more time in bed while depressed; severe fatigue, creating a sensation of leaden paralysis or extreme heaviness of arms or legs while depressed; rejection sensitivity as a trait throughout adulthood.

Our study attempts to validate this nosological definition against drug effect. Patients who meet these criteria, who have

147

not received as much as 45 mg of phenelzine (or its equivalent) or more than 150 mg of imipramine (or the equivalent) per day for two weeks during the current episode, are initially treated single-blind for 10 days with placebo medication. Those who fail to respond are randomly assigned to either phenelzine, imipramine, or placebo for a six-week trial. Dosage is increased stepwise so that patients on active drug receive phenelzine, 60 mg/day, or imipramine, 200 mg/day, for weeks three and four of the study. Depending on clinical response and side effects, daily doses can be increased to 75 and then 90 mg of phenelzine, or to 250 and then 300 mg of imipramine for the last two weeks of the study.

To date, of the approximately 60 of 120 patients who have completed the trial, 20% responded to placebo, 40% to imipramine, and 75% to phenelzine. If the current trend persists, the results will strongly suggest that this patient group specifically benefits from MAO inhibitors and therefore is a distinct subgroup of unipolar depressive illness.

Phenelzine in endogenous depression. Double-blind, placebo-controlled studies of largely endogenous depressive inpatients are summarized in Table 3. In deciding which studies to include in Table 3, we attempted to minimize arbitrary decisions. We used authors' descriptions of study samples when possible; when there was no description but the study was of inpatients, we assumed that the sample was predominantly endogenous, although this is clearly a shaky assumption.

Evidence for the utility of phenelzine in endogenous depressives is less convincing than for neurotic-atypical depressives. Strikingly, we could find only one inpatient study of MAO inhibitors vs placebo between 1965 and 1977. Thus, most of this work was done when study design methods, which are now routine, were relatively new. Several of the early studies involve too low doses and too short study periods.

The most compelling data suggesting a lack of utility of phenelzine for endogenous depressives come from the British Medical Research Council *(27)*. Criteria for entrance into their study were primary depressive disorder accompanied by one or more vegetative features. The 61 patients who received phenelzine did no better than patients receiving placebo. The group treated with imipramine was significantly more improved than the placebo group. A significantly greater percentage of imipramine-treated patients improved than did those treated with phenelzine. Given the results with imipramine, there is little question that the patients included in the study were, in fact, potential drug responders—a strong methodological point.

The other large collaborative studies have drawbacks that limit their interpretation. The dropout rate of the study by Raskin et al. *(39)* was so high as to lead to questions regarding the characteristics of those who actually completed it. In the study by Greenblatt et al. *(37)*, neither phenelzine nor imipramine was distinguishable from placebo. The fact that imipramine was ineffective suggests that the state hospital patients included in the study were refractory to medication, thereby precluding the possibility of detecting any effect for phenelzine, if one existed.

However, three placebo-controlled studies with small samples *(47–49)* do support the utility of phenelzine in endogenous depression. It is very difficult to demonstrate a weak drug effect over placebo in small samples; therefore, the fact that studies utilizing samples of 34, 31, and 17 subjects demonstrated phenelzine to be effective is compelling evidence that the drug does benefit some endogenous depressions. Agnew et al. *(50)*, in a study of only 11 patients, found an insignificant trend favoring phenelzine.

It is unlikely that MAO inhibitor–placebo trials will be done in severely ill endogenous depressives because of the unethical nature of withholding treatment from severely ill patients when a useful treatment has already been established. Therefore, further evidence about the utility of MAO inhibitors in endogenous depression will derive from trials without placebo control groups.

Davidson et al. *(51)* studied 21 inpatients treated with imipramine (maximum dose 150 mg/day) and 21 inpatients treated with phenelzine (maximum dose 90 mg/day) for three weeks. Although mean pretreatment scores on the Hamilton Depression Scale were greater than 25, only 10 of the patients were considered endogenous depressives. Both groups showed significant improvement (an average of 15 points on the Hamilton Scale, in both groups, after three weeks of treatment); unfortunately, however, the report is unclear as to the degree of improvement for the 10 endogenous depression patients in the sample. This study suggests that there may be some endogenous depression patients who respond to MAO inhibitors.

Quitkin et al. *(52)* reported on an open trial of five depressed bipolar endogenous depressive patients refractory to treatment with TCA (at daily doses exceeding 250 mg of imipramine or its equivalent) and lithium, who were given phenelzine at doses up to 90 mg/day. Five of the six clearly improved over a period of six weeks. This type of trial is limited by the fact that it does not control for the effect of time (the chance of spontaneous remission), but it does suggest that MAO inhibitors may be useful for some refractory endogenous depressives and that there may be a group of bipolar patients who specifically require MAO inhibitors. This hypothesis was proposed by Himmelhoch et al. *(53)*, who found that the combination of MAO inhibitors and lithium was useful in a group of refractory bipolar depressed patients.

In summary, the data do not unanimously deny or support the utility of phenelzine in endogenous depression. Further work is needed to help distinguish those patients with endogenous depression likely to respond to MAO inhibitors. Phenelzine is unlikely to be more useful than TCAs for most patients with endogenous depression, but it may play a role in the treatment of a subgroup of endogenous depressives, perhaps those who have such atypical features as hypersomnia or hyperphagia.

Other hydrazine MAO inhibitors. Some clinicians who have used several MAO inhibitors say that iproniazid is an outstanding drug. It has not been extensively tested under controlled conditions, partly because of its removal from the market before appropriate clinical testing methods were developed. Kiloh et al. *(54)* found it effective in endogenous depressives, although Wittenborn *(55)* found it useful only if no pretreatment paranoia was evident.

A recent study by Giller et al. *(56)* supports the utility of isocarboxazid. Thirty patients meeting DSM-III criteria for major depressive disorder and having Hamilton Depression Scale scores of 20 or greater, were treated with isocarboxazid, 40 mg per day, or placebo. The dose was adjusted double-blind to achieve 90% platelet inhibition. The mean daily dose after six weeks of treatment was 48 mg ($\pm$ 12 mg) of isocarboxazid. Seven of 13 study completers on active drug, but only one of 11 on placebo, were rated much improved. Further studies of this drug are required before adequate assessment is possible.

Significance of dose. Psychopharmacologic dose–response studies are difficult primarily because the effect of antidepressant drugs is small. That is, if 60 to 70% of patients respond to active drug treatment and 30 to 40% respond to placebo treatment, the effect attributable to the active drug is about 30%. In detecting differences in efficacy between two doses of an active agent, the difference will be even smaller. Therefore, this type of study requires large numbers of diagnostically homogeneous patients, with comparable illness and treatment histories. Such studies are difficult and expensive to conduct. The few that have been conducted do indicate that dose is a crucial issue in the somatic treatment of psychiatric disorders.

Two good studies offer guidelines for selecting the dose of phenelzine. As noted earlier, a study by Ravaris et al. (17) clearly demonstrated that 30 mg of phenelzine per day was not as effective as 60 mg/day. Tyrer et al. (57) did an extremely useful study in which they assessed the role of dose of phenelzine, acetylator status, and diagnosis in determining clinical outcome. Using the Present State Examination (58) for diagnostic classification, they divided patients with diagnoses of depressive neurosis, anxiety neurosis, and phobic anxiety into fast and slow acetylators and then randomized them into two fixed-dose schedules (maximum daily phenelzine dose either 45 or 90 mg) for a four-week trial. Those in the high-dose group showed greater improvement for several measures of outcome, including self ratings. This was true for all three diagnostic groups, and both fast and slow acetylators had roughly equal improvement. Contrary to earlier work, the trend was for fast acetylators to demonstrate greater improvement. The implications are clear: all patients who can tolerate it should receive at least 90 mg of phenelzine daily before a decision is made that the drug is ineffective.

Nonhydrazines

Tranylcypromine. Tranylcypromine is the other major MAO inhibitor currently used as an antidepressant in the United States. When several fatal hypertensive crises occurred early in its use, it was withdrawn from the U.S. market. However, once clinicians understood the role that tyramine-containing foods and other pressor substances played in the pathogenesis of paroxysmal hypertensive crises, the prescription information was revised, and the drug was again marketed.

In a well-designed outpatient study with tranylcypromine and placebo, Bartholomew (59) evaluated consecutively selected pairs of depressed patients matched by sex and age and by severity, duration, and type of depression. Patients whose depression was considered periodic and not precipitated were considered endogenous, and those whose illness was related to some stress were considered reactive. Depressions first appearing between ages 45 and 60 in persons with "rigid anancastic personality" were diagnosed as involutional. Patients assigned to tranylcypromine, 60 mg per day, did significantly better than those receiving placebo, although statistical significance was reached only when all patient subtypes were combined. Patients with reactive depression showed a nonstatistically significant higher improvement rate than those with endogenous depression. However, in five of six prospectively matched pairs of involutional depressives, the member receiving active drug improved more, suggesting that some endogenous depressives may also respond to tranylcypromine.

Only five other placebo-controlled studies of tranylcypromine have been reported. In two (59, 60) tranylcypromine was found superior to placebo by various measures. The sample studied by Khanna et al. (60) was described as females "diagnosed as depressed at regular staff meetings." Glick (61) demonstrated a significant drug effect only when a small group of patients randomly assigned to tranylcypromine was combined with a similar group tested with phenelzine. No sample description was reported other than that they were depressed outpatients. Gottfries (62) found nonsignificant trends favoring tranylcyrpomine. However, patients received the drug for only 15 days, too short a time to permit it to take full effect, and the 30 mg maximum daily dosage was low; these factors markedly reduce the likelihood of finding drug–placebo differences. In a more recent study, Himmelhoch et al. (63) found tranylcypromine more effective than placebo in anergic depressives. Although the number of studies contrasting tranylcypromine to placebo is relatively small, four of five found the drug to be superior.

In some studies the antidepressant effect of tranylcypromine was compared with that of TCAs and found to be approximately equal (64–66). Combining these data with those from the placebo–tranylcypromine studies strongly argues for the likelihood that tranylcypromine has antidepressant properties.

Occasionally, patients respond to tranylcypromine after being unresponsive to previous medications. When tranylcypromine was withdrawn from the market, some patients suffered a worsening of symptoms on other medications. When the drug was reintroduced, they responded again. Schiele *(67)* surveyed 55 psychiatrists and found 603 such patients. No test other than trial and error is available to identify these patients.

Tranylcypromine isomers. The dextro form of tranylcypromine is reportedly a more potent MAO inhibitor than the levo form, which is a more effective blocker of monoamine uptake *(68)*. Several studies have attempted to demonstrate different clinical effects of the two isomers *(69, 70)*. If different clinical efficacies were demonstrated, this would suggest which mechanism was more important in mediating the benefits of tranylcypromine. Unfortunately, results to date are contradictory, and the number of patients studied is too small to warrant conclusions.

Other nonhydrazine MAO inhibitors. Pargyline in a dose range of 75 to 150 mg per day was more effective than placebo for both a group of manic depressives and patients with involutional depression. In a group of endogenous inpatient depressives, 62% (18/29) had at least "marked improvement" with pargyline and less than 10% (1/13) responded to placebo *(71)*. One study found pargyline inferior to tranylcypromine in 40 hospitalized depressed patients *(72)*, but the pargyline doses may have been too low (50 to 150 mg per day) or the three-week study period may have been too short to show a maximal therapeutic effect.

Of the various other nonhydrazine MAO inhibitors studied, none has been extensively tested under controlled conditions, and is unlikely that these drugs will receive widespread clinical use.

Mebanazine (methylbenzylhydrazine) in preliminary open studies has been reported by Knott *(73)* and Kline and Sacks *(74)* to be an effective antidepressant. Wheatley *(75)*, however, in a placebo-controlled, four-week trial, failed to find it effective, perhaps because of the small (20 mg per day) dose or the fact that 65% of placebo-treated patients improved. In the controlled study by Barker et al. *(76)* the 76% reduction in severity score with placebo made contrasts with the group receiving mebanazine futile.

Modaline sulfate, which is not structurally related to present MAO inhibitors, had a beneficial effect in some depressed patients. Dunlop et al. *(77)* found biological evidence of MAO inhibition in those patients who were helped.

Most of the MAO inhibitors that were introduced over a decade ago are unlikely ever to play a prominent clinical role. Of heuristic interest, however, is the question of whether all drugs that inhibit MAO alter mood.

Selective MAO Inhibitors

Earlier we mentioned that there are at least two types of MAO: MAO_A and MAO_B. Unlike most of the available MAO inhibitors, which inhibit both forms of the enzyme, clorgyline is a relatively selective inhibitor of MAO_A, and N-α-dimethyl-N-(2-propinyl)-phenethylamine (Deprenyl) selectively inhibits MAO_B (8).

Demonstrating that certain depressives respond to one and not the other of these selective MAO inhibitors would have strong implications for establishing diagnostic validity. It would support the importance of MAO inhibition in mediating the antidepressant effect of these drugs, the monoamine theory of depression, and the possibility of pharmacological demonstration of specific subgroups.

The hysteroid dysphoric patient may be a case in point. This group of patients, primarily women, becomes acutely depressed in response to interpersonal rejection. These depressions are characterized by a leaden feeling, an increased appetite for sweets, and the need for sleep.

Klein (78) has suggested that these episodes bear a resemblance to the depression associated with amphetamine withdrawal, and that a derangement in regulation of phenylethylamine (PEA), an amphetamine-like substance occurring in the brain, might be responsible for the mood disorder seen in the hysteroid dysphoric.

Knoll (8) has demonstrated that Deprenyl potentiates the effects of PEA on a variety of in-vivo and in-vitro measures, but clorgyline, a relatively specific inhibitor of MAO_A, does not.

Therefore, if hysteroid dysphorics responded to Deprenyl (an MAO_B inhibitor that potentiates PEA) but not to clorgyline (an MAO_A inhibitor with no effect on PEA), this would suggest that PEA plays a specific role in this group of patients.

Theorizing aside, is there evidence that selective MAO inhibitors are effective? This is more complicated than it first appears, because only within a specific dose range are these drugs selective inhibitors. A drug that is a selective inhibitor at a dose at which it has no antidepressant properties and that has antidepressant

154

effects only at a dose at which it inhibits both forms of MAO may not be very different from currently available MAO inhibitors. Although an in-depth examination is beyond the scope of this review, the reader should be aware of the relevant questions: Is the drug effective? Is it effective at a dose at which it maintains its selectivity? (This may give clues as to which neurotransmitters are responsible for its efficacy.) If effective in a range in which it is no longer selective, does it nevertheless have advantages over the available MAO inhibitors?

Deprenyl. Deprenyl has been available for almost 20 years. Early pilot studies suggested it might be effective as an antidepressant *(79, 80)*. It appears to be a useful adjunct to L-dopa in the treatment of Parkinsonism, but few studies have been done concerning its efficacy in treating depression.

However, several recent studies also suggest that Deprenyl may be an active antidepressant. Mann et al. *(81)* recently reported a single-blind study of 25 patients who met Research Diagnostic Criteria for major depressive disorder and underwent a week of treatment with placebo, followed by four weeks of Deprenyl up to 20 mg per day. Ten of 12 nonendogenous and six of 13 endogenous depressive patients responded to Deprenyl. The six endogenous depression responders included five of the seven bipolars in the sample, but only one of the six endogenous unipolars studied. This study is significant in reporting an antidepressant effect of Deprenyl in a relatively low dose range, where the drug may be pharmacologically specific.

Mendlewicz and Youdim *(82)* reported a study in which 10 bipolar and four unipolar depressed patients were openly treated with 300 mg of 5-hydroxytryptophan (5-HTP), 75 mg of benserazide (a peripheral decarboxylase inhibitor), and 5 mg of Deprenyl three times a day for 32 days. Ten (seven bipolars and three unipolars) of the 14 patients showed a good antidepressant response to the drug combination. Then the effect of Deprenyl plus 5-HTP plus benserazide was compared with that of 5-HTP plus benserazide in a mixed unipolar–bipolar population in a double-blind placebo-controlled trial. In the former group, 14 patients responded and four did not. In the group without Deprenyl, 13 responded and eight did not. Overall, Deprenyl plus 5-HTP was significantly better than placebo, but not significantly better than 5-HTP alone. Note that, although the proportion of bipolars to unipolars was roughly equivalent in the three treatment groups, there were no differences in treatment response according to clinical diagnosis.

In contrast to these findings, Mendis et al. *(83)* studied 22 patients with primary depressive illness in a double-blind trial comparing the effects of doses of 10 mg of Deprenyl for one week followed by 20 mg for three weeks, with placebo; they found no significant difference between the two groups. In fact, only two of 11 patients on Deprenyl showed any marked improvement, in contrast to a trial of TCAs conducted in similar patients, of whom 50% showed marked improvement. Because this group showed a modest response to tricyclics, it may have been the wrong depressive population in which to study Deprenyl.

Quitkin et al. *(84)* did an open study of carefully diagnosed atypical depressives meeting Research Diagnostic Criteria for major, minor, or intermittent depression. Of 17 patients, 10 (59%) were "much improved" or "very much improved" on a clinical global rating, which is similar to the response rate obtained with phenelzine in this diagnostic group.

Eleven of 15 study patients were subsequently treated with phenelzine after completing the Deprenyl trial, stopping medication, and in the case of responders, relapsing. Seven Deprenyl responders received phenelzine, of whom six responded to this drug in doses up to 90 mg per day. The one phenelzine nonresponder among the Deprenyl responders could not tolerate 60 mg of phenelzine per day because of the side effects. Four Deprenyl nonresponders also received phenelzine; two responded and two did not.

A variety of antidepressants such as phenelzine and imipramine are suppressors of rapid eye movement (REM), and are useful in the treatment of narcolepsy. Deprenyl (10 mg per day) was totally ineffective during a two-week trial of 12 patients with narcolepsy *(85)*; unfortunately, greater doses were not tested.

Evidence for the antidepressant efficacy of Deprenyl so far is scanty, but promising. Clearly, controlled trials with well-defined patient groups are necessary before drawing any further conclusions.

Clorgyline. Only two controlled trials have been reported for clorgyline, a selective inhibitor of MAO_A. Herd *(86)* reported in 1969 that it was superior to amitriptyline, but the use of a phenothiazine along with clorgyline in the trial makes the results difficult to interpret. The low rate of response to amitriptyline, even among endogenously depressed patients, also makes conclusions difficult.

Wheatley *(87)* reported a randomized trial in a mixed group of outpatients who showed equivalent response to clorgyline and imipramine. The imipramine patients appeared to have a good response, lending support to the belief that this was a specific drug response, beyond the placebo response rate.

Several studies of clorgyline have been reported from the National Institute of Mental Health. Lipper et al. *(88)* reported a crossover trial between clorgyline and pargyline in which clorgyline was significantly more effective. Unfortunately, the effectiveness of pargyline as an antidepressant has not been established, making it a poor reference drug. Also, the improvement ratings were neither consistent nor impressive when considered in the light of the multiple comparisons made. The mean scores after treatment indicated that the average patient was still quite symptomatic, making it hard to assess the clinical significance of the statistical differences reported.

Pickar et al. *(89)* reported an inpatient trial of clorgyline, phenelzine, and pargyline, in which all three drugs produced an equal incidence of hypomania. Antidepressant efficacy was not reported, but the precipitation of hypomania with clorgyline suggests that it may be an antidepressant.

Potter et al. *(90)* reported a clinical series of five cases in which clorgyline, combined with lithium, may have prolonged the cycles and decreased the symptom severity of refractory, rapidly cycling bipolar patients.

In summary, there is suggestive but by no means persuasive evidence that clorgyline is an active antidepressant. Further controlled clinical trials in well-defined patient groups and with protocols that provide for adequate reference treatment need to be done.

Combined TCA–MAO Inhibitor Treatment

The combining of TCAs and MAO inhibitors to treat depressive disorders is another area that needs further study. Although several reports suggest that initial concerns about the toxicity of the combination were exaggerated *(2, 91)*, there are too few controlled studies. One controlled study of combined TCA–MAO inhibitor treatment found the drug combination less effective than electroconvulsive treatment in a group of refractory depressives *(92)*.

Two recent trials of combined treatment indicate the combination is safe but did not demonstrate any advantage as compared with either drug alone *(45, 93)*. However, one trial *(93)* was a pilot study with a small number of subjects and the other involved conservative doses *(45)*. A good trial of TCA–MAO inhibitor combination in refractory depressives is still indicated.

MAO Inhibition and Therapeutic Effect—Clinical Relevance

Inhibition of platelet MAO is supposedly an index of brain MAO inhibition. Robinson et al. *(33)*, studying the relationship of percent inhibition of platelet MAO and clinical improvement, found that 68% of the patients who achieved at least 80% MAO inhibition—but only 44% of those achieving less than 80% MAO inhibition—had a favorable response to phenelzine. Of those who achieved 90% inhibition, 79% improved. In addition, they found that with 60 mg of phenelzine daily, maximum platelet MAO inhibition took longer than two weeks to occur, which may account for the failure to demonstrate improvement in studies lasting only two or three weeks. This contention is supported by the finding that improvement with phenelzine did not reach a maximum until the fourth week. This relationship between improvement and at least an 80% inhibition of platelet MAO is supported in other studies by this group *(34)*.

A significant correlation (varying between 0.29 and 0.56) between phenelzine dose in milligrams per kilogram of body weight and percent platelet MAO inhibition was demonstrated at weeks two, four, and six, with both benzylamine and tryptamine as the substrate. There was also a correlation between dose in milligrams per kilogram and clinical effect. These findings, if confirmed, could become a useful guide in prescribing MAO inhibitors. Although perhaps not indicated for routine clinical use, studies of platelet MAO inhibition may be of value in treating patients refractory to standard MAO inhibitor doses. However, the group treated with 60 mg per day had a 71% improvement rate, and it is not clear whether taking into account other factors such as percent MAO inhibition or dose in milligrams per kilogram identifies a group with a significantly higher percentage of definite responders.

Several more-recent studies have used the percentage of platelet inhibition as a guide to prescribing MAO inhibitors. Giller et al. *(56)* adjusted the dosage of isocarboxazid to achieve 90% platelet MAO inhibition and suggest that this facilitates reaching optimal benefit from MAO inhibitors. However, only about 55% of their patients improved. Raft et al. *(44)* also suggested a relationship between percent of platelet MAO inhibition and therapeutic outcome.

We are skeptical about the relevance of platelet inhibition because Deprenyl doses of 10 mg per day virtually completely inhibit platelet MAO within 8 h *(94)*. At this dose, Deprenyl is at best a very weak antidepressant and its onset of effect takes place weeks after MAO inhibition. Therefore, the percentage of platelet inhibition may be a weak indicator of the relevant mechanisms of the benefits of MAO inhibitors.

Ultimately, the best rule to follow may be to increase the dose slowly (within a range for each drug) until clinical effects or intolerable side effects occur.

Acetylator Status and Response to MAO Inhibitors—
Clinical Relevance

Humans show genetic polymorphism for the liver enzyme acetyltransferase (acetyl-CoA acetyltransferase, EC 2.3.1.9), with about 60% slow and 40% fast acetylators *(10)*. The rate of acetylation is relevant in determining the type of side effects associated with isoniazid. Fast acetylators, with greater buildup of acetylated metabolites, are more likely to get isoniazid hepatitis. Slow acetylators, who have greater exposure to the parent compound, are more likely to get isoniazid peripheral neuropathy *(95, 96)*. Thus, acetylator status may conceivably account for some of the variance in determining side effects and therapeutic outcome with hydrazine MAO inhibitors.

The evidence that acetylator status significantly determines therapeutic outcome with phenelzine is weak. As mentioned earlier, Johnstone and Marsh did two studies *(11, 18)* that suggested that slow acetylators had a greater likelihood of benefiting from

MAO inhibitors. Three other studies, however, have failed to replicate this finding *(54, 97, 98)*.

A recent report by Paykel et al. *(99)* suggests a weak relationship between acetylator status and outcome with phenelzine. Our only reservation about this report is that slow acetylators on phenelzine were compared with slow acetylators on placebo, and fast acetylators on phenelzine were compared with fast acetylators on placebo. Because the worst outcome was in the slow acetylators on placebo, this increased the chance of finding drug–placebo differences for slow acetylators. The difference in improvement between fast and slow acetylators on phenelzine was of dubious significance. If slow acetylators have a slight advantage concerning their chance of benefiting from hydrazine MAO inhibitors, this appears to be a weak effect that is probably equalized in fast acetylators by increasing the dose.

Interesting New Leads

Several recent uncontrolled reports suggest new uses for MAO inhibitors that warrant further study. Maletzky *(100)* used phenelzine in treating patients addicted to amphetamine in much the same fashion as disulfiram is used with alcoholics. This carefully monitored program suggested that severe amphetamine abusers so treated were likely to abstain from amphetamine use. Unfortunately, no measure of the antidepressant effect of phenelzine was reported in this study, which would have enabled us to determine whether its effect in diminishing amphetamine abuse was the product of its antidepressant properties or was due to fear of hypertensive crises. Our clinical experience suggests that some severe abusers of amphetamine are in fact depressed and use amphetamine in an attempt to improve their mood. If some such patients were included in Maletzky's sample, the positive results might be due to the antidepressant properties of MAO inhibitors.

Larson and Rafaelson *(101)* have provided an interesting anecdotal report on the utility of long-term MAO inhibitor treatment in a group of 20 chronic depressives. These patients had been ill for an average of more than 10 years and were refractory to other somatic treatments. Their median duration of treatment with isocarboxazide was about four years with a dose range of 10–70 mg per day. It was the authors' impression that MAO inhibitors had significant long-term benefit for this group of patients. They report only two hypertensive crises while treating more than 200 patients with isocarboxazid. Clearly, further work on the long-term utility of MAO inhibitors in chronic depressives refractory to other treatments is indicated.

Other recent interesting reports suggest that MAO inhibitors may be effective for treating traumatic war neurosis (102), post-traumatic stress disorder (DSM-III), delusional depression (103, 104), Briquet's syndrome (105), and depression in the elderly (106). These leads require testing in formal controlled studies. The suggestion that delusional depressives may respond to MAO inhibitors indicates that these drugs may be effective in some endogenous depressions, although adequate tests of this issue are lacking.

Another interesting lead was reported by Nelson and Byck (107), whose patients, who had been nonresponsive to phenelzine, responded shortly after lithium was started. The rapidity of the response suggested that treatment with phenelzine had altered the sensitivity of serotonin receptors, which set the stage for rapid response when lithium was added to the therapeutic regime. This area also requires further study.

Overview of MAO Inhibitors

The evidence clearly establishes the value of phenelzine as an antidepressant for patients referred to as atypical or neurotic depressives, a heterogeneous syndrome that probably contains several diagnostic subtypes. This heterogeneity may account for some of the inconsistent results with phenelzine. While some endogenous depressives probably also respond to phenelzine, a review of placebo-controlled studies of phenelzine in such depressives does not clearly support or refute its utility in this group.

Questioning the relative efficacy of the TCAs vs the MAO inhibitors seems outdated. The assumption that the TCAs have a broader spectrum of effectiveness probably results from the fact that the majority of the earlier antidepressant studies were done on inpatients. Inpatients are more likely to be endogenous (endogenomorphic) depressives (108), and TCAs are in fact more likely to be effective for such samples. However, there are far more outpatients with heterogeneous, inadequately studied, difficult to classify, dysphoric syndromes who may well have symptoms responsive to MAO inhibitors. Therefore, the salient issue involves defining the population that benefits most from each drug class.

The utility of tranylcypromine is strongly suggested, but not as well supported, because of a paucity of controlled studies. The literature suggests that, like phenelzine, tranylcypromine is more useful in neurotic or reactive depressives. This conclusion is made by inference, and well-designed studies of tranylcypromine in endogenous depressives would be timely.

Evidence is accumulating that patients who appear phenomenologically similar may have depressive illness mediated by diverse biochemical mechanisms. This may account for those endogenous depressives who respond to MAO inhibitors rather than TCAs. Studies of patients refractory to TCAs should be conducted, in which the patients could be randomized to continue TCAs or be switched to MAO inhibitors. Results of such investigations would help identify characteristics of endogenous depressives who respond to MAO inhibitors.

We suggest that MAO inhibitors should be the first antidepressants used in depressed patients with atypical features such as lethargy, hypersomnolence, hyperphagia, rejection sensitivity, and reactivity of mood. This is only our clinical impression, no controlled trials having been completed that contrast TCAs and MAO inhibitors in this group of patients.

Others may disagree and first prescribe a trial of TCA in atypical depressives. Certainly, all atypical depressives failing to respond to TCAs should be given a trial of MAO inhibitors. In addition, depressed patients with more typical symptoms who fail to respond to TCA should also receive a trial of MAO inhibitors, unless electroconvulsive treatment is thought to take priority.

We thank Drs. W. Harrison, M. Liebowitz, P. McGrath, J. Stewart, and J. Rabkin for help in data gathering, and Mrs. P. Blackman for typing the manuscript. This work was supported in part by the National Institute of Mental Health, grant no. MH35279-01A1, and the Mental Health Clinical Research Center, grant no. MH30906-3.

References

1. Blackwell B, Maryley E, Price J, et al. Hypertensive interactions between monoamine oxidase inhibitors and food stuffs. *Br J Psychiatry* **113**, 349–365 (1967).
2. Ananth J, Luckins D. A review of combined tricyclic and MAOI therapy. *Compr Psychiatry* **18**, 221–230 (1977).
3. Yang HYT, Neff NH. The monoamine oxidases of brain: Selective inhibition with drugs and the consequences for the metabolism of the biogenic amines. *J Pharmacol Exp Ther* **189**, 733–740 (1974).
4. Youdim M. Multiple forms of monoamine oxidase and their properties. In *Psychopharmacology*, E Costa, M Sandler, Eds., Raven Press, New York, NY, 1972, pp 67–77.
5. Burger A, Yost WL. Arylcycloalkylamines: I. 2-Phenylcyclopropylamine. *J Am Chem Soc* **70**, 2198–2201 (1948).
6. Maass AR, Nimmo MJ. A new inhibitor of serotonin metabolism. *Nature* **184**, 547–548 (1959).
7. Tedeschi RE, Tedeschi DH, Ames PL, et al. Some pharmacological observations of tranylcypromine (SKF tran 385), a potent inhibitor of monoamine oxidase. *Proc Soc Exp Biol Med* **102**, 380–381 (1959).
8. Knoll J. Analysis of the pharmacological effect of selective MAOI. In *Monoamine Oxidase and Its Inhibition* (CIBA Found Symp 39), North-Holland Publ., Amsterdam, 1976, pp 135–161.
9. Evans DAP, Manley KA, McKusick V. Genetic control of isoniazid metabolism in man. *Br Med J* **ii**, 485–491 (1960).
10. Evans DAP, White TA. Human acetylation polymorphism. *J Lab Clin Med* **63**, 391–403 (1964).
11. Johnstone EC. The relationship between acetylator status and inhibition of monoamine oxidase, excretion of free drug and antidepressant response in depressed patients on phenelzine. *Psychopharmacologia* **46**, 289–294 (1976).
12. Marshall EF. The myth of phenelzine acetylation. *Br Med J* **ii**, 817 (1976).
13. Tilstone WJ, Margot P, Johnstone EC. Acetylation of phenelzine. *Psychopharmacology* **60**, 261–263 (1979).
14. Sanders GL, Rawlins MD. Phenelzine: Acetylator status and clinical response. *Br J Clin Pharmacol* **7**, 451–452 (1979).
15. MacLean R, Nicholson WJ, Pare CMB, et al. Effect of monoamine oxidase inhibitors on the concentration of 5-hydroxytryptamine in the human brain. *Lancet* **ii**, 205–208 (1965).
16. Pare CMB. Some clinical aspects of antidepressant drugs. In *The Scientific Basis of Drug Therapy in Psychiatry*, J Marks, CMB Pare, Eds., Pergamon Press, New York, NY, 1965, pp 103–113.

17. Ravaris CL, Nies A, Robinson DS, et al. A multiple-dose controlled study of phenelzine in depression-anxiety states. *Arch Gen Psychiatry* **33**, 347–350 (1976).
18. Johnstone EC, Marsh W. Acetylator status and response to phenelzine in depressed patients. *Lancet* **i**, 567–570 (1973).
19. Mountjoy M, Roth RF, Garside F, et al. A clinical trial of phenelzine in anxiety depressive and phobic neuroses. *Br J Psychiatry* **131**, 486–492 (1977).
20. Sargant W. Drugs in the treatment of depression. *Br J Med* **i**, 225–227 (1961).
21. Sargant W. Some newer drugs in the treatment of depression and their relation to other somatic treatments. *Psychosomatics* **1**, 14–17 (1960).
22. Klein DF, Davis JM. *Diagnosis and Drug Treatment of Psychiatric Disorders*, Williams and Wilkins Co., Baltimore, MD, 1969.
23. Spitzer R, Endicott J, Robins E. Research Diagnostic Criteria: Rationale and reliability. *Arch Gen Psychiatry* **35**, 773–782 (1978).
24. Roth M. Phobic-anxiety-depersonalization syndrome. *Proc R Soc Med* **52**, 587–595 (1959).
25. Hordern A. The antidepressant drugs. *N Engl J Med* **272**, 1159–1169 (1965).
26. Robinson DS, Nies A, Corcella J, Cooper TB. MAO inhibitors, new biochemical and clinical findings. *Psychopharmacol Bull* **17**, 154–157 (1981).
27. British Medical Research Council. Clinical trial of the treatment of depressive illness. *Br J Med* **i**, 881–886 (1965).
28. Blackwell B, Taylor D. An operational evaluation of monoamine oxidase inhibitors. *Proc R Soc Med* **60**, 830–834 (1967).
29. Robinson DS, Nies A, Ravaris L, et al. The monoamine oxidase inhibitor, phenelzine, in the treatment of depressive-anxiety states. *Arch Gen Psychiatry* **29**, 407–413 (1973).
30. Paykel ES. Classification of depressed patients. A cluster-analysis derived grouping. *Br J Psychiatry* **118**, 275–288 (1971).
31. West ED, Dally PJ. Effects of iproniazid in depressive syndromes. *Br Med J* **i**, 1491–1494 (1959).
32. Robinson DS, Nies A, Ravaris CL, et al. Treatment response to MAO inhibitors: Relation to depressive typology and blood platelet MAO inhibition. In *Classification and Prediction of Outcome of Depression*. (Symp Med Hoechst, vol 8), FK Schattauer Verlag, Stuttgart, F.R.G., 1974, pp 259–267.
33. Robinson DS, Nies A, Ravaris CL, et al. Clinical pharmacology of phenelzine: MAO activity and clinical response. In *Psychopharma-*

cology: A Generation of Progress, M Lipton, A DiMascio, KF Killam, Eds., Raven Press, New York, NY, 1978, pp 961–973.
34. Robinson DS, Nies A, Ravaris C, et al. Clinical pharmacology of phenelzine. *Arch Gen Psychiatry* **35,** 629–635 (1978).
35. Lascalles RG. Atypical facial pain and depression. *Br J Psychiatry* **112,** 651–659 (1966).
36. Hare EH, Dominian J, Sharpe L. Phenelzine and dexamphetamine in depressive illness. *Br Med J* **i,** 9–12 (1962).
37. Greenblatt M, Grosser GH, Wechsler H. Differential response of hospitalized depressed patients to somatic therapy. *Am J Psychiatry* **120,** 935–943 (1964).
38. Klein DF, Zitrin CM, Woerner M. Antidepressants, anxiety, panic and phobia. In *Psychopharmacology: A Generation of Progress* (see ref. *33*), pp 1401–1410.
39. Raskin A, Schulterbrandt JG, Reatig N, et al. Depression subtypes and response to phenelzine, diazepam and a placebo. *Arch Gen Psychiatry* **30,** 66–75 (1974).
40. Tyrer P, Candy J, Kelly D. Phenelzine in phobic anxiety: A controlled trial. *Psychol Med* **3,** 120–124 (1973).
41. Solyom L, Heseltine GFD, McClure DJ, et al. Behaviour therapy versus drug therapy in the treatment of phobic neurosis. *Can Psychiatr Assoc J* **18,** 25–32 (1973).
42. Ballenger J, Sheehan D, Jacobsen G. Antidepressant treatment of severe phobic anxiety. Read before the annual meeting of the American Psychiatric Association, Toronto, May 1977.
43. Johnstone EC. The relationship between acetylator status and inhibition of monoamine oxidase, excretion of free drug and antidepressant response in depressed patients on phenelzine. *Psychopharmacologia* **46,** 289–294 (1976).
44. Raft D, Davidson J, Wasik J, Mattox A. Relationship between response to phenelzine and MAO inhibition in a clinical trial of phenelzine, amitriptyline and placebo. *Neuropsychobiology* **7,** 122–126 (1981).
45. Young JPR, Lader MH, Hughes WC. A controlled trial of trimipramine, a monoamine oxidase inhibitor, and combined treatment in depressed outpatients. *Br Med J* **ii,** 1315–1317 (1979).
46. Rowan P, Paykel ES, Parker RR. Phenelzine and amitriptyline: Effects on symptoms of neurotic depression. *Br J Psychiatry* **140,** 475–483 (1982).
47. Hutchinson JT, Smedberg D. Phenelzine (Nardil) in the treatment of endogenous depression. *J Ment Sci* **106,** 704–710 (1960).
48. Rees L, Davies B. A controlled trial of phenelzine (Nardil) in the

treatment of severe depressive illness. *J Ment Sci* **107**, 560–566 (1961).

49. Schildkraut JJ, Klerman GL, Hammond R, et al. Excretion of 3-methoxy-4-hydroxy-mandelic acid (VMA) in depressed patients treated with antidepressant drugs. *J Psychiatr Res* **2**, 257–266 (1965).

50. Agnew PC, Baran ID, Klapman HJ, et al. A clinical evaluation of four antidepressant drugs (Nardil, Tofranil, Marplan and Deprol). *Am J Psychiatry* **118**, 160–162 (1961).

51. Davidson JRT, McLeod MN, Turnbull CD, Miller RD. A comparison of phenelzine and imipramine in depressed inpatients. *J Clin Psychiatry* **42**, 395–397 (1981).

52. Quitkin FM, McGrath P, Liebowitz ML, et al. Monoamine oxidase inhibitors in bipolar endogenous depressives. *J Clin Psychopharmacol* **1**, 70–73 (1981).

53. Himmelhoch JM, Detre TA, Kupfer DJ, et al. Treatment of previous intractable depressions with tranylcypromine and lithium. *J Nerv Ment Dis* **155**, 216–220 (1972).

54. Kiloh LG, Child JP, Latner G. A controlled trial of iproniazid in the treatment of endogenous depression. *J Ment Sci* **106**, 1139–1144 (1960).

55. Wittenborn JR. Factors which qualify the response to iproniazid and to imipramine. In *Prediction of Response to Pharmacotherapy*, JR Wittenborn, PRA May, Eds., Charles C Thomas, Springfield, IL, 1966, pp 125–146.

56. Giller E, Bialos D, Riddle M, et al. Monoamine oxidase inhibitor responsive depression. *Psychiatr Res* **6**, 41–48 (1982).

57. Tyrer P, Gardner M, Lambourn J, Whitford M. Clinical and pharmacokinetic factors affecting response to phenelzine. *Br J Psychiatry* **136**, 359–365 (1980).

58. Wing JK, Cooper JE, Sartorius N. *The Measurement in Classification of Psychiatric Symptoms*. Cambridge University Press, London, 1974.

59. Bartholomew AA. An evaluation of tranylcypromine in the treatment of depression. *Med J Aust* **49**, 655–662 (1962).

60. Khanna JL, Pratt S, Burdizk EG, et al. A study of certain effects of tranylcypromine, a new antidepressant. *J New Drugs* **3**, 227–232 (1963).

61. Glick BS. Double-blind study of tranylcypromine and phenelzine in depression. *Dis Nerv Syst* **25**, 617–619 (1964).

62. Gottfries CG. Clinical trials with the monoamine oxidase inhibitor tranylcypromine on a psychiatric clientele. *Acta Psychiatr Scand* **39**, 463–472 (1963).

63. Himmelhoch JM, Fuchs CZ, Symons BJ. A double-blind study of tranylcypromine of major anergic depression. *J Nerv Ment Dis* **170**, 678–684 (1982).

64. Spear FG, Hall P, Stirland JD. A comparison of subjective responses to imipramine and tranylcypromine. *Br J Psychiatry* **110**, 53–54 (1964).

65. Haydu GE, Whittier JR, Goldschmidt L, et al. Differential therapeutic results of three antidepressant medications according to fixed or functional schedules. *J Nerv Ment Dis* **139**, 475–478 (1964).

66. Hutchinson JT, Smedberg D. Treatment of depression: A comparative study effect of six drugs. *Br J Psychiatry* **109**, 536–538 (1963).

67. Schiele BC. The Parnate-specific patient. *Minn Med* **48**, 355–357 (1965).

68. Horn AS, Snyder SH. Steric requirements for catecholamine uptake by rat brain synaptosomes: Studies with rigid analogs of amphetamine. *J Pharmacol Exp Ther* **185**, 523–530 (1972).

69. Moises HW, Beckmann H. Antidepressant efficacy of tranylcypromine isomers: A controlled study. *J Neural Transm* **50**, 185–192 (1981).

70. Schiele BC, Zimmerman R. Tranylcypromine isomers, a controlled clinical trial. *Am J Psychiatry* **131**, 1025–1026 (1974).

71. Oltman JE, Friedman S. Pargyline in the treatment of depressive illnesses. *Am J Psychiatry* **120**, 493–494 (1963).

72. Janecek J, Schiele BC, Vestre ND. Pargyline and tranylcypromine in the treatment of hospitalized depressed patients. *J New Drugs* **3**, 309–316 (1963).

73. Knott F. A preliminary trial of mebanazine in depressive states. *J New Drugs* **5**, 345–347 (1965).

74. Kline NS, Sacks W. Relief of depression within one day using a MAO inhibitor and intravenous 5-HTP. *Am J Psychiatry* **120**, 274–275 (1963).

75. Wheatley D. A report from the British General Practitioner Research Group on mebanazine in the treatment of depression. *J New Drugs* **5**, 348–357 (1965).

76. Barker JC, Jan IA, Enoch MD. A controlled trial of mebanazine (Actomol) in depression. *Br J Psychiatry* **111**, 1095–1100 (1965).

77. Dunlop E, DeFelice EA, Bergen JR, et al. Relationship between MAO inhibition and improvement of depression. *Psychosomatics* **6**, 1–7 (1965).

78. Klein DF. Pathophysiology of depressive syndromes. *Biol Psychiatry* **8**, 119–120 (1974).

79. Varga E, Tringa L. Clinical trial of a new type of promptly acting psycho-energetic agent (phenyl-isopropyl methyl propinyl-HCl, E250). *Acta Med Acad Sci Hung* **23**, 289–295 (1967).

80. Tringa L, Haits G, Varga E. *Societes Pharmacologica Hungarica. Fifth Conferentia Hungarica pro Therapia et Investigatione in Pharmacologia*, GP Lesz-

kovszky, Ed., Publishing House of Hungarian Academy of Sciences, Budapest, pp 111–114.

81. Mann JJ, Francis A, Kaplan RD, et al. The relative efficacy of l-Deprenyl, a selective monoamine type-B inhibitor, in endogenous and nonendogenous depression. *J Clin Psychopharmacol* **2**, 54–57 (1982).

82. Mendlewicz J, Youdim MBH. Antidepressant potentiation of 5-hydroxytryptophan by l-Deprenyl, an MAO "Type B" inhibitor. *J Neural Transm* **43**, 279–286 (1978).

83. Mendis M, Pare CMB, Sandler M, et al. Is the failure of l-Deprenyl, a selective monoamine oxidase B inhibitor, to alleviate depression related to freedom from the "cheese effect"? *Psychopharmacology* **73**, 87–90 (1981).

84. Quitkin FM, Liebowitz ML, McGrath P, et al. An open trial of Deprenyl in atypical depressives. Presented at ACNP, Dec 1982. San Juan, Puerto Rico.

85. Schachter M, Price PA, Parks JD. Deprenyl in narcolepsy. *Lancet* **i**, 831–832 (1979). Letter.

86. Herd JA. A new antidepressant—M&B 9302. A pilot study and a double-blind controlled trial. *Clin Trials J* **6**, 219–225 (1969).

87. Wheatley D. Comparative trial of a new monoamine oxidase inhibitor in depression. *Br J Psychiatry* **117**, 573–574 (1970).

88. Lipper S, Murphy DL, Slater SL, Buchsbaum MS. Comparative behavioral effect of clorgyline and pargyline in man. *Psychopharmacology* **62**, 123–128 (1979).

89. Pickar D, Murphy DL, Cohen RM, et al. Selective and nonselective monoamine oxidase inhibitors. *Arch Gen Psychiatry* **39**, 535–540 (1982).

90. Potter WZ, Murphy DL, Wehr T, et al. Clorgyline: A new treatment for patients with refractory rapid-cycling disorder. *Arch Gen Psychiatry* **39**, 505–510 (1982).

91. Schuckit M, Robins E, Feighner J. Tricyclic antidepressants and monoamine antidepressants. *Arch Gen Psychiatry* **24**, 509–514 (1971).

92. Davidson J, McLeod M, Lawyone B, et al. A comparison of ECT and combined phenelzine–amitriptyline in refractory patients. *Arch Gen Psychiatry* **35**, 639–642 (1978).

93. White K, Pistole T, Boyd JL. Combined monoamine oxidase inhibitor–tricyclic antidepressant treatment: A pilot study. *Am J Psychiatry* **137**, 1422–1420 (1980).

94. Birkmayer W, Riederer D, Ambrozi L, Youdim MBH. Implications of combined treatment with madoper and l-Deprenyl in Parkinson's disease. *Lancet* **i**, 439–443 (1977).

95. Mitchell JR, Thorgeirsson UP, Black M, et al. Increased incidence

of isoniazid hepatitis in rapid acetylators: Possible relation to hydrazine metabolites. *Clin Pharmacol Ther* **18**, 70 (1975).

96. Devadatta S, Gangadharum PRJ, Andrews RH, et al. Peripheral neuritis due to isoniazid. *Bull World Health Org* **23**, 587 (1960).

97. Davidson J, McLeod MN, Blum RN. Acetylation phenotype platelet monoamine oxidase inhibition and the effectiveness of phenelzine in depression. *Am J Psychiatry* **135**, 467–469 (1978).

98. Marshall EF, Mountjoy CQ, Campbell IC, et al. The influence of acetylated phenotype on the outcome of treatment with phenelzine in a clinical trial. *Br J Clin Pharmacol* **6**, 247–254 (1978).

99. Paykel E, West PS, Rowan PR, Parker PR. Influence of phenotype on antidepressant effects of phenelzine. *Br J Psychiatry* **141**, 243–248 (1982).

100. Maletzky BM. Phenelzine as a stimulant drug antagonist: A preliminary report. *Int J Addictions* **12**, 651–665 (1977).

101. Larson JK, Rafaelson OJ. Long-term treatment of depression with isocarboxazide. *Acta Psychiatr Scand* **62**, 456–463 (1980).

102. Hogben GL, Cornfeld RB. Treatment of traumatic war neurosis with phenelzine. *Arch Gen Psychiatry* **38**, 440–445 (1981).

103. Minter RE, Verdugon M, Mandel MR. The treatment of delusional depression with tranylcypromine: A case report. *J Clin Psychiatry* **41**, 178 (1980).

104. Lieb J, Collins C. Treatment of depression with tranylcypromine. *J Nerv Ment Dis* **166**, 805–808 (1978).

105. Maany I. Treatment of depression associated with Briquet's syndrome. *Am J Psychiatry* **138**, 373–376 (1981).

106. Ashford JW, Ford CV. Use of MAO inhibitors in elderly patients. *Am J Psychiatry* **136**, 1466–1467 (1979).

107. Nelson JC, Byck R. Rapid response to lithium in phenelzine nonresponder. *Br J Psychiatry* **141**, 85–86 (1982).

108. Klein DF. Endogenomorphic depression. *Arch Gen Psychiatry* **31**, 447–454 (1974).

Lithium: Its Clinical Uses and Biological Mechanisms of Action

Ronald R. Fieve

Historical Uses

Lithium, a silvery-white substance, is the lightest of the 1A group of alkaline metals and one of the most reactive of elements. It was originally discovered by August Arfvedson in 1817, working in the Swedish laboratory of Berzelius. Although never found free in nature, lithium in mineral compounds and mineral waters is distributed throughout the world. Originally, its use may go back to early Greek and Roman times; Soranno during the second century in Greece and Caelius Aurelianus during the fifth century in Rome prescribed mineral water therapy, including specific alkaline springs for particular physical and mental illnesses. Geological surveys indicate that these springs may have contained large amounts of lithium; further, many of the springs developed by the Romans in southern and western Europe may have been similarly used during much earlier periods (1).

During the 19th and early 20th centuries, the specific presence of lithium in European and American mineral water spas that were used for drinking and bathing was highly sought after. At times, in fact, the word "Lithia" was added to the names of these springs, along with exaggerated figures for their lithium content, to attract the public interested in lithium's reputed medicinal properties. During the 1840s it had been discovered that lithium salts combined with uric acid in soluble form were able to dissolve urate deposits; during this period, therefore, lithium was used to treat renal calculi, gouty rheumatism, and mental illness. The use of lithium to treat these disorders was largely discontinued when newer and more effective treatments were discovered.

Early in this century lithium bromide was used as an antiepileptic *(2)*; in the 1920s it was thought to be the most hypnotic of all the bromides *(3)*. During the late 1940s lithium chloride in the United States became a popular salt substitute for patients on sodium-free diets, and was sold under the names of Westal, Foodsal, and Saltisalt. Among the patients who were then using lithium as a salt substitute and food seasoning were some with heart and kidney disease, conditions in which we now know lithium is particularly dangerous. When at least four deaths and many more serious but nonfatal poisonings were attributed to lithium in 1949, it was immediately banned from the American pharmacopeia and its use among American physicians prohibited *(4)*.

Ironically, during that same year, the Australian psychiatrist John F. Cade first discovered the therapeutic effect of lithium against mania *(5)*. Subsequently, Noack and Trautner *(6)* in Australia, and later Schou et al. *(7)* in Denmark and Maggs *(8)* in England, initiated the earliest clinical trials. The first systematic American clinical trials were undertaken by my colleagues and me at the New York State Psychiatric Institute *(9–12)*. Throughout the 1960s European and American investigators undertook numerous studies of lithium's effects on mania and depression and its prophylactic effects on bipolar and unipolar illness. These clinical studies, along with numerous pharmacologic and metabolic studies of lithium's basic properties, finally led the Lithium Task Force in America and the U.S. Food and Drug Administration (FDA) to approve the use of lithium in 1970 for the treatment of mania *(13)*.

Diagnosis of Bipolar and Unipolar States

For several decades American psychiatrists tended to confuse the diagnoses of manic depression (bipolar depression) with schizophrenia and the diagnoses of major depression (unipolar depression) with schizophrenia and dysthymia (neurotic depression) *(14)*. Thus, during the 1950s and until the late 1960s, most of the leading psychiatric teaching hospitals in America diagnosed schizophrenia much more frequently than manic depression, and manic depression was often mislabeled as schizophrenia. Throughout the 1960s, however, American psychiatry was undergoing several major revolutions—one in psychopharmacology and another in psychiatric diagnosis. At this time the lithium ion,

171

with its dramatic anti-manic effects, had a profound impact on diagnostic practice *(15)*, making it much easier to diagnose manic depression as a major mental illness different from schizophrenia. The evolution of the DSM III *(Diagnostic and Statistical Manual,* 3rd edition) of the American Psychiatric Association *(16)*, along with the SADS *(Schedule for Affective Disorders and Schizophrenia) (17)*, similarly led to a clearer separation in the minds of American psychiatrists between bipolar and unipolar affective states, schizophrenia, and other psychiatric disorders. Tables 1 and 2 illustrate the DSM III diagnostic profiles required for diagnosing mania and depression in 1983. Table 3 illustrates a further subclassification of affective disorders by which bipolar and unipolar illnesses are viewed as constituting a homogeneous illness with a multifactorial mode of genetic transmission *(18, 19)*. The spectrum of affective illnesses that results from gene–gene and gene–environmental interactions are thus subclassified by Fieve and Dunner into Bipolar I, II, Other, and Cyclothymic Personality, as well as Unipolar, Unipolar Other, and Depressive personality subgroups. The DSM III diagnostic classification system and the Fieve–Dunner spectrum subclassification, the concept of which has been reinforced by our study of morbid risk *(18)*, have led to a greater uniformity in results from psychiatric research studies at various laboratories, largely because of the improved reliability in psychiatric diagnosis among clinicians and researchers using these diagnostic instruments. Thus, research data from one center are now comparable with data from a similar diagnostic sample from a second center, making much more likely the discovery of new findings.

Current Lithium Therapy

Commercial Lithium Preparations

Several commercial preparations of lithium carbonate are available (Table 4), either in capsule or tablet form, as normal or slow-release preparations. The usual capsule/tablet comes in 300-mg quantities, but some are marketed as 150, 250, or 400 mg. Only Ciba-Geigy, Inc., markets lithium in the liquid form (752 mg of lithium citrate in 5 mL). Several pharmaceutical companies throughout the world are developing slow-release forms of lithium that will soon be added to the list.

Table 1. **DSM III Criteria for Diagnosis of Mania** *(16)*

One or more distinct periods of elevated, expansive, or irritable mood

Duration: at least one week of at least three of the following:
1. Restlessness, activity increase
2. Talkativeness
3. Racing of thoughts, flight of ideas
4. Grandiosity
5. Decreased need for sleep
6. Distractibility
7. Excessive involvement in activities of potentially painful consequences

Neither of the following dominates:
1. Preoccupation with mood—incongruent delusion or hallucination
2. Bizarre behavior

Not superimposed on schizophrenia, schizophreniform disorder, or paranoid disorder

Not due to organic mental disorder (e.g., substance intoxication)

Table 2. **DSM III Criteria for Diagnosis of Depression** *(16)*

Dysphoric mood

Duration: at least two weeks of at least four of the following:
1. Appetite/weight gain/loss
2. Psychomotor agitation or retardation
3. Loss of interest or pleasure in usual activities
4. Loss of energy/fatigue
5. Insomnia or hypersomnia
6. Self-reproach, inappropriate guilt, worthlessness
7. Diminished concentration, slowed thinking
8. Suicidal tendencies

Neither of the following dominates:
1. Preoccupation with mood—incongruent delusion or hallucination
2. Bizarre behavior

Exclusions:
1. Schizophrenic symptoms
2. Organic mental disorder
3. Residual-type schizophrenia
4. Simple bereavement

Table 3. Fieve–Dunner Subclassification of Unipolar and Bipolar Affective States in Rapid Cyclers[a]

Primary affective disorder

Bipolar	Unipolar
Bipolar I: hospitalized for mania	Unipolar: hospitalized for depression
Bipolar II: hospitalized for depression only	Unipolar other: outpatient treatment for depression
Bipolar other: outpatient treatment for depression or hypomania	Depressive personality: meets criteria for depression but never treated
Cyclothymic personality: meets criteria for hypomania but never treated	

[a] Rapid-cyclers: Those with four or more cyclical attacks per year.
Source: reference 19.

Table 4. Commercial Lithium Preparations[a]

Product name	Pharmaceutical co.	Quantity, mg[b]	Type[c]	Form
North America				
Carbolith	ICN, Canada	300	Conv	Cap
Eskalith	Smith, Kline & French USA	300	Conv	Cap, tab
Lithane	Dome, USA	300	Conv	Cap, tab
Lithane	Pfizer, Canada	300	Conv	Tab
Lithium carbonate	Philips Roxane, USA	300	Conv	Cap
Lithizine	Canapharm, Canada	150 & 300	Conv	Cap
Lithobid	Ciba-Geigy, USA	300	Slow-rel	Tab
Lithonate	Rowell, USA	300	Conv	Cap
Lithonate S	Ciba-Geigy, USA	752/5 mL[d]	Conv	Liq
Lithotabs	Rowell, USA	300	Conv	Tab
PFI-Lithium	Pfipharmecs, USA	300	Conv	Tab
British Commonwealth				
Camcolit	Norgine, England	250	Conv	Tab
Lithicarb	Protea, Australia	250	Conv	Tab
Lithium Phasal	Pharmax, England	300	Slow-rel	Tab
Manialith	Muir & Neil, Australia	250	Conv	Tab
Priadel	Delandale, England, and Protea, Australia	400	Slow-rel	Tab

[a] All available as carbonate salts except Lithonate S, which is citrate.
[b] Per tablet (tab) or capsule (cap).
[c] Conventional or slow-release.
[d] Liquid form.

Table 5. Dosage Schedule for Lithium Initiation and Therapy

Time	Treatment	Comment
Pretreatment	Physical examination, including laboratory tests and electrocardiogram	Caution against kidney, heart, and thyroid disease; actual and planned pregnancy; diabetes; and use of diuretics
Day 1	Initial low dosage (300–600 mg/day)	Tablet ingestion after breakfast and at bedtime
Day 7	Determination of serum lithium in blood sample 12 h after evening dose	Adjust dose to obtain serum lithium concentration of 0.6–1.0 mmol/L (doubling usually results in doubling of serum lithium in medically well patients)
Days 14, 21, 28	Determination of serum lithium	If indicated, dosage adjustment
Monthly for next 12 months, thereafter at longer intervals according to physician's instructions and patient's complaints (FDA prefers monitoring each one to two months)	Determination of serum lithium at every visit	Dosage is adjusted to patient's condition; serum lithium should not exceed 1.4 mmol/L

Source: adapted from Schou [20].

Dosage, Pretreatment Physical Exam, and Recommended Frequency of Lithium Determination for Outpatients and Inpatients

In our clinics, outpatients who are to begin treatment with lithium are first required to have a thorough physical examination (blood chemistries, urinalysis, and electrocardiogram) with particular emphasis on thyroid, kidney, and cardiac evaluations, as well as any existing or planned pregnancy. In patients who are physically well, the usual starting dose is 300–600 mg (i.e., one or two capsules) of lithium per day, taken regularly after breakfast and (or) at bedtime for the first seven days (see Table 5). Patients and families are given instructions on the possible side effects of lithium and are urged to call the physician immediately if any disagreeable symptoms or side effects ensue. One week later we make the first measurement of serum lithium 12 h after the last dose. At the end of the second, third, and fourth week additional serum lithium determinations are made, each 12 h after

175

Table 6. Recommended Frequency for Determination of Serum Lithium Concentration[a]

Determine the serum lithium concentration 12-h post-dose:

1. Weekly during the first month, every one or two months during the next 12 months, thereafter at longer intervals according to the doctor's instructions.
2. One week after a dosage increase.
3. Soon after an unexpected increase of the serum lithium concentration.

It is advisable to determine the 12-h post-dose serum lithium concentration several times weekly:

4. After start of treatment with low-salt diet.
5. After start of weight-loss diet.
6. After start of treatment with diuretics (extra caution needed).
7. After salt and fluid loss due to heavy sweating, diarrhea, vomiting, or any other medical cause.
8. During physical disease (influenza or other conditions with high temperature) and during the weeks afterwards.
9. After development of manic or depressive relapse.
10. After delivery.

It is wise to determine the serum lithium concentration every few weeks during the last part of pregnancy.

[a] Recommended by Fieve and Schou.

the last dose, and the dosage is adjusted so that the concentration of serum lithium is somewhere between 0.6 and 1.0 mmol/L (see Table 6).

At this point, a large majority of manic-depressive patients who had been initially hypomanic are considerably better clinically. If the patients were initially significantly depressed, they also receive an antidepressant along with the lithium, so that after four weeks 60 to 70% of depressed patients are out of their depression.

After this initial stage of clinical treatment and stabilization of serum concentration of lithium, the patients are seen monthly over the next year, and thereafter less frequently, provided the illness is stabilized and there are no complicating medical problems, manic-depressive relapses, or episodes of lithium toxicity.

Patients with acute mania require hospitalization during their early treatment phase and take higher lithium doses (usually in the range of 1800 mg per day) during the first two to three weeks of treatment to bring the acute manic state under control. During that period such patients are also given a phenothiazine to bring the acute psychotic process under immediate control, because lithium requires one to two weeks to take effect. Lithium concentrations in serum throughout the acute hospital stay are best maintained in the 1.0 to 1.4 mmol/L range; we advocate monitoring serum lithium concentration 12 h after the last dose, two to three times a week, during inpatient treatment of acute mania. The above dosage and serum lithium recommendations are used for most but not all young, healthy patients, although elderly patients and patients taking diuretics or having concomitant medical illnesses need individual lithium adjustment—usually less lithium intake and lower serum concentrations. In these groups of patients less lithium seems sufficient to keep the disease under control without producing intolerable side effects or lithium toxicity (20).

If, during the course of prophylactic treatment, the serum lithium concentrations increase or decrease, it is imperative to obtain a subsequent lithium determination shortly thereafter. Also, if for any reason a patient is required to go on a diet or be treated either with diuretics or low-salt diet, his 12-h postdose serum lithium concentrations must be determined once or twice weekly over a four- to eight-week period while his clinical state and serum lithium concentrations are being adjusted, to avoid relapses or serious toxicity. In the event that the laboratory finds a serum lithium concentration exceeding 1.5 mmol/L, the patient must be called at home and told to decrease his lithium intake and come in for an immediate check of the 12-h post-dose concentration the same or the next day. Meanwhile, the clinician must try to determine what factors may have contributed to this sudden increase in the lithium concentration. Often one finds that the patient has stopped eating, has gone on a low-fluid or low-salt diet, or is taking diuretics; is experiencing heavy sweating (especially in tropical climates); or is experiencing diarrhea or vomiting because of gastrointestinal or other systemic illnesses, with or without fever. Patients should be cautioned to have their lithium measured frequently during such physical illnesses, as well as before and after surgery. Lithium is usually discontinued three to seven days before a surgical procedure and reinstituted once fluids and food are taken orally again. Patients with poorly controlled manic-depressive illness or those with complications of alcoholism or drug abuse not under control are at high risk for toxicity and should advisedly have more frequent determinations of serum lithium similar to that described by Schou (20).

Indications for the Use of Lithium

Indications for the use of lithium include acute mania, the prophylaxis of bipolar manic depression, prophylaxis of recurrent unipolar depression, and, in some instances, the treatment of thyrotoxicosis, granulocytopenia, and inappropriate secretion of antidiuretic hormone. The FDA has not yet approved the use of lithium in the prophylaxis of recurrent unipolar depression, although most comparable regulatory agencies in Scandinavia and England have done so. With respect to possible but not yet proven uses of lithium, a number of studies indicate that some schizoaffective patients, particularly where a prominent manic component exists, do well either on lithium alone or in combination with a phenothiazine. Adolescents with emotionally unstable character disorders, characterized by rapid mood swings, drug-taking, impulsivity, and acting out against authority (21) seem to do well with lithium, as do children with a number of childhood affective disorders. Patients with premenstrual depression syndrome have been treated with lithium in several centers, but the resulting findings are controversial (22, 23). In my experience, manic depressives who also experience the premenstrual syndrome do dramatically better with their premenstrual depression symptoms when they come under lithium stabilization for their manic depressive illness. Some cases of episodic binge-drinkers and depressed alcoholics possibly benefit from lithium (24, 25). Children, adolescents, and adults with pathologically aggressive behavior—which can be viewed as equivalent to the paranoid manic state—do well on lithium if they comply, and a limited number of patients with migraine and (or) cluster headaches reportedly benefit from lithium therapy.

The Uses of Lithium in Acute Mania

Controlled Studies—Lithium vs Placebo

Table 7 lists the original studies in Denmark, England, and the United States involving a double-blind crossover design with lithium and placebo. Approximately 70–80% of patients with acute mania responded well to lithium carbonate, which in all cases was superior to placebo. Table 8 shows comparisons of lithium with antipsychotic drugs (usually chlorpromazine) in

Table 7. **Lithium Treatment of Acute Mania: Controlled Double-Blind Cross-over Studies of Lithium vs Placebo**

| | | Results | |
Study	No. of patients	Lithium	Placebo
Schou et al. (7)	38	14 good response, 18 partial	Not stated
Maggs (8)	28	Li$^+$ superior to placebo	
Fieve et al. (10)	35	28 of 35 had good response	Not stated
Bunney et al. (26)	2	2 of 2 responded	2 relapsed on placebo
Goodwin et al. (27)	12	8 of 12 had complete response to Li$^+$	5 of 8 Li$^+$ responders relapsed on placebo
Stokes et al. (28)	38	75% responded to Li$^+$ in 7–10 days	Not stated

Table 8. **Lithium Treatment of Acute Mania: Controlled Studies of Lithium vs Chlorpromazine (C)**

Study	No. of patients	Duration, weeks	Results
Johnson et al. (29)	28	3	Remission: Li$^+$ 78%, C 36%
Spring (30)	12	3	Remission: Li$^+$ 6 of 7, C 3 of 5
Platman (31)	23	3	No signif. diff., Li$^+$ superior
Johnson et al. (32)	21	3	Li$^+$ better
Prien et al. (33)	225	3	C better for highly active manics, Li$^+$ better for mildly active manics
Shopsin et al. (34)[a]	30	3	Li$^+$ best, then H, then C
Takahashi et al. (35)	77	5	Moderate improvement: Li$^+$ 68%, C 47%

[a] Lithium vs chlorpromazine vs haloperidol (H).

seven major controlled studies with acutely ill manic patients. The results in all cases favor lithium over chlorpromazine, except in the highly active, often psychotic manics in the Veterans' Administration multihospital study; in those patients, chlorpromazine in the early phases seemed to be preferred over lithium for controlling the violent and unmanageable manic state. Most clinicians agree that in severely hyperactive manic states (psychotic) lithium plus chlorpromazine constitutes the preferred method of beginning treatment; the phenothiazine is tapered off once the acute manic state has subsided. For mild to moderately active outpatient hypomanics, lithium alone is the preferred drug of choice for initial treatment and long-term prophylaxis.

Lithium as an Antidepressant vs Placebo or Tricyclic Antidepressant

The early American and European studies comparing lithium with placebo and (or) a tricyclic antidepressant showed that lithium had at most a mild antidepressant effect during the acute bipolar endogenous phase; the tricyclic antidepressants were much more effective (10). Data from subsequent American studies suggest that lithium has a stronger antidepressant effect during the bipolar depressed phase than was originally thought. In several studies (36–44), in fact, lithium was as effective as a tricyclic antidepressant (Table 9). Nonetheless, lithium has still not gained

Table 9. **Effectiveness of Lithium as an Antidepressant vs Placebo or Tricyclic Antidepressant**

Study	Diagnosis	No. of patients	Results
Hansen et al. (36)[a]	Endogenous depression	12	Several patients improved with Li^+, 1 relapsed with placebo
Fieve et al. (11)[b]	Bipolar	29	IMI more effective
Stokes et al. (28)[c]	Bipolar	18	Improvement with Li^+ not significantly superior to placebo after 10 days' Li^+ treatment
Goodwin et al. (37)[d]	Bi- and unipolar	52	69% remissions, most among bipolar patients
Mendels et al. (38)[e]	Bi- and unipolar	24	Li^+ as effective as DMI
Noyes et al. (39)[d]	Bi- and unipolar	22	59% responded to Li^+, 9 relapsed on placebo
Johnson (40)[d]	Endogenous depression	10	5 had marked improvement
Baron et al. (41)[d]	Primary affective disorder	23	5 unequivocal and 5 equivocal responses, mostly among bipolar patients
Watanabe et al. (42)[b]	Mixed group of affective disorders	68	Li^+ as effective as IMI
Mendels (43)[d]	Primary affective disorder	21	13 unequivocal improvements; 7 relapses with placebo, especially among bipolar patients
Worrall et al. (44)[b]	Bi- and unipolar	29	Li^+ better after two and three weeks

[a] Crossover with placebo. [b] Compared with imipramine (IMI). [c] Compared with placebo. [d] Placebo substitute. [e] Desimipramine (DMI) for control group.

acceptability by clinicians nor approval by the FDA as an effective antidepressant of the first order: i.e., it is rarely the first choice of an antidepressant in a severe bipolar or unipolar patient. Lithium plus an antidepressant appears to be the best combination for initial treatment of a bipolar patient who is in the moderate to severely depressed phase and who will subsequently require long-term lithium prophylaxis.

Lithium Prophylaxis of Bipolar Illness

Table 10 lists the major double-blind, controlled studies in which data were sufficiently well-presented to enable the reader to score lithium and placebo relapses (except in the Coppen and Hullin studies), both in the manic and depressed phase, while the patient was undergoing long-term prophylaxis. Table 11 shows that in all studies except the nonblind study of Persson (53) patients during the manic phase had considerably fewer manic relapses while on lithium than did patients on placebo. Table 11 likewise shows that bipolar patients on either lithium or placebo tended to have fewer relapses in the depressed phase while on lithium. Thus, it would appear that bipolar patients tend to have fewer relapses into both depression and mania while on lithium than when receiving a placebo.

Figure 1 illustrates the life-table probabilities that bipolar I patients will remain well on lithium or control (placebo or no lithium) maintenance therapy after their initial hospitalization for mania. (These data are taken from independent study populations: The New York State Psychiatric Institute's Lithium Clinic and a Veterans' Administration multihospital collaborative study.) From the Figure, the increased probability of remaining well on lithium vs no lithium is statistically significant at one year, two years, and thereafter. Moreover, the probabilities of remaining well in the lithium groups and in the control groups are similar in both studies despite the fact that the two populations are hundreds of miles apart and treated with different doctors, nurses, and hospital settings (54).

In the earlier cited prophylactic studies, which so dramatically demonstrated lithium's advantage over placebo, the different investigators (see Tables 10 and 11) used distinctly different experimental designs: double-blind randomization of patients to lithium/placebo at the beginning of treatment, with re-evaluation

Table 10. Lithium Prophylaxis Studies with Bipolar Patients

Investigator	Design	Trial period, months	Treatment	No. of patients	No. (and %) of total failures	p	No. of depressive failures	p	No. of manic failures	p
Baastrup et al. (45)	Discontinuation: failure = hospitalization or need for additional drugs	5	Lithium	28	0(0)		0		0	
			Placebo	22	12(55)	<0.001	6	<0.01	7	<0.01
Coppen et al. (46)	Start: failure = no major improvement	14	Lithium	17	3(18)		no data		no data	
			Placebo	21	21(100)	<0.001				
Hullin et al. (47)	Discontinuation	6	Lithium	18	1(5.5)		no data		no data	
			Placebo	18	6(33)	<0.02				
Cundall et al. (48)	Discontinuation	6	Lithium	12	4(33)		3		1	
			Placebo	12	10(83)	<0.05	5	N.S.	0	<0.05
Stallone et al. (49)[a]	Discontinuation–start	28	Lithium	25	11(44)		13		5	
			Placebo	27	25(92)	<0.001	16	N.S	16	<0.02
Prien et al. (50), VA-NIMH I	Discontinuation	24	Lithium	101	43(43)				32	
			Placebo	104	84(80)	<0.001	27	<0.001	71	<0.001
Prien et al. (51), VA-NIMH II	Discontinuation	24	Lithium	18	5(28)		4		2	
			Imipramine	13	10(77)	[b]	4	[c]	7	[d]
			Placebo	13	10(77)		8		5	
Fieve et al. (52)[e]	Discontinuation	53	Lithium	17	3(18)		2		1	
			Placebo	18	9(50)	<0.05	2	<0.01	7	<0.05

[a] Bipolar I and II (see Table 3). [b] Li vs Imi: p <0.02; Li vs Imi: NS. [c] Li vs Imi: NS; Li vs placebo: NS. [d] Li vs Imi: p < 0.02; Li vs placebo: NS; Imi vs placebo: NS. [e] Bipolar I. NS, not significant.

Table 11. Lithium Prophylaxis of Mania and Depression in Bipolar Patients

| | | | | Results (no. relapsed) | | | |
| | | | | Mania | | Depression | |
Study	Design	Duration	No. of patients	Lithium	Placebo	Lithium	Placebo
Baastrup et al. (45)	D/B random	5 mos	50	0 of 28	7 of 22	0 of 28	6 of 22
Coppen et al. (46)	D/B random	75 wks	39	6 of 17	17 of 22		
Cundall et al. (48)	D/B crossover	6 mos	13[a]	1 of 12	9 of 12	3 of 12	5 of 12
Persson (53)	Non-blind control, Li⁺ vs no medication		24	5 of 12	6 of 12	5 of 12	8 of 12
Prien et al. (50)	D/B random	2 yrs	205	32 of 101	71 of 104	16 of 101	27 of 105
Prien et al. (51)	D/B random, Li⁺ vs placebo vs imipramine[b]	2 yrs	44	2 of 18	5 of 13	4 of 18	8 of 13
Fieve et al. (52)	D/B random, Li⁺ vs placebo	Up to 4 yrs	35	10 of 17	17 of 18	5 of 17	8 of 18

[a] One dropout.
[b] Of 13 patients treated with imipramine for mania, seven relapsed; of 13 treated for depression, four relapsed.
D/B, double-blind.

183

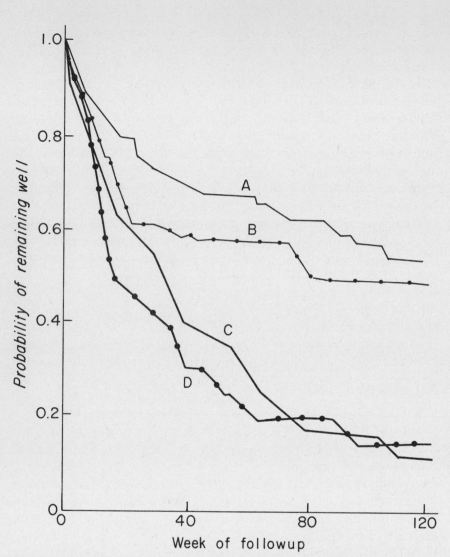

Fig. 1. Life-table probabilities of bipolar I patients remaining well on lithium or controlled maintenance therapy in two independent studies

(A) Li-treated patients in the Veterans Administration study (n = 117) and (B) in the New York State Psychiatric Institute study (n = 96); (C) Control patients in the VA study (n = 112) and (D) in the NY study (n = 38). Source: Fleiss et al. (54)

and global judgements at the end of the trial; double-blind randomization of patients previously treated with lithium to either continue lithium or receive placebo, followed by discontinuation of treatment after six months, at which point the number of relapses were scored; double-blind crossover between lithium and placebo; and life-table analysis. Nevertheless, all arrived at the same conclusion.

Several studies attempted to compare the long-term prophylactic effects of lithium with a second tricyclic drug in bipolar illness. In the study by Prien et al. (51), nine of 18 cases relapsed on lithium, 11 of 13 relapsed on placebo, and 11 of 13 relapsed on imipramine. This suggests that lithium is superior to both placebo and imipramine in the long-term prophylaxis of bipolar illness. Quitkin et al. (56) obtained similar results. The number of manic relapses in these studies among patients on imipramine suggested that imipramine might in fact induce a manic relapse. In the study by Coppen et al. (57), lithium was compared with maprotiline over a one-year period; although the numbers are too small for any statistical analysis, the trend was in favor of lithium. A much larger study comparing an antidepressant with placebo and with lithium in bipolar illness is needed for us to draw definitive conclusions. However, such a study is ethically difficult to conduct now that we know of lithium's high degree of efficacy and the high morbidity of manic-depressive patients when placed on placebo.

Prophylaxis of Recurrent Unipolar Depression

Table 12 lists the six major double-blind controlled prophylactic studies of lithium and placebo in unipolar recurrent depression. In all studies, except those of Fieve et al. (52, 58) and Cundall et al. (48), the number of patients relapsing into hospitalizable depressions were much greater in the placebo groups than in the lithium groups. The Cundall group involved only four patients on lithium and four on placebo, which makes any conclusions difficult. In the four-year study of Fieve et al. (52, 58), hospitalizable relapses of patients given lithium and placebo were comparable among this seriously ill unipolar group. However, when multiple and more sensitive outcome indices were added to the single gross index of rehospitalization, lithium was clearly superior to placebo in preventing depressive relapse.

Four or five subsequent studies have compared the prophylactic efficacy of antidepressants with lithium and placebo in preventing unipolar depressive relapse. In two separate studies by Coppen et al. (57, 59), who compared lithium with maprotiline and mianserin, lithium appeared superior, even though the antidepressant

185

Table 12. Unipolar Prophylaxis: Double-Blind Trials with Lithium

Study	Design	Duration, months	Indices	No. receiving each treatment	No. (and %) of failures		
					Total	Depressive	Manic
Baastrup et al. (45)	Discontinuation	5	Hosp/add med.	Li = 17	0 (0)[a]	0(0)[a]	0
				Pl = 17	9(53)	9(53)	0
Coppen et al. (46)	Before–after	14	No improv. over pre-treatment	Li = 11	1(9)[a]	Not indicated	Not indicated
				Pl = 15	12(80)		
Cundall et al. (48)	Discontinuation	6	Hosp/add med.	Li = 4	3(75)	3(75)	0
				Pl = 4	2(50)	2(50)	0
Prien et al., VA-NIMH I (50)	Random assign[b]	24	Hosp/add med.	Li = 27	13(48)[a]	12(44)[a]	3(11)
				Pl = 26	24(92)	24(92)	2(8)
				IMI = 25	12(48)	12(44)	1(4)
Coppen et al. (57)	Random assign[b]	24			Li statistically superior to Ludiomil (maprotiline)		
Fieve et al. (52, 58)	Random assign[b]	48	Rating scales[c]	Li = 14	8(57)	8(57)	0
				Pl = 14	9(64)	9(64)	0

[a] Statistically significant at p = 0.01 or better.
[b] Some patients previously on lithium.
[c] Additional outcome indices were: Mean no. of months in study: 20.52 (Li), 9.00 (Pl); frequency of depressive episodes per patient year: 0.59 (Li), 1.60 (Pl); global scale (mean): 1.87 (Li), 2.17 (Pl); no. of hospitalizations: 2 (Li), 4 (Pl); average duration of depression (days): 86.25 (Li), 75.00 (Pl); dropouts: 2 (Li), 3 (Pl). Global scale, no. of hospitalizations, and duration of depression are indicators of severity of illness. Pl, placebo.

did have some power to prevent depressive relapse (See Table 13). In the other studies *(60, 61)* in which a tricyclic antidepressant was compared with lithium (or, in some instances, placebo), the former appeared to be almost as effective as lithium in preventing a recurrent depressive relapse: in all instances either lithium or the antidepressant was superior to placebo. To date, the overall data, including a recent study by Peselow et al. *(110)*, do not sufficiently answer the question of the comparative effectiveness of lithium alone, an antidepressant alone, or lithium plus an antidepressant in preventing unipolar depressive relapse. A larger, multihospital VA study by Prien et al. is in its late stages of analysis, the results of which will soon be published.

Ordinary clinical practice by most psychopharmacologists or lithium experts indicates that most patients with recurrent unipolar depression are initially treated with lithium alone by the lithium proponents, or with tricyclic antidepressants alone by the psychopharmacologists whose work has been more in the antidepressant field. Unipolar depressed patients whose cycles are clear and regular would probably benefit initially from a trial with lithium. Unipolar patients who have atypical symptoms—particularly those with hyperphagia and hypersomnia—would probably benefit more from an initial trial of monoamine oxidase (MAO) inhibitor. Unipolar patients with typical endogenous symptoms and infrequent attacks would probably benefit most from prophylactic treatment with tricyclics.

Figure 2 illustrates the life-table probabilities for recently hospitalized unipolar patients who were placed on no lithium (controls). These patients were studied at the Lithium Clinic of the New York State Psychiatric Institute (Columbia Presbyterian Medical Center) *(55)*. The probability of remaining well is higher at the end of one and two years for the lithium group than for the placebo group; however, the trend does not quite reach statistical significance. These results suggest, as is commonly known in clinical practice, that lithium has a stronger prophylactic effect in bipolar than unipolar illness. Nevertheless, in the latter it exerts a substantial prophylactic effect.

Table 14 compares rapid-cyclers and nonrapid-cyclers with respect to lithium's efficacy in comparison with placebo *(62)*. Rapid-cyclers on placebo tend to drop out of the study much more rapidly than nonrapid-cyclers. By definition, the mean number

Table 13. Treatment of Recurrent Unipolar Depression: Prophylaxis with Antidepressants vs Lithium or Placebo

Study	Design and duration[a]	No. of patients	Results (no. relapsed)		
			Lithium	Antidepressant	Placebo
Bialos et al. (60)	D/B random, AMI vs placebo after stability on AMI for avg. 3.7 yrs; followed for 15 wks	17	—	0 of 7	8 of 10
Prien et al. (50)	D/B random for 2 yrs (Li vs placebo vs IMI)	78	12 of 27	12 of 25	24 of 26
Coppen et al. (57)	D/B random for 1 yr (Li vs MAP)	30	3 of 12 (3 d/o)	6 of 8 (7 d/o)	—
Coppen et al. (59)	D/B random for 1 yr (Li vs MIAN)	41	0 of 15 (5 d/o)	7 of 13 (8 d/o)	—
Quitkin et al. (56)	D/B random for 11 mos (stable 6 mos) (Li vs IMI vs Li + IMI vs placebo)	27	2 of 7 (Li); 2 of 8 (Li + IMI)	5 of 6 (IMI)	6 of 6
Brit. Med. Res. Council (61)	D/B random for 3 yrs: (a) Severe depression (Li vs AMI) (b) Mild recurrent depression (Li vs AMI vs placebo)	107	36 of 56 (1 excl)	31 of 47 (3 excl)	—
		29	4 of 12	4 of 7 (1 d/o)	8 of 9

[a] D/B, double-blind; AMI, amitryptiline; IMI, imipramine; MAP, maprotiline; MIAN, mianserin. d/o, dropouts; excl., excluded.

188

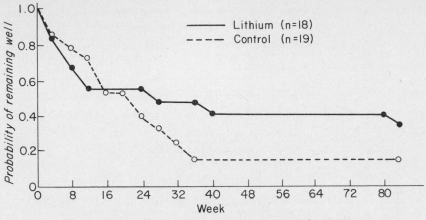

Fig. 2. Lithium vs nonlithium course in unipolar patients

Source: Fleiss et al. *(55)*

of months in remission before the first episode is much smaller for the rapid-cycler groups (four attacks per year on lithium and seven per year on placebo) than for the nonrapid-cycler groups on each treatment. Also, by definition, the mean number of manic and depressive episodes per patient year is going to be greater for rapid-cyclers than for nonrapid-cyclers, whether on lithium or placebo. Our overall studies on rapid-cyclers indicate that a trial of 12–18 months at a sufficiently high, stable concentration of serum lithium is needed to establish whether the rapid-cycling patient will come under lithium control. Approximately 50% of rapid-cyclers become stabilized on lithium alone during this pe-

Table 14. **Comparisons between "Rapid Cyclers" and non-"Rapid Cyclers"**

	Rapid cyclers		Nonrapid cyclers	
	Lithium	Placebo	Lithium	Placebo
Mean no. of months in study	36.50	7.25	14.80	16.80
Mean no. of months in remission before first episode	1.75	3.00	12.90	13.81
Mean no. of manic episodes per patient-year	0.32	1.66	0.00	0.18
Mean no. of depressive episodes per patient-year	4.54	1.97	0.49	0.37
No. of patients	2	4	10	16

Source: Dunner et al. *(62)*.

riod. The remaining 50% divide into two groups: 25% who respond to lithium and (or) Tegretol (carbamazepine), Synthroid (L-thyroxin), chlorgyline, an MAO inhibitor, or a tricyclic; and 25% who have a poor prognosis and do not seem to respond to any drug combination as yet available. One study suggests that tricyclics tend to perpetuate the rapid-cycling patient and in fact augment the frequency of the cycles rather than bring them under stabilization (63).

Finally, the positive prognostic indicators of lithium's prophylactic efficacy include:

1. A definite diagnosis of bipolar I primary affective disorder.

2. The occurrence of fewer than four affective episodes in one year (nonrapid-cycling).

3. Psychotic features during mania.

4. Grandiose-elated picture during the manic episodes.

Table 15. **Incidence (%) of Lithium Side Effects**

	Euthymic patients		Noneuthymic patients	
Symptom	Lithium only (n = 69)	Lithium plus psychotropics (n = 21)	Lithium only (n = 14)	Lithium plus psychotropics (n = 23)
Excessive urination	37.6	57.1	14.3	47.8
Hand tremor	24.6	61.9[a]	50.0	65.2
Thirst	23.2	28.6	35.7	73.9
Dry mouth	17.4	42.9[b]	14.3	78.3[b]
Nausea	8.7	0.0	28.6	30.4
Diarrhea	10.1	14.3	21.4	21.7
Lightheadedness	0.0	14.3	21.4[c]	17.4
Dazed feeling	0.0	14.3	21.4[c]	30.4
Dizziness	8.7	4.8	14.3	13.0
Constipation	1.4	28.6[b]	28.6[c]	52.2
Skin rash	7.2	4.8	0.0	4.3
Vomiting	2.9	0.0	7.3	4.3
Abdominal pain	2.9	4.8	21.4[c]	17.4
Fatigue	8.7	28.6	57.1	34.8
Incoordination	0.0	0.0	7.3	13.0
Drowsiness	4.3	14.3	35.7[c]	43.5
Blurred vision	4.3	4.8	7.3	8.7
Muscle weakness	0.0	9.5	21.4	26.1

[a] Significantly different from lithium alone (same mood state), $p < 0.01$, or [b] $p < 0.05$.
[c] Significantly different from lithium alone (euthymic mood), $p < 0.05$.
Source: Bone et al. (64).

5. A family history of bipolar illness.

6. A positive response by an affectively ill family member to lithium.

Lithium Side Effects and Toxicity

During the early treatment phases with lithium, which usually last two to four weeks, and later during the prophylactic and maintenance phases, which may go on for years, some mild side effects may come and go. A study of our lithium clinic population (Table 15) showed that the most commonly observed side effects were excessive urination, hand tremor, dry mouth, thirst, occasional nausea, and diarrhea (64). Mild to moderate side effects with lithium may be seen in several organ systems of the body, including gastrointestinal, neuromuscular, central nervous system, cardiovascular, thyroid, and kidney. Five to 10% of patients on long-term lithium develop hypothyroidism and goiter; this can be treated easily with thyroid replacement, continuing the lithium as before. Fifteen to 20% develop weight gain, which may be corrected by restricting caloric intake. Weight gain is thought to be attributed mostly to lithium's effect on glucose metabolism and in some instances the retention of fluids. Patients with cardiovascular disease may infrequently have a tendency to show pulse irregularity and reversible T-wave changes on the electrocardiogram. Patients with central nervous system disease (i.e., senility, etc.) tend to develop neurotoxicity, electroencephalographic changes, and seizures more than medically well patients. Patients with renal disease, as reflected by decreased glomerular filtration rate and increased serum creatinine, may easily develop lithium toxicity; further lithium treatment may accelerate the glomerular defect and most certainly creates a high-risk for lithium toxicity.

Most patients experience the effects of lithium on kidney function as symptoms of increased thirst and polyuria. The cause of the lithium-induced polyuria and concentrating defect in the kidneys is most likely the suppression of antidiuretic hormone. Several reports of histological examination of kidney tissue have revealed structural changes in some lithium-treated patients (65), but these studies were inadequately controlled (66). So far, the results from most centers indicate that, even when lithium is given for decades, the glomerular function of the kidneys is not affected in normal kidneys *(67–70).* For the few patients who have had previous kidney disease or damage from taking other drugs, additional lithium treatment may accelerate a downhill course. Patients with excessive urine production or dehydration while on lithium must be made aware of the increased risk to develop lithium intoxication and should therefore increase their fluid intake. All patients on lithium should have kidney function checked once or twice yearly. In those with increased concentrations of serum creatinine, more frequent measurements of serum lithium and repeated serum creatinine are called for, while the patient is maintained on lower doses of lithium; these patients must make extra efforts to remain well-hydrated.

Lithium toxicity may develop insidiously in patients who fail to ingest adequate salt or fluids or who have increasing kidney disease for other medical reasons. Serious toxicity and death may occur in patients who develop intercurrent infections, nausea, vomiting, diarrhea, and high temperature, or who begin diuretics without the careful supervision of a physician. Patients who ingest too much lithium orally or who go on crash diets with fluid or salt deprivation may also become toxic. Signs of lithium toxicity include apathy, poor concentration, impaired consciousness, confusion with cerebellar ataxia, incoordination, and neuromuscular fasciculations, along with hyperactive tendon reflexes. Patients with severe lithium toxicity often develop gross tremor of the hands, arms, and often the jaw, along with nausea, vomiting, diarrhea, and finally convulsions, delirium, and coma. These symptoms are usually accompanied by significant electroencephalogram alterations.

The treatment of lithium toxicity is the same as for barbiturate poisoning: intravenous re-establishment of fluid and electrolyte balance, and the administration of an antiepileptic agent, mannitol, and aminophylin to promote lithium diuresis. In severe cases of lithium poisoning, kidney dialysis is indicated. Antibiotics should be given, especially to elderly patients, because a frequent cause of death during lithium toxicity is pneumonia.

Mechanisms of Action of the Lithium Ion on Major Target Systems

The mechanism of action of the lithium ion is currently one of the most fascinating biochemical research areas in psychiatry.

The discovery of how this simple ion stabilizes a major mental illness will indeed constitute a major breakthrough. The neurobiology of the lithium ion can be best understood by reviewing its basic physical chemistry. In the following sections I will discuss its biological effects on membrane transport; electrolyte balance; the structure and activity of enzymes; neurotransmitter synthesis, metabolism, and release; and receptor binding (71–76).

Membranes

The physical properties of lithium that determine its action on membranes are listed in Table 16. Lithium (atomic no. 3), with sodium and potassium, calcium and magnesium, belongs

---

Table 16. **Physical Properties of Lithium Relevant to Its Action on Membranes**

Size (lightest alkali ion): atomic mass, 6.94 amu; ionic radius, 0.08 nm
Charge: monovalent cation
Electrical field density: greatest electrical density at its surface; high ionization potential, like Na^+ and K^+
Energy of hydration:[a] greatest of the alkali ions
Other: Li^+ competes with Na^+, and K^+, Mg^{2+}, and Ca^{2+}, and substitutes for Na^+ and K^+ in biological tissues to maintain the nerve-impulse conduction; interacts with NH_4^- groups, including those of the biogenic amines

[a] Energy needed to strip off water molecules.

---

to the group I alkali metals. Its physiochemical properties can thus be understood in terms of the properties of these other four naturally occurring biological cations. Lithium has the same charge as sodium (monovalent) and potassium, but is closer to sodium with respect to its ionic radius (lithium 0.08, sodium 0.1, potassium 0.13 nm) and its charge density. Lithium also has approximately the same ionic radius as magnesium (0.07 nm) and approximately the same charge density as calcium. Lithium especially competes for calcium-binding sites in most biological systems, the explanation for which has been studied by numerous physical chemists, including Eigen, Eisenman, Lehn, and Winkler (see ref. 71). Lithium competes with these four biological cations in nerve tissues that maintain nerve impulse conduction, perhaps by attaching itself to a binding site, which in turn may produce biochemical changes in the system either by direct action of the lithium ion on the macromolecular structure or by displacement of one of the other biological cations. Furthermore, the interaction of lithium with ammonium groups, including those of the biogenic amines, may alter the biochemistry of these important neurotransmitter substances.

Lithium thus substitutes for sodium, extracellularly, and may pass rapidly through sodium channels of cell membranes during impulse conduction. It may also block the narrow potassium channels, thereby affecting electrolyte gradients on either side of the cell membrane, while still permitting impulse conduction to continue. By competing for calcium-binding sites, lithium could affect the calcium-dependent release of neurotransmitters, such as norepinephrine, or the calcium-dependent production of cyclic AMP. Lithium's action on microcellular sites may directly alter the tertiary structure of macromolecules such as those that make up membranes, hormones, receptor sites, enzyme chains, and chromosomes. These latter protein substances are functionally sensitive to local concentrations of the other four biological cations. By altering the conformation of the macromolecules, lithium may indirectly affect the ionic selectivity on either side of the membrane, the response to neurotransmitter hormones, and the complex process of energy production needed to transport neurotransmitter hormones and other protein substances across the cell membrane, the latter giving rise ultimately to genetic expression.

Microenvironmental changes in pH, ionic strength, and osmolality may also result as a consequence of lithium's acting on cellular sites (72) Cellular protein carriers bind to or transport sodium, potassium, calcium, and magnesium, permitting neurotransmitter hormones to cross the membrane. Lithium may alter the macromolecular structure of these protein membrane carriers for neurotransmitters, which often have allosteric sites for binding sodium and can thus bind lithium.

Keeping in mind the physical properties of lithium, its cellular sites of action, and its microenvironmental effects, one can better understand how lithium is transported across the cell membrane. Figure 3 illustrates four principal lithium transport pathways in human erythrocytes, as proposed by Pandey et al. (73). Tosteson (74) has reviewed the four major types of molecular movement

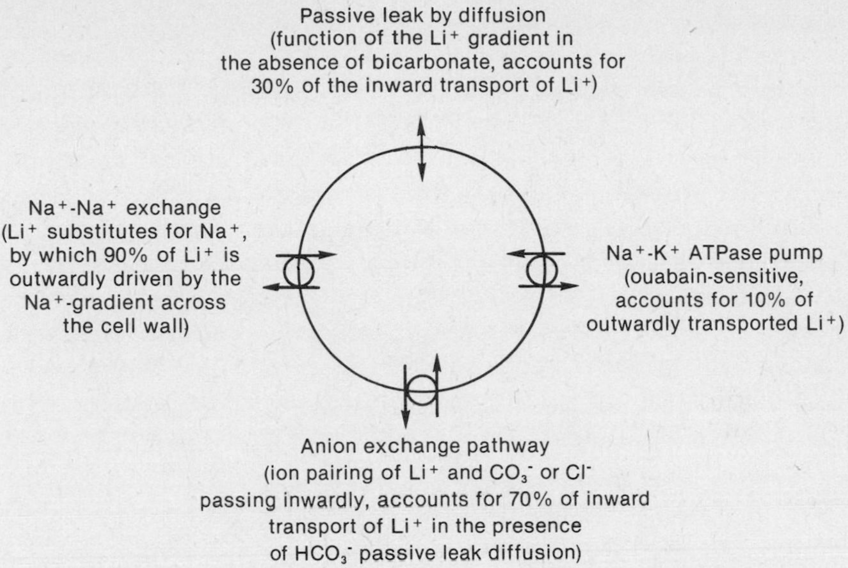

Passive leak by diffusion
(function of the Li+ gradient in
the absence of bicarbonate, accounts for
30% of the inward transport of Li+)

Na+-Na+ exchange
(Li+ substitutes for Na+,
by which 90% of Li+ is
outwardly driven by the
Na+-gradient across
the cell wall)

Na+-K+ ATPase pump
(ouabain-sensitive,
accounts for 10% of
outwardly transported Li+)

Anion exchange pathway
(ion pairing of Li+ and CO_3^- or Cl-
passing inwardly, accounts for 70% of inward
transport of Li+ in the presence
of HCO_3^- passive leak diffusion)

Fig. 3. Mechanisms of action of lithium on membranes: Proposed Li+ transport pathways in human erythrocytes

Source: Pandey et al. *(73)*

across biological membranes mediated by the protein carriers located in the lipid layers of the membranes as follows:

1. Passive leak by diffusion, in which there is a selected movement of ions down channels, depending on their relative concentrations and electrical potential gradients on either side of the membrane.

2. Pump mechanisms, including those of the sodium/potassium pump and the calcium pump (present in the membrane), which convert energy into movement of the four cations against concentration gradients.

3. Ion transport in the form of exchange diffusion, as in the saturable sodium–sodium exchange mechanism.

4. Co-transport (two substances moving together), as in the ion pairing that occurs in the anion-exchange pathway.

Lithium passing inwardly with either carbonate or chloride accounts for approximately 70% of the inward transport; 90% of the outward transport is accounted for by the sodium–lithium exchange mechanism, whereby lithium is moved outwardly across the cell against its concentration gradient.

Electrolytes

Lithium is absorbed through the gastrointestinal tract and enters the plasma to be distributed among tissues and cells; it reaches a steady-state after approximately two weeks of constant ingestion of the same dose under conditions of normal kidney function. Lithium is filtered through the glomerular membrane, reabsorbed in the proximal tubules with no distal tubular reabsorption and no secretion taking place, and ultimately excreted by the kidneys. Study of the acute effects of lithium administration in humans reveals that on days 1 and 2 natriuresis, kaluresis, and diuresis take place, followed by a retention of sodium on about day 3 *(77).* During days 6 and 7, a new state of metabolic balance and equilibrium begins, a steady-state of lithium being achieved between 10 and 14 days.

Body composition studies in affective disorders before, during, and after lithium therapy at the Metabolic Ward of the New York State Psychiatric Institute show that the ratio of extracellular to intercellular water content is significantly less in male patients than in controls *(78).* In both sexes, residual sodium concentration was greater in depressed patients than in controls, but the intercellular potassium content was the same in depressed patients as in controls. Body composition was studied in six patients before lithium therapy, after 17 days of lithium, and 17 days after discontinuance of administration of the drug. The significant changes included a decrease in body weight during therapy, and a decrease in body water content and an increase in residual sodium concentration after the drug treatment was discontinued. This finding of increased residual sodium in depressed patients now appears to be supported by findings at other centers. The increase in residual sodium content in depression implies that intracellular content may also be increased (residual sodium consists of bone sodium plus intracellular sodium, of which bone sodium remains relatively constant). The increased residual sodium and therefore increased intracellular sodium could possibly reflect the combined activities of the membrane pumps of different tissues. Sodium transport can be altered by interference with sodium/potassium ATPase and events at the membrane, which are in turn influenced by cortisol, catecholamines, and aldosterone, all of which are reported to undergo perturbations in the affective disorders.

In the six patients above who underwent measurements of body composition before, during, and after lithium therapy, both body weight and total body water decreased progressively. The time sequence implies that the effect of lithium on total body water takes longer than seven days to reach a peak and longer than 17 days to subside when the drug is discontinued. This interval coincides with clinical observations on the time-course of lithium-induced polyuria. During therapy with lithium carbonate, body composition has been associated with an increase in residual sodium content. This change was statistically significant when the value of sodium before lithium carbonate therapy was compared with the value 17 days after discontinuance of the drug. From this one can infer that 17 days is insufficient for the effect of lithium carbonate on residual sodium content to reach a peak and that it takes longer than 17 days for the effect of the drug to subside once lithium therapy has been discontinued. It seems possible that the increased residual sodium seen in depression and in its alteration with lithium therapy represents an increase in bone sodium (78).

Additional long-term effects of lithium demonstrated during metabolic studies of humans include increased plasma concentration of calcium and magnesium, decreased urinary excretion of calcium ion (79), decreased serum phosphate, and a decreased uptake of phosphate into bone, accompanied by a decrease in bone density (80).

Erythrocyte/Plasma Ratio of Lithium

Because of the pronounced effects of lithium on overall electrolyte balance and electrolyte concentration gradients on either side of the cell membrane, several investigators have studied the ratio of lithium content in erythrocytes and plasma, hoping that effects occurring at the erythrocyte membrane might give clues to lithium's mechanism of action. Several dozen important studies were reported during the 1970s, the most consistent and important of which demonstrate that the lithium erythrocyte/plasma ratio is stable within an individual patient (81). However, there is considerable interindividual variation, related to the genetically determined activity of this system (82); variations of this activity presumably reflect differences in the number of transport sites per cell.

In addition, in vitro determinations of lithium–sodium exchange mechanisms indicate less activity in erythrocytes from patients during lithium treatment than when no lithium is given *(83)*. Variations in the activity of the lithium–sodium exchange mechanisms may also account for interindividual variations of erythrocyte/plasma ratios.

Although considerable excitement was generated by claims that lithium erythrocyte/plasma ratios might be predictive of lithium response or might be used as a diagnostic test for unipolar or bipolar disorders, these studies have not been replicated *(84)*. Measurements of erythrocyte lithium during periods of lithium toxicity, however, seem to be quite useful, the intracellular lithium content often being a better indicator of the degree of lithium toxicity at its peak and during the period of recovery (Fieve, Meltzer, and Dunner, unpublished data). During recovery, plasma concentrations of lithium may not reflect the tissue concentration of lithium, despite the discontinuance of lithium administration.

Enzymes

Lithium is known to stimulate enzyme activity when sodium is the activator and to inhibit enzyme activity when potassium is the enzyme activator, probably by competing with sodium, potassium, and ammonium sites on the enzyme itself to alter the rate at which the enzyme processes its substrate. *(71)*. Lithium also interferes with intermediary metabolism, including increasing urinary excretion of alpha-ketoglutaric acid, tricarboxylic acid, and other metabolites *(85)*, and affecting lipid metabolism, liver hexokinase activation of liver adenyl cyclase, and protein kinase. In addition, lithium appears to stimulate glycogen synthesis and the action of pyruvate kinase, probably by blocking production of cyclic AMP and inhibition of adenylate cyclase *(86)*.

Clinical reports published over the past decade suggest that lithium may affect erythrocyte, plasma, and platelet enzymes in humans. In two such studies *(87, 88)*, lithium treatment increased the activity of erythrocyte ATPase, and another study by Fieve et al. *(89)* indicated that erythrocyte acetylcholinesterase increased in lithium-treated manic depressives. Increases in monoamine oxidase from lithium treatment have been reported by both Bucard et al. (1975) and Fieve et al. *(90)*. No effects on catechol-*O*-methyltransferase *(91)* nor dopamine β-hydroxylase *(92)* were reported.

These findings are interesting, but the studies are still controversial and need replication. However, the effects of lithium on enzyme activity remain undisputed and may, in fact, ultimately account for lithium's mode of action.

Neurotransmitters

Dozens of laboratory studies have been undertaken to better understand the effect of lithium on norepinephrine, serotonin, and dopamine synthesis, metabolism, and degradation. The catecholamine hypothesis and the accompanying serotonin hypothesis have remained the main theoretical models for understanding the manic-depressive syndrome. Kety, in fact, has proposed that both norepinephrine and serotonin metabolism may be involved in the manic-depressive process and in its genetic expression (see ref. 71). He has suggested that serotonin may play a homeostatic role at the synapse, dampening the effects of other transmitters such as the catecholamines. In such a model, manic depression would be viewed primarily as a deficiency in the serotonin-governed stabilization of mood, in which the normal fluctuations mediated by norepinephrine or other transmitters go out-of-bounds. Thus, both mania and depression might be prevented or treated by a single agent that potentiated the action of serotonin. Clearly the original catecholamine hypothesis of manic depression is not sufficient to explain why lithium appears to correct both the manic and depressive phases of the cycle (93, 94). Lithium does increase the intracellular degradation of norepinephrine to deaminated O-methylated metabolites (95, 96), and both stimulates and inhibits amine re-uptake into synaptosomes (97). Lithium may also cause a decrease in brain concentrations of norepinephrine (98–100), a decreased synthesis and a decreased turnover, or no changes, depending on whether the studies have been performed acutely or chronically. Furthermore, lithium stimulates serotonin turnover and inhibits stimulus-induced release of norepinephrine (101, 102) or serotonin (103–105). In experiments with animals and humans (106, 107), lithium changes brain and spinal fluid concentrations of amine precursors, amines, and amine metabolites; platelet serotonin uptake is inhibited, and the post-synaptic receptor processes are altered. Current information on the role of these neurotransmitter hormones in various behavioral processes is still very rudimentary; however, the catecholamine and serotonin hypotheses of affective disorder have been most important, stimulating a wealth of scientific data that have been instrumental in conceptualizing lithium's ultimate mode of action.

Receptors

Lithium-binding sites may be either identical with or closely bound to neurotransmitter or other hormone-receptor sites (71). Thus, lithium decreases kidney response to aldosterone, resulting in decreased conservation of sodium. Lithium also causes a decreased kidney response to antidiuretic hormone, resulting in polyuria and at times nephrogenic diabetes insipidus (72). In addition, lithium causes decreased thyroid response to thyrotropin (108), presumably by inhibiting thyrotropin-stimulated adenylate cyclase (a) by altering the hormone-receptor site microenvironment, (b) by substituting for an important enzyme cofactor such as sodium, potassium, calcium, or magnesium, or (c) possibly by blocking the effects of cyclic AMP at any step in the biosynthetic pathway. This, in turn, would result in a secondarily increased concentration of thyrotropin (thyroid-stimulating hormone) and could explain the production of goiter in animals and humans, the decreased concentration of serum thyroxin, the decreased release of ^{131}I, and transient increases in thyrotropin (72). The latter altered indices are seen in at least 30–40% of lithium-treated patients.

In summary, lithium's effects on lowering the hormone-induced stimulation of adenylate cyclase activity so that less cyclic AMP is produced could explain both the decreased kidney response to antidiuretic hormone and the decreased thyroid response to thyrotropin (71). Belmaker has written an important review of the subject (109).

Summary of Potential Mechanism of Lithium Action

The genetic defect of manic-depressive illness is hypothetically localized at the cell membrane in the form of an altered protein carrier, enzyme, or specific receptor. Lithium may correct this defect by shifting sodium and potassium transport (ion concentrations) at the cell membrane which, in turn, alters enzyme activity. Lithium competes with calcium and magnesium in ion-dependent, neurotransmitter-release processes, altering the release of neurotransmitter hormones into the synaptic cleft. This may lead to normal nerve-impulse conduction and remission of the manic-depressive illness.

References

1. Fieve RR. Lithium in psychiatry. *Int J Psychiatry* **9**, 375–412 (1970).
2. *Practitioner* **2**, 130 (1909).
3. Culbreth DMR. *Materia Medica and Pharmacology*, 7th ed., 1927, p 743.
4. Corcoran AC, Taylor RD, Page IH. Lithium poisoning from the use of salt substitute. *J Am Med Assoc* **139**, 685–688 (1949).
5. Cade JFJ. Lithium salts in the treatment of psychotic excitement. *Med J Aust* **36**, 349–352 (1949).
6. Noack CH, Trautner EM. Lithium treatment of maniacal psychosis. *Med J Aust* **38**, 219–222 (1951).
7. Schou M, Juel-Nielson N, Strömgren E, Voldby H. The treatment of manic psychoses by the administration of lithium salts. *J Neurol Neurosurg Psychiatry* **17**, 250 (1954).
8. Maggs R. Treatment of manic illness with lithium carbonate. *Br J Psychiatry* **109**, 56–65 (1963).
9. Wharton RN, Fieve RR. The use of lithium in the affective psychoses. *Am J Psychiatry* **123**, 706–712 (1966).
10. Fieve RR, Platman SR, Plutchik RR. The use of lithium in affective disorders: I. Acute endogenous depression. *Am J Psychiatry* **125**, 487–491 (1968).
11. Fieve RR, Platman SR, Plutchik R. The use of lithium in affective disorders: II. Prophylaxis of depression in chronic recurrent affective disorder. *Am J Psychiatry* **125**, 492–498 (1968).
12. Gattozzi D. *Lithium in the Treatment of Mood Disorders*, NIMH, Bethesda, MD, 1970, p 2.
13. Gershon S, Shopsin B. *Lithium: Its Role in Psychiatric Research and Treatment*, Plenum Press, New York, NY, 1973.
14. Gurland BJ, Fleiss JL, Cooper RE, et al. Cross-national study of diagnosis of the mental disorders: Some comparisons of diagnostic criteria from the first investigation. *Am J Psychiatry* **125** (Apr Suppl), 30–39 (1969).
15. Dunner DL, Fieve RR. The Li ion: Its impact on diagnostic practice. In *Psychiatric Diagnosis: Exploration of Biological Predictors*, Spectrum Publications, New York, NY, 1978, pp 233–244.
16. *Diagnostic and Statistical Manual*, 3rd ed., RL Spitzer, Ed., Am Psych Assoc, Washington, DC, 1980.
17. Spitzer RL, Endicott J. *Schedule for Affective Disorders and Schizophrenia*. N.Y. State Psychiatric Institute, New York, NY, 1978.

18. Fieve RR, Go R, Dunner DL. A family study of morbid risk for affective disorders in first degree relatives of bipolar and unipolar probands. Submitted for publication.
19. Fieve RR, Dunner DL. Unipolar and bipolar affective states. In *The Nature and Treatment of Depression,* FF Flach, SC Draghi, Eds., Wiley Publications, New York, NY, 1975.
20. Schou M. *Lithium Treatment of Manic Depression,* S. Karger, Basel, Switzerland, 1978.
21. Rifkin A, Quitkin FM, Blumberg AG, et al. Lithium carbonate in emotionally unstable character disorder. *Arch Gen Psychiatry* **27,** 519–523 (1972).
22. Sletten IW, Gershon S. *Compr Psychiatry* **7,** 197–206 (1966).
23. Singer K, Cheng R, Schou M. *Br J Psychiatry* **124,** 50–51 (1974).
24. Wren JC, Kline NS, Cooper TB, et al. *Clin Med J* **81,** 33–37 (1974).
25. Merry J, Reynolds CM, Bailey J, Coppen A. Prophylactic treatment of alcoholism by lithium carbonate. *Lancet* **ii,** 481–482 (1976).
26. Bunney WE Jr, Goodwin FK, David JM, Fawcett JA. A behavioral–biochemical study of lithium treatment. *Am J Psychiatry* **125,** 499 (1968).
27. Goodwin FK, Murphy DL, Bunney WE Jr. Lithium carbonate treatment in depression and mania. *Arch Gen Psychiatry* **21,** 486 (1969).
28. Stokes PE, Stoll PM, Shamorian CA, Patton MJ. Efficacy of lithium in the acute treatment of manic depressive illness. *Lancet* **i,** 1319–1325 (1971).
29. Johnson G, Gershon S, Hekimian LJ. Controlled evaluation of lithium and chlorpromazine in the treatment of manic states: An interim report. *Compr Psychiatry* **9,** 563 (1968).
30. Spring GK. Some current thoughts on lithium carbonate in manic depressive illness, based on a double-blind comparison with chlorpromazine. *Psychosomatics* **12**(5), 1970.
31. Platman SR. A comparison of lithium carbonate and chlorpromazine in mania. *Am J Psychiatry* **127,** 351 (1970).
32. Johnson G, Gershon S, Burdock E, et al. *Br J Psychiatry* **119,** 267–276 (1971).
33. Prien RF, Caffey EM Jr, Klett CJ. *Arch Gen Psychiatry* **27,** 182–189 (1972).
34. Shopsin B, et al. Psychoactive drugs in mania. *Arch Gen Psychiatry* **32,** 34–42 (1975).
35. Takahashi R, et al. Comparison of efficacy of lithium carbonate and chlorpromazine in mania. *Arch Gen Psychiatry* **32,** 1310–1318 (1975).
36. Hansen CJ, Retboll K, Schou M. Lithium in psychiatry. A review. *J Psychiatr Res* **6,** 67–95 (1968).

37. Goodwin FK, Murphy DL, Dunner DL. Lithium response in unipolar vs bipolar depression. *Am J Psychiatry* **129**, 44–47 (1972).
38. Mendels J, Secunda SK, Dyson WC. A controlled study of the antidepressant effects of lithium. *Arch Gen Psychiatry* **26**, 154–157 (1972).
39. Noyes R, Dempsey GM, Blum A. Lithium treatment of depression. *Compr Psychiatry* **15**, 187–193 (1974).
40. Johnson G. Antidepressant effect of lithium. *Compr Psychiatry* **15**, 43–47 (1974).
41. Baron M, Gershon ES, Rudy V. Lithium carbonate response in depression, prediction by unipolar/bipolar illness, average evoked response, catechol-*O*-methyl transferase and family history. *Arch Gen Psychiatry* **32**, 1107–1111 (1975).
42. Watanabe S, Ishino H, Otsuki S. Double blind comparison of lithium carbonate and imipramine in treatment of depression. *Arch Gen Psychiatry* **32**, 659–668 (1975).
43. Mendels J. Lithium in the treatment of depression. *Am J Psychiatry* **133**, 373–377 (1976).
44. Worrall EP, Moody JP, Peet M, et al. Controlled studies of the acute antidepressant effects of lithium. *Br J Psychiatry* **135**, 255–262 (1979).
45. Baastrup PC, Poulsen JC, Schou M, et al. Prophylactic lithium: Double-blind discontinuation in manic-depressive and recurrent-depressive disorders. *Lancet* **ii**, 326–330 (1970).
46. Coppen A, Noguera R, Bailey J, et al. Prophylactic lithium in affective disorders: Controlled trial. *Lancet* **ii**, 275–279 (1971).
47. Hullin RP, McDonald R, Allsopp NE. Prophylactic lithium in recurrent affective disorders. *Lancet* **i**, 1044–1046 (1972).
48. Cundall RL, Brooks PW, Murray LG. A controlled evaluation of lithium prophylaxis in affective disorders. *Psychol Med* **2**, 308–311 (1972).
49. Stallone F, Shelley E, Mendlewicz J, et al. The use of lithium in affective disorders. III. A double-blind study of prophylaxis in bipolar illness. *Am J Psychiatry* **130**, 1006–1010 (1973).
50. Prien RF, Caffey EM, Klett CJ. Prophylactic efficacy of lithium carbonate in manic-depressive illness. *Arch Gen Psychiatry* **28**, 337–341 (1973).
51. Prien RF, Klett CJ, Caffey EM. Lithium carbonate and imipramine in prevention of affective episodes. A comparison in recurrent affective illness. *Arch Gen Psychiatry* **29**, 420–425 (1973).
52. Fieve RR, Kumbaraci T, Dunner DL. Lithium prophylaxis of depression in bipolar I, bipolar II, and unipolar patients. *Am J Psychiatry* **133**, 925–929 (1976).

53. Persson G. Lithium prophylaxis in affective disorders: An open trial with matched controls. *Acta Psychiatr Scand* **48**, 462–479 (1973).
54. Fleiss JL, Prien RF, Dunner DL, et al. Actuarial studies of the course of manic-depressive illness. *Compr Psychiatry* **19**, 355–361 (1978).
55. Fleiss JL, Dunner DL, Stallone F, Fieve RR. The life table: A method for analyzing longitudinal studies. *Arch Gen Psychiatry* **33**, 107–112 (1976).
56. Quitkin F, Kane J, Rifkin A, et al. Prophylactic lithium carbonate with and without imipramine for bipolar I patients. *Arch Gen Psychiatry* **38**, 902–909 (1981).
57. Coppen AJ, Montgomery SA, Gupta RK, et al. A double-blind comparison of lithium carbonate and maprotiline in the prophylaxis of the affective disorders. *Br J Psychiatry* **128**, 479–485 (1976).
58. Fieve RR, Dunner DL, Kumbaraci T, Stallone F. Lithium carbonate in affective disorders. IV. A double-blind study of prophylaxis in unipolar recurrent depression. *Arch Gen Psychiatry* **32**, 1541–1544 (1975).
59. Coppen A, Chose K, Rao R, et al. Mianserin and lithium in the prophylaxis of depression. *Br J Psychiatry* **133**, 206–210 (1978).
60. Bialos D, Giller E, Jatlow P, et al. Recurrence of depression after discontinuation of long-term amitriptyline treatment. *Am J Psychiatry* **139**, 325–329 (1982).
61. British Medical Research Council. Continuation therapy with lithium and amitriptyline in unipolar depressive illness. A controlled trial. *Psychol Med* **11**, 409–416 (1981).
62. Dunner DL, Patrick V, Fieve RR. Rapid cycling manic-depressive patients. *Compr Psychiatry* **18**, 561–566 (1977).
63. Wehr TA, Goodwin FK. Rapid cyclings in manic depression induced by tricyclic antidepressants. *Arch Gen Psychiatry* **36**, 555–559 (1979).
64. Bone S, Roose SP, Dunner DL, Fieve RR. Incidence of side-effects in patients on long-term lithium therapy. *Am J Psychiatry* **137**, 103–104 (1980).
65. Hestbech J, Hansen HE, Amidsen A, et al. Chronic renal lesions following long term treatment with lithium. *Kidney* **12**, 205–213 (1977).
66. Hullin RP, Coley VP, Birch NJ, et al. Renal function after long term treatment with lithium. *Br Med J* **i**, 1457–1459 (1979).
67. Colt EW, Kimbrell D, Fieve RR. Renal impairment, hypercalcemia and lithium therapy. *Am J Psychiatry* **138**, 683–684 (1981).
68. Decina P, Oliver JA, Sciacca RR, et al. Effect of lithium therapy on glomerular filtration rate. *Am J Psychiatry*, in press.
69. Vestergaard P, Amdisen A, Hansen HE, Schou M. Lithium treatment and kidney function. *Acta Psychiatr Scand* **60**, 504–520 (1979).

70. Vestergaard P, Schou M, Thomsen K. Monitoring of patients in prophylactic lithium treatment. *Br J Psychiatry* **140**, 185–187 (1982).
71. Bunney WE, Murphy DL, Eds. *The Neurobiology of Lithium. Neurosci Res Prog Bull* **14**, no. 2 (April 1976).
72. Singer J, Rotenberg D. Mechanisms of lithium action. *N Engl J Med* 254–260 (1973).
73. Pandey GN, Javaid JL, Davis JM, Tosteson DC. Mechanism of lithium transport in red blood cells. *Physiologist* **19**, 321 (1976).
74. Tosteson DC. Lithium and mania. *Sci Am*, 164–174 (April 1981).
75. Sheard MH. The biological effects of lithium. *TINS*, 85–86 (April 1980).
76. Schou M. Mode of action of lithium. In *Handbook of Biological Psychiatry*, Van Pragg, Ed., Marcel Dekker, New York, NY, 1981, pp 805–824.
77. Baer L, Platman SR, Fieve RR. The role of electrolytes in affective disorders. *Arch Gen Psychiatry* **22**, 108–113 (1970).
78. Colt EWD, Dunner DL, Wang J, et al. Body composition in affective disorder before, during and after lithium carbonate therapy. *Arch Gen Psychiatry* **39**, 577–581 (1982).
79. Mellerup ET, Lauritsen B, Dam H, Rafaelsen OJ. Lithium effects on diurnal rhythm of calcium, magnesium, and phosphate metabolism in manic-melancholic disorder. *Acta Psychiatr Scand* **53**, 360–370 (1976).
80. Christiansen C, Baastrup PC, Transbøl I. Osteopenia and dysregulation of divalent cations in lithium-treated patients. *Neuropsychobiology* **1**, 344–354 (1975).
81. Mendels J, Ramsey TA, Frazer A. Intracellular lithium concentration, diagnosis, and clinical response. Paper presented at meeting of Am Psych Assoc, Toronto, Canada, May, 1977.
82. Dorus E, Pandex GN, Davis JM. Genetic determinant of lithium ion distribution. *Arch Gen Psychiatry* **32**, 1097–1102 (1975).
83. Schreiner HC, Dunner DL, Meltzer HL, Fieve RR. The relationship of the lithium erythrocyte:plasma ratio to plasma lithium level. *Biol Psychiatry* **14**, 207–213 (1979).
84. Mendels J, Frazer A. Intracellular lithium concentration and clinical response: Towards a membrane theory of depression. *J Psychiatr Res* **10**, 9–18 (1973).
85. Bond PA, Jenner FA. The effects of lithium on organic acid excretion. In *Lithium Research and Therapy*, FN Johnson, Ed., Academic Press, London, 1975, pp 499–506.
86. Mellerup ET, Rafaelsen OJ. Lithium and carbohydrate metabolism. *Ibid*, pp 381–389.
87. Naylor GJ, Dick DAT, Dick EG, Moody JP. Lithium therapy and

erythrocyte membrane cation carrier. *Psychopharmacologia (Berlin)* **37**, 81–86 (1974).

88. Hokin-Neaverson M, Spiegel DA, Lewis WC. Deficiency of erythrocyte sodium pump activity in bipolar manic-depressive psychosis. *Life Sci* **15**, 1739–1748 (1974).

89. Fieve RR, Milstoc M, Kumbaraci T, Dunner DL. The effect of Li on red blood cell cholinesterase activity in patients with affective disorders. *Dis Nerv Syst* **37**, 241–243 (1976).

90. Fieve RR, Kumbaraci T. Platelet monoamine oxidase activity in affective disorder. *Biol Psychiatry* **15**, 473–478 (1980).

91. Dunner DL, Levitt M, Kumbaraci T, Fieve RR. Erythrocyte catechol-*O*-methyltransferase activity in primary affective disorder. *Biol Psychiatry* **12**, 237–244 (1977).

92. Levitt M, Dunner DL, Mendlewicz J, et al. Plasma dopamine β-hydroxylase activity in affective disorders. *Psychopharmacologia (Berlin)* **46**, 205–210 (1976).

93. Milstoc M, Teodoru CV, Fieve RR, Kumbaraci T. Cholinesterase activity and the manic depressive patients. *Dis Nerv Syst* **36**, 197–199 (1975).

94. Bunney WE Jr, Gershon ES, Winokur G. X linkage in manic-depressive psychosis. *Neurosci Res Prog Bull* **14**, 46–53 (1976).

95. Schildkraut JJ, Schanberg SM, Kopin IJ. The effects of lithium ion on ^{3}H-norepinephrine metabolism in brain. *Life Sci* **5**, 1479–1483 (1966).

96. Schildkraut JJ, Logue MA, Dodge GA. Effects of lithium salts on turnover and metabolism of norepinephrine in rat brain. *Psychopharmacologia (Berlin)* **14**, 135–141 (1969).

97. Colburn RW, Goodwin FK, Bunney WE Jr, Davis JM. Effects of lithium on the uptake of noradrenaline by synaptosomes. *Nature* **215**, 1395–1397 (1967).

98. Corrodi H, Fuxe K, Schou M. The effect of prolonged lithium administration on cerebral monoamine neurons in the rat. *Life Sci* **8** (Pt I), 643–651 (1969).

99. Stern DN, Fieve RR, Neff NH, Costa E. The effect of lithium chloride administration on brain and heart norepinephrine turnover rates. *Psychopharmacologia (Berlin)* **14**, 315–322 (1969).

100. Schildkraut JJ. Pharmacology—the effects of lithium on biogenic amines. In *Lithium: Its Role in Psychiatric Research and Treatment.* S Gershon, B Shopsin, Eds., Plenum Press, New York, NY, 1973, pp 51–73.

101. Bogdanski DF, Tissari A, Brodie BB. The effects of inorganic ions on uptake, storage and metabolism of biogenic amines in nerve endings. In *Psychopharmacology: A Review of Progress 1957–1967.* DH

Efron, JO, Cole, J Levine, JR Wittenborn, Eds. PHS Publ. No. 1836, U.S. Government Printing Office, Washington, DC, 1968, pp 17–26.

102. Katz RI, Kopin IJ. Release of norepinephrine-^{3}H evoked from brain slices by electrical field stimulation—calcium dependency and the effects of lithium, ouabain and tetrodotoxin. *Biochem Pharmacol* **18**, 1935–1939 (1969).

103. Mandell AJ, Knapp S. Neurobiological mechanisms in lithium prophylaxis of manic-depressive disease: An hypothesis. In *Chemical Tools in Catecholamine Research,* **2.** O Almgren, A Carlsson, J Engel, Eds., North-Holland Publishing Co., Amsterdam, 1975, pp 9–16.

104. Mandell AJ, Knapp S. A model for the neurobiological mechanisms of action involved in lithium prophylaxis of bipolar affective disorder. In *Aminergic Hypotheses of Behavior: Reality or Cliché?* BK Bernard, Ed., NIDA Res. Monograph Series, no. 3, Washington, DC, 1975, pp 97–197.

105. Knapp S, Mandell AJ. Effects of lithium chloride on parameters of biosynthetic capacity for 5-hydroxytryptamine in rat brain. *J Pharm Exp Ther* **193**, 812–823 (1975).

106. Goodwin FK, Sack RL, Post RM. Clinical evidence for neurotransmitter adaptation in response to antidepressant therapy. In *Neurobiological Mechanisms of Adaptation and Behavior.* AJ Mandell, Ed., Raven Press, New York, NY, 1975, pp 33–45.

107. Goodwin FK, Wehr T, Sack RL. Studies on the mechanism of action of lithium in man. A contribution to neurobiological theories of affective illness. In *Lithium in Psychiatry: A Synopsis.* A Villeneuve, Ed., Presses Univ. Laval, Quebec, 1976, pp 23–48.

108. Berens SC, Wolff J. The endocrine effects of lithium. In *Lithium Research and Therapy,* FN Johnson, Ed., Academic Press, London, 1975, pp 443–472.

109. Belmaker RH. Receptors, adenylate cyclase, depression and lithium. *Biol Psychiatry* **16**, 333–349 (1981).

110. Peselow et al. Lithium tricyclics and lithium in the prophylaxis of unipolar illness. *IRCS Med Sci* **8**, 524–525 (1980).

New Antidepressants

J. O. Cole

The number of new antidepressant drugs now or soon to be available in the United States is growing rapidly. A recent talk on this subject was preceded by a slide showing a terrified depressed patient holding his hands over his ears in dread with the caption stating, "What, another new antidepressant!" The situation is nowhere near *that* bad and is, in fact, almost wholly good, but there are a good many new drugs around with more to come.

One cannot, without encyclopedic knowledge and remarkable awareness of new compounds under testing by drug companies, really cover all the possible new antidepressants on the market or in advanced clinical trial here or in Europe or Japan. I will therefore focus on the more recently marketed U.S. antidepressant drugs, trimipramine (Surmontil), amoxapine (Asendin), maprotiline (Ludiomil), and trazodone (Desyrel), plus alprazolam (Xanax), a benzodiazepine marketed for anxiety but with probable antidepressant efficacy. I will also discuss mianserin, nomifensine, bupropion (Wellbatrin), oxaprotiline, and synaptamine, investigational antidepressants known to me through review articles, meetings, or personal involvement in studies. This paper will cover both the available literature and our experiences at McLean Hospital in treating inpatients and outpatients with the various drugs mentioned.

Trimipramine

Trimipramine is an old drug in Europe, where it has been in wide clinical use for many years. It is new in the United States, where it was first marketed about three years ago. In most respects it is a quite standard tricyclic, and was developed so long ago that data on such issues as biogenic amine re-uptake, receptor binding, plasma concentrations, etc. were not available at the time it appeared in the U.S. This deficiency is now being corrected. It seems to be a relatively weak inhibitor of norepinephrine re-uptake with potent H_1 antihistamine effects (1). Like imipramine, it should have an active desmethyl metabolite, which might have other activities. It is moderately sedative, about like doxepin, and about as anticholinergic as imipramine (2). It is said not to affect REM sleep. Trimipramine has been the subject of several double-blind studies comparing it both with placebo, and with other standard tricyclics. It seems to be as safe and as effective as the other older drugs, with the same assets and liabilities as other tricyclics (3–5). Work is now under way to characterize the drug's properties in more depth; perhaps special advantages may appear. At the moment, it is considered a somewhat sedative tricyclic in the imipramine–doxepin range. It has been well tolerated in elderly depressions in an ongoing study at McLean. Trimipramine's special virtue is its reasonably extensive use in combination with monoamine oxidase inhibitors (6).

Amoxapine

This tricyclic antidepressant is new, developed mainly in the U.S., and is a metabolite of a potent antipsychotic, loxapine. Its pharmacology resembles that of the other tricyclic antidepressants with a couple of interesting exceptions. It is a dopamine-blocking agent and antagonizes the effects of d-amphetamine in laboratory animals; it also seems to have less effect on cardiac function in toxic dosages. Overdosage in humans is characterized by overactivity of the central nervous system and convulsions, but not cardiac arrhythmias. Its effects on biogenic amine re-uptake are said to resemble those of nortriptyline, affecting both norepinephrine and serotonin (7, 8).

Six studies reportedly show that amoxapine is superior to placebo in depression. The three studies available to me (9–11) bear this out. Two of these studies plus six others document that amoxapine is somewhat more rapid in its onset of action than is imipramine or amitriptyline (7–12). The effective dose of amoxapine is about twice that of the older tricyclics, and its side effects are roughly comparable with those of older tricyclics.

In a recent review of amoxapine's properties, Donlon (13) notes that the effective dose is about twice that of standard tricyclics, and that it is as effective as the older drugs. Its sedative and anticholinergic properties resemble those of imipramine, except that neurological, extrapyramidal side effects, predictable from the drug's neuroleptic action, are uncommon, although lactation, akathisia, and swollen tongue have been reported. Neither Donlon nor other reviewers are confidant that the claims of rapid onset of action are fully justified.

Cohen et al. *(14)* have recently reported that patients on therapeutic doses of amoxapine have plasma concentrations of neuroleptic, as measured by radioreceptor assay, quite comparable with those found in patients on loxapine. In vitro, amoxapine is as potent as loxapine by this method, and one of amoxapine's metabolites, 7-hydroxyamoxapine, is as potent as haloperidol. All this makes one afraid that patients on amoxapine will be at risk for developing tardive dyskinesia in the long run and extrapyramidal side effects in the shorter run.

I have now used amoxapine in more than 50 patients, with extraordinarily mixed results. Its effects are, or seem to be, far more variable from patient to patient than those of any other antidepressant I have used. A few, mainly treatment-resistant, patients have responded dramatically within a day or three, often showing an amphetamine-like psychic stimulation, even to the extent that the euphoria will wear off in a few hours and be re-established by a second dose. In other patients amoxapine is either markedly sedative or unpleasantly agitating, and has caused a sudden and remarkable surge of food craving in two bulimics. Nevertheless, I have found it useful in occasional treatment-resistant depressions where a rapid mood response was devoutly to be desired.

The longer-range problems with the drug, in my hands, have included the emergence of full-blown Parkinsonism and akathisia in a few patients, usually after they have been on the drug several weeks. Often by that time the stimulant effect has gone and the drug is sedative. One wonders whether the drug is not a stimulant antidepressant, conceivably by blocking presynaptic dopamine receptors, early in treatment, then shifts to being a neuroleptic later, with neurological side effects occurring after one or two months, late enough to have been missed in standard four-week controlled studies. I also have a strong, but unproven, suspicion that amoxapine responders will do very well for a month or two, after which their response gradually fades and no manipulation of dose, up or down, reinstates the improvement. In two patients, I have been able to get a second good response to the drug after they had been off it for three or more months. I have not found anticholinergic side effects a problem at all, perhaps because I have used the drug in low doses in outpatients. A logical but unproven implication of the drug's mixed tricyclic–neuroleptic pharmacology is that it might be the drug of choice in psychotic depressions and depressed schizoaffectives. This hypothesis has not been seriously tested, however. The marked stimulation seen in some patients early in treatment makes me fear that it will precipitate mania in some patients. I have heard of convulsions occurring during overdose in two local patients.

In summary, amoxapine is effective but odd, a neuroleptic as well as an antidepressant, sometimes but not reliably fast acting, highly variable in its sedative–stimulant profile, and low in anticholinergic effects. It may have less cardiac effects than older drugs in overdose but can cause hyperstimulation and seizures. It could cause tardive dyskinesia.

Maprotiline

Maprotiline, a tetracyclic antidepressant, widely used and extensively studied in Europe and recently marketed in the U.S., may, in fact, be less different from the tricyclics than some of the other new drugs, its fourth ring being attached like a handle to the center ring of a typical tricyclic structure. Nevertheless, this modification may fix or stabilize the molecule in a useful way.

Maprotiline is active in standard animal tests for tricyclic antidepressants. It has anticholinergic properties but probably less effect on cardiovascular systems than tricyclics. It blocks norepinephrine re-uptake but has no effect on serotonin re-uptake, a property that makes it most like desipramine among our older standard drugs. On the other hand, it does not potentiate amphetamine effects, whereas all tricyclics except amoxapine do. Maprotiline has antiaggression effects on several animal models, a unique property for an antidepressant. It increases REM sleep, whereas imipramine and amitriptyline reduce REM sleep. It is sedative in animals (15, 16).

In clinical trials at low dosages (usually 150 mg a day), in comparison with imipramine or amitriptyline at similar dosages, it was at least equally effective as imipramine in 12 studies involving over 600 patients and at least as effective as amitriptyline in 18 studies involving over 1000 patients. In three studies maprotiline was significantly superior to amitriptyline in clinical efficacy by one or more measures, and in one study amitriptyline was superior by one measure. In two studies maprotiline was clinically superior to imipramine in efficacy. In other studies maprotiline elicited significantly fewer side effects than amitriptyline (two studies) or imipramine (three studies).

Double-blind placebo-controlled studies carried out before the drug's marketing in the U.S. confirmed its efficacy in depression (17–19). As with amoxapine, several of the available controlled studies comparing maprotiline with imipramine and, less commonly, with amitriptyline, suggest a somewhat more rapid onset of clinical response in maprotiline-treated patients (20).

Clinically, we have found maprotiline to be a useful drug, probably a bit more sedative than desipramine and with anticholinergic effects intermediate to those of desipramine and imipramine. It may be less cardiotoxic than the older tricyclics. In our studies we found it works rapidly in patients with low concentrations of 24-h urinary 3-methoxy-4-hydroxyphenylglycol (21).

Maprotiline has been suspected of being more likely than older tricyclics to cause both skin rashes and grand mal seizures. The skin rashes are a minor problem in our hands, but we have encountered seizures in several patients, almost exclusively patients given more than 250 mg a day or who had a history of seizures or abnormal electroencephalograms. In one case, however, the seizure was almost certainly not due to abnormally high plasma concentrations of the drug: the patient's dose had been increased to 400 mg a day because his response at 300 mg was clearly subtherapeutic.

Oxaprotiline

This hydroxy derivative of maprotiline has been the subject of a multicenter double-blind study comparing it with amitriptyline and placebo (22). Oxaprotiline appears to be an effective antidepressant with very little sedative effect and few anticholinergic effects, except for an unexplained tendency to induce constipation.

Trazodone

The chemical structure of this drug, a 5-triazolo[4,3-a]pyridine, is unique, being unrelated to any existing psychoactive drug. It is inactive in standard animal screening tests for antidepressants. It antagonizes the effects of amphetamine in animals and has alpha-adrenergic blocking activity. Although it is a serotonin antagonist peripherally, trazodone potentiates serotonin activity in the brain. It is a weak but highly selective inhibitor of serotonin re-uptake, and is without anticholinergic effects in animals (23, 24).

The drug, discovered by an Italian firm in 1967, was originally studied as an anti-anxiety agent. European studies (involving small numbers of patients) suggest that the drug is equal to amitriptyline (two studies) and equal to imipramine (two studies). One study showed it to be superior to placebo in patients with mixed anxiety and depression; another showed it equivalent to desipramine in patients primarily diagnosed as endogenously depressed. In the latter study desipramine worsened anxiety symptoms while trazodone improved them. One Italian study, involving very high dosages of trazodone (mean, 468 mg a day by the third week), found trazodone to be slightly less effective than imipramine. A Canadian study found trazodone equivalent to amitriptyline in depressed patients (23).

In a recently completed 10-hospital double-blind four-week study involving 263 depressed patients, trazodone was compared with imipramine and placebo (25). Both trazodone (47% improved) and imipramine (57% improved) were superior to placebo (25% improved). Trazodone had significantly fewer anticholinergic side effects, about one-third as many as did imipramine, but was twice as likely to cause sedation. Neurological side effects were also three times as common on imipramine as on trazodone.

Two parallel controlled studies in "neurotic" depressed outpatients, in which trazodone, amitriptyline, and placebo were compared, found trazodone significantly superior to placebo (26); one study found trazodone superior to placebo on more measures than for amitriptyline (27). In the two outpatient studies differences in anticholinergic side effects between trazodone and amitriptyline were not detected by physicians' ratings, but patients' ratings in one study indicated a significant difference in favor of trazodone.

In a double-blind one-year study of outpatients, comparing imipramine with trazodone, more patients did well on trazodone than on imipramine (28). In a recent study in elderly depressions (29), trazodone and imipramine were both more effective than placebo; more imipramine-treated patients dropped out of the study, however, and imipramine caused more anticholinergic side effects.

At McLean, we administered trazodone to 26 patients with primary or secondary depressions who had failed to improve on or failed to be able to tolerate previous treatment courses with standard antidepressants (a mean of nine prior unsuccessful trials of tricyclics, monoamine oxidase inhibitors, lithium, or electroconvulsive therapy per patient). Three patients were also unable to tolerate trazodone, but of the others, 45% improved within the first four weeks and 63% within three months. Anticholinergic side effects were essentially absent (present in only one patient). Sedation occurred in 43% of the trials but was easily handled by dosage adjustment. A few patients reported headaches and dizziness (30).

Trazodone seems to have minimal effects on the cardiovascular system at conventional dosages. It occasionally causes brief postural hypotension about an hour after an oral dose if taken on an empty stomach, but no sustained hypotension of the type seen with tricyclics occurs. A recent Food and Drug Administration (FDA) warning was issued after a confusing study in which patients with pre-existing cardiac disease were given trazodone. Holter monitor records, scored before and after trazodone administration, showed increased numbers of premature ventricular contractions in some of the trazodone-treated patients; others showed fewer. The meaning of this "finding" is obscure.

Minimal data exist on the number of suicidal or accidental overdoses with trazodone. What there is looks reassuring: a number of patients have survived large overdoses when trazodone was taken alone, and only sedation was a consequence. Better data would be helpful, but my guess is that trazodone is safer in overdose than other currently marketed antidepressants, if taken alone.

In my clinical experience with trazodone since it has been commercially available, some mildly depressed outpatients feel remarkably improved on rather low doses (100–150 mg a day), with few or no side effects and early (within three to five days) response. This may, of course, be a placebo effect, but I doubt it. The most frequent limiting side effect of the drug is sedation, but in a few patients it doesn't even improve sleep. "Anticholinergic" side effects do occur—patients occasionally have marked dry mouth, constipation, and urinary problems, but this is less common than in patients on tricyclics and must be an alpha-adrenergic or serotonergic effect, because trazodone otherwise lacks anticholinergic properties. Three of my patients have had trazodone-induced difficulties with memory and concentration; again, this effect looks, but can't be, anticholinergic.

In summary, trazodone is a useful, somewhat sedative nontricyclic antidepressant that is often well tolerated and effective in patients who don't tolerate or respond to tricyclics. It may be preferable in patients at risk for suicidal overdosing and may be better tolerated as a maintainance therapy.

Nomifensine

Nomifensine, a tetrahydroisoquinoline, has three phenol rings, but they are arranged quite differently from standard tricyclic antidepressants. In animal testing, nomifensine has not only the actions of conventional antidepressants but also clear amphetamine-like effects on activity and stereotypy in animals. Hence, it is not surprising that the drug is an inhibitor of dopamine re-uptake as well as of norepinephrine. It has little effect on serotonin re-uptake. Nomifensine has low anticholinergic activity in animals. Its cardiovascular effects are less pronounced than those of the standard tricyclics. In quantitative electroencephalograms of humans, nomifensine resembles desipramine in its effects (31).

In depressed patients receiving between 75 and 225 mg a day, nomifensine is more effective than placebo. Two brief crossover studies showed that after only one week nomifensine was superior to placebo. Three American studies, two in depressed outpatients and one in depressed geriatric outpatients, have all shown the drug to be significantly better than placebo, by the 10th day in one study and by the third week in the other two (32). The drug was said to have been especially good in reducing symptoms of retardation and anergia and improving ratings of cognitive functioning, but data were not presented.

At least 17 controlled studies have compared nomifensine with standard tricyclic antidepressants. In two studies it was significantly less effective than the standard drugs (doxepin and imipramine), and tended to show less efficacy than imipramine in two others. On the other hand, it produced more improvement (global ratings) than amitriptyline in one study, relieved anxiety in depressed patients better than desipramine in another study, and was more effective than imipramine in a third. The remaining studies showed equivalent effectiveness for both nomifensine and the standard drug, usually at comparable dosages (31–33).

In overdose with suicidal intent, convulsions can occur but serious cardiovascular changes are not observed. Sedation, coma, and excitement do appear (31).

In humans, nomifensine has a half-life of about 2 h. It has active metabolites, which also seem to have short half-lives. This should make serious adverse effects fade rapidly but also suggests that frequent daily dosages are more essential than with most standard antidepressants. However, three studies (two uncontrolled) support the idea that a single daily dose of nomifensine is effective (34).

Pohl and Gershon, in a recent review of nomifensine (35), agree that nomifensine has been shown to be an effective antidepressant without anticholinergic, sedative, or cardiac side effects and without effect on seizure threshold in laboratory animals. It does not affect psychological or psychomotor performance in normal individuals (36), and overdose has not been associated with serious cardiovascular side effects or convulsions. It is at present not clear when this interesting drug will become available in the U.S.

Mianserin

This new drug has four rings and thus is technically "tetracyclic," but bears little resemblance to maprotiline; it is a tetracyclic piperazino-azepine. On initial pharmacological testing it showed behavioral effects but none to clearly identify it as any specific type of psychoactive drug. In laboratory animals it behaves like neither a tricyclic antidepressant nor a monoamine oxidase inhibitor (37, 38). Studied in migraine patients, because of its

Periactin (cyproheptadine)-like antihistamine properties, it relieved depression in a few headache patients. Its effects on the quantitative electroencephalogram in normal subjects resembled those of amitriptyline (39). Consequently, it was tried in depressed patients and has proved useful. Mianserin decreases brain concentrations of norepinephrine while increasing the turnover of norepinephrine, a set of actions opposite to those of the tricyclics. It does not block re-uptake of norepinephrine or serotonin. Mianserin, a potent inhibitor of histamine-sensitive adenylate cyclase, antagonizes the central hypotensive effect of clonidine but does not interfere with the hypotensive action of guanethidine, effects with which tricyclics do interfere. Mianserin is less cardiotoxic in animals than are the tricyclics or maprotiline. Anticholinergic effects in animals and normal volunteers are essentially absent. This drug is clearly sedative. Its half-life is 10 to 17 hours. Brogden et al. (37) suggest that effective plasma concentrations of mianserin in humans are < 70 ng/mL.

Mianserin has been studied fairly extensively in controlled double-blind studies (37–40), being compared with amitriptyline in 11 studies, and in one case, with Limbitrol (an amitriptyline–chlordiazepoxide combination). In 10 of the studies, the two drugs were equal in efficacy; in the one study involving elderly depressions, mianserin was more effective than amitriptyline. In eight of these studies mianserin had fewer side effects.

Mianserin was compared with imipramine in four studies, two of which also included a placebo group. In all studies the two antidepressants were comparable in efficacy, and in one of the placebo-controlled studies, but not the other, both drugs were more effective than placebo. In two of the studies mianserin caused more side effects, particularly drowsiness, than did imipramine. Mianserin, generally at dosages of 60 mg a day (20 mg of mianserin is about equivalent to 50 mg of amitriptyline), causes more early sedation than either amitriptyline or imipramine. In two studies comparing mianserin with benzodiazepines, mianserin was more effective in relieving depression. During a large (340 patient) open trial in Switzerland, 80% of the depressed patients had "good" or "excellent" outcomes. In a recent study in outpatient elderly depressed patients, mianserin was as effective as amitriptyline and more effective than placebo but lacked amitriptyline's effects of mild impairment of tests of cognition and memory (41).

Mianserin taken alone in overdose has not resulted in death and seems to cause mainly drowsiness, without eliciting convulsions or serious cardiotoxicity. It does not prevent recurrence in bipolar patients and may produce mania; six of 10 bipolar patients who were shifted from lithium to mianserin became manic within a three-month period (42).

Mianserin seems to be a safe, reasonably effective sedative antidepressant with minimal anticholinergic and cardiac effects and a complex and different profile of pharmacological actions. It is at present unclear whether mianserin will soon become available in the U.S.; it is widely used in Europe. An analog, synaptamine, currently in clinical trial in the U.S., appears to be less sedative than mianserin.

Alprazolam

Alprazolam is a benzodiazepine with a triazolo group attached to the central ring. It resembles diazepam in animal tests, being generally much more potent but only slightly more toxic. It has anti-anxiety effects in mice and rats (open field test, conditioned suppression), and increases beta activity in electroencephalograms of animals and man. It is a muscle relaxant, but no more so than diazepam, and induces sleep, but only at higher dosages. An anticonvulsant, it can cause barbiturate-type physical dependence in animals but shows only limited cross-dependence with phenobarbital. To achieve physical dependence, very high and very frequent dosages are required. Alprazolam is not active in standard tests for antidepressants or antipsychotics. It has no anticholinergic properties. In short, there is no reason to expect that alprazolam would have antidepressant properties except that it shares its triazolo group with trazodone, another atypical apparent antidepressant (43).

Alprazolam, developed initially as an anti-anxiety drug (43, 44), was marketed in 1982 for use in generalized anxiety in doses ranging from 0.25 mg three times daily to an upper limit of 4 mg a day. Roughly 1 mg of alprazolam is equivalent to 10 mg of diazepam in anti-anxiety effect. During the multi-center controlled trials, the manufacturer's staff noted that alprazolam looked a bit better than diazepam overall and was significantly better than diazepam in patients diagnosed as "mixed anxiety and depression." This observation led to a series of controlled and uncontrolled studies of alprazolam in depression. Although much of this work is unpublished, the studies tend to show that 3 mg of alprazolam is as effective as 150 mg of imipramine in outpatient depressions and causes fewer side effects. The one published study by Rickels et al. *(45)* agrees in general with this, but the high rate of placebo response in their study obscured many drug effects. Chouinard et al. *(44)* have found alprazolam efficacious in panic disorders, in which conventional benzodiazepines are usually ineffective but antidepressants are useful.

In our experience at McLean, evaluating alprazolam in treatment-resistant depressed inpatients and outpatients, the drug is clinically an antidepressant. About a third of the patients treated show a clear and often striking improvement in their depression, of an order rarely seen with other benzodiazepines. Some patients require 6–8 mg to respond; others can't tolerate doses exceeding 2 mg a day without overwhelming sedation. The responders, at high or low dosages, are often remarkably unsedated by the drug. Side effects other than sedation are rare; occasionally, patients have become agitated when being tapered off the drug and have required a shift to a benzodiazepine (with a longer half-life) for this purpose.

In summary, alprazolam does seem to have a place in the treatment of depression, sometimes being very effective. It has no common side effects other than sedation and is now available in pharmacies, albeit for use in generalized anxiety. A lingering worry exists about the potential for physical dependency of the benzodiazepine type.

Bupropion

Bupropion is a novel unicyclic developed in the search for a drug that could pass the then-usual antidepressant screening tests but lack anticholinergic and cardiovascular effects. Bupropion, an aminoketone, not only meets these criteria, but also is nonsedating and appears not to be associated with the long-term weight gain often seen with the older antidepressants. Several multi-center double-blind studies have been completed but not published. One, by Zung et al., is in press *(48)* and confirms the drug's antidepressant efficacy. Although the drug has an amphetamine-like structure, it was not judged euphoriant when compared with *d*-amphetamine in a group of casual drug abusers *(49)*. It seems to be well tolerated and useful in maintainance therapy in depressed patients intolerant of tricyclic antidepressants *(50)*. It is rumored that bupropion was approved as effective by the FDA's Psychopharmacology Advisory Committee; such an action does not commit the FDA to release the drug, but does suggest that the drug might become available before too long.

Bupropion, is a novel, nonsedative antidepressant with low side effects but no clear mechanism of action. Its effect on dopamine re-uptake appears to occur at too high a concentration in plasma to explain its antidepressant properties.

Conclusions

Although there are other new antidepressants I have not covered in this paper (e.g., Zimelidine, an Astra drug with specific inhibition of serotonin re-uptake; Fluoxetine, a Lilly drug with similar properties; Deprenyl, a Hungarian monoamine oxidase inhibitor specific to the enzyme MAO_B and noninducive of "cheese" reactions), even the ones discussed here greatly expand clinicians' range of possible choices in treating either fresh or treatment-resistant depressions. In fact, there are now enough new drugs and possible drug combinations for an inventive psychopharmacologist to spend several years trying to find the "right" drug for a completely treatment-resistant patient, thereby providing hope and support if not a cure.

Of the available drugs now marketed in the U.S., trazodone and alprazolam seem the most "different"—in the good sense. Amoxapine is also very different, but its neuroleptic properties are worrisome. Maprotiline is a good and effective drug but not markedly different from the older tricyclics; trimipramine, though clearly effective, has yet to find a unique niche.

References

1. Baldessarini R. Overview of recent advances in antidepressant pharmacology: Part II. *McLean Hosp J* **7**, 1–27 (1982).
2. Cole JO, Schatzberg AF. Antidepressant drug therapy. To be pre-

sented at the American Psychiatric Association meeting, New York, NY, May, 1983. (In press.)

3. Pauker N. Trimipramine: A safe, effective antidepressant. *Psychiatr Ann* **11**, 18–20 (1981).
4. Settle E, Ayd F. Trimipramine: Twenty years' worldwide clinical experience. *J Clin Psychiatry* **41**, 266–274 (1980).
5. Rickels K, Gordon P, Weise C, et al. Amitriptyline and trimipramine in neurotic depressed outpatients: A collaborative study. *Am J Psychiatry* **127**, 208–218 (1970).
6. White K, Simpson G. Combined MAOI–tricyclic antidepressant treatment: A reevaluation. *J Clin Psychopharmacol* **1**, 264–282 (1981).
7. Amoxapine: A new tricyclic antidepressant. *Int Drug Ther Newsl* **15**, 33–40 (1980).
8. Donlon P, Biertuemphel H, Willenbring M. Amoxapine and amitriptyline in the outpatient treatment of endogenous depression. *J Clin Psychiatry* **42**, 11–51 (1981).
9. Smith R. Amoxapine, imipramine and placebo in depressive illness. *Curr Ther Res* **18**, 346–353 (1975).
10. Fabre L, McLendon D, Gainey A. Double-blind placebo-controlled comparison of amoxapine and imipramine in depressed outpatients. *Curr Ther Res* **22**, 611–619 (1977).
11. Wilson I, Loosen P, Pettus C, et al. A double-blind comparison of amoxapine, imipramine and placebo in the treatment of depression. *Curr Ther Res* **22**, 620–627 (1977).
12. Kiev A, Okerson L. Comparison of the therapeutic efficacy of amoxapine with that of imipramine. *Clin Trials J* **16**, 68–72 (1979).
13. Donlon P. Amoxapine: A newly marketed tricyclic antidepressant. *Psychiatr Ann* **11**, 23–27 (1981).
14. Cohen B, Harris P, Altesman R, Cole J. Amoxapine: Neuroleptic as well as antidepressant? *Am J Psychiatry* **139**, 1165–1167 (1982).
15. Pinder R, Brogden R, Speight T, Avery G. Maprotiline: A review of its pharmacological properties and therapeutic efficacy in mental depressive states. *Drugs* **13**, 321–287 (1977).
16. Wells BG, Gelenberg AJ. Chemistry, pharmacology, pharmacokinetics, adverse effects and efficacy of the antidepressant maprotiline hydrochloride. *Pharmacotherapy* **1**, 121–139 (1981).
17. Claghorn JL. Study of maprotiline (Ludiomil) and imipramine in depressed outpatients. *Curr Ther Res* **22**, 446–452 (1977).
18. Logue JN, Sachais BA, Feighner JP. Comparisons of maprotiline with imipramine in severe depression: A multicenter controlled trial. *J Clin Pharmacol* **19**, 64–74 (1979).
19. Van der Velde C. Maprotiline versus imipramine and placebo in neurotic depression. *J Clin Psychiatry* **42**, 138–141 (1981).

20. Silverstone T. The relative speed of onset of the antidepressant effect of maprotiline. In *New Directions in Antidepressants: Ludiomil,* FF Flach, Ed., Excerpta Medica, Princeton, 1981, pp 39–44.

21. Schatzberg A, Cole J. Maprotiline: A review of its biochemical and pharmacological properties. Presented at the Cornell Medical Center, 1981.

22. Roffman M, Gould EE, Brewer SJ, et al. A double-blind comparative study of oxaprotiline with amitriptyline and placebo in moderate depression. *Curr Ther Res* 32, 247–256 (1982).

23. Ayd F. Trazodone: A unique broad spectrum antidepressant. *Int Drug Ther Newsl* 14, 33–40 (1979).

24. Riblet L, Taylor D. Pharmacology and neurochemistry of trazodone. *J Clin Psychopharmacol* 1, 17.S–22.S (1981).

25. Gershon S, Mann J, Newton R, Gunther B. Evaluation of trazodone in the treatment of endogenous depression: Results of a multicenter double-blind study. *J Clin Psychopharmacol* 1, 39.S–44.S (1981).

26. Goldberg H, Finnerty R. Trazodone in the treatment of neurotic depression. *J Clin Psychiatry* 41, 430–434 (1980).

27. Goldberg H, Rickels K, Finnerty R. Treatment of neurotic depession with a new antidepressant. *J Clin Psychopharmacol* 1, 35.S–38.S (1981).

28. Feighner JP, Merideth C, Hendrickson G. Maintenance antidepressant therapy: A double-blind comparison of trazodone and imipramine. *J Clin Psychopharmacol* 1, 45.S–48.S (1981).

29. Gerner R, Estabrook W, Steuer J, Jarvik L. Treatment of geriatric depressions with trazodon, imipramine and placebo: A double-blind study. *J Clin Psychiatry* 41, 216–220 (1980).

30. Cole JO, Schatzberg A, Sniffin C, et al. Trazodone in treatment-resistant depression: An open study. *J Clin Psychopharmacol* 1, 49.S–54.S (1981).

31. Brogden R, Heel R, Speight T, Avery G. Nomifensine: A review of its pharmacological properties and therapeutic efficacy in depressive illness. *Drugs* 18, 1–24 (1979).

32. Matz R. Clinical trials with nomifensine in the U.S.A. In *Nomifensine* (R. Soc. of Med., Int. Cong. and Symp. Ser., No. 25), Grune and Stratton, New York, NY, 1980, pp 73–80.

33. *Op. cit.,* entire volume.

34. Hanks G, Magnus R, Myskova I, Mathur G. Antidepressants in single daily doses: Studies with nomifensine. *Ibid.,* pp 87–94.

35. Pohl R, Gershon S. Nomifensine: A new antidepressant. *Psychiatr Ann* 11, 39–43 (1981).

36. Taeuber K, Zapf R, Rupp W, Badian M. Pharmacodynamic comparison of the acute effects of nomifensine, amphetamine and placebo in healthy volunteers. *Int J Clin Pharmacol Biochem* 17, 32–35 (1979).

37. Brogden R, Heel R, Speight T, Avery G. Mianserin: A review of its pharmacological properties and therapeutic efficacy in depressive illness. *Drugs* **16**, 273–301 (1978).
38. Peet M, Behagel H. Mianserin: A decade of scientific development. *Br J Clin Pharmacol* **5** (Suppl 1), 51–91 (1978).
39. Itil T, Pulvan N, Hsu W. Clinical and EEG effects of GB94, a tetracyclic antidepressant. *Curr Ther Res* **14**, 395–413 (1972).
40. Drykoningen G, Rees W, Ogara C, Eds. *Progress in the Pharmacotherapy of Depressions,* Excerpta Medica, Amsterdam, 1979.
41. Branconnier R, Cole J, Ghazvinian S, Rosenthal S. Treating the depressed elderly patient: The comparative behavioral pharmacology of mianserin and amitriptyline. In *Typical and Atypical Antidepressants: Clinical Practice,* Raven Press, New York, NY, 1982, pp 195–212.
42. Coppen A, Ghose K, Rama RV, Peet M. Mianserin in the prophylactic treatment of bipolar affective illness. *Int Pharmacopsychiatry* **12**, 95–99 (1977).
43. Investigators' brochure, Upjohn Co., Kalamazoo, MI, 1981.
44. Chouinard G, Annable L, Fontaine R, Solyom L. Alprazolam in the treatment of generalized anxiety and panic disorders: A double-blind placebo controlled study. *Psychopharmacology* **77**, 229–233 (1982).
45. Rickels K, Cohen D, Csanalosi I, et al. Alprazolam and imipramine in depressed outpatients: A controlled study. *Curr Ther Res* **32**, 157–164 (1982).
46. Soroko FE, Mehta NB, Maxwell RA, et al. Bupropion hydrochloride [*(dl)* α-*tert*-butylamino-3-chloropropiophenone HCl]: A novel antidepressant agent. *J Pharm Pharmacol* **29**, 767–770 (1977).
47. Ferris RM, Cooper BR, Maxwell RA. Studies concerning the mechanism of the antidepressant activity of buproprion. *J Clin Psychiatry* (1983) (in press).
48. Zung WWK, Brodie HKH, Fabre L, et al. Comparative efficacy and safety of bupropion and placebo in the treatment of depression. *Psychopharmacology* (1983) (in press).
49. Miller L, Griffith J. A comparison of bupropion, dextroamphetamine and placebo in mixed substance abusers. *Psychopharmacology* (1983) (in press).
50. Gardner EA. Bupropion: Long-term preventative care in depressed patients intolerant to tricyclic antidepressants. Scientific Exhibit, American Psychiatric Association annual meeting, 1982, Toronto, Canada.

Discussion—Session III

QUESTION: Please comment on the adjunctive use of tryptophan to maximize lithium in partial responders.

DR. FIEVE: Some scanty data in the old literature suggest lithium as an antidepressant, but it never really panned out to be so, by most of the controlled studies. In a study we did on lithium plus nardil, the lithium potentiated monoamine oxidase (MAO) inhibitor action. Numerous clinicians use tryptophan as a sleep-inducing amino acid.

DR. POTTER: We have not been impressed by the clinical efficacy of adding tryptophan; the biochemical changes, if any, are very unpredictable. The range of tryptophan dose used is probably critical, because at one level the tryptophan will block the uptake of tyrosine into the central nervous system and thereby alter norepinephrine metabolism.

Q: What effect does lithium carbonate have on seizure threshold, and please compare its mechanism with the use of carbamazepine?

DR. FIEVE: Lithium traditionally lowers the seizure threshold. We did a study on that, in the early 1960s, and found about 10 to 15% of manic-depressives had an altered electroencephalogram to begin with. This is pretty close to the proportion in the normal population. Lithium altered the seizure threshold in these patients even more.

Tegretol (carbamazepine) is another drug still in the experimental stage. A couple of studies from Japan suggested that carbamazepine may have some prophylactic value in manic depression. The mechanism of action is still just speculative; certainly no clinical trial on that has held up, as far as I am concerned. Some studies at NIMH showed that carbamazepine did affect manic-depressive cyclical phases. I have used Tegretol on manic-depressive patients who had failed on lithium, and I am not, frankly, that impressed with it. It is certainly not a drug of choice. If I have a rapid-cycling patient who has failed on all the easier treatments, I may try it, but there are certain hazards. You have got to monitor blood concentrations repeatedly, and the drug does produce an agranulocytosis. I think its future as a treatment modality is limited.

Q: Would you comment further on the use of lithium in premenstrual depression syndrome? Is it necessary to achieve the same blood concentrations as for bipolar illness, or is 300 mg a day or so effective?

DR. FIEVE: In the early 1960s a study was published on lithium and its effectiveness in premenstrual tension. Lithium modified the depressed, whining, angry, irritable state that certain women encounter periodically every 28 days, beginning three or four days before the menstrual period and lasting into it, then disappearing. A later study, however, could not really corroborate those results. Anecdotally, I have gotten responses from women who came in, first and foremost, as manic-depressives, but then related in their history that they also had premenstrual depression syndrome; in that group of patients I have had some very excellent results. But this is a select group of patients who have, primarily, an affective disorder with major highs and lows and, secondarily, 28-day premenstrual depression syndrome. I have no data on patients with primary premenstrual depression syndrome but without the affective disorder. In addition, no one has done a really well-designed double-blind study with diuretics vs hormone treatment vs lithium in patients with premenstrual depression syndrome. It should be done; it would be a very important study. But there are no solid data on that as of today.

Q: What is the duration of lithium treatment?

DR. FIEVE: I prefer to play down the duration of lithium treatment with patients. They almost always ask me, "Do I have to be on this forever?" I do not think anybody can really tell a patient that. When dealing with a young woman or man in the early twenties, who has had a single episode or attack, I tell the patient and the family that, after this is over, we will taper the lithium dose off. If a patient has had two or more attacks, serious ones, then I usually want to give the drug prophylactically—which I discuss with the patient and the family. No one can say forever, but we have found that most patients in this age bracket who have had two or more attacks, particularly serious ones, such that they went into the hospital with mania or depression, will have recurring attacks throughout their lifetime.

Q: Please comment about the nephrotoxicity of lithium and its implications.

DR. FIEVE: Three to five years ago, there was what we call the lithium scare, when several publications from Denmark reported histological studies on patients who had died of lithium poisoning; these findings seemed to indicate an interstitial nephritis, actual damage to kidney tissue. Because we were alarmed, we started working with creatinine clearances in patients we were treating with lithium. I really want to mention this to you in the clinical laboratory, because after working with creatinine clearance for about a year, we gave it up as totally useless as an outpatient test. (As an inpatient test it is another matter; it certainly has value when you can control the measurement of the patient's 24-h urine.) We then switched to monitoring serum creatinine; in about 100 patients whom I had had on lithium for as long as 25 years, we checked their serum creatinine values over the past five to 10 years. Only four of those patients had a slightly increased concentration of serum creatinine, which led me to doubt that lithium was doing any serious damage to the kidneys. Subsequently, I think we can conclude that certainly lithium causes functional changes: it causes polyuria, and it creates a concentrating defect in the kidney that does not correct itself as soon as lithium is no longer given. But as far as lithium's doing substantial damage to the kidneys, so that you would change how you give it to a well patient or alter how much you give, I do not think there is any good evidence for this.

What we can say is that you must monitor kidney function closely. You must first get a history of kidney disease. Patients who have had previous kidney damage are high risk for lithium nephrotoxicity. Those patients who have had serious lithium poisonings, where they have gone up to 1.8, 2.5 mmol/L, and so forth, are a high-risk group. We now think it may be better not to give all the lithium at night because of lithium peaking; that may have some risk factor connected with it.

Q: Would measuring lithium in erythrocytes be a better indicator of a patient's status?

DR. FIEVE: Measurements of erythrocyte/plasma ratios of lithium were very popular about six or seven years ago. The current situation is essentially that the erythrocyte/plasma ratio index for lithium has no relationship to diagnosis or to predictive ability of whether the patient will be a lithium responder or not. However, it has some value in patients who are lithium-toxic. High plasma lithium seems to increase the concentration of intracellular lithium substantially. Perhaps this is a good indicator, particularly if it helps identify the course of the resolution of the toxicity better than the plasma concentration of lithium. Measurement of erythrocyte lithium may be of some research value, certainly, and perhaps also of some value in severe lithium poisoning.

DR. POTTER: If I understand correctly, there is a subpopulation of people who will achieve very high erythrocyte concentrations of lithium. This may be under some sort of genetic control, so that a certain fraction of the population will have an atypical response. Dr. Fieve, do you have any idea what fraction of the population would be in this subgroup?

DR. FIEVE: No, but one study did show that the erythrocyte/plasma lithium ratio is determined by genetic expression. Probably this is related to the number of transport sites located on the cell membrane, which varies from individual to individual. The ratio is constant in the individual patient over time, but there is tremendous interindividual variation in the erythrocyte/plasma ratio. Therefore, in a group of people, some will have high ratios and some will have low ratios. To date I do not believe this subset with high ratios have turned out to be better lithium responders than other patients with lower ratios.

Q: Please comment on the use of tryptophan and pyridoxin in atypical depression with or without use of MAO inhibitors.

DR. COLE: A few studies show that L-tryptophan is, in fact, better than placebo in outpatient depression. Most of the studies throw in something else—pyridoxin or some anti-gout medication to try to decrease liver metabolism of tryptophan. I have used tryptophan clinically when I do not know what else to do, or sometimes to try to avoid using a real hypnotic. Every now and then someone gets a little better. I tend not to use the adjuvants. One of my patients on lithium and tryptophan was a brittle, borderline depressive, obsessional woman. She clearly feels better on one to one-and-a-half 500-mg tryptophan pills a day, which must be titrated very carefully, plus lithium, and she has been doing fine for two years. I tend to think maybe it works; you occasionally find a responder.

Q: Please expand on the effect of tricyclics in worsening certain depressions.

DR. POTTER: This issue is directed to a subset of rapid cyclers, whom the clinical research centers are seeing more and more. In a subset of bipolar patients, tricyclics actually produce clear signs and symptoms of worsening. Another big question is the case of using lithium alone—is it good enough? In an extended Italian series, in which 450 cyclic patients were studied, about one-fourth clearly had worsening of their cycling illness associated with tricyclic use.[1] This was quite clear, and I do not think it needs to be reproven.

Q: Would you comment on the pretreatment use of determining MAO activities in children and adults with attention-deficit disorder, in dysthymic, endogenously depressed patients?

DR. COLE: Dr. Schildkraut, who has the most baseline data on platelet MAO and depression, found that a high MAO activity correlates with features of atypical depression. Otherwise, it has no predictor validity and is generally used only if you want to see when people get to 80% inhibition. As far as I know, it has no confirmed predictive value for anything. I do not know much about attention-deficit disorder children on MAO inhibitors; I do not know if anybody has tried those. My experience is that a patient who fails on a tricyclic and has a clear endogenous depression is likely to do well on an MAO inhibitor.

Q: Would you comment on the addictive potential of alprazolam?

DR. COLE: The manufacturer says that anxious patients on alprazolam at 2 mg or so a day, for as long as a year, stopped without withdrawal effects. Some people on a higher dose had trouble getting off the drug because they got pretty jumpy and restless. I have not seen a full-blown barbiturate-type withdrawal syndrome, but it is worth watching for. This being a relatively short half-life drug, a couple of my patients have had trouble getting off of it, but when I shifted them to Tranxene, which has a longer half-life, they came off more easily.

DR. POTTER: One of our patients had seizures coming off of this drug. I think it carries a risk of this problem during withdrawal.

[1] Kukopulos A, Reginaldi D, Laeldomada P, et al. Course of the manic-depressive cycle and changes caused by treatments. *Pharmakopsychiatry* 13, 156–167 (1980).

Q: Please comment on methodologies for measuring MAO inhibitors.

DR. ORSULAK: MAO inhibitors per se are not measured. Several older studies involved attempts to measure plasma concentrations of phenelzine or acetylphenelzine and some of the other drugs. Clinical effect is not related to plasma concentration of the drugs per se, because they are essentially irreversible MAO inhibitors. They are bound to the enzyme, and their circulating concentration in plasma, once that binding occurs, is not related to clinical effect.

In some cases inhibition of platelet MAO is monitored by measuring platelet MAO rather than the concentration of the drug itself. Thus one is measuring the pharmacological effect. To date, the only way to do that has been a radiometric assay for platelet MAO. We obviously cannot measure MAO in the brain, so we measure it in the peripheral source, platelets. Some time in the last year or so, an HPLC procedure for the measurement of MAO activity was published, in which the product of the enzyme reaction, rather than the uptake of a radiometric substrate, was measured. Additional work is going on to develop new methodologies for this, but so far the radiometric assay is still used in virtually all cases.

DR. POTTER: A good point in the paper by Klein and Quitkin was that Deprenyl, which in low doses is a selective MAO_B inhibitor, markedly inhibits platelet MAO, independent of clinical outcome. Inhibition of MAO_B, the form found in platelets, is therefore not clearly associated with response. Probably the MAO_A enzyme is the more important form. If I were to bet money on a clinically relevant variable, I would come back to the time-honored 3-methoxy-4-hydroxyphenylglycol (MHPG), because in this particular instance, inhibition of MAO_A will reduce the urinary MHPG. One observes about an 80% decrease of urinary MHPG with inhibition of MAO_A. To study the relationship between enzyme inhibition and response, one should be following the concentration of MHPG, not the platelet MAO.

Organ-Specific Representation and Neuropepetides in Central Autonomic Functions: A Prospect for Pharmacotherapy

Harvey J. Karten

The field of biological psychiatry has emerged as a dynamic branch of medicine after many years of uncertain status. As young residents in psychiatry, more than 20 years ago, we were equipped with our wits, a naive understanding of psychodynamics, and a strong belief in the value of ideas as our most powerful of tools. In those days, biological psychiatry was, by current parlance, an alternative life style; at best it seemed a socially acceptable euphemism for electroshock and the use of three or four drugs that were, often distressingly, more effective in the treatment of psychotic patients than were our hardest sought insights. The role of the brain in behavior was more allegorical than tangible.

The availability of a new series of drugs for the treatment of severe psychiatric disorders altered the character of clinical psychiatry for all time. "Tranquilizers" and psychotropic drugs profoundly affect behavior; their action on the central nervous system is indisputable. The prospect of developing a biological psychiatry based on an understanding of the biology and biochemistry of the brain is ever more tantalizing. Yet even now, more than 20 years after these drugs were introduced, we still have only a fragmentary concept of how and where such drugs exert their actions. One of the most striking features of many of these drugs, however, is the inseparability of behavioral effects from the effects on autonomic functions. In many fields of medical practice, "psychotropic" drugs have been recognized as effective tools for exploring and regulating cardiovascular, pulmonary, exocrine secretory, and other autonomic and basal ganglionic functions. Indeed, one of the most persistent problems has been the lack of pharmacologic agents that exert a "purely behavioral" effect. We might suggest several reasons for this difficulty:

1. The commonality of occurrence of various transmitters and receptors in several unrelated systems is so widespread that any drug that alters a particular transmitter or receptor provokes changes in all systems. "Selective or preferential" effects may be attributable to quantitative differences in the occurrence of particular transmitters, receptors, or receptors subtypes.

2. The systems are inseparable, and the behavioral system "requires" the autonomic system for its integrated output.

3. There is no such thing as a "purely behavioral" effect. Behavior is so essential a product of the nervous system that it does not and cannot exist separate of all the individual neural circuits that keep an organism alive and functional.

One of the persistent obstacles, however, in attempts to formulate a neurobiological hypothesis of affective states is the lack of a concept of the physiological nature of emotions. Though we generally agree that affective states include a sense of awareness of our "visceral responses" to various situations, it is not at all clear whether such visceral awareness *is* the emotional state, *confirms and reinforces* the emotional state, or is merely *epiphenomenal* to emotional states. The classical neurobiological approach to this problem has been to identify those areas of the brain most directly involved in the control of autonomic and neuroendocrine functions. Fortunately for those of us involved in research on the brain, they happen to be areas that are also profoundly affected by almost all "psychotropic" drugs.

Identification of the particular neural circuits mediating the central and peripheral neural control of visceral organs is essential to understanding the mechanism of action of psychotropic drugs upon the autonomic nervous system. The dorsal motor nucleus of the vagal nerve (DMN) and its associated sensory nucleus of the tractus solitarius (nTS) are major links between the brain and periphery, regulating the functions of cardiopulmonary, gastrointestinal, and several endocrine and exocrine systems. Our knowledge is still distressingly sparse regarding the nature of the visceral sensory information conveyed to the rostral neuraxis and its precise zone of termination. Conversely, does the DMN-nTS receive inputs from hypothalamic and caudal brainstem structures? Do these inputs terminate on organ-specific subsets of the

DMN-nTS—i.e., do certain hypothalamic neurons control selected viscera? If so, are they ending on sensory, internuncial, or motor neurons of the DMN-nTS? Are they excitatory or inhibitory? What are the specific transmitters/peptides or trophic substances contained within these pathways?

In the past, physiologic interpretation of the role of afferent and efferent projections of the vagal complex was obscured by our lack of knowledge of the precise peripheral organs innervated by specific subsets of the DMN-nTS. In constrast to the visual or somatosensory systems, where well-defined topographic projections have long been recognized, sensory and motor representation of discrete visceral end organs has been poorly defined, largely because of technological difficulties in analyzing this system.

Recent dramatic advances in anatomical, histochemical, and pharmacological techniques have provided tools for a greatly refined analysis of the autonomic nervous system. The three major techniques used in the present analysis provide sensitive methods for (a) tracing anterograde projections of axons from the cells of origin to their terminal fields, by using either axonal transport of radioactive isotopes with subsequent processing of the tissue for autoradiography or large protein molecules whose presence can be visualized with various histochemical methods; (b) identifying the location of cells whose processes project into a particular region, by using the retrograde transport of horseradish peroxidase; and (c) immunohistochemical methods for identifying the presence of unique transmitters and transmitter-related compounds. Using various combinations of these methods, Dr. Katz and I (1–4) and Kalia and Mesulam (5, 6) have now demonstrated:

1. A discrete topographic representation of visceral organs within the DMN. Different organs are innervated by cytoarchitecturally distinct types of cells.

2. A discrete sensory organotopic map with the nTS.

3. Descending hypothalamic projections that terminate on selected functionally specific subsets of the DMN-nTS complex.

4. Striking differential distributions of various transmitter/peptide substances in various organ-specific subsets of the DMN-nTS complex.

5. Marked differences in the distribution of receptors in various subsets of this complex.

6. Various inputs to this complex, both central and peripheral,

which contain differing specific transmitters and transmitter-related compounds.

The vagal nerve plays a vital role in the regulation of many visceral organs, including the heart, lungs, gastrointestinal tract, and endocrine and exocrine pancreas. The motor fibers of the vagal nerve arise from two central nuclei, the DMN and the ventral motor nucleus of the vagus (nucleus ambiguus). The sensory fibers of the vagal nerve terminate in the nTS, which lies immediately lateral to the DMN. Despite the heterogeneity of viscera innervated by the vagal nerve, and the relatively small size of the vagal motor and sensory nuclei, each peripheral visceral organ is discretely represented in a restricted region of both the motor and sensory nuclei of the vagus.

Figure 1 is a schematic drawing illustrating the general pattern of organization of the DMN-nTS complex in the pigeon. The vagal complex of the pigeon is more highly developed and differentiated than in most other laboratory animals. The results obtained with this animal, however, appear to be directly applicable to understanding the organization of the vagal complex of mammals. The DMN is a prominent longitudinal collection of preganglionic motor neurons composed of cytologically distinct subnuclei. In conjunction with axons of the nucleus ambiguus, the DMN forms the motor component of the vagal nerve. The sensory axons of the vagal nerve have their cell bodies in the nodose, jugular-superior, and petrosal ganglia of the vagal nerve. Their central axons terminate within the sensory nucleus of the vagal nerve, also known as the nTS. The nTS may be subdivided into two longitudinal columns, a medial tier and a lateral tier (nTSm and nTSl). Within each tier, groups of small neurons are organized into numerous subgroups.

The medial–lateral dichotomy reflects an underlying segregation in relationship to function. The lateral division of the nTS is concerned mainly with cardiopulmonary inputs, including pulmonary stretch receptors, arterial baroreceptors, chemoreceptors, etc. The medial division of the nTS is mainly concerned with sensory input from various portions of the gastrointestinal tract. Each region of the gastrointestinal tract is represented in a continuous map within the medial nTS. A correspondingly precise motor representation of visceral organs is found within the DMN and the nucleus ambiguus.

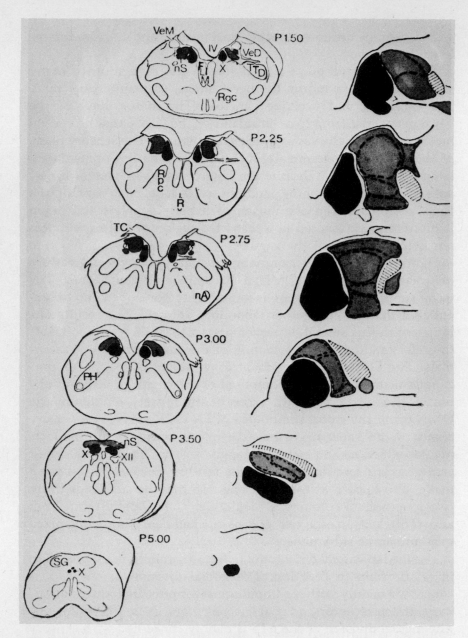

Fig. 1. A schematic drawing illustrating the location and general pattern of organization of the DMN-nTS complex in the pigeon

This nuclear complex is located at the caudal end of the brainstem and extends into the spinal cord. The DMN *(black)* lies immediately lateral to the midline, the nTS *(gray)* lateral to DMN and partially surrounding the tractus solitarius itself *(hatched region)*

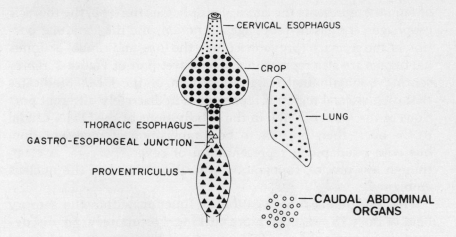

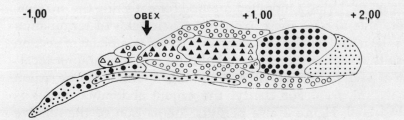

Fig. 2. The *upper* drawing is a representation of the esophagus, proventriculus of the stomach, lung, and caudal abdominal organs; the *lower* drawing is a reconstruction in a sagittal plane of the DMN, showing the topographic representation of the peripheral viscera within the DMN complex

Rostral levels of the neuraxis are to the right, spinal cord to the left. The overlying numbers indicate the relative stereotaxic coordinates

An example of the precision of the topography of motor representation within the DMN of the vagus is shown in Figure 2. Horseradish peroxidase (EC 1.11.1.7) was placed on individual branches of the vagal nerve at their points of innervation of individual visceral organs. After suitable periods, the pigeons were killed and the brains were examined for evidence of retrograde transport of the horseradish peroxidase back to the motor neurons innervating each particular visceral end organ. The upper portion of Figure 2 represents the cervical esophagus, the crop, the thoracic esophagus, the gastro-esophageal junction, and the glandular portion of the stomach (proventriculus); the lung and caudal abdominal organs are also represented. The lower part of Figure 2, representing a longitudinal (sagittal) section of the DMN, indicates that each visceral region is represented in discretely different portions of the rostral DMN. In the subdivisions of the DMN caudal to the obex, there appears to be a replication of representation, but with overlapping representation of several viscera. A clear, though less precise, topography was also evident in the nucleus ambiguus.

The topographical segregation of function within the sensory field of the nTS was even more striking. Fortuitously, we discovered that horseradish peroxidase, when placed upon a peripheral branch of the vagal nerve, would be transported retrogradely not only to the sensory neurons of the vagal ganglia (nodose, jugular-superior, and petrosal ganglia) but also into the central branches of the ganglia. Using a modified method for detecting the enzyme, we were able to trace these axons into their fields of termination within the nTS. Figure 3 diagrams in a transverse plane of section the results of such an experiment, indicating the topographic localization of each individual visceral end organ with both the region of DMN and nTS. For clarity, the caudal abdominal vagus is not illustrated. Figure 3 also permits comparison of the relative regional representation of both motor and sensory components within the DMN and nTS, respectively. Note that sensory representation of the gastrointestinal tract is localized within the medial portions of the nTS; in contrast, the lung is represented in the lateral region of nTS.

Another clear example of the segregation of organ representation is demonstrated in Figure 4, showing the localization of aortic arch chemo- and baroreceptors. The baroreceptors of the aortic and carotid systems play an extremely important role in regulation of the cardiovascular system, and appear to play a major role in the genesis of central hypertension. Once again using the horseradish peroxidase transganglionic method, we demonstrated (7) the central terminal localization of the sensory fibers innervating the aortic arch sensory receptors. These axons were found only

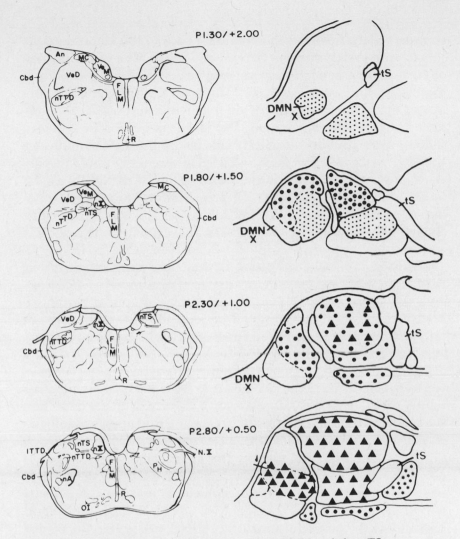

Fig. 3. Transverse sections of the region of the DMN and the nTS

The caudal abdominal vagus is not represented in this illustration for purposes of clarity. Symbols used for organ representation are the same as those shown in Fig. 2. This figure also permits comparison of the relative regional representation of both motor and sensory components within the DMN and nTS, respectively. See also legend to Fig. 4

within a limited dorsal region of the lateral tier of the nTS. The area of termination was clearly separate from the majority of the pulmonary sensory fibers, although some pulmonary afferents extend into the dorso-lateral subnuclei. Histochemical studies of this region have demonstrated the presence of discrete populations

237

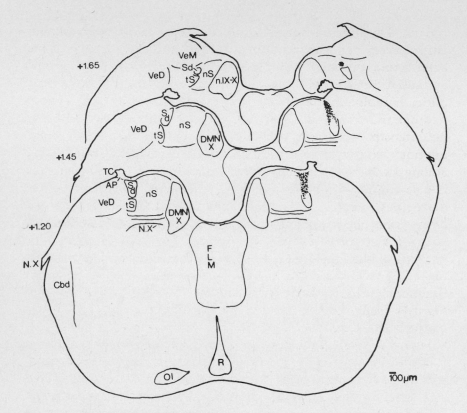

Fig. 4. Camera lucida drawings of transverse brain stem sections through the rostrocaudal extent of the aortic nerve projection area

Stippling illustrates the sharply restricted distribution of horseradish peroxidase-filled aortic arch afferents within the nucleus solitarius. The projection to only one side of the brain is shown. AP, area postrema; DMN X, dorsal motor nucleus of the vagus nerve; FLM, fasciculus longitudinalis medialis; n.IX-X, motor nucleus of the glossopharyngeal nerve, including the rostral extent of DMN X; N.X, vagus nerve; OI, nucleus olivaris inferior; R, nucleus raphe; Sd, subnucleus sulcalis dorsalis; TC, taenia choroidea; VeM, medial vestibular nucleus; tS, nTS

of catecholamine-containing neurons within the sensory region in receipt of baroreceptor inputs, possibly contributing to the known important role of catecholamines in the regulation of blood pressure, atrial receptors, etc. *(7–9)*.

Studies such as these demonstrate that visceral organ sensory and motor representations are, in many regards, as precise as those of the visual and general somatosensory system. These studies also provide the basic framework for a series of experiments regarding the pharmacologic substrates regulating visceral organ control. Despite the relatively small size of the vagal complex, almost every major transmitter substance thus far discovered has been found there. To date, this includes acetylcholine; gamma-aminobutyric acid; glutamate; biogenic amines, including dopamine, norepinephrine, epinephrine, and serotonin; and various neuropeptides, including enkephalin, substance P, somatostatin, neurotensin, vasoactive intestinal polypeptide, pancreatic polypeptide, cholecystokin, and oxytocin/vasopressin/mesotocin, amongst others. An equally dazzling array of receptor substances is also found within the DMN-nTS complex, including benzodiazepines, opiates, and others. Histological techniques for the localization of each of these substances reveal an extraordinarily complex pattern of specific distribution for each of them. The analysis of the DMN-nTS complex for each compound has thus far only provided a crude idea of their distribution within specific functional subsets. Even these studies, however, have revealed highly selective distributions, often within organ-specific subsets of the nuclear complex.

Figure 5 *(lower)* indicates the differential density of substance P within the vagal motor complex. Correspondingly selective distributions have now been found for many of the neuropeptides *(10)*, often limited to organ-specific subsets of the vagal complex. Thus (e.g.) oxytocin-containing axons of hypothalamic origin selectively terminate on pulmonary and baroreceptor sensory terminal fields, and on motor neurons innervating the distal abdominal viscera *(11)*. Several neuropeptides have also been found within neurons of the sensory ganglia, including substance P, vasoactive intestinal polypeptide, and cholecystokinin-octapeptide. A distinct subset of neurons of the nodose ganglion, which innervate the aortic arch baroreceptors, were found to contain substance P. Pickel et al. (personal communication), using combined electron microscopic immunohistochemical techniques and autoradiography of axonally transported radioisotopes, have recently demonstrated that sensory fibers originating in the nodose ganglion terminate directly upon catecholaminergic neurons of the lateral tier of nTS. Although their studies do not directly demonstrate that these fibers were the sensory processes of cells innervating the aortic arch, the results are sufficiently tantalizing to provoke speculation regarding the direct activation of catecholaminergic neurons by specific peptidergic sensory neurons.

PERIPHERAL ORGAN REPRESENTATION WITHIN THE VAGAL MOTOR COMPLEX

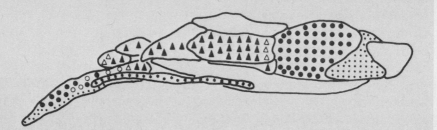

DISTRIBUTION OF SUBSTANCE P-CONTAINING FIBERS WITHIN THE VAGAL MOTOR COMPLEX

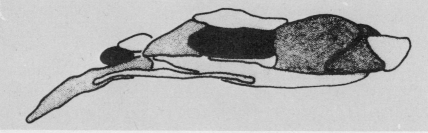

Fig. 5. *Upper,* pattern of visceral organ representation; *lower,* representation of the differential density of substance P within the vagal motor complex

The DMN is represented in sagittal plane; rostral levels of the neuraxis are to the right, spinal cord to the left. The differential density of distribution of substance P corresponds to specific organ subsets of the DMN. Symbols as in Fig. 2, except that ○ represents the thoracic esophagus

Conclusion

The discovery of a precise viscerotopic representation within the sensory-motor nuclei of the vagal nerve and the unique localization of various transmitters provide a framework for the development of a rational pharmacology for the central regulation of individual viscera. The anticipated development of various pharmacologic agents capable of regulating various transmitters and neuropeptides may provide a means of treating functional disorders of the cardiovascular, pulmonary, gastrointestinal, and related endocrine systems. The prospective development of targeted pharmacologic agents capable of selectively acting on various peptidergic receptors may provide the next major therapeutic tool in treatment of disorders of the autonomic nervous system. Further progress in understanding the fundamental anatomy and physiology of these systems can only further benefit our search for an understanding of the complex relationship of telencephalic limbic structures and the regulation of the autonomic nervous system.

I thank Drs. David M. Katz, Kent Keyser, Rodrigo O. Kuljis, Anton Reiner, and Nicholas Brecha for their many helpful discussions during the course of this research. This research was supported by grants from the National Institutes for Health, NINCDS (12078) and NEI (02164). I extend special thanks to Ms. Christine Laverack for her unstinting efforts and excellent technical assistance during all stages of this research.

References

1. Katz DM, Karten HJ. Substance P in the vagal sensory ganglia: Localization in cell bodies and pericellular arborizations. *J Comp Neurol* **193,** 549–564 (1980).
2. Katz DM, Karten HJ. Subnuclear organization of the dorsal motor nucleus of the vagus nerve in the pigeon, *Columba livia. J Comp Neurol* **217,** 31–46 (1983).
3. Katz DM, Karten HJ. Topographic representation of peripheral target organs within the dorsal motor nucleus of the vagus nerve of the pigeon, *Columba livia. J Comp Neurol,* in press (1983).
4. Katz DM, Karten HJ. Visceral representation within the nucleus of the tractus solitarius in the pigeon, *Columba livia. J Comp Neurol,* **218,** 42–73 (1983).
5. Kalia M, Mesulam M. Brain stem projections of sensory and motor components of the vagus complex in the cat. I. The cervical vagus and nodose ganglion. *J Comp Neurol* **193,** 435–465 (1980).
6. Kalia M, Mesulam M. Brain stem projections of sensory and motor components of the vagus complex in the cat. II. Laryngeal, tracheobronchial, pulmonary, cardiac and gastrointestinal branches. *J Comp Neurol* **193,** 467–508 (1980).
7. Katz DM, Karten HJ. The discrete anatomical localization of vagal aortic afferents within a catecholamine-containing cell group in the nucleus solitarius. *Brain Res* **171,** 187–195 (1979).

8. Armstrong DM, Pickel VM, Joh TH, et al. Immunocytochemical localization of catecholamine synthesizing enzymes and neuropeptides in area postrema and medial nucleus tractus solitarius of rat brain. *J Comp Neurol* **196**, 505–518 (1981).

9. Jacobowitz DM, MacLean PD. A brainstem atlas of catecholaminergic neurons and serotonergic perikarya in a pygmy primate *(Cebuella pygmaea)*. *J Comp Neurol* **177**, 397–416 (1978).

10. Katz DM, Karten HJ. Substance P-like immunoreactivity (SPLI) and target organ representation within the nucleus solitarius (nS) and vagal motor nucleus (DMN X). *Soc Neurosci* **5**, 530 (1979). Abstract.

11. Keyser KT, Karten HJ, Cabot JB. Descending hypothalamic oxytocin/mesotocin projections end preferentially on pulmonary and baroreceptor regions of the n. solitarius. *Soc Neurosci* **8**, 513 (1982). Abstract.

Multiple Dopamine Receptors—Their Role in Schizophrenia

Ian Creese

Several lines of evidence—primarily pharmacological—suggest an association of central nervous system dopaminergic neuronal systems in the etiology of schizophrenia. Chronic abuse of stimulants such as amphetamine, which are known to enhance dopaminergic activity in the brain, can lead to a paranoid psychosis that is almost indistinguishable from classic paranoid schizophrenia. Furthermore, acute administration of amphetamine will exacerbate the symptomotology of a schizophrenic and initiate a recurrent psychosis in a schizophrenic in remission (discussed in detail in ref. 28). On the other hand, schizophrenic symptomotology can be reduced by reserpine, which depletes brain dopamine, and by antipsychotic, neuroleptic drugs such as Haldol (haloperidol) or Thorazine (chlorpromazine), which we now know act by blocking dopamine postsynaptic receptors, thereby decreasing dopamine's actions in the brain.

The evidence that neuroleptic, antipsychotic drugs act by blocking postsynaptic dopamine receptors was initially circumstantial. Most data were gathered in animal studies in which the effects of dopamine agonists were blocked by the administration of neuroleptic drugs. However, interference with many other mechanisms could also diminish enhanced dopaminergic tone that had been exogenously produced. The major idea that stimulated the research I will discuss was to discover the biochemical mechanism of action of neuroleptic drugs and thereby perhaps uncover a potential biochemical locus involved in the etiology of schizophrenia. In these studies neuroleptic drugs were radioactively labeled so that very small quantities could be measured in various brain regions. If these drugs bound to dopamine receptors, my coworkers and I hoped to demonstrate a high degree of pharmacological specificity of the binding of these radioactively labeled neuroleptic drugs. Indeed, we found that potent neuroleptics such as haloperidol or spiperone (a drug not yet used in the United States) did label dopamine receptors in a number of brain areas; moreover, the potencies of the drugs at the binding sites labeled by these neuroleptics were predictive of their antipsychotic potencies in humans and their antidopaminergic activities in animals. These studies demonstrated conclusively that the major antipsychotic activity of the drugs was mediated through their binding to, and hence blockade of, postsynaptic dopamine receptors.

If indeed schizophrenia is the result of an enhanced dopaminergic activity, this activity should be demonstrable in the schizophrenic brain. However, studies investigating dopaminergic activity in terms of presynaptic mechanisms, e.g., increased release of dopamine or decreased metabolism of dopamine, were negative. This left only one potential site for an enhanced dopaminergic tone—an increased sensitivity of the postsynaptic dopamine receptor. Studies in postmortem schizophrenic brains indeed demonstrated that schizophrenics had as many as twice the number of dopamine receptors as controls had. Was this increased number of dopamine receptors etiologic in the disease process? If so, this would be potentially the first demonstration that a psychiatric disease could be directly related to a very specific biochemical defect.

Unfortunately, the answer to this question is still unclear. Since the introduction of chlorpromazine in the early 1950s, schizophrenics have been treated chronically with neuroleptic drugs, often for many years. One result of this chronic neuroleptic treatment is the development of a side effect called tardive dyskinesia. Characterized by protrusion of the tongue with marked chewing movements and constant movement of the extremities, this motor disorder is persistent and even worsens if the neuroleptic drugs are stopped. The only alleviation is to increase the dose of neuroleptic drugs, which, in turn, leads to enhanced tardive dyskinesia later. Animal studies investigating the etiology of this vicious circle suggested that the continuous blockade of dopamine receptors by a neuroleptic drug hypersensitizes the receptors, resulting in the subsequent motor side effects. Indeed, radioligand-binding studies demonstrated that just a few weeks of treatment with neuroleptic drugs increased the number of dopamine receptors in the areas of the brain associated with motor control. Thus, it is unclear whether the increase in dopamine receptors in schizophrenics is part of the disease process itself or is merely iatrogenic—the result of the chronic treatment with neuroleptics. This area of research is still very controversial. One study has demonstrated that patients who are drug-free at the time of death and who have been drug-free for a number of weeks before death have normal numbers of dopamine receptors, whereas other studies show that patients who are drug-naive have more dopamine receptors than do controls. More data must be collected before we can draw a definite conclusion.

This area of research has become even more complicated in the past few years. Multiple subtypes of dopamine receptors have been discovered, much like muscarinic and nicotinic cholinergic receptors or alpha and beta adrenergic receptors. Apparently, there are at least two major subtypes of dopamine receptors, one associated with the stimulation of adenylate cyclase (EC 4.6.1.1) and one with the inhibition of this enzyme. Other potential receptor sites have been proposed, including one of special interest that may identify the presynaptic autoreceptors on dopamine terminals that regulate the synthesis and release of dopamine. At the moment, we do not know how these receptors might change after chronic treatment with neuroleptic drugs and what their involvement might be in the etiology of schizophrenia or in the antipsychotic action and side effects produced by neuroleptic drugs. The therapeutic precedence set by the identification of distinct subtypes of adrenoreceptors, histamine receptors, and cholinergic receptors portends an exciting future for studies of dopamine receptors.

Anatomy of Dopaminergic Systems

The nigrostriatal pathway, which accounts for about 70% of the total brain content of dopamine, has become an obvious focus of research (Figure 1). The existence of the nigrostriatal pathway was strongly indicated by the observations of Hornykiewicz (re-

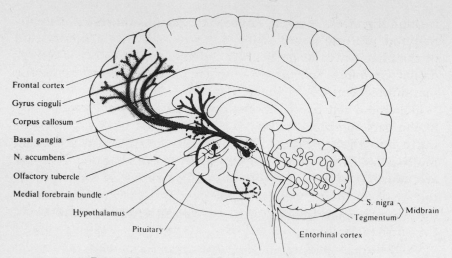

Fig. 1. Major dopamine pathways in human brain

viewed in ref. *63*), who demonstrated that patients with Parkinson's disease displayed a concomitant loss of dopamine in the striatum or basal ganglia, along with the degeneration of cells in the substantia nigra, pars compacta. The other major dopamine pathway originates from a group of cells in the ventrotegmental area surrounding the interpeduncular nucleus and innervates the olfactory tubercle and adjacent limbic and cortical structures. The substantia nigra and ventrotegmental dopamine cell groups are frequently referred to as the A-9 and A-10 nuclear groups, respectively, following the original designation by Dahlstrom and Fuxe *(45)* in their pioneering fluorescence histochemical studies. Since the introduction of the more sensitive glyoxylic acid fluorescence histochemical method *(93)*, immunohistochemical studies, and orthograde and retrograde nerve circuit tracing *(6)*, it is becoming clear that the dopamine systems are more complex than originally envisaged.

Ontogenetic and mapping studies have now demonstrated that the A-9 and A-10 nuclear groups are more correctly described as a continuum, with the more laterally situated cells predominantly innervating the striatum and the more medial cells predominantly innervating the "mesocortical" areas. The striatal projection includes the caudate nucleus, putamen, and globus pallidus, whereas the terminal areas of the mesocortical projection

246

include the medial frontal, anterior cingulate, entorhinal, perirhinal, and piriform cortex. Also apparent is a strong innervation of the olfactory tubercle, septum, nucleus accumbens, and amygdaloid complex. This pathway is frequently referred to as the mesolimbic, cortical, or limbic dopamine system.

Dopamine cell bodies in the substantia nigra are found only in the pars compacta, although their dendritic trees extend ventrally into the pars reticulata. The cells are medium sized and multi-polar. The pronounced varicosities within the dendritic tree are unusual, which some propose are indicative of the dendritic release of dopamine (10). Pathways for substance P and γ-aminobutyric acid from the striatum and globus pallidus feed back to the substantia nigra.

Dopamine innervation in the cortex appears to be to the deeper layers, in contrast to the norepinephrine input, which is to the more superficial layers (9, 95). A dopaminergic innervation to the spinal cord, probably originating from the substantia nigra, has recently been described (12, 23, 24).

Of the other dopamine pathways, the tuberohypophyseal system has received most attention and will be discussed below. Two other dopamine pathways originate in hypothalamic areas: the incerto-hypothalamic and periventricular systems (11, 94). The periglomerular cells of the olfactory bulb (62) and the innerplexiform cells of the retina (50) both also appear to utilize dopamine as a transmitter. In the periphery some small, intensely fluorescent cells in sympathetic ganglia are thought to be dopaminergic (91), and dopaminergic nerves have recently been described in the kidney (7, 49). However, although other structures in the periphery such as the stomach, parathyroids, and carotid bodies are known to be responsive to dopamine, no other dopaminergic neurones have yet been identified.

The role of these various pathways in schizophrenia is not known. A reasonable guess, however, is that the nigrostriatal pathway, which is part of the extrapyramidal motor system, is involved in the motoric symptoms seen in some forms of schizophrenia (catatonia) and in the parkinsonian side effects of neuroleptic drugs. The mesolimbic and mesocortical pathways, on the other hand, brain areas classically associated with intellectual function and emotionality, are involved in the more cardinal psychiatric symptoms of the disease.

Pharmacological Characterization of Dopamine Receptors

Before discussing the biochemical characteristics of dopamine receptors, I will describe the basic pharmacology of various dopaminergic drugs.

Principal Behavioral and Biochemical Actions of the Principal Dopaminergic Agents

In general, behavioral experiments in animals have concentrated on the effects of dopaminergic agents on motor behavior (see *52, 72*). Dopamine agonists (Figure 2), acting at dopamine receptors in the striatum and nucleus accumbens, increase locomotor activity and stereotyped behavior in intact rodents; when injected unilaterally into the striatum, these drugs produce turning to the contralateral side. The dopamine agonist most frequently used in all types of experiments—whether behavioral, physiological, or biochemical—is apomorphine. This alkaloid of the aporphine class easily crosses the blood–brain barrier, although its duration of action is relatively short. In rodents it stimulates both locomotor

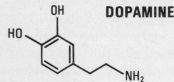
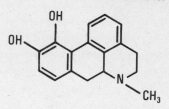
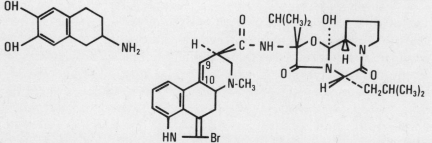

Fig. 2. Major dopaminergic agonists

activity and "stereotyped" behavior—repetitious movements such as rearing, sniffing, or gnawing, maintained in one location. In humans, dogs, and other animals with a chemoreceptive trigger zone in the area posttrema, apomorphine produces nausea and intense vomiting. Interestingly, in low doses apomorphine has a sedative action, through its possible interaction with autoreceptors (discussed later), rather than the stimulant action associated with higher doses.

As we shall see, biochemical experiments have demonstrated distinct dopamine receptors in both the central nervous system and the periphery that are linked in a stimulatory or inhibitory fashion to adenylate cyclase. In addition, peripheral administration of agonists decreases dopamine turnover in neurons of the striatonigral projection by acting at presynaptic dopamine autoreceptors. In the anterior pituitary, agonists act on dopamine receptors to decrease prolactin secretion. Apomorphine acts as a partial agonist of the dopamine-stimulated adenylate cyclase activity and as a full agonist in decreasing striatal dopamine turnover and pituitary release of prolactin.

Although dopamine itself does not penetrate the blood–brain barrier, its concentration in the brain can be raised in vivo by administering the dopamine precursor L-dopa. Simultaneous treatment with a decarboxylase inhibitor that does not cross the blood–brain barrier eliminates peripheral side effects by allowing L-dopa to be converted to dopamine only in the central nervous system. L-Dopa is one of the major therapeutic agents in the treatment of Parkinson's disease, where tremor, akinesia, and rigidity result from degeneration of nigrostriatal dopamine neurons. Presumably, extra dopamine is synthesized from L-dopa in the remaining intact dopaminergic neurons.

The other principal dopaminergic agonist, used mainly in biochemical studies, is 2-amino-6,7-dihydroxy-1,2,3,4-tetrahydronaphthalene (ADTN), another agent that does not cross the blood–brain barrier.[1] Bromocryptine, an ergot derivative, acts as an agonist in suppressing prolactin secretion, effecting rotational behavior, and alleviating parkinsonian symptoms; however, it acts as an

---

[1] Abbreviations used: ADTN, 2-amino-6,7-dihydroxy-1,2,3,4-tetrahydronaphthalene; NPA, N-propylnorapomorphine; cAMP, cyclic AMP; K_D, apparent dissociation constant; B_{max}, maximum number of binding sites; R_H and R_L, high-affinity and low-affinity binding sites, respectively.

antagonist of the dopamine-stimulated adenylate cyclase. It is used in treating Parkinson's disease and galactorrhea caused by pituitary tumors.

Amongst dopamine antagonists, phenothiazines and butyrophenones have received the greatest attention (Figure 3). Because antipsychotic or neuroleptic drugs are used to treat schizophrenia, the biochemical interactions of dopamine antagonists with dopamine receptors are of widespread interest (see *32, 74*). Dopamine antagonists specifically decrease avoidance behavior in rats and

FLUPHENAZINE

CHLORPROMAZINE

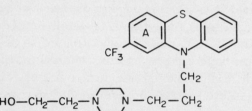
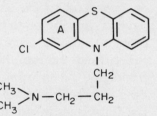

HALOPERIDOL

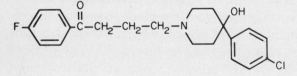

Fig. 3. Major dopaminergic antagonists

monkeys without affecting escape responses to noxious stimuli. This paradigm is used as a sensitive screen for potential antipsychotic agents. Chlorpromazine, the first neuroleptic identified, is still one of the phenothiazines in widest use, despite its sedative properties. Since its introduction in the early 1950s, many hundreds of other phenothiazines have been synthesized in the hope of finding more potent and specific agents. Thioridazine (Mellaril), the most widely used neuroleptic, is about as potent as chlorpromazine. The other principal phenothiazines used in clinical practice now include fluphenazine (Prolixin) and trifluoperazine (Stelazine), both of which are one to two orders of magnitude more potent than chlorpromazine. Within the second major class of dopamine antagonists, the butyrophenones, haloperidol was the first agent identified as being antipsychotic; it is about as potent therapeutically as fluphenazine. The other butyrophenone important for biochemical experiments is spiperone (spiroperidol). Of the other antipsychotic agents that appear to be dopamine antagonists, the thioxanthenes (e.g., flupentixol) are closely similar in structure to the phenothiazines. Butaclamol (a dibenzocycloheptane derivative) exists as optical isomers: only the (+)isomer of butaclamol is active in blocking dopamine-mediated effects in vivo and in vitro, whereas the (−)isomer is virtually inactive. As we shall see, the stereospecificity of this compound has been an important tool in delineating dopamine-receptor mechanisms. Several dopamine antagonists are of interest because of their inability to inhibit the dopamine-stimulated adenylate cyclase. The substituted benzamide antipsychotics, including sulpiride, tiapride, and metaclopramide, exhibit dopamine antagonist activity by a number of indices, yet are inactive at the dopamine-stimulated cyclase-linked receptor. Domperidone, a butyrophenone-like compound, shows the same selectivity, but does not cross the blood–brain barrier; clinically, it is utilized to increase gastric emptying, probably via antagonism of gastric dopamine receptors.

Because these structurally diverse compounds owe their differing activities to the degree of selectivity they display for the various dopamine receptor subtypes, their preferences can be utilized to identify distinct dopamine receptors. Among dopaminergic agents, the antagonists—haloperidol, spiroperidol, domperidone, pimozide, tiapride, sulpiride, flupentixol—and the agonists—lysergic acid diethylamide (LSD), dihydroergocryptine, dopamine, apomorphine, ADTN, and N-propylnorapomorphine (NPA)—are all available in tritiated form for use in receptor-binding studies.

The D-1 Dopamine Receptor

The enzyme adenylate cyclase is linked to several neurotransmitter and hormone receptors in the periphery. Activation of the enzyme results in conversion of ATP to cyclic AMP (cAMP), which initiates a cascade of events that may result in (e.g.) voltage changes across neuronal membranes, leading to alterations in neuronal activity. In the early 1970s Greengard first demonstrated that cAMP could act as a second messenger for dopamine (for a review, see ref. *58*). In the bovine superior cervical ganglion, dopamine mediates a slow inhibitory postsynaptic potential, which can be mimicked by the exogenous application of cAMP. Crucial biochemical studies confirm the presence of adenylate cyclase in this tissue, which is activated by dopamine. In the neostriatum, a similar accumulation of cAMP after exposure to dopamine has been reported *(77)*. In striatal homogenates, dopamine at 100 μmol/L elicited maximal stimulation of cAMP accumulation; at 2 μmol/L the effect was about half of the maximal. Localization of the dopamine-stimulated adenylate cyclase in brain tissue was also consistent with association with dopamine receptors, the activity being found only in regions that are rich in dopamine innervation (corpus striatum, olfactory tubercle, and nucleus accumbens).

Greengard's group, and later Iversen *(70)* and colleagues, evaluated the effects of neuroleptic drugs on the dopamine-stimulated adenylate cyclase. The phenothiazines were effective competitive inhibitors of the enzyme *(22, 71, 102)*, there being a general parallel between the pharmacological potencies of phenothiazines as dopamine antagonists in animals and humans and their influences on the cyclase. There were, however, marked discrepancies of responses to the butyrophenones and other neuroleptics *(70, 142)*. For example, haloperidol, which clinically and pharmacologically is about 10- to 100-fold more potent than chlorpromazine, appeared weaker than, or at best equal to, chlorpromazine in its effect on the cyclase. Furthermore, spiroperidol, which is about fivefold more potent than haloperidol in intact animals and schizophrenics, was weaker than both haloperidol and chlorpromazine in inhibiting the dopamine-stimulated activity of adenylate cyclase. Similarly, the potent antipsychotic sulpiride was almost devoid of inhibitory potency.

These discrepancies, initially overlooked, raised the possibility that butyrophenones might not block dopamine receptors at all, but rather might act in some other system and influence dopaminergic activity indirectly. This would presumably be related to the marked difference in chemical structure between phenothiazines and butyrophenones despite their pharmacological similarities. This hypothesis was reinforced by computer modeling stud-

Table 1. Functional Classification of Dopamine-Receptor Subtypes

	D-1	D-2
Prototype receptor location	Parathyroid gland	Anterior and intermediate pituitary glands
Adenylate cyclase linkage	Stimulatory	Inhibitory or unlinked
Agonists		
Dopamine	Full agonist (micromolar potency)	Full agonist (nanomolar potency)
Apomorphine	Partial agonist (micromolar potency)	Full agonist (nanomolar potency)
Antagonists		
Phenothiazines	Nanomolar potency	Nanomolar potency
Thioxanthenes	Nanomolar potency	Nanomolar potency
Butyrophenones	Micromolar potency	Nanomolar potency
Substituted benzamides	Inactive	Nano–micromolar potency
Dopaminergic ergots	Antagonists or partial agonists (micromolar potency)	Full agonists (nanomolar potency)

Modified from Kebabian and Calne *(76)*.

ies, which demonstrated that, whereas the phenothiazine molecule could easily take on a conformation mimicking the extended or *trans*-conformation of dopamine *(51)*, butyrophenones were no more likely to take up the dopamine-mimicking conformation than any other *(149)*. An alternative hypothesis, not considered initially, was that more than one type of dopamine receptor existed. Thus, butyrophenones would exhibit weak affinity for the receptor responsible for eliciting an increase in cAMP but would exhibit higher potencies at those dopamine receptors responsible for the behavioral and clinical effects of the drugs. This hypothesis now seems the more tenable one. Indeed, Kebabian and Calne *(76)*, in their recent seminal review of the pharmacological classification of dopamine receptors, divided dopamine receptors into two general categories, D-1 and D-2 receptors. Upon agonist activation, D-1 receptors are responsible for stimulating dopamine-sensitive adenylate cyclase (Table 1). The location for the prototype D-1 receptor is the parathyroid gland, where dopamine agonists stimulate cAMP synthesis concomitantly with release of parathyrin (parathyroid hormone) *(2, 14, 15)*. For a more detailed discussion of the dopamine-sensitive stimulation of adenylate cyclase, see reviews by Miller and McDermed *(103)* and Schmidt *(126)*.

The D-2 Dopamine Receptor

In contrast to D-1 receptors, D-2 receptors are functionally classified as not enhancing adenylate cyclase activity upon agonist occupation. Instead, the consequences of D-2 receptor stimulation are either to decrease or to have no effect on the formation of cAMP (Table 1). Prototype D-2 receptors exist in the anterior and intermediate pituitary glands, and in neither of these tissues does dopamine elicit its physiological effects through the stimulation of cAMP synthesis. Indeed, Kebabian and colleagues (109, 110) have elegantly shown that, in the intermediate pituitary, dopamine inhibits the beta adrenergic agonist-stimulated synthesis of cAMP, leading to a diminution of hormone release (see below), whereas in the anterior pituitary, dopamine inhibits vasoactive intestinal peptide stimulation of adenylate cyclase (115).

The pharmacological profile of D-2 receptors is clearly distinct from that of D-1 receptors (Table 1). Agonists consistently demonstrate higher affinities in eliciting a biochemical or physiological response at D-2 receptors than at D-1 receptors. Apomorphine is a potent agonist with full intrinsic activity at D-2 receptors, in contrast to its partial agonist activity at D-1 receptors. Similarly, various dopaminergic ergots (e.g., bromocryptine, lisuride, lergotrile) are full, potent (effective at nanomolar concentrations) agonists at D-2 receptors but only weak, partial agonists or antagonists at D-1 receptors. Although phenothiazines and thioxanthenes are potent antagonists of D-2 receptors, they exhibit equally high affinity for D-1 receptors and thus are not useful for discriminating between these subtypes. In contrast, butyrophenones and related drugs (e.g., domperidone) are very potent antagonists of D-2 receptors but exhibit only weak affinity for D-1 receptors. Similarly, substituted benzamides (e.g., sulpiride), which are inactive at D-1 receptors, exhibit potent behavioral dopamine antagonism and moderate affinity at D-2 receptors.

Dopamine Autoreceptors

The term autoreceptors refers to presynaptic dopamine receptors on dopamine terminals and the dendrites of dopamine neurons in the substantia nigra (124). It is fairly clear that none of these receptors stimulate adenylate cyclase activity (D-1), and at least some of the autoreceptors on nigral dopamine neuron dendrites are D-2 receptors *(112, 121)*. Some pharmacological evidence, however, suggests that presynaptic autoreceptors on dopamine terminals are a separate receptor subtype from D-1 and D-2 receptors, dopamine autoreceptors being clearly more sensitive to dopamine agonists than are postsynaptic D-1 and D-2 receptors. Recent electrophysiological studies also demonstrate that some cell body autoreceptors are more sensitive to dopamine agonists than postsynaptic receptors in the striatum *(140)*. Autoreceptors on substantia nigra dopamine cell bodies mediate the inhibition of the firing rates of these cells. These cells were six- to 10-fold more sensitive to iontophoretically applied dopamine and intravenous apomorphine than the majority of spontaneously active rat striatal cells, which were inhibited by dopamine agonists. In addition, autoreceptors and postsynaptic receptors may show differential sensitivity to some antagonists *(124, 152)*.

Dopamine autoreceptors localized on nerve terminals and neuronal soma influence dopaminergic synaptic activity by decreasing, via local negative-feedback mechanisms, *(a)* the rate of dopamine biosynthesis, *(b)* impulse-induced release of transmitter, and *(c)* cell firing rate. The preferential sensitivity of pre- vs postsynaptic dopamine receptors is already being used in clinical studies. Although it has not been conclusively demonstrated that the effects of low doses of apomorphine are mediated by preferential stimulation of dopamine autoreceptors, administration of apomorphine has resulted in many beneficial effects: reduction of alcohol craving, antimanic effects, antipsychotic effects in schizophrenics, reduction in the symptoms of tardive dyskinesia, induction of drowsiness or sleep, and alleviation of the symptoms of Huntington's chorea and Tourette's syndrome (reviewed in Meltzer, *101*). The alleviation of psychotic symptoms in schizophrenics by low doses of a dopamine agonist *(25, 141)*, obviously of great clinical interest, would be difficult to comprehend were it not for the conceptual framework of autoreceptors. As of yet, no clinical studies have suggested preferential presynaptic activity of dopamine antagonists. However, development of antipsychotic drugs devoid of presynaptic blocking activity might obviate the increase in dopamine synthesis and release observed after administration of dopamine antagonists. Some of the mesocortical dopamine systems lack autoreceptors *(5)*; thus the development of a selective autoreceptor agonist may allow for the specific reduction of dopamine release in the nigrostriatal system. This could conceivably control the occurrence of tardive dyskinesia (see below) without the necessity of neuroleptic withdrawal, thus allowing for the continued blockade of dopamine receptors in the mesocortical areas, to alleviate schizophrenia.

Direct Receptor Characterization: Radioligand-Binding Studies

Since 1975 the elegantly simple radioligand-binding technique has allowed direct examination of various neurotransmitter and drug interactions with dopamine receptors. The simplification obtained through elimination of such factors as alteration of neurotransmitter synthesis or activation of a second messenger has been the chief advantage of this approach in the study of receptors. This simplification, however, also presents a major challenge: to demonstrate that the binding sites identified in vitro have functional physiological relevance. Of utmost importance, and often of considerable difficulty, is the demonstration that receptor binding sites can be clearly associated with some biological function. Although problems remain, this correspondence between binding sites and their function, both in terms of behavior and biochemistry, is steadily being established for the dopamine receptors.

Further investigations with radioligand-binding studies of the pharmacological profiles described in the previous section have elucidated the characteristics of individual receptor subtypes and how they may change in schizophrenia and during drug therapy. With standard filtration assay technique, a radiolabeled agent is useful for identifying only receptors for which it has approximately nanomolar affinity (see ref. *8*). Thus, although D-1 receptors should be labeled by radioactive phenothiazines and thioxanthenes, these agents would also bind D-2 sites. Therefore, butyrophenones, [^{3}H]spiroperidol, [^{3}H]haloperidol, and [^{3}H]domperidone, should be fairly selective ligands for D-2 receptors because of their lower affinities for D-1 receptors.

At first approximation one might predict that only the D-2 receptor would bind ^{3}H-labeled agonists such as apomorphine or the ergots. However, other factors must be considered: agonist affinity for a particular receptor-mediated response may not quantitatively predict agonist affinity for that receptor as determined by radioligand-binding studies in membrane preparations because of factors such as spare receptors or differing intrinsic activities. Indeed, D-1 receptors can exist in two conformational states, having low or high affinity for agonists in membrane preparations. The existence of a third dopamine-receptor subtype, "D-3," which is characterized by its high affinity for agonists, has been suggested for labeled autoreceptors *(146)* and will also be considered.

In studies of radioligand binding, one must demonstrate that the binding under measurement involves a physiological or pharmacological receptor. Because receptors are present in extremely small numbers and because radioligands can adhere to many membrane components, uptake sites, other "irrelevant" neurotransmitter receptors, and even inorganic materials, one must exercise considerable caution in interpreting data. Radioligand-binding studies should therefore satisfy the following criteria to reduce the probability of a false-positive receptor identification *(16):*

1. Specific binding must be saturable and reversible; that is, specific binding must be established with a competitive agent of high affinity and high specificity for the putative receptor of interest. For example, spiroperidol and (+)butaclamol bind with high affinity not only to dopamine receptors but also to serotonin receptors. Therefore, in tissues that might contain both types of receptors, butaclamol does not provide a satisfactory "blank" for the determination of specific binding of [^{3}H]spiroperidol to dopamine receptors. Under ideal conditions specific binding should be significantly greater than nonspecific binding. Without signal-to-noise ratios greater than or equal to one, little reliance can be placed on the data.

2. The regional localization of ^{3}H-labeled ligand-binding sites must correspond to known innervation and must not be demonstrated in regions lacking innervation or physiological sensitivity to the neurotransmitter.

3. The pharmacological specificity of antagonists should not differ greatly from in vivo pharmacological or behavioral studies; drugs that are inactive in pharmacological measurements of receptors should show little affinity for the ^{3}H-labeled ligand-binding sites.

4. Finally, it is important to demonstrate that uptake mechanisms have not confounded the assays, and that the radioligand itself, not a metabolite, is bound.

In a typical radioligand-binding assay, membranes are incubated with low concentrations of a ^{3}H-labeled ligand of high specific activity. After binding has reached equilibrium, the ^{3}H-labeled ligand bound to the membranes is separated from the free ligand in the incubation mix, commonly by centrifugation or by rapid filtration through glass-fiber filters under reduced pressure. The ^{3}H-labeled ligand remaining on the membranes is the total of ligand both specifically bound to the putative receptor and non-specifically bound to the various possible components described above. The amount of nonspecific binding is measured in parallel sets of test tubes containing, in addition to the usual reagents, excess amounts of a nonradioactive drug known to block the receptors of interest; for dopamine receptors, more often than not, this is (+)butaclamol. Specific binding is then determined by simple subtraction. Receptor number and affinity for the radio-ligand are determined by conducting saturation experiments uti-lizing increasing concentrations of radioligand. The affinity of nonradioactive drugs is determined in "competition" experiments, in which increasing concentrations of the nonradioactive drug are incubated with a fixed low concentration of radioligand (*cf.* Figure 4).

The Pituitary D-2 Receptor

The pituitary provides a relatively simple starting point for the discussion of dopamine receptors in the central nervous sys-tem. In contrast to multiple receptor subtypes in the brain, the pituitary has only a single type of dopamine receptor. This recep-tor exhibits two agonist-binding states, which are controlled by the presence or absence of guanine nucleotides and various cat-ions. Our understanding of the pituitary dopamine receptor is a recent development that has been instructive in the delineation of other dopamine receptor subtypes.

Release of some pituitary hormones is regulated by dopamine originating from the tuberohypophyseal neuron system. The cell bodies of this system, located in the hypothalamic arcuate and periventricular nuclei, project axons ventromedially to the median eminence (reviewed in ref. *104*). Some axons continue beyond the median eminence and traverse the pituitary stalk to directly innervate the posterior and intermediate pituitary. The physiological significance of this innervation has heretofore been unclear, but recent evidence (discussed later) suggests that dopamine regulates release of α-melanotropin and β-endorphin from the intermediate lobe and possibly oxytocin release from the posterior pituitary (105). Other axons terminate within the median eminence and the pituitary stalk in close approximation to the capillaries that form the hypophyseal portal vessels. Dopamine released from these terminals is transported in the portal blood to the anterior pituitary, where it inhibits the release of prolactin. Indeed, the release of prolactin from the anterior pituitary appears to be under tonic inhibitory hypothalamic control; moreover, convincing evidence suggests that dopamine may be the only inhibitory hypothalamic factor controlling the secretion of prolactin (reviewed in refs. 100, 154). Briefly, dopamine and dopamine agonists suppress prolactin secretion in vivo, from the isolated pituitary gland in vitro, and from dispersed pituitary cells in culture. Correspondingly, dopamine antagonists stimulate prolactin secretion in vivo and block the inhibiting action of dopamine agonists in vitro. Moreover, the stereoselectivity and rank order of potency of catecholamines, phenothiazines, and related drugs in regulating prolactin release in vitro directly implicate the presence of specific dopamine-receptor sites in the anterior pituitary.

Accordingly, several groups (19, 20, 34, 40) have used radioactive dopamine agonists and antagonists to identify a high-affinity, stereoselective, saturable dopamine receptor in preparations of anterior pituitary membrane. The rank order of agonists and antagonists for competing with radioligand binding to the dopamine receptor agrees closely with their rank order in inhibiting or disinhibiting prolactin release. In addition, immunocytochemical evidence indicates that these dopamine receptors are largely confined to the mammotroph cells (57, 153).

The radiolabeled dopamine antagonist, [³H]spiroperidol, has previously been shown to bind exclusively to dopamine receptors in the anterior pituitary of cattle (34), sheep (41), and rats (145). In bovine anterior pituitary membranes, the specific binding of [³H]spiroperidol is saturable and of high affinity. Analysis of the saturation data indicates a homogeneous population of binding sites with a dissociation constant (K_D) of approximately 0.3 nmol/ L. The maximum number of binding sites (B_{max}) is about 4 pmol/ g of tissue—only 20% of the number of sites detected in bovine

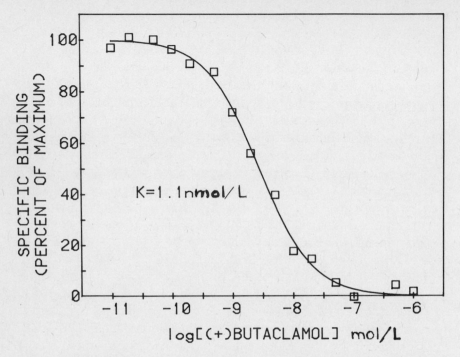

Fig. 4. Computer-fitted curve for a (+)butaclamol/[³H]spiroperidol competition experiment with bovine anterior pituitary membranes

The data points are from a single representative experiment. The computer-drawn curve represents the best fit to the data, given a single homogeneous binding site; the assumption of a two-site model does not improve the fit. The pseudo-Hill coefficient is n = 0.99. K = dissociation constant of the binding site = 1.1 nmol/L

caudate. Using [³H]spiroperidol as the radioligand produces antagonist competition curves that exhibit monophasic, mass-action characteristics with pseudo-Hill coefficients equal to 1 *(136).* For example, Figure 4 shows the experimental data and the resulting computer-modeled competition curve for the antagonist (+)butaclamol. The nonlinear least-squares curve-fitting program used can analyze the data in terms of one or more classes of binding sites *(48, 111).* For (+)butaclamol the best curve model corresponds to a single homogeneous receptor state with a K_D of 1.1 nmol/L.

In contrast, agonist competition curves with [³H]spiroperidol correspond to heterogeneous sites with pseudo-Hill coefficients

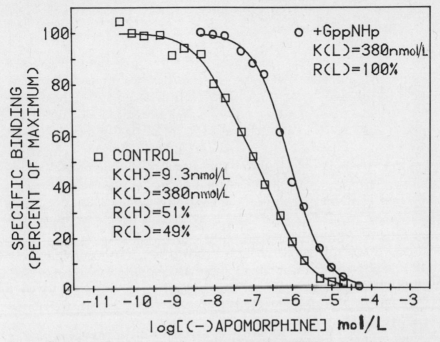

Fig. 5. Computer-fitted curves for a (—)apomorphine/[³H]spiroperidol competition experiment with bovine anterior pituitary membranes

The (—)apomorphine control curve is best fitted by assuming a two-site model, whereas in the presence of guanyl-5'-ylimidodiphosphate (GppNHp), 0.1 mmol/L, a one-site model is sufficient to explain the data. When the two curves are analyzed simultaneously and constrained to share the same K_L value, there was no worsening of the fit. K_L and K_H, dissociation constants for the low- and high-affinity binding sites (R_L and R_H), respectively, in nanomoles per liter

of less than unity. As shown in Figure 5, in the absence of guanine nucleotides, the curve for (—)apomorphine vs [³H]spiroperidol (control curve) is shallow (pseudo-Hill coefficient = 0.58); the computer analysis indicates that the data are best explained by a two-site (or two-state) binding model. The K_D for the high- and the low-affinity binding sites/states (R_H and R_L) are designated K_H and K_L, respectively. Interestingly, the two sites/states are present in membranes in approximately equal proportions. In the presence of a saturating concentration of guanyl-5'-ylimidophosphate, a nonmetabolizable analog of the guanine nucleotide GTP, the (—)apomorphine curve is shifted to the right and its slope steepens (pseudo-Hill coefficient = 0.94). Computer analysis

261

of these data now indicates a single homogeneous population of binding sites, for which the affinity for (−)apomorphine is not significantly different from the K_L value of the control curve (Figure 5). Three additional agonists, (±)ADTN, (−)NPA, and dopamine give qualitatively identical results *(136)*.

Recently, we have characterized the binding of the radiolabeled agonist [³H]NPA to dopamine receptors in bovine anterior pituitary membranes *(134, 136)*. The identification of high-affinity ³H-labeled agonist binding in a tissue with no direct dopaminergic innervation reinforces our hypothesis *(35)* that under our assay conditions ³H-labeled agonists can label "postsynaptic" receptors. One of the more striking findings with this radioligand is that its B_{max} is approximately 50% of that of [³H]spiroperidol, suggesting that [³H]NPA labels the high-affinity agonist site/state (R_H) seen in agonist/[³H]spiroperidol curves. This is further supported by the finding that agonist/[³H]NPA competition curves are homogeneous, with single affinities that do not differ significantly from the K_H values obtained from the corresponding agonist/[³H]spiroperidol curve. Furthermore, saturating concentrations of guanine nucleotides completely abolish the specific [³H]NPA binding to pituitary membranes.

Two major explanations for these data are available. One is that the R_H and R_L sites represent two discrete dopamine receptors, i.e., two separate protein molecules. The two receptors would have identical affinity for all antagonists but differential affinity for all agonists. In addition, guanine nucleotides would inhibit agonist binding to the R_H receptor in some "allosteric" fashion. The second possibility is that the R_H and R_L sites actually represent high- and low-affinity agonist-binding states of a single receptor molecule. In this model, guanine nucleotides would regulate an interconversion between the high- and the low-affinity states. Evidence supporting this latter possibility is shown in Figure 6. In this experiment, bovine anterior pituitaries were first dispersed into single whole cells via collagenase treatment and then used directly in the binding experiment *(138)*. Strikingly, the (−)apomorphine/[³H]spiroperidol curve is now steep (pseudo-Hill coefficient = 0.86) and resembles the curve for (−)apomorphine/[³H]spiroperidol + guanyl-5'-ylimidophosphate (Figure 5); moreover, exogenous (added) guanine nucleotides no longer affect the (−)apomorphine/[³H]spiroperidol curve. The finding that the

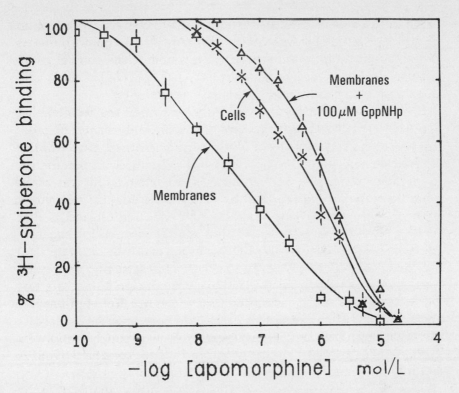

Fig. 6. Competition curve for [³H]spiroperidol binding by (−)apomorphine in intact bovine anterior pituitary cells and membranes

From Sibley et al. *(138)*

(−)apomorphine competition curve does not appear to be maximally shifted and steepened in intact cells may be attributable to a nonsaturating concentration of intracellular GTP at the receptor. Thus, in whole cells, endogenous GTP may regulate agonist binding in a fashion identical to that of exogenous GTP in membrane preparations. Also, specific binding of [³H]NPA is not detectable in intact cells, which directly confirms the absence of a detectable R_H state in these cells. However, membranes prepared from these cells exhibit the same binding properties as membranes directly prepared from the whole gland, thus indicating that the lack of high-affinity agonist binding is not the result of possible receptor degradation during the collagenase-mediated dispersion. Therefore, the R_H and R_L sites are presumably not functionally discrete receptor molecules; otherwise, they would *both* be demonstrable in whole cells as well as in membranes.

Recently, Hoffman and Lefkowitz *(61, 88)* have examined in detail the radioligand–receptor binding characteristics of the β-adrenergic receptor system in frog erythrocytes. Their data with frog erythrocyte β receptors are qualitatively identical to our dopamine-receptor data from the anterior pituitary. That is, agonist/ ^{3}H-labeled antagonist competition curves indicate two affinity states in membranes, with the high-affinity state being dispelled with exogenous guanine nucleotides and being undetectable in intact cells *(78)*.

De Lean et al. *(48)* have proposed a ternary complex model to explain the binding data in the frog erythrocyte system:

$$A + R \rightleftharpoons AR$$

$$AR + N \rightleftharpoons ARN$$

This model is similar to the floating receptor *(73)* or two-step models *(13)* previously described. Briefly, agonists (A) or antagonists can bind to the receptor (R) to form an initial drug–receptor complex (AR). The binding of agonists, however, induces a conformational change in the receptor so that it can now couple to a third membrane component (N). It is this ternary complex (ARN) that is responsible for the high-affinity agonist binding state. Limbird et al. *(92)* have provided evidence that the third component is the guanine nucleotide-binding protein of the adenylate cyclase complex. The ternary complex of agonist, receptor, and nucleotide-binding protein is then presumably responsible for activating adenylate cyclase in the presence of GTP. This complex is formed only transiently, however, its dispersal being rapidly induced by the endogenous GTP in intact cells. Although high-affinity binding of ^{3}H-labeled agonists is not demonstrable under equilibrium conditions in intact cells, it probably does occur upon initial exposure to the ligand.

The application of this model to the anterior pituitary dopamine-receptor system is extremely attractive. However, dopamine does not appear to increase adenylate cyclase activity in the anterior pituitary *(21, 101, 106, 127;* however, see also ref. *1)*; on the contrary, recent evidence suggests that dopamine may actually decrease cAMP formation in the anterior pituitary *(47, 56, 82, 118, 119, 123)*, and can reverse the activation of adenylate cyclase by vasoactive intestinal peptide *(115)*. Thus, the consequences of agonist–receptor complexation may be to decrease mammotroph cAMP content and thus to decrease prolactin release. This hypothesis is additionally supported by recent work suggesting that increased mammotroph cAMP enhances prolactin release (46, 114).

Some of the biochemical mechanisms involved in the dopaminergic regulation of hormone release have been better elucidated in the intermediate pituitary. The intermediate pituitary is composed predominantly of corticotropic cells that synthesize and secrete a variety of peptides related to β-lipotropin and corticotropin, including β-endorphin and α-melanotropin. Interestingly, Vale et al. (151) showed that dopamine agonists could inhibit the release of β-endorphin from cultures of rat neurointermediate pituitary cells, whereas cAMP analogs and phosphodiesterase inhibitors stimulated this release. This latter stimulation was blocked by dopamine agonists, suggesting that dopamine may regulate β-endorphin secretion by decreasing cAMP. More detailed studies of intermediate pituitary corticotroph regulation have been performed by Kebabian and colleagues (26, 27, 109, 110). Using dispersed cells from rat intermediate pituitaries, they demonstrated that β-adrenergic agonists, cAMP analogs, and phosphodiesterase inhibitors enhanced the secretion of α-melanotropin. Activation of the β receptor was accompanied by an increase in corticotropic cAMP. Strikingly, dopamine inhibited the basal and isoproterenol-enhanced release of α-melanotropin as well as the isoproterenol-induced accumulation of cAMP. When adenylate cyclase activity was measured directly in homogenates of the intermediate pituitary, dopamine agonists inhibited the basal as well as the isoproterenol-stimulated cyclase activity. The inhibition of the response to isoproterenol was noncompetitive, because dopamine inhibited the maximum isoproterenol-stimulated increase in cyclase activity without affecting the concentration (EC_{50}) of isoproterenol that stimulated 50% production of cAMP. Evidence suggesting that the mechanism of action by dopamine is distal to the beta receptor came from radioligand-binding experiments with the β antagonist ^{125}I-labeled hydroxybenzylpindolol. Dopamine or dopamine agonists had no direct effect on the binding of the β antagonist, nor did they interfere with the ability of β agonists to compete with it for binding.

Recently we have directly labeled the dopamine receptor in

bovine intermediate pituitary membranes by using [³H]-spiroperidol and [³H]NPA *(135)*. The dopamine-receptor binding characteristics in this tissue are remarkably similar to those in the anterior pituitary. For example, agonist/[³H]spiroperidol curves are shallow (pseudo-Hill coefficients <1), but shift and steepen in the presence of GTP. Additionally, there are approximately twice as many sites for binding [³H]spiroperidol as for [³H]NPA. These observations suggest the presence of identical dopamine receptors in the anterior and intermediate pituitaries; by the biochemical and pharmacological criteria outlined above (ref. *76,* and Table 1), those receptors can therefore be classified as D-2.

Dopamine Receptors in the Central Nervous System

The very first dopamine-receptor binding studies utilized [³H]dopamine and [³H]haloperidol as ligands *(18, 29, 130)* in the examination of receptors in mammalian striatum. [³H]Haloperidol bound to a site with high affinity, very much like the D-2 receptor since described in anterior pituitary *(29, 130)*. Bovine striatum also possessed high-affinity sites for [³H]dopamine and other agonist ligands that, unlike the R_H state of the pituitary D-2 receptor, had very low (approximately micromolar) affinity for butyrophenones *(17, 29, 131)*. This led to the suggestion that mammalian striatum contained two distinct dopaminergic binding sites *(55)*. Much of the controversy of the last few years within this area of research has centered around the neuronal localization of these two sites and their relationship to the dopamine-stimulated adenylate cyclase and autoreceptors.

[³H]Butyrophenone Binding: Labeling D-2 Receptors

Several lines of evidence suggest that at least the majority of high-affinity binding sites for [³H]butyrophenones in the striatum are identical to the D-2 pituitary receptor. The K_D for [³H]spiroperidol binding to dopamine receptors in striatum, determined under a variety of conditions in rat, bovine, and human striatal membranes, is in excellent agreement with the value obtained in bovine anterior pituitary *(34, 53, 64, 90, 122)*. However, there are approximately five- to 10-fold more receptors in the striatum. As in pituitary, ³H-labeled agonist ligands can, under appropriate conditions, label these same sites with high affinity (see below), and the affinity of agonists is reduced by guanine nucleotides with a specificity similar to that of pituitary *(39, 157)*. All D-2 receptors appear to be postsynaptic to the nigrostriatal terminals since they are not decreased by 6-hydroxydopamine lesions, which remove this pathway *(31)*. Striatal kainic acid lesion, which destroys the intrinsic striatal neurons, removes about 50% of the D-2 receptors *(128)*. The remaining D-2 receptors are located on the presynaptic terminals of the cortical input to the striatum and may regulate glutamate release from these neurons. The sensitivity of these D-2 receptors to GTP may be different from that of the D-2 receptors in the pituitary or on the intrinsic striatal neurons *(38)*.

Biochemically, the function of the striatal D-2 receptor is not known, although it now seems certain that it is not positively linked to the dopamine-stimulated adenylate cyclase. This D-2 site displays a much different pharmacological specificity *(29, 67)*, ontogenetic timecourse *(117)*, and regional *(122)* and cellular distribution (see below) than the dopamine-stimulated adenylate cyclase. This contention has further been supported by irreversible inhibition studies with phenoxybenzamine *(59)*. That the striatal D-2 receptor mediates the inhibition of a hormone-stimulated adenylate cyclase (as suggested for the pituitary D-2 receptors) is purely conjectural at this time. It should be borne in mind, however, that sensitivity to guanine nucleotide is at least consistent with such a hypothesis.

On the behavioral level, by contrast, the functional relevance of the striatal D-2 receptors is extremely well documented. The affinities of a number of structurally diverse dopamine antagonists for butyrophenone-binding sites correlate highly with their molar potencies in antagonism of apomorphine- ($r = 0.94$, $p < 0.001$) and amphetamine-induced ($r = 0.92$, $p < 0.001$) stereotyped behavior in rat *(32)*. Blockade of apomorphine-induced emesis in dog also correlates closely with D-2 binding-site affinities. This latter test may avoid the complicating factor of differential drug distribution, by being presumed to involve dopamine receptors in the area postrema of the brainstem, where the blood–brain barrier is less effective. Of greatest clinical importance is the correlation between the potencies of these drugs as antipsychotic agents in humans, and their potencies in competition for

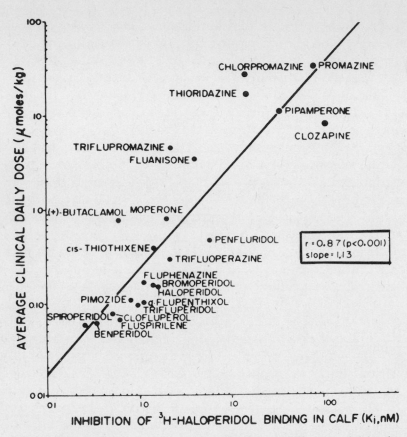

Fig. 7. Correlation of neuroleptic drug affinity for [³H]haloperidol-binding sites in bovine striatal membranes with average dosages for antipsychotic activity in humans

x-axis, inhibition constant (K_i), nmol/L. From Creese et al. (30)

[³H]butyrophenone binding (30, 132) (Figure 7). The affinity of an antagonist for [³H]butyrophenone binding is thus a powerful predictor of in vivo dopamine receptor antagonism and antipsychotic activity. The nanomolar affinities of the antipsychotic drugs for dopamine-receptor binding sites are also commensurate with the plasma concentrations of these drugs at therapeutic dose, as measured by the neuroleptic radioreceptor assay or other methods (37). A similar analysis indicates that the anti-parkinsonian effects of dopamine agonists are also mediated through butyrophenone-labeled D-2 receptors (125, 147).

[³H]Thioxanthene Binding: Labeling D-1 Receptors

A high-affinity striatal binding site for [³H]flupentixol *(42, 66–68)* and [³H]piflutixol *(69)* appears from competition studies to be the D-1 receptor (linked to adenylate cyclase stimulation). The potencies of many dopaminergic antagonists from a variety of structural classes in inhibiting dopamine-stimulated adenylate cyclase activity correlate well with their potencies in displacing [³H]thioxanthenes. For example, thioxanthenes, which possess very high affinity for [³H]flupentixol-binding sites, also have nanomolar potency in the inhibition of the dopamine-stimulated adenylate cyclase. Butyrophenone affinity for both the dopamine-stimulated adenylate cyclase and [³H]flupentixol-binding sites are one to two orders of magnitude lower. Detailed displacement studies have revealed that a minor portion, about 20%, of the specific binding of these thioxanthene ligands is to D-2 receptors *(42, 69)*. [³H]Thioxanthene binding can be directed to label the putative D-1 receptor exclusively, by including an appropriate "masking" drug, i.e., low concentrations of unlabeled butyrophenones in the assay to saturate the D-2 receptors, allowing selective competition studies of the D-1 sites. Agonists are active in stimulating cyclase in the micromolar range. However, as might be expected of a receptor linked to stimulation of adenylate cyclase, agonists exhibit a high-affinity (nanomolar) displacement of between 25 and 50% of specific [³H]flupentixol binding. This high-affinity binding is GTP-sensitive, so that in the presence of guanine nucleotides all agonist displacement occurs in the micromolar range *(137)*.

³H-Labeled Agonist-Binding Sites

Putative dopamine receptors in striatum have also been identified by the binding of tritiated dopamine agonists, including [³H]dopamine itself *(81)*. Unlike the binding of the [³H]-butyrophenone ligands, that of the ³H-labeled agonist ligands is markedly dependent on assay conditions. Under some conditions, tritiated agonist ligands bind to striatal D-2 receptors with high affinity *(148)*, as they do in anterior pituitary. A subset of the ³H-labeled agonist-binding sites, however, differs from both the butyrophenone-labeled D-2 binding sites and dopamine-stimulated adenylate cyclase in that butyrophenones have micromolar affinities whereas agonists have nanomolar affinities for these sites. Thus, it has been proposed that these agonist-binding sites, termed "D-3," represent yet another distinct dopamine receptor, the auto-receptor (146).

The function of the "D-3" sites is unclear. Drug affinities at these sites do not correlate with antipsychotic (30) or anti-parkin-sonian (147) activities. Lesion studies have suggested that the "D-3" sites may represent autoreceptors on nigrostriatal terminals. In the rat striatum, "D-3" sites were decreased 50% by 6-hydroxy-dopamine lesions of the nigrostriatal dopamine pathway (113, 144, 145), suggesting that such "D-3" binding labels the presynap-tic dopamine autoreceptors on the degenerated nigrostriatal termi-nals (113, 129, 144, 145). However, nigrostriatal denervation pro-duces a concomitant depletion of striatal dopamine. We have demonstrated that a reserpine-induced depletion of dopamine produces a comparable decrease in "D-3" binding independent of presynaptic terminal degeneration (Leff and Creese, submitted for publication). This loss in binding, or that caused by 6-hydroxy-dopamine lesions, is recovered by pre-incubating the striatal membranes with dopamine or with the supernate from control striatal membrane preparations. Therefore we suggest that the loss of "D-3" binding after 6-hydroxydopamine lesions results from the depletion of endogenous dopamine rather than the de-generation of terminals and their putatively associated autore-ceptors.

Other recent studies have suggested that the addition of dopa-mine to pre-incubations of washed or dopamine-depleted striatal membrane homogenates increases "D-3" binding (3, 60). In these studies the pre-incubation of the membrane homogenates was a crucial variable in the improved expression of all [³H]dopamine-specific binding. As has been suggested by Hamblin and Creese (60), this pre-incubation in the presence of (endogenous) dopa-mine and divalent cations may promote the dissociation and wash-out of endogenous guanine nucleotides from guanine nucleotide binding sites, which regulate dopamine agonist binding to D-2 and "D-3" binding sites by decreasing agonist affinity. This resem-bles the mechanism by which agonist pre-incubations appear to enhance agonist binding to some β-adrenergic receptors (83). Irrespective of mechanism, these data indicate that 6-hydroxy-dopamine denervation and reserpine treatments appear to reduce specific "D-3" binding by eliminating the usual pre-incubation-induced enhancement of this binding seen in control tissues containing endogenous dopamine.

In β-adrenergic systems associated with the stimulation of cAMP production, a high-affinity agonist-binding state of the receptor existing in membrane preparations is guanine nucleotide-sensitive (89, 156). Our recent studies indeed suggest that D-1 dopamine receptors demonstrate high- and low-affinity agonist-binding states, in much the same way as D-2 receptors that are modulated by guanine nucleotides (137). We suggest, therefore, that "D-3" binding may, at least in part, label the high-affinity agonist state of the D-1 receptor. This is reinforced by a series of corroborative findings. Firstly, "D-3" binding is reduced by striatal kainic acid lesion, which removes striatal intrinsic neurons that contain D-1 receptors. Secondly, agonist displacement of [^{3}H]flupentixol binding to D-1 receptors is biphasic, with the K_H of the high-affinity displacement phase matching the K_D of direct binding of ^{3}H-labeled agonists to "D-3" sites. Thirdly, both types of agonist binding (displacement of [^{3}H]flupentixol binding to D-1 receptors or ^{3}H-labeled agonist binding to "D-3" sites) are equivalently sensitive to GTP. Fourthly, antagonists' affinities at "D-3" sites correlate highly with antagonist affinities at D-1 receptors.

Functional and Clinical Implications of Dopamine Receptor Regulation

Dopamine receptors are dynamic macromolecules under the influence of a large variety of numerous factors; they appear to be subject to regulatory mechanisms similar to those that modulate other neurotransmitter and hormone receptors. The pharmacological manipulation of these regulatory mechanisms may prove to be a sensitive means of therapy in the numerous psychiatric and neurological diseases in which dysfunction of the dopamine system has been implicated. Furthermore, disruptions of the normal regulatory mechanisms may be etiologic in neurologic and psychiatric diseases and side effects of neuroleptic drugs.

Dopaminergic Denervation and Receptor Blockade

In Parkinson's disease, the dopamine cells in the substantia nigra degenerate, progressively denervating the striatum and resulting in the characteristic syndrome of bradykinesia, rigidity, and tremor. This syndrome can be mimicked in animals by producing lesions in the nigrostriatal pathway through use of 6-hydroxydopamine, a toxin selective for catecholamine neurons. Studies of radioligand binding to dopamine receptors have clearly demonstrated that the supersensitive behavioral responsiveness exhibited by lesioned rats to dopamine agonists is accompanied by an increase in the number (but no change in the affinity) of D-2 dopamine receptors in the striatum (31), a classic example of degeneration-induced postsynaptic receptor supersensitivity. Investigations of the dopamine-stimulated adenylate cyclase are controversial, with studies reporting both increases and no change in activity after denervation (for a review, see ref. 36). Seeman and colleagues (86) found 50% increases in the number of dopamine receptors in patients who died with Parkinson's disease. These patients were not treated with L-dopa before their death— a crucial variable, because L-dopa therapy may itself alter receptor number (see below).

One might anticipate that pharmacological blockade would produce postsynaptic supersensitivity similar to that produced by denervation, and indeed this occurs in both humans and animals (reviewed in ref. 36). In schizophrenic patients, who are often treated for many years with antipsychotic medication, tardive dyskinesia, a disabling syndrome characterized by abnormal repetitive movements of the face and extremities, develops in a significant proportion (4). Klawans (79) suggested that tardive dyskinesia might be directly caused by an "up-regulation" of dopamine receptors in the extrapyramidal motor system, because the disorder can be temporarily inhibited by increasing the dose of neuroleptic drug and is exacerbated by reducing the antipsychotic medication. Chronic neuroleptic treatment of animals for periods as short as a day to as long as many months also results in behavioral changes suggestive of a dopamine-receptor supersensitivity. In support of this hypothesis, receptor-binding studies involving both ^{3}H-labeled antagonists and agonists have demonstrated that after one or more weeks of neuroleptic treatment, followed by a brief withdrawal period, there is a 20 to 35% increase in striatal antagonist-binding sites and a smaller increase in agonist-binding sites (reviewed in refs. 36, 107). In very long-term treatment regimens of six months or more, which more closely simulates the dosage of human schizophrenic patients, [³H]butyrophenone-binding sites increase by as much as 65% (116).

Recent evidence suggests that motor abnormalities may not be inevitable sequelae of neuroleptic medication. Reversal of super-sensitivity by dopamine agonists has potential as a treatment of tardive dyskinesia. Given that behavioral and receptor supersensi-tivity that develops after chronic neuroleptic treatment can be reversed by subsequent treatment of animals with L-dopa (54, 96), those investigators have suggested that "down-regulation" of the supersensitive receptors was the therapeutic factor. Evi-dence that "down-regulation" may occur in humans was demon-strated in the brains of patients with Parkinson's disease (86). Patients who were not receiving L-dopa before death showed sig-nificantly more dopamine receptors than controls or patients who were receiving L-dopa therapy.

In addition, lithium appears to exert a "stabilizing" effect on dopamine receptors, preventing not only the behavioral supersen-sitivity seen after chronic administration of neuroleptics but also the increase in dopamine receptors that accompanies it (80, 120). These findings may have profound implications for the treatment of tardive dyskinesia as well as for that of affective disorders.

Dopamine Receptors in Schizophrenia

Schizophrenia has been hypothesized to be associated with in-creased dopaminergic neurotransmission. Supporting evidence in-cludes the worsening of schizophrenic symptoms by the adminis-tration of amphetamine (a drug that enhances dopaminergic neurotransmission) and the induction of psychosis after chronic amphetamine abuse (28). On the other hand, inhibiting the syn-thesis or storage of dopamine ameliorates schizophrenic symp-toms. Of relevance to clinical studies investigating the role of changes in dopamine receptors in the etiology of schizophrenia are six postmortem studies reporting significant (50–200%) in-creases in [³H]butyrophenone binding in the brains of schizo-phrenic patients (43, 44, 85, 87, 97, 98). Most of these patients had been previously treated with antipsychotic medication. Thus it is unclear whether the observed receptor increase is a primary cause of the disease process or simply iatrogenic, e.g., the result of chronic treatment with neuroleptics. On the other hand, the few "neuroleptic-free" or "neuroleptic-naive" schizophrenics examined do exhibit greater densities of dopamine receptors than do the normal controls (87, 116).

These results are both exciting and tantalizing. The demonstration that a psychiatric illness is the result of a deficit in receptor regulation would markedly change current psychiatric concepts and have a major clinical impact. We have recently completed a very large study (99) in which brain tissue was obtained at autopsy from more than 70 patients who had had a hospital diagnosis of schizophrenia. In postmortem samples of caudate nucleus and nucleus accumbens from 48 of the patients, there were significant increases in both the maximum number (B_{max}) of binding sites (Figure 8) and the apparent dissociation constant (K_D) for [³H]spiroperidol. The increase in apparent K_D probably reflects the presence of residual neuroleptic drugs, because this increase was reversed by "washing" the brain membranes.

Changes in the B_{max} value, however, seem to reflect genuine alterations in the density of dopamine receptors. As observed by Owen et al. (116), the increases in the B_{max} value in the psychotic group were most noticeable in the caudate nucleus, where patients who received neuroleptic medication until death exhibited about a 70% increase in [³H]spiperone-binding sites, whereas the increase was approximately 50% in the nucleus accumbens (Figure 8). The most striking observation, however, was that the abnormality in the B_{max} value was seen only in patients who had received neuroleptic medication until death (Figure 8); there was no significant difference in B_{max} values between controls and those patients who had been untreated with neuroleptic drugs for one month or more before death. These findings were true in both brain areas.

There is a small but statistically significant ($p < 0.02$) increase in dopamine concentration in the nucleus accumbens in the psychotic group (n = 57), being greatest in the subgroup of schizophrenic patients in whom the onset of illness occurred early in life (between the age of 15 and 24 years). In this group, dopamine concentrations were increased by 43% over control values. A similar small but statistically significant ($p < 0.05$) increase in dopamine concentrations in the caudate (n = 64) was also exaggerated in the "early-onset schizophrenia" subgroup. In a small number of patients who had been free of neuroleptic medication for more than one month before death, dopamine values in the caudate

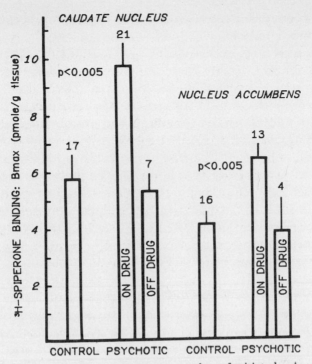

Fig. 8. Changes in maximum number of tritiated spi-perone-binding sites (B_{max}) in caudate nucleus and nucleus accumbens in schizophrenic patients

On drug, patients receiving neuroleptic medication until time of death; *off drug,* patients who had not received neuroleptic medication for at least one month before death

nucleus and nucleus accumbens were similar to those observed in the overall psychotic group.

An unexpected finding was that in the psychotic group, but not in the control group, there was a significant negative correlation between age at death and dopamine concentrations in both the caudate nucleus and nucleus accumbens. This observation clearly affects the interpretation of the finding that the dopamine concentration was most sharply increased in the early-onset schizophrenia subgroup, because in this group a disproportionately large number of patients died relatively early in life. Thus, it is difficult to determine whether age at onset of illness or age at death is the more important factor in determining postmortem dopamine values in the psychotic group.

Our findings suggest, but do not prove, that drug treatment may be responsible for the increases in dopamine receptors observed in postmortem samples obtained from patients dying with schizophrenic illness. It seems less likely that drug history is the determining factor responsible for the observed changes in brain dopamine content. In any case, the increases in brain dopamine content in patients with schizophrenia are not easy to interpret. They do not seem to be consistently associated with increased concentrations of dopamine metabolites in postmortem brain samples and thus do not necessarily imply any increase in synaptic use of this monoamine. The present results emphasize the difficulties likely to be encountered in interpreting the results of postmortem biochemical analyses of human brain. The paradoxical age-dependent changes in biochemical variables in schizophrenia patients suggest that future studies should use carefully age-matched populations and perhaps focus on those patients who die at a relatively early age.

Chronic Stimulation of Receptors

Acute or chronic treatment with agonists might well be expected to lead to both a behavioral and receptor subsensitivity, as is the case in many other neurotransmitter/hormone systems. However, the chronic treatment of rats and guinea pigs with amphetamine leads to a paradoxical increase in behavioral sensitivity to subsequent amphetamine or apomorphine treatments *(133, 155)*. The behavioral supersensitivity may indicate that low doses of agonists preferentially activate presynaptic autoreceptors and decrease dopamine release. This decreased dopamine presynaptic activity would then be compensated for by a postsynaptic receptor supersensitivity. This may represent one mechanism by which amphetamine can induce psychosis.

Too few receptor-binding studies have been conducted at present to allow any firm conclusions to be drawn about agonist-induced receptor changes. We have found that amphetamine treatment for five days (2.5 mg/kg of body weight, four times per day) paradoxically decreases by 20% the maximum number of [^{3}H]spiroperidol-binding sites in rat striatum, with a smaller but significant decrease in ^{3}H-labeled agonist (NPA) binding *(139)*. Similar findings have been reported by Howlett and Nahorski *(65)*. In contrast, Muller and Seeman *(108)* have not been able to demonstrate changes in [^{3}H]haloperidol binding in response to apomorphine or amphetamine administration (10 mg/kg per day) for 14 days, although they did find a 25% decrease in [^{3}H]apomorphine binding. All of these studies are inconclusive because chronic administration of amphetamine causes marked changes in concentration of dopamine, norepinephrine, and serotonin. It is thus unclear whether the apparent behavioral supersensitivity these animals demonstrate is due solely to dopaminergic mechanisms, or whether it is the result of interactions between multiple neuronal systems.

Radioreceptor Assays

The routine monitoring of blood concentrations of some drugs is an important tool and often a necessary aid in the clinical management of disease. Tardive dyskinesia may be associated with high blood concentrations of neuroleptics that accumulate, even in patients maintained on a recommended dose (4, 75). Large interindividual differences in the bioavailability of neuroleptics present less than optimal conditions for the treatment of schizophrenia. Thus the recommended dosage may be either too low to achieve therapeutic results or unnecessarily high. Further, it is important to determine whether patients who are unresponsive to therapy are receiving a potentially detrimental dosage. Because neuroleptic drugs (or their therapeutically active metabolites) are clinically efficacious in proportion to their potency in blocking brain D-2 receptors, one can directly measure the concentration of neuroleptic drugs in plasma or serum by their inhibition of [^{3}H]haloperidol or [^{3}H]spiroperidol binding to D-2 receptors in a sample of rat or bovine caudate membrane (37, 150). No extraction procedure is necessary because the small volumes (15–30 μL) of plasma or serum do not interfere with binding and because the neuroleptics compete with [^{3}H]butyrophenone binding at concentrations much lower than their usual therapeutic concentrations in blood.

Radioreceptor assays have several advantages and may be routinely conducted for large patient populations. Because the assay is selective for neuroleptics, it can therefore be used with samples from patients receiving other drugs (33). Among other drug classes, only the dopaminergic ergots and a few tricyclic antidepressants (84) compete significantly in these assays; however, these agents are not usually prescribed for schizophrenics. Therapeutically active metabolites of neuroleptics will be detected in this assay because they, too, compete for dopamine receptor binding. This is a major advantage of the radioreceptor assay, because some metabolites produced in vivo are active in blocking dopamine-receptor activity, yet would have to be individually identified to be detected by fluorometric, immunologic, or chromatographic methods. In addition, the radioreceptor procedure is highly sensitive: with haloperidol, for example, as little as 2.5 ng of total serum haloperidol per milliliter can be readily detected (37).

Utilization of this application of the radioligand-binding technique will make possible better control of the degree of blockade of dopamine receptors by dopamine-antagonist drugs. This has great clinical utility, particularly in ensuring that patients are not overmedicated and thus will not become more likely to develop untoward side effects.

Concluding Comments

The interpretation of early dopamine-receptor binding studies with striatal membranes was difficult—the data did not describe a system containing a single set of homogeneous receptors. Several approaches have now allowed the clear division of dopamine receptors in the central nervous system into subtypes. Among the most important advances have been the examination of binding characteristics in other tissues, such as anterior pituitary, and the use of discrete lesions to remove particular presynaptic or postsynaptic cellular elements. Such studies have now characterized two dopamine-receptor subtypes, D-1 and D-2, which have the characteristics shown in Table 2.

This classification is, as yet, preliminary; a number of questions remain. For instance, the possibility that a portion of the ^{3}H-labeled agonist "D-3" binding sites may label autoreceptors has not yet been rigorously excluded. Also, other classes of dopamine-receptor sites, such as those having high affinity for substituted benzamides, may be further elucidated in future studies. Additionally, the degree to which D-2 receptors on corticostriate terminals and intrinsic striatal neurons may differ is as yet uncertain.

Uncertainties also exist with respect to the function of each dopamine-receptor subtype. It is still not clear, for example, that D-2 receptors increase in schizophrenic patients independent of the effects of chronic neuroleptic treatment; thus, the involvement of dopamine receptors and their regulation in this disorder remains

Table 2. **Characteristics of Dopaminergic Binding Sites**

	D-1		D-2	
	"D-3" R_H ⇌	R_L	R_H ⇌	R_L
Usable radioligands				
[³H]Thioxanthenes	+	+	+	+
[³H]Butyrophenones	−	−	+	+
³H-Labeled agonists	Nanomolar	Micromolar	Nanomolar	Micromolar
Butyrophenone affinity	Micromolar	Micromolar	Nanomolar	Nanomolar
Adenylate cyclase association	Stimulatory		Inhibitory or unassociated	
Guanine nucleotide sensitivity	++	−	+	−
Function	Parathyrin release; striatum unknown		Inhibition of pituitary hormone release; dopamine-mediated behavioral responses and their antagonism by neuroleptics	
Striatal location	Intrinsic neurons		Intrinsic neurons and corticostriate afferents	
Pituitary location	No		Yes	

obscure. In addition, although there is a clear role for D-1 receptors in stimulating—and for some D-2 receptors in inhibiting—adenylate cyclase activity, their subsequent biochemical and physiological functions are unknown. The availability of selective agonists and antagonists has been central to the past therapeutic and experimental advances in the field of dopaminergic transmission. The advent of even more selective D-1, D-2, and autoreceptor agents may allow not only the resolution of the above questions, but also better pharmacological treatment of disorders involving these receptor subtypes.

References

1. Ahn HM, Gardner E, Makman MH. Anterior pituitary adenylate cyclase: Stimulation by dopamine and other monoamines. *Eur J Pharmacol* **53**, 313–317 (1979).
2. Attie MF, Brown EM, Gardner DG, et al. Characterization of dopamine-responsive adenylate cyclase of bovine parathyroid cells and its relationship to parathyroid hormone secretion. *Endocrinology* **107**, 1776–1781 (1980).
3. Bacopolous NG. Acute changes in the state of dopamine receptors; in vitro monitoring with ³H-dopamine. *Life Sci* **29**, 2407–2414 (1981).
4. Baldessarini RJ, Tarsy D. Relationship of the actions of neuroleptic

drugs to the pathophysiology of tardive dyskinesia. *Int Rev Neurobiol* **21**, 1–45 (1979).

5. Bannon MJ, Reinhard JF Jr, Bunney EB, Roth RH. Unique response to antipsychotic drugs is due to absence of terminal autoreceptors in mesocortical dopamine neurones. *Nature* **296**, 444–446 (1982).

6. Beckstead RM, Domesick VB, Nauta WJH. Efferent connections of the substantia nigra and ventral tegmental area in the rat. *Brain Res* **175**, 191–217 (1979).

7. Bell C, Lang WJ, Laska F. Dopamine-containing vasomotor nerves in the dog kidney. *J Neurochem* **31**, 77–83 (1978).

8. Bennett JP Jr. Methods in binding studies. In *Neurotransmitter Receptor Binding,* HI Yamamura, SJ Enna, MJ Kuhar, Eds., Raven Press, New York, NY, 1978, pp 57–90.

9. Berger B, Tassin JP, Blanc G, et al. Histochemical confirmation for dopaminergic innervation of the rat cerebral cortex after destruction of the noradrenergic ascending pathways. *Brain Res* **81**, 332–337 (1974).

10. Bjorklund A, Lindvall O. Dopamine in dendrites of substantia nigra neurons: Suggestions for a role in dendritic terminals. *Brain Res* **83**, 531–537 (1975).

11. Bjorklund A, Lindvall O, Nobin A. Evidence of an incerto-hypo-thalamic dopamine neurone system in the rat. *Brain Res* **89**, 29–42 (1975).

12. Blessing WW, Chalmers JP. Direct projection of catecholamine (presumably dopamine)-containing neurons from hypothalamus to spinal cord. *Neurosci Lett* **11**, 35–40 (1979).

13. Boeynaems JM, Dumont JE. The two-step model of ligand–receptor interaction. *Mol Cell Endocrinol* **7**, 33–47 (1977).

14. Brown EM, Attie MF, Reen S, et al. Characterization of dopa-minergic receptors in dispersed bovine parathyroid cells. *Mol Pharmacol* **18**, 335–340 (1980).

15. Brown EM, Carrol RJ, Aurbach GD. Dopaminergic stimulation of cyclic AMP accumulation and parathyroid hormone release from dispersed bovine parathyroid cells. *Proc Natl Acad Sci USA* **74**, 4210–4213 (1977).

16. Burt DR. Criteria for receptor identification. In *Neurotransmitter Receptor Binding, op cit* (ref *8),* pp 41–55.

17. Burt DR, Creese I, Snyder SH. Properties of [³H]haloperidol and [³H]dopamine binding associated with dopamine receptors in calf brain membranes. *Mol Pharmacol* **12**, 800–812 (1976).

18. Burt DR, Enna SJ, Creese I, et al. Dopamine receptor binding in the corpus striatum of mammalian brain. *Proc Natl Acad Sci USA* **72**, 4655–4659 (1975).

19. Calabro MA, MacLeod RM. Binding of dopamine to bovine anterior pituitary gland membranes. *Neuroendocrinology* **25**, 32–46 (1978).
20. Caron MC, Beaulieu M, Raymond V, et al. Dopaminergic receptors in the anterior pituitary gland. *J Biol Chem* **253**, 2244–2253 (1978).
21. Clement-Cormier YC, Heindel JJ, Robison GA. Adenylyl cyclase from a prolactin producing tumour cell: The effect of phenothiazines. *Life Sci* **21**, 1357–1364 (1977).
22. Clement-Cormier YC, Kebabian JW, Petzold GL, Greengard P. Dopamine-sensitive adenylate cyclase in mammalian brain: A possible site of action of antipsychotic drugs. *Proc Natl Acad Sci USA* **71**, 1113–1117 (1974).
23. Commissiong JW, Gentleman S, Neff SH. Spinal cord dopaminergic neurons: Evidence for an uncrossed nigrospinal pathway. *Neuropharmacology* **18**, 565–568 (1979).
24. Commissiong JW, Neff NH. Current status of dopamine in the mammalian spinal cord. *Biochem Pharmacol* **28**, 1569–1573 (1979).
25. Corsini GU, Del Zompo M, Marconi S, et al. Evidence for dopamine receptors in the human brain mediating sedation and sleep. *Life Sci* **20**, 1613–1618 (1977).
26. Cote TE, Grewe CW, Kebabian JW. Stimulation of the D-2 dopamine receptor in the intermediate lobe of the rat pituitary gland decreases the responsiveness of the beta-adrenoceptor: Biochemical mechanism. *Endocrinology* **108**, 420–426 (1981).
27. Cote T, Munemura M, Eskay RL, et al. Biochemical identification of the beta-adrenoceptor and evidence for the involvement of a cyclic AMP system in the beta-adrenergic-induced release of alpha-melanocyte stimulating hormone in the intermediate lobe of the rat pituitary gland. *Endocrinology* **107**, 108–116 (1980).
28. Creese I. *Stimulants: Neurochemical, Behavioral and Chemical Perspectives*, Raven Press, New York, NY, 1983.
29. Creese I, Burt DR, Snyder SH. Dopamine receptor binding: Differentiation of agonist and antagonist states with ^{3}H-dopamine and ^{3}H-haloperidol. *Life Sci* **17**, 993–1002 (1975).
30. Creese I, Burt DR, Snyder SH. Dopamine receptor binding predicts clinical and pharmacological potencies of antischizophrenic drugs. *Science* **192**, 481–483 (1976).
31. Creese I, Burt DR, Snyder SH. Dopamine receptor binding enhancement accompanies lesion-induced behavioral supersensitivity. *Science* **197**, 596–598 (1977).
32. Creese I, Burt DR, Snyder SH. Biochemical actions of neuroleptic drugs: Focus on the dopamine receptor. In *Handbook of Psychopharmacology* **10**, LL Iversen, SD Iversen, SH Snyder, Eds., Plenum Press, New York, NY, 1978, pp 37–89.

33. Creese I, Lader S, Rosenberg B. A radioreceptor assay for neuroleptic drugs. In *Clinical Pharmacology in Psychiatry—Neuroleptic and Antidepressant Research,* E Usdin, SG Dahl, LF Gram, O Lingjaerde, Eds., Macmillan Press, New York, NY, 1981, pp 79–109.

34. Creese I, Schneider R, Snyder SH. ³H-Spiroperidol labels dopamine receptors in pituitary and brain. *Eur J Pharmacol* **46,** 377–381 (1977).

35. Creese I, Sibley DR. Radioligand binding studies: Evidence for multiple dopamine receptors. *Commun Psychopharmacol* **3,** 385–395 (1979).

36. Creese I, Sibley DR. Regulation of dopamine receptors. In *Psychopharmacology and Biochemistry of Neurotransmitter Receptors,* HI Yamamura, RW Olsen, E Usdin, Eds., Raven Press, New York, NY, 1980, pp 387–410.

37. Creese I, Snyder SH. A novel, simple and sensitive radioreceptor assay for antischizophrenic drugs in blood. *Nature* **270,** 180–182 (1977).

38. Creese I, Usdin TB, Snyder SH. Guanine nucleotides distinguish between two dopamine receptors. *Nature* **278,** 577–578 (1979).

39. Creese I, Usdin TB, Snyder SH. Dopamine receptor binding regulated by guanine nucleotides. *Mol Pharmacol* **16,** 69–76 (1979).

40. Cronin MJ, Roberts JM, Weiner RI. Dopamine and dihydroergocryptine binding to the anterior pituitary and other brain areas of the rat and sheep. *Endocrinology* **103,** 302–309 (1978).

41. Cronin MJ, Weiner RI. [³H]Spiroperidol (spiperone) binding to a putative dopamine receptor in sheep and steer pituitary and stalk median eminence. *Endocrinology* **104,** 307–312 (1979).

42. Cross AJ, Owen F. Characteristics of ³H-*cis*-flupenthixol binding to calf brain membranes. *Eur J Pharmacol* **65,** 341–347 (1980).

43. Crow TJ, Cross AJ, Johnstone EC, et al. Abnormal involuntary movements in schizophrenia: Are they related to the disease process of its treatment? Are they associated with changes in dopamine receptors? *J Clin Psychopharmacol* **2,** 336–340 (1982).

44. Crow TJ, Johnston EC, Owen F, et al. Dopaminergic mechanisms in schizophrenia. *Life Sci* **23,** 563–568 (1978).

45. Dahlstrom A, Fuxe K. Evidence for the existence of monoamine-containing neurons in the central nervous system. I. Demonstration of monoamines in the cell bodies of brain stem neurons. *Acta Physiol Scand* **232** (Suppl 62), 1–55 (1964).

46. Dannies PS, Gautvik KM, Tashjian AH. A possible role of cyclic AMP in mediating the effects of thyrotropin-releasing hormone on prolactin release and on prolactin and growth hormone synthesis in pituitary cells in culture. *Endocrinology* **98,** 1147–1159 (1976).

47. De Camilli P, Macconi D, Sdada A. Dopamine inhibits adenylate

cyclase in human prolactin-secreting pituitary adenomas. *Nature* **278**, 252–254 (1979).

48. De Lean A, Stadel JM, Lefkowitz RJ. A ternary complex model explains the agonist-specific binding properties of the adenylate cyclase-coupled beta-adrenergic receptor. *J Biol Chem* **255**, 7108–7117 (1980).

49. Dinerstein RJ, Vannice J, Henderson RC, et al. Histofluorescence techniques provide evidence for dopamine-containing neuronal elements in canine kidney. *Science* **205**, 497–499 (1979).

50. Ehinger B. Biogenic amines as transmitters in the retina. In *Transmitters in the Visual Process*, SL Bonting, Ed., Pergamon Press, Oxford, 1976, pp 145–163.

51. Feinberg AP, Snyder SH. Phenothiazine drugs: Structure–activity relationships explained by a conformation that mimics dopamine. *Proc Natl Acad Sci USA* **72**, 1899–1903 (1975).

52. Fielding S, Lal H. Behavioral actions of neuroleptics. In *Handbook of Psychopharmacology* **10**, *op cit* (ref *32*), pp 91–128.

53. Fields JZ, Reisine TD, Yamamura HI. Biochemical demonstration of dopaminergic receptors in rat and human brain using [^{3}H]spiroperidol. *Brain Res* **136**, 578–584 (1977).

54. Friedhoff AJ, Bonnet K, Rosengarten H. Reversal of two manifestations of dopamine receptor supersensitivity by administration of L-dopa. *Chem Pathol Pharmacol* **16**, 411–423 (1977).

55. Furchgott RF. Pharmacological characterization of receptors: Its relation to radioligand-binding studies. *Fed Proc Fed Am Soc Exp Biol* **37**, 115–120 (1978).

56. Giannattasio G, DeFerrari ME, Spada A. Dopamine-inhibited adenylate cyclase in female rat adenohypophysis. *Life Sci* **28**, 1605–1612 (1981).

57. Goldsmith PC, Cronin MJ, Weiner RI. Dopamine receptor sites in the anterior pituitary. *J Hist Cytochem* **27**, 1205–1207 (1979).

58. Greengard P. Possible role for cyclic nucleotides and phosphorylated membrane proteins in postsynaptic actions of neurotransmitters. *Nature* **260**, 101–108 (1976).

59. Hamblin M, Creese I. Phenoxybenzamine treatment differentiates dopaminergic ^{3}H-ligand binding sites in bovine caudate membranes. *Mol Pharmacol* **21**, 41–51 (1982).

60. Hamblin MW, Creese I. ^{3}H-Dopamine binding to rat striatal D-2 and D-3 sites: Enhancement by magnesium and inhibition by sodium. *Life Sci* **30**, 1587–1595 (1982).

61. Hoffman BB, Lefkowitz RJ. Radioligand binding studies of adrenergic receptors: New insights into molecular and physiological regulation. *Ann Rev Pharmacol Toxicol* **20**, 581–608 (1980).

62. Hokfelt T, Halasz N, Ljungdahl A, et al. Histochemical support for a dopaminergic mechanism in the dendrites of certain periglomerular cells in the rat olfactory bulb. *Neurosci Lett* **1**, 85–90 (1975).

63. Hornykiewicz O. Dopamine and brain function. *Pharmacol Res* **18**, 925–964 (1966).

64. Howlett DR, Nahorski SR. A comparative study of [^{3}H]haloperidol and [^{3}H]spiroperidol binding to receptors on rat cerebral membranes. *FEBS Lett* **87**, 152–156 (1978).

65. Howlett DR, Nahorski SR. Acute and chronic amphetamine treatments modulate striatal dopamine receptor binding sites. *Brain Res* **161**, 173–178 (1979).

66. Hyttel J. A comparison of the effect of neuroleptic drugs on the binding of ^{3}H-haloperidol and ^{3}H-*cis(Z)*-flupenthixol and on adenylate cyclase activity in rat striatal tissue in vitro. *Prog Neuro-Psychopharmacol* **2**, 329–335 (1978).

67. Hyttel J. Effects of neuroleptics on ^{3}H-haloperidol and ^{3}H-*cis(Z)*-flupenthixol binding and on adenylate cyclase activity in vitro. *Life Sci* **23**, 551–556 (1978).

68. Hyttel J. Further evidence that ^{3}H-*cis(Z)*flupenthixol binds to the adenylate cyclase-associated dopamine receptor (D-1) in rat corpus striatum. *Psychopharmacology* **67**, 107–109 (1980).

69. Hyttel J. Similarities between the binding of ^{3}H-piflutixol and ^{3}H-flupentixol to rat striatal dopamine receptors in vitro. *Life Sci* **28**, 563–569 (1981).

70. Iversen LL. Dopamine receptors in the brain. *Science* **188**, 1084–1089 (1975).

71. Iversen LL, Rogawski MA, Miller RJ. Comparison of the effects of neuroleptic drugs on pre- and postsynaptic dopaminergic mechanisms in the rat striatum. *Mol Pharmacol* **12**, 251–262 (1976).

72. Iversen SD. Brain dopamine systems and behavior. In *Handbook of Psychopharmacology* **8**, LL Iversen, SD Iversen, SH Snyder, Eds., Plenum Press, New York, NY, 1977, pp 333–384.

73. Jacobs S, Cuatrecasas P. The mobile receptor hypothesis and "cooperativity" of hormone binding. *Biochim Biophys Acta* **433**, 482–495 (1976).

74. Jansen PAJ, Van Bever WFM. Structure activity relationships of the butyrophenones and biphenylbutylpiperidines. In *Handbook of Psychopharmacology* **10**, *op cit* (ref *32*), pp 1–36.

75. Jeste DV, Rosenblatt JE, Wagner RL, et al. High serum neuroleptic levels in tardive dyskinesia. *N Engl J Med* **300**, 1184 (1979).

76. Kebabian JW, Calne DB. Multiple receptors for dopamine. *Nature* **277**, 93–96 (1979).

77. Kebabian JW, Petzold GL, Greengard P. Dopamine-sensitive

adenylate cyclase in caudate nucleus of rat brain and its similarity to the "dopamine receptor." *Proc Natl Acad Sci USA* **79**, 2145–2149 (1972).

78. Kent RS, De Lean A, Lefkowitz RJ. A quantitative analysis of beta-adrenergic receptor interactions: Resolution of high and low affinity states of the receptor by computer modeling of ligand binding data. *Mol Pharmacol* **17**, 14–23 (1980).

79. Klawans HL. The pharmacology of tardive dyskinesias. *Am J Psychiatry* **130**, 82–86 (1973).

80. Klawans HL, Weiner WJ, Nausieda PA. The effect of lithium on an animal model of tardive dyskinesia. *Prog Neuro-Psychopharmacol* **1**, 53–60 (1977).

81. Komiskey HL, Bossart JF, Miller DD, et al. Conformation of dopamine at the dopamine receptor. *Proc Natl Acad Sci USA* **75**, 2641–2643 (1978).

82. LaBrie F, Ferland L, DiPaolo T, et al. Modulation of prolactin secretion by sex steroids and thyroid hormones. In *Central and Peripheral Regulation of Prolactin Function*, RM MacLeod, U Scapagnini, Eds., Raven Press, New York, NY, 1980, pp 97–113.

83. Lad PM, Nielsen TB, Preston MS, et al. The role of the guanine nucleotide exchange reaction in the regulation of the beta-adrenergic receptor and in the actions of catecholamines and choleratoxin on adenylate cyclase in turkey erythrocyte membranes. *J Biol Chem* **255**, 988 (1980).

84. Lader S. A radioreceptor assay for neuroleptic drugs. *Immunoassay* **1**, 57–67 (1980).

85. Lee T, Seeman P. Elevation of brain neuroleptic/dopamine receptors in schizophrenia. *Am J Psychiatry* **137**, 191–197 (1980).

86. Lee T, Seeman P, Rajput A, et al. Receptor basis for dopaminergic supersensitivity in Parkinson's disease. *Nature* **273**, 59–61 (1978).

87. Lee T, Seeman P, Tourtellotte W, et al. Binding of ^{3}H-neuroleptics and ^{3}H-apomorphine in schizophrenic brains. *Nature* **274**, 897–900 (1978).

88. Lefkowitz RJ. Modification of adenylate cyclase activity by alpha- and beta-adrenergic receptors: Insights from radioligand binding studies. In *Psychopharmacology and Biochemistry of Neurotransmitter Receptors*, *op cit* (ref *36*), pp 155–170.

89. Lefkowitz RJ, Williams LT. Catecholamine binding to the beta-adrenergic receptor. *Proc Natl Acad Sci USA* **74**, 515–519 (1977).

90. Leysen JE, Gommeren W, Laduron PM. Spiperone: A ligand of choice for neuroleptic receptors. 1. Kinetics and characteristics of *in vitro* binding. *Biochem Pharmacol* **27**, 307–316 (1978).

91. Libet B. The SIF cell as a functional dopamine-releasing interneuron

in the rabbit superior cervical ganglion. In *SIF Cells: Structure and Function of the Small, Intensely Fluorescent Sympathetic Cells,* Fogarty Int. Ctr. Proc. 30, DHEW-NIH 76–942, 1976, pp 163–177.

92. Limbird LE, Gill DM, Lefkowitz RJ. Agonist-promoted coupling of the beta-adrenergic receptor with the guanine nucleotide regulatory protein of the adenylate cyclase system. *Proc Natl Acad Sci USA* **77,** 775–779 (1980).

93. Lindvall O, Bjorklund A. The glyoxylic acid fluorescence histochemical method: A detailed account of the methodology for the visualization of central catecholamine neurons. *Histochemistry* **39,** 97–127 (1974).

94. Lindvall O, Bjorklund A. Organization of catecholamine neurons in the rat central nervous system. In *Handbook of Psychopharmacology* **9,** L Iversen, S Iversen, SH Snyder, Eds., Plenum Press, New York, NY, 1977, pp 139–231.

95. Lindvall O, Bjorklund A, Divac I. Organization of catecholamine neurons projecting to the frontal cortex in the rat. *Brain Res* **142,** 1–24 (1978).

96. List SJ, Seeman P. Dopamine agonists reverse the elevated ^{3}H-neuroleptic binding in neuroleptic-pretreated rats. *Life Sci* **24,** 1447–1452 (1979).

97. MacKay AVP, Bird ED, Iversen LL, et al. Dopaminergic abnormalities in postmortem schizophrenic brain. In *Long-Term Effects of Neuroleptics,* F Cattabeni, G Racagni, PF Spano, E Costa, Eds., Raven Press, New York, NY, 1980, pp 325–333.

98. MacKay AVP, Bird ED, Spokes EG, et al. Dopamine receptors and schizophrenia: Drug effect or illness? *Lancet* **ii,** 915–916 (1980).

99. MacKay AVP, Iversen LL, Rossor M, et al. Increased brain dopamine and dopamine receptors in schizophrenia. *Arch Gen Psychiatry* **39,** 991–997 (1982).

100. MacLeod RM, Nagy I, Login IS, et al. The role of dopamine, cAMP, and calcium in prolactin secretion. In *Central and Peripheral Regulation of Prolactin Function, op cit* (ref *82*), pp 27–41.

101. Meltzer HY. Clinical evidence for multiple dopamine receptors in man. *Commun Psychopharmacol* **3,** 457–470 (1979).

102. Miller RJ, Horn AS, Iversen LL. The action of neuroleptic drugs on dopamine-stimulated adenosine cyclic 3',5'-monophosphate production in rat neostriatum and limbic forebrain. *Mol Pharmacol* **10,** 759–766 (1974).

103. Miller RJ, McDermed J. Dopamine-sensitive adenylate cyclase. In *The Neurobiology of Dopamine,* AS Horn, J Korf, BHC Westerink, Eds., Academic Press, New York, NY, 1979, pp 159–177.

104. Moore RY, Bloom FE. Central catecholamine neuron systems: Anat-

omy and physiology of the dopamine systems. *Ann Rev Neurosci* **1**, 129–169 (1978).

105. Moos F, Richard P. Effects of dopaminergic antagonist and agonist on oxytocin release induced by various stimuli. *Neuroendocrinology* **28**, 138–144 (1979).

106. Mowles TF, Burghardt B, Burghardt C, et al. The dopamine receptor of the rat mammotroph in cell culture as a model for drug action. *Life Sci* **22**, 2103–2108 (1978).

107. Muller P, Seeman P. Dopaminergic supersensitivity after neuroleptics: Timecourse and specificity. *Psychopharmacology* **60**, 1–11 (1978).

108. Muller P, Seeman P. Pre-synaptic subsensitivity as a possible basis for sensitization by long-term dopamine mimetics. *Eur J Pharmacol* **55**, 149–157 (1979).

109. Munemura M, Cote TE, Tsuruta K, et al. The dopamine receptor in the intermediate lobe of the rat pituitary: Pharmacological characterization. *Endocrinology* **107**, 1683–1686 (1980).

110. Munemura M, Eskay RL, Kebabian JW. Release of alpha-melano-cyte-stimulating hormone from dispersed cells of the intermediate lobe of the rat pituitary gland: Involvement of catecholamines and adenosine 3',5'-monophosphate. *Endocrinology* **106**, 1795–1803 (1980).

111. Munson PJ, Rodbard D. Ligand: A versatile computerized approach for characterization of ligand-binding systems. *Anal Biochem* **107**, 220–239 (1980).

112. Murrin LC, Gale K, Kuhar MJ. Autoradiographic localization of neuroleptic and dopamine receptors in the caudate-putamen and substantia nigra: Effects of lesions. *Eur J Pharmacol* **60**, 229–235 (1979).

113. Nagy JI, Lee T, Seeman P, et al. Direct evidence for presynaptic and postsynaptic dopamine receptors in brain. *Nature* **274**, 278–281 (1978).

114. Naor Z, Snyder G, Fawcett CP, et al. Pituitary cyclic nucleotides and thyrotropin-releasing hormone action: The relationship of adenosine 3',5'-monophosphate and guanosine 3',5'-monophosphate to the release of thyrotropin and prolactin. *Endocrinology* **106**, 1304–1310 (1980).

115. Onali P, Schwartz, JP, Costa E. Dopaminergic modulation of adenylate cyclase stimulation of vasoactive intestinal peptide (VIP) in anterior pituitary. *Proc Natl Acad Sci USA* **78**, 6531–6534 (1981).

116. Owen F, Cross AJ, Waddington JL, et al. Dopamine-mediated behaviour and ³H-spiperone binding to striatal membranes in rats after nine months' haloperidol administration. *Life Sci* **26**, 55–59 (1980).

117. Pardo JS, Creese I, Burt DR, et al. Ontogenesis of dopamine receptor binding in the corpus striatum of the rat. *Brain Res* **125**, 376–382 (1977).

118. Pawlikowski M, Karasek E, Kunert-Radek J, et al. Effects of dopamine on cyclic AMP concentration in the anterior pituitary gland in vitro. *J Neural Transm* **50**, 179–184 (1981).

119. Pawlikowski M, Karasek E, Kunert-Radek J, et al. Dopamine blockade of the thyroliberin-induced cyclic AMP accumulation in rat anterior pituitary. *J Neural Transm* **45**, 75–79 (1979).

120. Pert A, Rosenblatt J, Swit C, et al. Long-term treatment with lithium prevents the development of dopamine receptor supersensitivity. *Science* **201**, 171–173 (1978).

121. Quik M, Emson PC, Joyce E. Dissociation between the presynaptic dopamine-sensitive adenylate cyclase and [^{3}H]spiperone binding sites in rat substantia nigra. *Brain Res* **167**, 355–375 (1979).

122. Quik M, Iversen LL. Regional study of ^{3}H-spiperone binding and the dopamine-sensitive adenylate cyclase in rat brain. *Eur J Pharmacol* **56**, 323–330 (1979).

123. Ray KP, Wallis M. Is cyclic adenosine 3':5'-monophosphate involved in the dopamine-mediated inhibition of prolactin secretion? *J Endocrinol* **85**, 59p (1980).

124. Roth RH. Dopamine autoreceptors: Pharmacology, function and comparison with post-synaptic dopamine receptors. *Commun Psychopharmacol* **3**, 429–445 (1979).

125. Schachter M, Bedard P, Debono AG, et al. The role of D-1 and D-2 receptors. *Nature* **286**, 157–159 (1980).

126. Schmidt MJ. Perspectives on dopamine-sensitive adenylate cyclase in the brain. In *Neuropharmacology of Cyclic Nucleotides,* GC Palmer, Ed., Urban & Schwarzenberg, Baltimore, MD, 1979, pp 1–52.

127. Schmidt MJ, Hill LE. Effects of ergots on adenylate cyclase activity in the corpus striatum and pituitary. *Life Sci* **20**, 789–798 (1977).

128. Schwarcz R, Creese I, Coyle JT, et al. Dopamine receptors localized on cerebral cortical afferents to rat corpus striatum. *Nature* **271**, 766–768 (1978).

129. Seeman P. Brain dopamine receptors. *Pharmacol Rev* **32**, 229–313 (1980).

130. Seeman P, Chau-Wong M, Tedesco J, et al. Brain receptors for antipsychotic drugs and dopamine: Direct binding assays. *Proc Natl Acad Sci USA* **72**, 4376–4380 (1975).

131. Seeman P, Lee T, Chau-Wong M, et al. Dopamine receptors in human and calf brains, using [^{3}H]apomorphine and an antipsychotic drug. *Proc Natl Acad Sci USA* **73**, 4354–4358 (1976).

132. Seeman P, Lee T, Chau-Wong M, et al. Antipsychotic drug doses

and neuroleptic/dopamine receptors. *Nature* **261**, 717–719 (1976).

133. Segal DS, Weinberger SB, Cahill J, et al. Multiple daily amphetamine administration: Behavioral and neurochemical alterations. *Science* **207**, 904–907 (1980).

134. Sibley DR, Creese I. Multiple pituitary dopamine receptors: Effects of guanine nucleotides. *Soc Neurosci Abstr* **5**, 352 (1979).

135. Sibley DR, Creese I. Dopamine receptor binding in bovine intermediate lobe pituitary membranes. *Endocrinology* **107**, 1405–1409 (1980).

136. Sibley DR, Creese I. Anterior pituitary dopamine receptors: Demonstration of interconvertible high and low affinity states of D-2 dopamine receptor. *J Biol Chem* **257**, 6351–6361 (1982).

137. Sibley DR, Leff SE, Creese I. Interactions of novel dopaminergic ligands with D-1 and D-2 dopamine receptors. *Life Sci* **31**, 637–645 (1982).

138. Sibley DR, Mahan LC, Creese I. Dopamine receptor binding on intact cells: Absence of high affinity agonist-receptor binding state. *Mol Pharmacol* **23**, 295–302 (1983).

139. Sibley DR, Weinberger S, Segal DS, et al. Multiple daily amphetamine administration decreases both ^{3}H-agonist and ^{3}H-antagonist dopamine receptor binding. *Experientia* **38**, 1124–1125 (1982).

140. Skirboll LR, Grace AA, Bunney BS. Dopamine auto- and postsynaptic receptors: Electrophysiological evidence for differential sensitivity to dopamine agonists. *Science* **206**, 80–82 (1979).

141. Smith RC, Tammanga CA, Haraszti J, et al. Effects of dopamine agonists in tardive dyskinesia. *Am J Psychiatry* **134**, 763–768 (1977).

142. Snyder SH, Creese I, Burt DR. The brain's dopamine receptor: Labeling with [^{3}H]dopamine and [^{3}H]haloperidol. *Psychopharmacol Commun* **1**, 663–673 (1975).

143. Sokoloff P, Martres MP, Schwartz J-C. ^{3}H-Apomorphine labels both dopamine postsynaptic receptors and autoreceptors. *Nature* **288**, 283–286 (1980).

144. Sokoloff P, Martres MP, Schwartz J-C. Three classes of dopamine receptor (D-2, D-3, D-4) identified by binding studies with ^{3}H-apomorphine and ^{3}H-domperidone. *Naunyn-Schmiedebergs Arch Pharmacol* **315**, 89–102 (1980).

145. Stefanini E, Dejoto P, Marchisio A, et al. [^{3}H]Spiroperidol binding to a putative dopaminergic receptor in rat pituitary gland. *Life Sci* **26**, 583–587 (1980).

146. Titeler M, List S, Seeman P. High affinity dopamine receptors (D$_3$) in rat brain. *Commun Psychopharmacol* **3**, 411–420 (1979).

147. Titeler M, Seeman P. Antiparkinsonian drug doses and neuroleptic receptors. *Experientia* **34**, 1490–1492 (1978).

148. Titeler M, Seeman P. Selective labeling of different dopamine recep-

tors by a new agonist ^{3}H-ligand: ^{3}H-*N*-Propylnorapomorphine. *Eur J Pharmacol* **56**, 291–292 (1979).

149. Tollenaere JP, Moereels H, Koch MHJ. On the conformation of neuroleptic drugs in the three aggregation states and their conformational resemblance to dopamine. *Eur J Med Chem* **12**, 199–211 (1977).

150. Tune LE, Creese I, DiPaulo JR, et al. Clinical state and serum neuroleptic levels measured by radioreceptor assay in schizophrenia. *Am J Psychiatry* **137**, 187–190 (1980).

151. Vale W, Rivier J, Guillemen R, et al. Effects of purified CRF and other substances on the secretion of ACTH and beta-endorphin-like immunoactivities by cultured anterior or neurointermediate pituitary cells. In *Central Nervous System Effects of Hypothalamic Hormones and Other Peptides*, R Collu, A Barbeau, J Ducharne, J Rochefort, Eds., Raven Press, New York, NY, 1979, pp 163–176.

152. Walters JR, Roth RH. Dopaminergic neurons: An in vivo system for measuring drug interactions with presynaptic receptors. *Nauyn-Schmiedebergs Arch Pharmacol* **296**, 5–14 (1976).

153. Weiner RI, Cronin MJ, Cheung CY, et al. Anterior pituitary dopamine receptors and prolactin. In *Catecholamines: Basic and Clinical Frontiers*, E Usdin, IJ Kopin, J Barchas, Eds., Pergamon Press, New York, NY, 1979, pp 1218–1220.

154. Weiner RI, Ganong WF. Role of brain monoamines and histamine in regulation of anterior pituitary secretion. *Physiol Rev* **58**, 905–976 (1978).

155. Weiner WJ, Goetz CG, Nausieda PA, et al. Amphetamine-induced hypersensitivity in guinea pigs. *Neurology* **29**, 1054–1057 (1979).

156. Williams LT, Lefkowitz RJ. Slowly reversible binding of catecholamine to a nucleotide-sensitive state of the beta-adrenergic receptor. *J Biol Chem* **252**, 7207–7209 (1977).

157. Zahniser NR, Molinoff PB. Effect of guanine nucleotides on striatal dopamine receptors. *Nature* **275**, 453–455 (1978).

β-Adrenergic Receptor Subtypes: Localization and Regulation

Anders Hedberg and Perry B. Molinoff

Characterization of Receptor Subtypes

A variety of effects are observed when tissues are exposed to either of the two endogenous catecholamines, epinephrine and norepinephrine. Ahlquist, in 1948, attempted to explain these results by postulating the existence of two subclasses of adrenergic receptors, called α- and β-adrenergic receptors (4). When coexisting in a tissue such as the uterus, these receptors mediate functionally antagonistic effects. Thus, stimulation of α-adrenergic receptors gives rise to contraction of uterine or vascular smooth muscle, while relaxation of these muscles follows stimulation of β-adrenergic receptors. On the other hand, both α- and β-adrenergic receptors cause relaxation of the intestine.

Studies in vitro or in situ make it possible for an investigator to assess the responses to various natural and synthetic catecholamines, and to rank a series of compounds in terms of potency, as measured in studies of a given physiological effect. Experiments of this type, involving a variety of tissues containing β-adrenergic receptors, led Lands and coworkers (10) in 1967 to propose the existence of two subclasses of β-adrenergic receptors, β_1- and β_2-adrenergic receptors. Effects of catecholamines on adipose and cardiac tissue involved β_1 receptors, whereas vascular and bronchiolar smooth muscle appeared to contain β_2-adrenergic receptors. Similar studies by Langer (11) led to the identification of two subtypes of α-adrenergic receptors: many of the postsynaptic excitatory effects of norepinephrine involved α_1 receptors, whereas in the periphery, so-called α_2-adrenergic receptors were inhibitory autoreceptors.

With the introduction of specific antagonists, the accuracy of receptor characterization increased markedly. Investigation of differential blockade of the responses to various agonists led to an extensive mapping of the distribution of β_1- and β_2-adrenergic receptors. Studies of this type led to the conclusion that the two receptor subtypes may coexist in the same organ. Experiments with tissue from cat heart led Carlsson et al. (6) to conclude that the chronotropic effects of catecholamines on the atria were mediated by both β_1- and β_2-adrenergic receptors. More recently, they demonstrated (7) that the inotropic effects of catecholamines on cat ventricular myocardium were mediated predominantly by β_1-adrenergic receptors.

Studies of the effects of selective stimulation and inhibition of adrenergic receptors provide an invaluable means of evaluating the functional importance of drugs active at receptors. However, the ability to study directly the interaction between a receptor and a high-affinity ligand labeled with ^3H or ^{125}I has greatly increased our ability to quantify the properties of catecholamine receptors. The main virtue of this approach is that one can study the interactions of agonists or antagonists with receptors in the absence of complications inherent in studies of intact preparations.

In practice, one identifies radioactively labeled compounds that bind reversibly and stereospecifically to the receptors in question. The binding is concentration-dependent, while binding of the radioligand to other, nonreceptor sites in the same tissue is generally nonsaturable. Nonspecific binding is assessed by carrying out duplicate assays in the presence of a high concentration of a competing ligand. The reliability of the determinations is improved if the competing ligand and the radioligand are structurally dissimilar. Saturation curves of specific binding (total binding minus nonspecific binding) are analyzed according to Scatchard (17), to estimate the affinity of the receptor for the radioligand (K_d) and the density of receptors in the tissue (B_{max}). These experiments can be carried out with membranes prepared after homogenization of the tissue or, in some cases, with viable cells maintained in tissue culture.

A different set of techniques is used to assess the interactions of a receptor with a competing ligand. In these experiments, the binding of a fixed concentration of the radioligand is measured in the presence of various concentrations of a competing ligand.

The concentration of a competing ligand that inhibits 50% of the binding of the radioligand (EC_{50}) provides an estimate of the affinity of the receptor for the competing ligand. The EC_{50} value can be converted into a K_d value mathematically (8). Studying a variety of ligands allows one to define comprehensively the pharmacological properties of a receptor.

An added complexity occurs if assays involve tissues that contain more than one class of receptor with a high affinity for a radioligand. Under these conditions, competition experiments are likely to produce displacement curves with low slopes (low Hill coefficients) if the competing ligand has a higher affinity for one class of receptors than the other. If both classes of receptors have the same affinity for the competing ligand, displacement curves will follow simple mass-action principles with Hill coefficients equal to 1. Experiments of this type usually involve nonselective radioligands, identified by linear Scatchard plots.

Localization of β_1- and β_2-Adrenergic Receptors

In the Central Nervous System

The radioligand [^{125}I]iodohydroxybenzylpindolol (^{125}I-IHYP) has been used to study β-adrenergic receptors in the central nervous system (18). Minneman et al. (12, 13) and Hedberg et al. (9) studied the interactions of various competing ligands with receptors labeled with ^{125}I-IHYP in several brain regions and other tissues of rats and other mammals. These experiments showed that ^{125}I-IHYP was nonselective; i.e., β_1- and β_2-adrenergic receptors had the same affinity for the radioligand. To assess the selectivity of these receptors for a variety of agonists and antagonists, we measured the inhibition or stimulation of adenylate cyclase (EC 4.6.1.1) activity in the heart, which contains primarily β_1-adrenergic receptors, and in the lung, which contains predominantly β_2-adrenergic receptors. Studies of the inhibition of the binding of ^{125}I-IHYP by β_1-selective antagonists, such as metoprolol and practolol, and agonists selective for β_2-adrenergic receptors, including zinterol and salmefamol, led to the development of a quantitative means of assessing the densities and properties of these two receptor subtypes in tissues that contained both β_1-and β_2-adrenergic receptors (9, 12, 13). In most cases, the tissues or brain regions studied contained both classes of receptors, but in a few cases, tissues contained only a single subtype. For example, the left ventricular myocardium of cat and guinea pig heart contains only β_1 receptors, and cat soleus muscle and rat liver appear to contain only β_2 receptors (12). All of the brain regions studied contained both β_1- and β_2-adrenergic receptors, although the distributions of these two subclasses of receptor differed. β_2-Adrenergic receptors appeared to be relatively homogeneously distributed, in that the density of these receptors varied by only two- to threefold. The highest concentration of β_2 receptors was in the cerebellum; the lowest, in the hippocampus and diencephalon. The density of β_1-adrenergic receptors, on the other hand, differed widely in various regions of the rat brain, the highest density being in the cerebral cortex and the lowest in the cerebellum. The ratio of the densities of β-adrenergic receptor subtypes in the cerebellum varied, depending on the age of the animal, from 25- to 100-fold (13, 16).

The homogeneous distribution of β_2-adrenergic receptors led to the suggestion that these receptors are localized primarily on glial cells or on vascular smooth muscle, whereas β_1-adrenergic receptors are associated with heterogeneously distributed neuronal elements. The hypothesis regarding β_2-adrenergic receptors would be consistent with the hypothesis that these receptors are stimulated by epinephrine released from the adrenal gland into the circulation. The low affinity of β_2-adrenergic receptors for the neurotransmitter norepinephrine makes it unlikely that these receptors respond to endogenously released norepinephrine. The concentration of epinephrine in the central nervous system is relatively low, and circulating epinephrine does not readily cross the blood–brain barrier.

To test this hypothesis, Minneman et al. (14) studied the effect of manipulations that alter the amount of neuronally released catecholamines having access to receptors. Administration of 6-hydroxydopamine to neonatal rats results in destruction of the sympathetic nerve terminals, thereby reducing the amount of transmitter that can reach postsynaptic receptors. This effect of 6-hydroxydopamine appears to be permanent, in that no recovery of norepinephrine was observed as long as three months following administration of the neurotoxin. Studies of β-adrenergic receptors in the cerebral cortex after the neonatal administration of

6-hydroxydopamine showed a 65% increase in the density of β_1-adrenergic receptors, with no change in the density of β_2 receptors. In other experiments, the tricyclic antidepressant desmethylimipramine, which acts to block the re-uptake of norepinephrine, was administered. This treatment, which would be expected to increase the amount of neurotransmitter having access to receptors, resulted in a decrease of 40% in the density of β_1-adrenergic receptors, with no change in the density of β_2 receptors. Neither of these manipulations had a marked effect on circulating amounts of epinephrine. These experiments led us to conclude that β_1-adrenergic receptors are regulated by neuronally released norepinephrine, and that β_2-adrenergic receptors either do not receive a catecholaminergic input or are not regulated by manipulations that affect the degree of receptor occupancy.

The cerebellum contains Purkinje cells, which receive a dense noradrenergic input from the locus ceruleus. In contrast to the cerebral cortex, the cerebellum contains predominantly (>90%) β_2-adrenergic receptors. The administration of propranolol or 6-hydroxydopamine had no effect on the total density of β-adrenergic receptors in this tissue. The density of β_1-adrenergic receptors, however, increased two- to threefold after the administration of these agents. In an attempt to define the cellular localization of β_1-adrenergic receptors in rat cerebellum, Minneman et al. *(15)* studied the effects of cerebellar degranulation induced by X-irradiation directed at the neonatal rat cerebellum. This procedure destroys late-maturing cerebellar interneurons, including the granule, basket, and stellate cells; the large, early-maturing Purkinje neurons are resistant, however *(5, 19)*. Following X-irradiation, 70–80% of the β-adrenergic receptors in the cerebellum were lost, a decrease almost entirely attributable to the disappearance of β_2-adrenergic receptors. The density of β_1-adrenergic receptors in the cerebellum was the same in treated and nontreated animals, suggesting that β_1-adrenergic receptors are localized on Purkinje cells in this tissue.

In Peripheral Organs

The distribution of β_1- and β_2-adrenergic receptors in the cat and guinea pig atrium and in the corresponding left ventricular myocardium, determined in our studies of radioligand binding *(9)*, confirmed the distribution previously suggested by Carlsson et al. *(7).* Both β_1- and β_2-adrenergic receptors were found in the atria, but the ventricles of both species contained only β_1-adrenergic receptors. In preliminary experiments, we have also observed both β_1- and β_2-adrenergic receptors in atrial biopsies of patients undergoing bypass surgery (Hedberg, Kempf, Josephson, and Molinoff, unpublished). These findings have important clinical implications, in that they suggest that β_2-selective agonists will result in a tachycardia, so that it will not be possible to identify agents that will cause bronchiolar dilatation via stimulation of β-adrenergic receptors without inducing increases in heart rate.

Studies of β-Adrenergic Receptors in Humans

In experiments with human lymphocytes, a readily accessible tissue in which chronic effects of drug administration can be assessed in longitudinal studies, the administration of propranolol increased the density of β-adrenergic receptors on lymphocytes by 40% *(1).* This increase in the density of receptors may contribute to the delayed side effects observed when propranolol administration is abruptly discontinued. In a similar series of investigations *(3),* the agonists terbutaline and ephedrine were administered to normal subjects, resulting in a rapid and pronounced decrease in the density of receptors. This may account for the tachyphylaxis that is observed following the chronic administration of agonists *(3).* The underlying hypothesis of these studies was that changes in receptor density on lymphocytes are relevant to changes occurring in solid, relatively inaccessible tissues such as the heart and lung. To address this question, Aarons and Molinoff *(2)* studied the effect of the administration of propranolol to rats. The drug was administered by chronic infusion with Alzet minipumps. There was an increase in the density of β-adrenergic receptors in the heart and lung, and in lymphocytes, which suggests that the lymphocyte does indeed represent a useful model system with which to study chronic drug effects in humans. It is interesting that increases in β_1- and β_2-adrenergic receptors were seen both in the hearts and lungs of animals treated with propranolol. Presumably the effects of propranolol are mediated at least partly through blockade of the effects of circulating epinephrine.

Conclusions

Studies of the binding of radioactively labeled compounds and the inhibition of this binding by various competing ligands have led to quantitative determination of the densities and properties of β-adrenergic receptors, including the β_1- and β_2-adrenergic receptor subtypes, in a variety of mammalian tissues. The results suggest that these receptors are affected by changes in neuronal activity, such that decreases in receptor occupancy lead to compensatory increases in the density of receptors, whereas increasing receptor occupancy leads to compensatory decreases in the density of receptors. Studies with circulating lymphocytes show that these phenomena occur in humans as well as in animals. Results of studies of chronic drug administration lead to the conclusion that the delayed side effects seen on abrupt withdrawal of β-adrenergic receptor antagonists, and the tachyphylaxis seen on chronic administration of agonists, may be explained in terms of changes in the densities of receptors.

This research was supported by U.S. Public Health Service grant NS 18479.

References

1. Aarons RD, Nies AS, Gal J, et al. Elevation of β-adrenergic receptor density in human lymphocytes after propranolol administration. *J Clin Invest* **65**, 949–957 (1980).
2. Aarons RD, Molinoff PB. Changes in the density of beta adrenergic receptors in rat lymphocytes, heart and lung after chronic treatment with propranolol. *J Pharmacol Exp Ther* **221**, 439–443 (1982).
3. Aarons RD, Nies AS, Gerber JG, Molinoff PB. Decreased beta adrenergic receptor density on human lymphocytes after chronic treatment with agonists. *J Pharmacol Exp Ther* **224**, 1–6 (1983).
4. Ahlquist RP. Studies of the adrenotropic receptors. *Am J Physiol* **153**, 586–600 (1948).
5. Altman J, Anderson WJ. Experimental reorganization of the cerebellar cortex. II. Effects of elimination of most microneurons with prolonged X-irradiation started at four days. *J Comp Neurol* **149**, 123–152 (1973).
6. Carlsson E, Åblad B, Brändstrom A, Carlsson B. Differentiated blockade of the chronotropic effects of various adrenergic stimuli in the cat heart. *Life Sci* **11**, 953–958 (1972).

7. Carlsson E, Dahlöf C-G, Hedberg A, et al. Differentiation of cardiac chronotropic and inotropic effects of β-adrenoceptor agonists. *Naunyn-Schmiedeberg's Arch Pharmacol* **300**, 101–105 (1977).
8. Cheng Y-C, Prusoff WH. Relationship between the inhibition constant (K_i) and the concentration of inhibitor which causes a 50 percent inhibition (IC_{50}) of an enzyme reaction. *Biochem Pharmacol* **22**, 3099–3108 (1973).
9. Hedberg A, Minneman KP, Molinoff PB. Differential distribution of beta-1 and beta-2 adrenergic receptors in cat and guinea-pig heart. *J Pharmacol Exp Ther* **212**, 503–508 (1980).
10. Lands AM, Arnold A, McAuliff JP, et al. Differentiation of receptor systems activated by sympathomimetic amines. *Nature (London)* **214**, 597–598 (1967).
11. Langer SZ. Presynaptic regulation of catecholamine release. *Biochem Pharmacol* **23**, 1793–1800 (1974).
12. Minneman KP, Hedberg A, Molinoff PB. Comparison of beta adrenergic receptor subtypes in mammalian tissues. *J Pharmacol Exp Ther* **211**, 502–508 (1979).
13. Minneman KP, Hegstrand LR, Molinoff PB. Simultaneous determination of beta-1 and beta-2 adrenergic receptors in tissues containing both receptor subtypes. *Mol Pharmacol* **16**, 34–46 (1979).
14. Minneman KP, Dibner MD, Wolfe BB, Molinoff PB. β_1- and β_2-adrenergic receptors in rat cerebral cortex are independently regulated. *Science* **204**, 866–868 (1979).
15. Minneman KP, Pittman RN, Yeh HH, et al. Selective survival of β_1-adrenergic receptors in rat cerebellum following neonatal X-irradiation. *Brain Res* **209**, 25–34 (1981).
16. Pittman RN, Minneman KP, Molinoff PB. Alterations in β_1- and β_2-adrenergic receptor density in the cerebellum of aging rats. *J Neurochem* **35**, 273–275 (1980).
17. Scatchard G. The attractions of proteins for small molecules and ions. *Ann NY Acad Sci* **51**, 660–672 (1949).
18. Sporn JR, Molinoff PB. β-Adrenergic receptors in rat brain. *J Cyclic Nucleotide Res* **2**, 149–161 (1976).
19. Woodward DJ, Hoffer BJ, Altman J. Physiological and pharmacological properties of Purkinje cells in rat cerebellum degranulated by postnatal X-irradiation. *J Neurobiol* **5**, 283–304 (1974).

The Laboratory and the Practicing Clinical Psychiatrist

Alan H. Rosenbaum

The diagnosis of depression is often difficult because of the varied and multiple presentations of depressive illness. Further, numerous illnesses and medications will cause a depressive picture.

Every patient first must be given a physical examination and a laboratory evaluation. Hyper- or hypothyroidisms, high or low cortisol production, liver disease, and cancer of the pancreas can present with depression. Further, changes in sodium, magnesium, and calcium concentrations can bring about personality changes. In the elderly, one must also check for anemia and for deficiencies of B_{12} and folate, which can present with loss of energy, weakness, and possibly dementia.

Because depression runs in families, a thorough personal and family psychiatric history must be taken. Depression can be precipitated by losses (i.e., of loved ones, limbs, etc.), severe viral infections, surgical procedures, and drug use [i.e., reserpine, Aldomet (methyldopa), Inderal (propranolol)], or can be seasonal, spring and fall being common times of onset. As one gets older, depression can become more frequent.

The presentation can be as clear as a sudden change in mood and energy, or as subtle as a preoccupation with one's glasses or ability to urinate; it can be as bizarre as increased sexuality, especially in the elderly. Because of the complexity of presentation, the use of biological markers analyzed by the laboratory to help diagnose and subtype depressive disorders is of extreme importance.

Tests Involving Hormones

The most studied of these tests is the dexamethasone suppression test (DST).[1] Several studies indicate that a significant proportion of patients with endogenous depression fail to suppress their cortisol production with a test dose of dexamethasone (1–7). However, the test lacks sensitivity, and some depressives are hypersecreters of cortisol although their cortisol is suppressed by dexamethasone (8). Further, some outpatient studies have been unable to distinguish between controls and outpatient depressives, mostly because of the lack of suppression in their controls (9).

In a recent control study of the DST, our collaborative group studied 38 controls, ages 20 to 78 years, in comparing a competitive protein binding assay with a radioimmunoassay (RIA). Because the competitive protein binding assay had not been set up to detect values < 50 μg/L (5.0 μg/dL; the suggested cutoff value for normals), we had to extrapolate for values < 50 μg/L. Because of this lack of sensitivity, the cutoff value in this assay for nonsuppression in controls was 70 μg/L, after 1 mg of dexamethasone was given at 2300 hours and blood concentrations of cortisol were determined the following day at 0800, 1600, and 2300 hours. With the RIA procedure, however, 50 μg/L was a suitable cutoff for normals. In fact, for those under 65 years of age, 40 μg/L appeared to be a good cutoff at 0800 and 1600 hours and 50 μg/L at 2300 hours. Controls older than 65 did not suppress as well, especially at 2300 hours, which brings into question the value of that measurement as a diagnostic aid, especially in the elderly (10).

Some have suggested that anxiety may increase cortisol values. To investigate this possibility, we studied 22 patients who met criteria for generalized anxiety disorder and had a Hamilton Anxiety Rating Scale > 18 (moderate anxiety). After a week of placebo, 24-h urine collections for cortisol were obtained. We found no difference between the controls and the moderate to severely anxious patients, indicating there had been no excessive cortisol production (11).

Lack of specificity has also been a question because of increased concentrations of cortisol associated with weight loss, surgery,

---

[1] Abbreviations used: DST, dexamethasone suppression test; RIA, radioimmunoassay; MHPG, 3-methoxy-4-hydroxyphenylglycol.

and drug withdrawal *(6)*. To elucidate further a report that alcoholics in the first week of hospitalization have shown lack of dexamethasone suppression *(12)*, our group studied 52 alcoholic patients three weeks after hospitalization for their drinking problem. We did find excessive cortisol secretions in 60% of them vs 9% of controls at 0800 hours, and in 42% of those with 24-h urine collection values > 100 μg/24 h vs 3% of controls. The DST with 2 mg of dexamethasone showed suppression in all but four patients, two of whom complained of depression *(13)*.

Given a 40 μg/L cutoff with a standardized RIA technique for subjects under 65 years of age, the DST appears to be useful, detecting approximately 50% of the cases of endogenous depression. Before taking the test, a patient must be allowed several days of normal diet, or three to four weeks if in drug withdrawal. Sedating drugs can produce misleading suppression of cortisol concentrations.

The DST may also be useful in subtyping depressive disorders. A recent paper by Rothchild et al. *(14)* indicates that patients with unipolar psychotic depressive disorders may have very high concentrations of cortisol, > 100 μg/L, after taking dexamethasone, whereas bipolar psychotic depressive disorders may give normal DST results. Further, cortisol production in patients with bipolar disorders in general may also be suppressed by dexamethasone, whereas unipolar depressives may have abnormal results *(7)*.

Finally, normalization of DST results appears to correlate with symptomatic improvement and may be useful in predicting early relapse *(15–17)*.

Other tests. The thyroliberin stimulation test for thyrotropin can be used in two ways: *(a)* a blunted response, namely, a change of < 5 milli-int. units/L, may indicate a significant biological depression or mania *(18–21)*; *(b)* once the patient has been treated and responds, the test may be an indicator of whether to stop the medication—in earlier reports, a return to normal values indicated medication could be discontinued and the patient would not relapse readily *(15, 22)*. More work needs to be done in this area because some studies indicate that a blunted response occurs in a significant percentage of normals and, therefore, the test lacks specificity *(23)*. However, other studies indicate increased sensitiv-

301

ity for the diagnosis of endogenous depression by using the DST and the thyroliberin stimulation test together *(23)*.

Other hormone studies, such as growth hormone *(24)* and prolactin *(25)*, must be tested further before they can be used as biological markers of depression.

Catecholamines

Cortisol and thyroxin are regulated by different catecholamines, indoleamines, and acetylcholine. Corticotropin-releasing hormone (corticoliberin), produced in the hypothalamus, releases corticotropin from the pituitary, which in turn releases cortisol from the adrenal gland; the cortisol then feeds back into the brain at the hypothalamus and pituitary to turn off production. This entire process is regulated by norepinephrine, which has both a positive and negative effect on corticoliberin. Further, serotonin seems to have an inhibitory effect, and acetylcholine a marked stimulatory effect. Studies in which normal persons are given intravenous physostigmine, an anticholinesterase inhibitor that increases acetylcholine, show that they may become depressed and have abnormal DST results *(26)*. In our experience, patients who are in partial remission may often have normal DST results, although they still don't feel quite right, especially when using drugs like Mellaril (thioridazine), Thorazine (chlorpromazine), or Elavil (amitriptyline), which have significant anticholinergic action.

Norepinephrine having been linked to abnormal production of cortisol, we did a study to measure the major metabolite of norepinephrine, namely, 3-methoxy-4-hydroxyphenylglycol (MHPG), in 24-h urine samples. For people with severe depression, there was a straight-line relationship between MHPG production and cortisol production for the same 24-h period. This relationship did not hold true for those with mild to moderate depressions, those with anxiety disorders, and normal subjects *(27)*.

As several investigators have already indicated, MHPG production may be a way of subtyping—but not diagnosing—depressive disorders. We found that normals had a wide range of MHPG concentration, which generally included all of the abnormal values found for our depressive disorders (bipolar and unipolar depressions). Therefore, we found this test of little use for diagnosing depression. However, once a diagnosis was made, based on clinical observation and the DST, we were able to use the test for MHPG to subtype the depressive disorders (28, 29).

We found that people with bipolar/schizoaffective depressive disorders had low MHPG values (mean ± SE: 1373 ± 110 μg/24 h), whereas those with unipolar depressions had mean values of 2147 (SE 104) μg/24 h. We noted two groups with values above 1950 μg/24 h, who appeared to have unipolar depressions. We subdivided this group into 1950 to 2500 μg/24 h and > 2500 μg/24 h, on the basis of a differential response to treatment and the fact that the group > 2500 μg/24 h had very high concentrations of urinary cortisol (27, 30–32). Of those patients with values < 1950 μg/24 h, 17 of 25 responded quite well to treatment with antidepressants. Those 17 patients responded rapidly—in less than two weeks—and had a sustained response. Where values ranged from 1950 to 2500 μg/24 h, only one of 14 patients responded. For those with values > 2500 μg/24 h, five of 13 patients responded; their response was slower, and not always quite as sustained. This led us to conclude there were three subtypes of depressive disorders (29).

Measuring Antidepressants

Measuring plasma concentrations of antidepressants has been of questionable value for a number of years. Åsberg et al. (33) indicated a curvilinear relationship between nortriptyline and response to treatment. Their patients who had values within a certain range (therapeutic window) seemed to respond; if there was too much drug, the patient deteriorated. Although several groups have attempted to duplicate these findings with different antidepressants, they have not been successful. However, they did find that a minimum drug concentration is needed for therapeutic response (34, 35).

Perhaps one reason for the discrepancy can be illustrated in our findings, where patients with 24-h urinary MHPG concentration < 1950 μg responded to the usual dosage of approximately 150 mg of antidepressant per day and had blood concentrations of the drug in the range of 185 ng/dL. Those who responded in the high-MHPG group responded to doses approximately double that of the lower MHPG group and required drug concentrations in blood that were also approximately twice those of the low-

MHPG group *(31)*. This could indicate that the response depends not only on the blood content but also on the type of depression.

At this time, routine testing of plasma concentrations of antidepressants does not seem to be indicated. However, it is recommended where: *(a)* there is a lack of response (to see if the drug is being absorbed); *(b)* there is significant toxicity; *(c)* the patient is elderly or has heart problems. If the patient does respond to drugs, it might be worth checking the drug concentration once during treatment to determine what concentration is therapeutic for him or her. Routine monitoring of blood values on a weekly or monthly basis is not indicated, however.

Monitoring Lithium

When first monitoring lithium, measurements should be taken at least two or three times in the first week to make sure the patient does not become toxic. Particular care must be taken with the elderly, who often respond to lower doses than younger patients and become toxic at plasma values above 1.0 mmol/L rather readily.

Further, other problems can ensue with the use of lithium, namely, hypothyroidism, which occurs from 1 to 4% of the time in patients with low normal thyroid function, or a history of thyroiditis. These patients are particularly susceptible to developing hypothyroidism or a goiter and should be monitored for this particular problem. Approximately six weeks after initial treatment, a sample for assessing thyroid function (by measuring thyroxin and thyrotropin) should be drawn; this should be repeated every six months *(36)*.

In view of reports of deteriorating kidney function, which have not, however, been substantiated by large-scale studies, concentrations of serum creatinine and creatinine clearance must be measured periodically. We assess creatinine clearance for elderly patients before they begin treatment, and use a value of 50 mg/min as the minimum clearance. Serum creatinines are measured every six months; if the serum creatinine is increasing, we order another test of creatinine clearance.

Some patients also develop nephrogenic diabetes insipidus; these patients are not able to concentrate their urine because of lithium's blockade of antidiuretic hormone (vasopressin) at the kidney. The frequent urination can become quite an inconvenience and make it difficult for these patients to maintain an adequate lithium concentration: they drink so much, they wash the lithium out of their system. Determination of this particular syndrome can be easily clarified with a 12-h fast and (or) use of vasopressin to see if they can concentrate their urine. If they do develop the syndrome and have difficulty maintaining adequate lithium concentrations, the lithium dosage should be decreased, if possible, or a diuretic should be used to stabilize the lithium value and cut down on the nephrogenic diabetes insipidus (37).

A side effect of lithium that has come to recent attention is that of increasing the concentrations of calcium, magnesium, and parathyrin (38). These analytes must be monitored throughout treatment. Patients probably should have calcium measured every six months to make sure no abnormality is developing. Some investigators have been concerned lithium might produce osteoporosis. Lithium does replace calcium in bone, although no pathological fractures have been found related to this.

Lithium can produce serious toxicity and endanger the patient. At high enough concentrations, lithium becomes toxic to the kidney, being no longer cleared in the urine, and thereby produces a vicious circle of escalating lithium concentrations (39). The rule of thumb used by Amdisen (40) is that if lithium cannot be decreased to less than 1 mmol/L within 30 h, dialysis may well be indicated.

To monitor lithium when a patient is toxic, samples should be drawn approximately every 3–4 h until the lithium concentration is less than 1.0 mmol/L. If dialysis is required, lithium concentrations must be taken down to 0.6 mmol/L by dialysis and kept down. Otherwise, lithium values in the therapeutic range in serum will keep the lithium in the cells in the toxic range. Serum values above 0.8 mmol/L probably indicate the need for further dialysis. Repeated dialysis may be necessary to keep the patient out of danger (40).

Summary

In summary, when one first sees a patient with depression, the patient must have a complete physical and laboratory evaluation. A complete history must be taken to seek precipitating factors for recurrent depressive disorders and for family history of depression. One must also look at the patient's previous sustained response to drug treatment as an indicator of significant biological-type depression. Patients should then have a dexamethasone suppression test if significant depression appears present; this test is relatively simple and requires a minimum effort by the patient.

With this evidence, the patient may then be treated with an antidepressant. If the patient has a lack of response, then plasma concentrations should be measured to make sure the drug is being absorbed. If the patient does not respond to an adequate course of treatment—namely, three weeks at an adequate dose, and adequate plasma concentration—alternative treatments may be indicated. Monoamine oxidase inhibitors may then be used as well as lithium as alternative treatments. If a patient is hospitalized, it would be appropriate, especially if the patient is resistant to treatment, to consider 24-h urine collections for cortisol and MHPG, and thyroliberin stimulation for thyrotropin to confirm the diagnosis and to subtype the depressive disorder. If a patient has a high MHPG concentration, a combination of lithium plus a tricyclic antidepressant or a phenothiazine plus a tricyclic may be in order, previous studies having shown poor response to tricyclics alone. If lithium is used, the laboratory again is called on, to determine baseline levels of kidney function (serum creatinine and creatinine clearance in the elderly or those with a history of kidney problems), thyroid status, and electrolytes.

Therefore, the laboratory is extremely important for diagnosing and subtyping the disorder, and for monitoring the therapeutic and toxic concentrations of medication.

References

1. Carroll BJ, Curtis GC, Mendels J. Neuroendocrine regulations in depression. I. Limbic system adrenocortical dysfunction. *Arch Gen Psychiatry* **33,** 1039–1044 (1976).
2. Carroll BJ, Curtis GC, Mendels J. Neuroendocrine regulations in depression. II. Discrimination of depressed from nondepressed patients. *Arch Gen Psychiatry* **33,** 1051–1057 (1976).
3. Stokes PE, Pick GR, Stoll PM, et al. Pituitary adrenal function in depressed patients: Resistance to dexamethasone suppression. *J Psychiatr Res* **12,** 271–281 (1975).
4. Schlesser MA, Winokur G, Sherman BM. Genetic subtypes of unipo-

lar primary depressive illness distinguished by hypothalamic pituitary adrenal axis activity. *Lancet* **i**, 739–741 (1979).

5. Brown WA, Johnston R, Mayfield D. The 24-hour dexamethasone suppression test in a clinical setting: Relationship to diagnosis, symptoms, and response to treatment. *Am J Psychiatry* **136**, 543–547 (1979).

6. Carroll BJ, Feinberg M, Greden JF, et al. A specific laboratory test for the diagnosis of melancholia. Standardization, validation and clinical utility. *Arch Gen Pscchiatry* **38**, 15–22 (1981).

7. Schatzberg AF, Rothschild AJ, Stahl JB, et al. The dexamethasone suppression test: Identification of subtypes of depression. *Am J Psychiatry* **140**, 88–91 (1983).

8. Asnis GM, Sachar EJ, Halbreich U, et al. Cortisol secretion and dexamethasone response in depression. *Am J Psychiatry* **138**, 1218–1221 (1981).

9. Amsterdam JD, Winokur A, Caroff SN, et al. The dexamethasone suppression test in outpatients with primary affective disorder and healthy control subjects. *Am J Psychiatry* **139**, 287–291 (1982).

10. Rosenbaum AH, Schatzberg AF, MacLaughlin RA, et al. The dexamethasone suppression test in normal control subjects: Comparison of two assays. Submitted to *Am J Psychiatry,* 1983.

11. Rosenbaum AH, Maruta T, Schatzberg AF, et al. Urinary free cortisol and MHPG levels in anxious patients and normal controls. Presented at Society of Biological Psychiatry Annual Meeting, New Orleans, May 1981.

12. Oxenkrug GF. Dexamethasone test in alcoholics. *Lancet* **ii**, 795 (1978). Letter.

13. de La Fuente JR, Rosenbaum AH, Morse RM, et al. The hypothalamic pituitary adrenal axis in alcoholics. *Alcoholism* **7**, 35–37 (1983).

14. Rothschild AJ, Schatzberg AF, Rosenbaum AH, et al. The DST as a discriminator among subtypes of psychotic patients. *Br J Psychiatry* **141**, 471–474 (1982).

15. Targum SD. The application of serial neuroendocrine challenge studies in the management of depressive disorder. *Biol Psychiatry* **18**, 3–19 (1983).

16. Albala AA, Greden JF, Tarika J, et al. Changes in serial dexamethasone suppression tests among unipolar depressives receiving electroconvulsive treatment. *Biol Psychiatry* **16**, 551–560 (1981).

17. de La Fuente JR, Rosenbaum AH. Neuroendocrine dysfunction and blood levels of tricyclic antidepressants. *Am J Psychiatry* **137**, 1260–1261 (1980).

18. Kirkegaard C. The thyrotropin response to thyrotropin releasing hormone in endogenous depression. *Psychoneuroendocrinology* **6**, 189–212 (1981).

19. Extein I, Pottash ALC, Gold MS, et al. Using the protirelin test to distinguish mania from schizophrenia. *Arch Gen Psychiatry* **39**, 77–81 (1982).

20. Gold MS, Pottash ALC, Ryan N, et al. TRH-induced TSH response in unipolar, bipolar, and secondary depressions: Possible utility in clinical assessment and differential diagnosis. *Psychoneuroendocrinology* **5**, 147–155 (1980).

21. Loosen PT, Prange AJ Jr, Wilson IC, et al. Thyroid stimulating hormone response after thyrotropin releasing hormone in depressed, schizophrenic, and normal women. *Psychoneuroendocrinology* **2**, 137–148 (1977).

22. Kirkegaard C, Norlem N, Lauridsen UB, et al. Prognostic value of thyrotropin-releasing hormone test in endogenous depression. *Acta Psychiatr Scand* **52**, 170–177 (1975).

23. Rubin RT, Marder SR. Biological markers in affective and schizophrenic disorders: A review of contemporary research. In *Affective and Schizophrenic Disorders: New Approaches to Diagnosis and Treatment,* MR Zales, Ed., Brunner/Mazel Publishers, New York, NY, 1983, pp 53–100.

24. Carroll BJ. Neuroendocrine dysfunction in psychiatric disorders. In *Psychopharmacology: A Generation of Progress,* MA Lipton, AD Mascio, KF Killam, Eds., Raven Press, New York, NY, 1978, pp 487–497.

25. Judd LL, Risch SC, Parker DC, et al. Blunted prolactin response: A neuroendocrine abnormality manifested by depressed patients. *Arch Gen Psychiatry* **39**, 1413–1416 (1982).

26. Carroll BJ, Greden JF, Rubin RT, et al. Neurotransmitter mechanism of neuroendocrine disturbance in depression. *Acta Endocrinol Suppl* **220**, 13 (1978).

27. Rosenbaum AH, Maruta T, Schatzberg AF, et al. Toward a biochemical classification of depressive disorders. VII. Urinary free cortisol and urinary MHPG in depressions. *Am J Psychiatry* **140**, 314–318 (1983).

28. Schatzberg AF, Orsulak PJ, Rosenbaum AH, et al. Toward a biochemical classification of depressive disorders. V. Heterogeneity of unipolar depressions. *Am J Psychiatry* **139**, 471–475 (1982).

29. Schildkraut JJ, Orsulak PJ, Schatzberg AF, et al. Biochemical discrimination of subgroups of depressive disorders based on differences in catecholamine metabolism. In *Biological Markers in Psychiatry and Neurology,* E Usdin, I Handin, Eds., Pergamon Press, Oxford and New York, 1982, pp 22–33.

30. Rosenbaum AH, Schatzberg AF, Maruta T, et al. MHPG as a predictor of antidepressant response to imipramine and maprotiline. *Am J Psychiatry* **137**, 1090–1092 (1980).

31. Schatzberg AF, Rosenbaum AH, Orsulak PJ, et al. Toward a biochemical classification of depressive disorders. III. Pretreatment urinary MHPG levels as predictors of response to treatment with maprotiline. *Psychopharmacology (Berlin)* **75**, 3–38 (1981).

32. Schatzberg AF, Orsulak PJ, Rosenbaum AH, et al. Toward a biochemical classification of depressive disorders. IV. Pretreatment urinary MHPG levels as predictors of antidepressant response to imipramine. *Commun Psychopharmacol* **4**, 441–445 (1980).

33. Åsberg M, Cronholm B, Sjoquist F, et al. Relationship between plasma level and therapeutic effect of nortriptyline. *Br Med J* **iii**, 331–334 (1971).

34. Glasman AH, Perel JM, Shostak M, et al. Clinical implications of imipramine plasma levels for depressive illness. *Arch Gen Psychiatry* **34**, 197–204 (1977).

35. Nelson JC, Jatlow P, Quinlan DM, et al. Desipramine plasma concentration and antidepressant response. *Arch Gen Psychiatry* **39**, 1419–1422 (1982).

36. Jefferson JW, Greist JH, Eds. *Primer of Lithium Therapy,* Williams and Wilkins Co., Baltimore, MD, 1977.

37. Forest JN. Lithium-induced polyuria: Celluar mechanisms and response to diuretics. In *Lithium Controversies and Unresolved Issues,* TB Cooper et al., Eds., Excerpta Medica, Amsterdam, Oxford, 1979, pp 632–641.

38. Franks RD, Dubovsky SL, Lifshitz M, et al. Long-term lithium carbonate therapy causes hyperparathyroidism. *Arch Gen Psychiatry* **39**, 1074–1077 (1982).

39. Thomsen K. Toxic effects of lithium on the kidney. In *Lithium Controversies and Unresolved Issues, op cit* (ref *37),* pp 619–631.

40. Amdisen A. The standardized twelve-hour serum or plasma concentration (12h-stSLi) in lithium therapy and the use of lithium concentration in lithium intoxication. The vital necessity of continuous self-supervision. *Ibid,* pp 304–332.

Role of the Clinical Laboratory in the Management of Psychiatric Illness: Perspectives for Therapeutic Drug Monitoring

Peter I. Jatlow

In the simplist and narrowest sense, the role of the clinical laboratory in the management of mental illness can be defined as that of determining, on demand, various psychotherapeutic drugs, endogenous neurotransmitters and their metabolites, neurotropic enzymes, and hormones in biological fluids. In these days of financial constraints, however, a more prudent and selective approach may be indicated.

Some laboratory tests have been of considerable value to research on the biology of normal brain function as well as mental illness, and on the mechanisms of actions of psychotherapeutic drugs. However, not all tests, as yet, have a clearly defined role in clinical practice. It is important that psychiatrists, understandably anxious to enter the space age of biochemical diagnosis and management, not confuse these aspects. The substantial economic overlay, in both burden and profit, associated with these tests further complicates the picture.

Technological advances have permitted the accurate measurement of many psychotropic drugs and endogenous compounds of interest to psychiatry. The contribution of measurements of urinary 3-methoxy-4-hydroxyphenylglycol (MHPG)[1] to better understanding of the biological heterogeneity of depression, for example, has already been thoroughly discussed (1–5). As yet,

---

[1] Abbreviations used: MHPG, 3-methoxy-4-hydroxyphenylglycol; TCA, tricyclic antidepressant; HPLC, "high-pressure" liquid chromatography; CP-E, chlorpromazine equivalents; MPH, methylphenidate.

however, this measurement does not have a well-established role in the clinical management of depression, although data relating excretion of urinary MHPG to selectivity of response to various antidepressants are provocative. Moreover, techniques for measurement of MHPG—gas chromatography, gas chromatography–mass spectrometry, or "high-pressure" liquid chromatography (HPLC)—are currently too cumbersome to be optimal for routine use.

The dexamethasone suppression tests *(6, 7)* and thyrotropin stimulation tests *(8, 9)* are good examples of new applications of established endocrine-function tests to psychiatric diagnosis. These tests have also provided new insights into the involvement of the hypothalamic–pituitary–adrenal axis in depression. The proper use of these function tests is critically dependent on the specificity and accuracy of the methods used by the laboratory, as has been recently emphasized for serum cortisol in association with the dexamethasone suppression test. The use of studies of neuroendocrine function to facilitate the diagnosis of the depressive syndromes has also been covered in detail elsewhere and will not be further considered here.

Rather, I will limit my discussion to the therapeutic monitoring of psychotherapeutic drugs other than lithium, with emphasis on the tricyclic antidepressants and antipsychotic drugs. Because our laboratory has also been involved with studies of methylphenidate in children with attention-deficit disorder, I will also briefly discuss this.

The relationship between plasma concentrations of a psychotherapeutic drug and clinical response or toxicity, or for that matter the correlation between any laboratory test and clinical state, may be studied by appropriately designed experiments. On the other hand, proof that measurement of a drug is of direct medical benefit to patients is a more elusive goal. Attempts to establish this for psychotherapeutic drugs such as the tricyclic antidepressants and antipsychotic agents have been particularly difficult. These drugs are effective at relatively low plasma concentrations; require cumbersome, expensive assays; and demonstrate relatively complex metabolism, in most instances having one or more active metabolites of variable potency.

In comparison, lithium concentrations in serum are simple to measure accurately. Most laboratories already had the instrumentation and technical skills required for its measurement at the time this test became relevant for the management of lithium therapy. Few manipulations are required, excellent precision and specificity are obtainable, the assay is relatively inexpensive compared with other drug assays, and no active metabolites complicate interpretation of the data. The pharmacokinetics of lithium and guidelines for sampling and interpretation of plasma concentrations have been well established; consequently, there has been relatively little controversy concerning indications and justification for the routine monitoring of lithium concentrations, at least as compared with measurements for the antidepressant drugs. In the following discussion I will attempt to put present knowledge and opinions about the utility of plasma drug measurements into perspective with present-day laboratory capabilities.

Tricyclic Antidepressants

Except for lithium, tricyclic antidepressants (TCAs) have received the most attention in therapeutic monitoring. Certainly a large body of data is available regarding plasma concentrations of the TCAs. Therapeutic monitoring of the antidepressants has been the subject of a great many competent and comprehensive reviews (10–17), and several new reviews, it seems, are published yearly. The emergence of new antidepressants of various chemical structures for clinical use has complicated this topic. Knowledge about the pharmacokinetics, metabolism, and therapeutic plasma concentrations of these new compounds is far from complete, and it may be unreasonable to expect the clinical laboratory to respond to each with appropriate analytical methodology. The problem is not dissimilar to that occurring with antiarrhythmics and beta blockers. Although I will discuss only the most widely used of the traditional tricyclics, the concepts, if not the specific details, should be applicable in general to the less widely used and newer compounds.

Methodology

Although details of analytical procedures will not be presented here, some understanding of the options available are relevant to any discussion of the indications and justifications for measurement of the TCAs, because the nature of the methodology strongly determines the cost and ease of providing this service.

Much, if not most, large-scale therapeutic monitoring of other drugs is based on immunoassays, particularly nonisotopic techniques. Such assays are generally efficiently applied to large numbers of samples, can be automated, and require relatively little technical expertise. Immunoassays have been less successfully applied to the TCAs or, for that matter, to other psychotropic drugs that have one or more major circulating metabolites. Radioimmunoassays have been used to monitor the TCAs (18–26), but usually have the major limitation of cross reactivity by metabolites. In particular, most antibodies show cross reactivity, but different affinities, for the tertiary-amine TCAs and their secondary-amine metabolites, although the production of antibodies with equal reactivity toward amitriptyline and nortriptyline has been reported (21). Because the relative proportions of parent compound and active metabolite show enormous interindividual variation, assays involving such antibodies cannot provide accurate estimations of the total compound without preliminary separation of parent drug and metabolites, as has been accomplished by Brunswick et al. (25, 26) for imipramine–desipramine and amitriptyline–nortriptyline. Radioimmunoassay should be suitable for clinical monitoring of patients treated initially with the secondary amines, e.g., nortriptyline and desipramine; however, in the United States, the tertiary amines are more commonly prescribed.

Many earlier studies utilized gas chromatographs equipped with mass spectrometric (27–31) or nitrogen detectors (32–35), and gas chromatography–mass spectrometry with selective-ion monitoring and stable-isotope-labeled internal standards remains the state of the art. More recently, HPLC has been increasingly applied to TCA measurements (37–40). In general, HPLC is a more versatile tool; analyses are somewhat simpler to perform and more trouble-free and precise. Unlike immunoassays, however, chromatographic procedures may suffer from interference from other, unrelated drugs and their metabolites. Because patients treated with TCAs may concurrently receive antipsychotics as well as nonpsychotropic medications, the clinician should provide the laboratory with a complete drug history.

HPLC is also well suited to the analysis of the unconjugated hydroxylated metabolites of the TCAs, should this become rele-

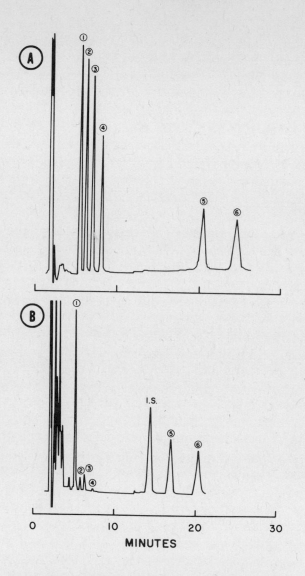

Fig. 1. HPLC chromatograms of *(A)* a mixture containing (1) *trans*-10-OH nortriptyline, (2) *trans*-10-OH amitriptyline, (3) *cis*-10-OH nortriptyline, (4) *cis*-10-OH amitriptyline, (5) nortriptyline, and (6) amitriptyline, 100 ng/mL each; *(B)* an extract of plasma from a patient receiving amitriptyline

I.S., the internal standard, is desipramine. The six peaks (A_{205nm}) in *A* and *B* have identical relative retention times, but differ in absolute retention time because slightly different acetonitrile concentrations were used in the mobile phase. From Bock et al. *(41)*, used with permission vant *(41, 42)*. Figure 1 illustrates such an assay. Using HPLC, a single efficient technologist might complete 15–20 analyses per day with a coefficient of variation of about 5% within the "therapeutic range." In addition, HPLC, in contrast to immunoassay, is more readily and quickly adapted to the analysis of new compounds. Given the rapid introduction of new compounds with antidepressant activity, this may present a relevant consideration in selecting a methodology.

Therapeutic Ranges and Correlations of Plasma Concentrations with Clinical State

Besides adequate analytical methodology, the other essential prerequisite to therapeutic drug monitoring is the availability of information about the interpretation of plasma concentrations. Probably the most frequent type of inquiry to the clinical laboratory about therapeutic drug monitoring concerns therapeutic ranges. Requests for drug measurements do not, a priori, assume knowledge of therapeutic ranges by the requester, nor do they assume that such knowledge even exists. Those who are experienced in clinical psychopharmacology, and in the use of drug concentrations, know how to use this type of information to best advantage, and how to integrate it with other clinical data. In general, however, once published, therapeutic ranges are accepted literally and considered to be precise. Most clinical laboratories, hospital and commercial, list normal and therapeutic ranges, and include them on their reports. Some even list "toxic" drug concentrations without further clarification. These data are generally taken from the literature, from articles that do not always agree with one another (Table 1). Although the original articles are themselves generally clear and explicit as to the limitations of the data and study design, such data can be misinterpreted when taken out of context and put into lists as isolated information.

The magnitude of the problem is illustrated in Table 2, which shows the therapeutic ranges listed in the catalogs of various commercial laboratories. These are not fly-by-night operations but large laboratories of considerable reputation and well-established high ethical standards. Quoted ranges, obtained from a laboratory handbook, from a laboratory report, or over the phone from a clerk, can be misleading without further qualification. Moreover, the usual format does not indicate whether the upper or lower

Table 1. **Purported Range of Plasma Concentrations (ng/mL) for Therapeutic Effects of Various Tricyclic Antidepressants**

Amitriptyline/nortriptyline

   60–220 *(1)*
   > 200 *(2)*
   80–200 *(3)*
   > 120 *(4)*
   95–250 *(5)*

Imipramine/desipramine

   > 20 *(6)*
   > 180 *(7)*
   > 45 imipramine, > 75 desipramine *(8)*

Nortriptyline

   60–140 *(1)*
   50–139 *(9, 10)*
   50–150 *(11)*
   > 100 *(12)*
   up to 175 *(11)*
   > 200 poorer response *(13)*

Source: Hollister *(119)*, used with permission. Nos. in parentheses refer to references cited in Hollister's paper.

Table 2. **Published Therapeutic Ranges from Five Laboratories**

Imipramine, ng/mL	Desipramine, ng/mL
125–275 (toxic > 500)	
50–160	50–250
150–300 (toxic > 1000)	20–160 (toxic > 1000)
180–250 (toxic > 300)	150–300 (toxic > 300)
50–250	50–200

---

therapeutic limits are known with equal confidence; which, if any, side effects are correlated with above-range concentrations; nor which psychiatric diagnoses correlate with the indicated therapeutic ranges.

At this conference considerable attention has been focused on the classification of depression. Speakers have emphasized that depression is biologically heterogeneous, and that this may have implications for the optimal selection of treatment. In addition, antidepressants are used for treatment of various nonaffective disorders. Nonetheless, while methods and concepts related to the subclassification of depression are still undergoing study and refinement, most published data showing a good correlation between plasma concentrations and clinical response refer to "endogenous depression." For lack of any better alternative, these same therapeutic ranges are in practice sometimes extrapolated to all types of conditions, even though there may be no scientific basis for doing so.

Regardless of the relative validity of the various ranges for therapeutic concentrations of the TCAs, those in the laboratory responsible for drug monitoring programs should be aware of the limitations that have been discussed. They should also be prepared to explain these uncertainties when asked about the therapeutic ranges for their laboratory. I have highlighted these problems as a caveat, not as an obstacle. The absence of *definitive* therapeutic ranges does not preclude the constructive use of measurements of plasma concentrations of psychotherapeutic drugs for clinical care.

Reported therapeutic ranges. Despite widely publicized and accepted therapeutic ranges, reports of the correlation, and of the lack of correlation, between plasma TCA concentrations and response continue to proliferate. Some studies have involved outpatients; others, more seriously ill inpatients. Most, but not all, have been fixed-dose studies. Some have included washout periods and have excluded placebo responders; some have not. Some have been restricted to a narrow diagnostic category, e.g., nondelusional endogenous depression; some are more casual in this regard. Some have used state-of-the-art analytical methodology; others, cruder methods. These considerable variations in experimental design make comparisons and definitive conclusions difficult.

A therapeutic window of 50–150 ng/mL for nortriptyline appears to be reasonably well established. Studies by various groups appear to confirm that the concentration/therapeutic response relationship for nortriptyline is curvilinear, with poorer response being seen at plasma concentrations above and below the therapeutic window (43, 44). Several studies have also indicated a good relationship between *total* TCA concentrations and clinical response during treatment with the tertiary TCAs, amitriptyline and imipramine (45–48). The ranges of about 150–300 and 125–250 ng/mL as optimal *total* concentrations during treatment with imipramine and amitriptyline, respectively, are widely used. Yet some recent studies still dispute the existence of a clinically useful relationship between plasma concentration and response for both drugs (49–51). Patients treated with tertiary amines have at least two (or, if the hydroxylated metabolites are included, four) active compounds in their plasma. The parent compounds (tertiary and secondary amines) show quantitative differences in their effects on re-uptake of norepinephrine and serotinin. "Depression" apparently comprises a biologically heterogeneous group of syndromes that may differ in their responsiveness to the various TCAs. It is therefore not surprising that data on the clinical correlates of plasma concentrations of the tertiary amines are inconclusive.

Nelson et al. (52, 53) in collaboration with our laboratory have been studying the clinical correlation of desipramine concentrations with clinical response, major adverse reactions, and side effects in carefully characterized hospital inpatients. Interpretation of desipramine concentrations is not confounded by the need to sum results for two active compounds with possibly different mechanisms of action and different therapeutic routes. Desipramine, for example, is a relatively selective blocker of norepinephrine re-uptake; with the possible exception of 2-OH desipramine, it has no active metabolites.

We have studied the relationship between treatment response and plasma concentrations of desipramine in 30 hospital inpatients with nondelusional unipolar depression who met DSM III (Diagnostic and Statistical Manual of Mental Disorders, 3rd ed.) criteria for major depressive disorders with melancholia (52). Patients who responded during the first week of hospitalization were excluded from the study. Patients who did not sustain their response for one month after discharge were not considered drug responders but were assumed to have responded to hospitalization. A desipramine concentration of 115 ng/mL provided the best demarcation between responders and nonresponders: 84% (8/9) of those whose plasma concentration exceeded this value responded, as compared with only 14% (3/18) with a lower concentration (significant by the Fisher exact test, $p < 0.001$). Several of the responders had concentrations above 300 ng/mL, which would be inconsistent with the type of curvilinear concentration–response relationship that has been demonstrated for nortriptyline, and suggested for desipramine *(54)*. But more relevant to the issue of whether therapeutic monitoring is useful, 10 of the nonresponders whose desipramine concentrations had been below 125 ng/mL improved when their dose and plasma concentrations were increased.

Toxicity. A common reason for measuring concentrations of drugs in plasma, in general, is to evaluate and manage possible drug toxicity. The assumption is that side effects are likely to be associated with drug concentrations that exceed the upper limit of a predefined therapeutic range; however, this assumption has not been demonstrated conclusively for the TCAs. Following acute overdose, major cardiac conduction defects and toxicity to the central nervous system have been related to concentrations greater than 1000 ng/mL *(55, 56)*. The occurrence of side effects during chronic therapy, however, has been less convincingly correlated with plasma concentrations. Åsberg et al. *(57)* reported a positive correlation between nortriptyline concentrations and subjective side effects. Braithwaite et al. *(58)*, in one of the earlier studies of plasma concentrations, found no correlation with side effects, but a very recent study *(59)* reported very high concentrations of amitriptyline in patients with delerium. Desipramine concentrations have been reported to correlate weakly with conduction defects *(60)* and with inhibition of salivation *(61)*, but not with reports of dry mouth. Glassman et al. *(62)* reported that orthostatic hypotension was not associated with drug concentrations in patients receiving desipramine. I cite these studies to indicate that specifying certain concentrations of TCAs as toxic without further details is relatively meaningless.

Nelson et al. *(53)*, in a study at our institution of 84 inpatients receiving desipramine, differentiated between major adverse reactions sufficiently severe to require interruption of treatment and subjective side effects. As in the Glassman study *(62)*, orthostatic hypotension occurred early, and at relatively low concentrations of desipramine. Other adverse reactions generally occurred in patients older than 60 years, who were also receiving antipsychotic medication, but did not correlate with desipramine concentrations.

Similarly, most subjective side effects correlated better with severity of depression than with drug concentrations in plasma. These population statistics do not, however, mean that side effects are not related to drug concentrations in individuals. Plasma concentrations may be helpful in determining whether desipramine dosage can be reduced, without falling below the apparent lower threshold for good therapeutic response. They would appear to be less useful for predicting or preventing toxicity.

Hollister (63) attempted to assess the usefulness of measuring plasma TCAs in routine clinical practice. Plasma concentrations were unusually low in 19 of 126 patients, 10 of whom probably were noncompliant. Plasma concentrations of amitriptyline and nortriptyline did not correlate with therapeutic response but, as the author emphasized, less than half of the patients in this study, which was intentionally unstructured, had a primary depressive disorder. Hollister concluded that monitoring plasma concentrations could be useful in detecting unexpectedly low concentrations in patients with a poor response. In a subsequent controlled study, Hollister et al. (64) divided into two groups 20 depressed outpatients treated with nortriptyline. A "blind" group was managed purely on the basis of clinical judgment, whereas the "feedback" group had their dosages adjusted with knowledge of the plasma concentrations. The number of days spent within the therapeutic plasma concentration range was the same for the two groups, as was the degree of clinical improvement. Therapeutic response did not correlate with the amount of time spent in the therapeutic range. The authors thus felt that "routine" monitoring of plasma concentrations was not indicated.

Extrapolating data derived from an outpatient population to more seriously ill inpatients may not be entirely fair. Although monitoring plasma concentrations in outpatients may not improve long-term results in aggregate, rapidity of response can shorten hospital stay. Attainment of a broadly defined therapeutic concentration might be more consistently obtained by adjusting doses on the basis of early (24 h after first dose) concentration. Even steady-state concentrations can usually be evaluated before an optimal therapeutic response is achieved. Considering that each adjustment of therapy may require one to two additional weeks before therapeutic response can be determined, economic as well as clinical benefits seem possible. Approximating from usual hospital and laboratory charges, saving one patient day should fund about 10 assays for plasma TCA concentrations. Studies quantifying the benefits of TCA monitoring of inpatients have not yet been reported.

Prediction of Steady-State Concentrations from Early Measurements

Traditionally, therapeutic monitoring of drugs is performed after a steady-state concentration has been achieved, that is, after at least four to five half-lives. With a few exceptions, the published therapeutic ranges are for steady-state trough concentrations. The half-lives of most tricyclics are approximately 18–24 h (protriptyline, an exception, has a $t_{1/2}$ of about 72 h); steady-state concentrations are reached about five to seven days after initiation of therapy or dose adjustment. Because the $t_{1/2}$ is long relative to the dosing intervals, the time of sampling is less critical than for many other drugs. With TCAs, most reported data are based on a.m. trough (pre-dose) sampling, to minimize the effect of variation in absorption rates.

Recently, considerable interest has focused on measuring plasma concentrations 24 h after a test dose to predict, roughly, steady-state concentrations. Subsequent dosages can be tailored to achieve a steady-state concentration within the therapeutic range. This strategy assumes linear kinetics and no change in drug clearance during the course of therapy, an approach that appears to be valid for imipramine, desipramine, and nortriptyline, which have all shown a reasonably good correlation between 24-h and steady-state concentrations (65–67). Although slightly better predictions can be made from using multiple samples and traditional kinetics calculations, the improvement in accuracy does not appear to justify the increased cost, inconvenience, and discomfort to the patient.

The clinical benefits of this approach to dosage optimization are obvious. Patients ordinarily take about one week to achieve steady-state concentrations, and longer before therapeutic response can reasonably be assessed; if the dose has to be adjusted, another similar time interval is required for re-evaluation of steady-state concentration and response. If the dose can be optimized shortly after the onset of therapy, an earlier response and shorter hospitalization can be anticipated for some patients.

The implications of this therapeutic strategy relate directly to the clinical laboratory. Ordinarily, measurement of plasma concentrations of TCAs for therapeutic monitoring cannot be considered an urgent type of assay. The therapeutic indices of these drugs are wide compared with, for example, those for the cardiac glycosides or many antiarrhythmic agents; thus the clinical laboratory can reasonably perform such an assay once or twice a week, or the hospital or clinician can send samples to a distant laboratory. If 24-h drug concentrations are to be used for early optimization of dosage, however, turnaround time becomes more important. A week's delay in obtaining data would defeat the purpose or at least greatly reduce the effectiveness of this approach. The technology currently available in the clinical laboratory for analysis of the TCAs is not well suited to the prompt but economical analysis of a single sample or small number of samples.

A second laboratory consideration is technical, but one the clinician should be aware of. The 24-h plasma drug concentrations after a 50- or 100-mg test dose will be much lower than those anticipated at steady-state. Therefore, the methods used to measure such concentrations should be precise and accurate at concentrations less than 50 ng/mL and calibrated accordingly. Errors of 10–20 ng/mL, which are of only modest clinical consequence in the therapeutic range, would cause substantial errors in predicting steady-state concentrations from the very much lower 24-h drug concentrations.

Protein Binding

Any discussion of therapeutic drug monitoring will touch on the issue of protein binding of drugs and the potential utility of free drug concentrations. The occasional requests for measurements of free drug sometimes have a rational basis, but apparently at other times are done to be fashionable and demonstrate that one is *au courant* with the literature. Because nonprotein-bound or "free" or diffusible concentrations of drugs in plasma are, at least conceptually, a more appropriate correlate of drug concentration at the receptor site, they are considered more reflective of pharmacodynamics or clinical effects. The TCAs are highly protein bound (>80%), although different studies indicate considerable variation (68–71). These differences probably reflect methodological problems related to choice of technique, sample collection, and, possibly, instability of binding proteins (72).

Analysis of total rather than free drug concentrations is sometimes cited as an explanation for inconsistencies in studies of the clinical significance of drug concentrations. However, no data definitively show that plasma concentrations of free TCAs correlate with clinical measures any better than total concentrations do. Variations in drug concentrations secondary to genetically determined differences in hepatic elimination of the TCAs are apparently of greater magnitude and consequence than interindividual differences in protein binding.

Many basic drugs, including the TCAs, bind with high affinity to α_1-acid glycoprotein (orosomucoid). The free fraction (percentage free) of such drugs has been shown to correlate negatively with serum concentrations of this glycoprotein (73). The serum concentration of α_1-acid glycoprotein increases in response to acute inflammatory conditions. Rutledge et al. (74) have reported that in patients with acute myocardial infarcts, α_1-acid glycoprotein is increased and the free fraction of another basic drug, lidocaine, is decreased; they suggest that this information should be considered in interpretation of total drug concentrations. Because α_1-acid glycoprotein concentrations are measurable by immunoassay with far greater ease than are free drug concentrations, measurement of the binding protein may be an easier, albeit indirect, way to infer possible alterations of drug binding in appropriate patients.

Measuring free drug concentrations involves much more than minor modifications of standard procedures for assaying total drug. Rather, the use of complex, labor-intensive, isotopic techniques is required, involving equilibrium dialysis or sometimes ultrafiltration. The accuracy of such methods, as applied to TCAs, is still uncertain. Information on the interpretation and clinical utilization of data for free drug values is still lacking. In general, alterations in the protein binding of drugs such as the TCAs do not alter absolute free drug concentrations and are probably of limited clinical significance. Although when evaluating total concentrations it may be prudent to take into account factors that may alter protein binding, the measurement of free TCA concentrations in plasma for purposes of clinical care does not, at our present state of knowledge, appear to be an appropriate use of clinical laboratory resources.

In the interest of completeness, I will mention the so-called "Vacutainer artifact." Spuriously low plasma concentrations of various highly protein-bound basic drugs (75) including the TCAs (76) were measured in blood samples collected in some types of

Vacutainer Tubes® (Becton Dickinson). Tris(2-butoxyethyl) phosphate eluted from the stoppers of the tubes and displaced various drugs from their plasma protein (orosomucoid) binding sites *(75)*. Subsequent uptake of drug into erythrocytes resulted in lowered concentrations of the drugs in plasma. This effect may now be only of historical interest: the manufacturer indicates that the plasticizer has been eliminated from the stoppers, and more recent studies suggest that the problem no longer exists *(77)*. In any event, clinical laboratories probably should evaluate any commercial blood-collection system before putting it into use.

Hydroxylated Metabolites

Measurement of the secondary-amine metabolites for clinical evaluation of plasma drug concentrations after treatment with the tertiary amines is generally accepted, but there is less certainty regarding the hydroxylated metabolites. Most of the latter are excreted as glucuronide conjugates; however, only the unconjugated compounds are of possible relevance in therapeutic monitoring.

The unconjugated hydroxylated metabolites of TCAs are pharmacologically active, blocking norepinephrine and serotonin reuptake in vitro and showing cardiac and behavioral effects in animals *(78–80)*. The pharmacology of the hydroxylated TCAs has been well reviewed in the literature *(79)*. Whether these derivatives are clinically effective as antidepressants has not been established, and may be demonstrable only indirectly, or by inference.

Several questions regarding measurement of the hydroxylated TCA metabolites are particularly relevant to the clinical laboratory. Is knowledge of plasma concentrations of the hydroxylated TCAs more useful than that of the parent compounds alone? If so, should these metabolites be measured in all instances, or only for assistance with difficult cases? What concentrations of hydroxylated TCAs are desirable? How should concentrations be interpreted? Should they be summed with the concentrations of the parent compounds, and, if so, should therapeutic ranges of total "active" drug be established? Is available methodology adequate for measurement of hydroxylated TCAs and would its use appreciably add to the cost of monitoring the TCAs? Would the extra cost be justified by additional clinical benefit?

Most of the data on these derivatives are for the 10-hydroxyl-

324

ated metabolites of amitriptyline and the 2-hydroxylated metabolites of imipramine and desipramine. Amitriptyline and its *N*-demethylated metabolite, nortriptyline, are ring-hydroxylated at either the *cis* or *trans* position, each yielding two distinct 10-OH metabolites. Patients receiving amitriptyline thus have four circulating unconjugated hydroxylated metabolites, in addition to the parent tertiary and secondary amines; these geometric isomers can be well separated with reversed-phase HPLC (see Figure 1). Hydroxylation is stereoselective so that the *trans*-hydroxylated compounds, particularly 10-OH-nortriptyline, predominate in plasma and urine *(41, 83)*. In a study of 27 patients receiving amitriptyline, we found that, although all four unconjugated compounds were present, *trans*-10-OH-nortriptyline always predominated *(41)*, exceeding the concentrations of amitriptyline and nortriptyline, as well as the other three unconjugated metabolites, and accounting for about 33% of the total concentrations of the six compounds (Table 3). The ratio of concentrations of hydroxylated metabolites to those of total parent compounds showed considerable variation, ranging from 0.32 to 2.44. Hydroxylation rate appears to be genetically determined and for nortriptyline has been reported to correlate with hydroxylation of the model drug debrisoquine *(83)*. In individuals, however, the proportions of the various compounds were fairly constant over time. Should the hydroxylated metabolites be clinically active, it might be informative to measure unconjugated *trans*-10-OH-nortriptyline, the predominant circulating compound in patients receiving amitriptyline. On the other hand, the clinical laboratory probably need not measure the very low concentrations of the other three hydroxylated metabolites of amitriptyline.

The 2-hydroxylated metabolites of imipramine and desipramine also reach substantial concentrations. Steady-state concentrations of these derivatives have been evaluated by Potter et al. *(84)*, and by our laboratory *(42)*. Potter et al. reported that plasma concentrations of unconjugated 2-OH-desipramine averaged about 50% of the total desipramine concentrations, but that absolute and relative concentrations of 2-OH-desipramine showed a wide range of variation among individuals. In a similar study of patients receiving desipramine *(42)*, we obtained a mean unconjugated metabolite-to-parent ratio of 0.48, but with a 150-fold range (Figure 2). However, if the small group of slow hydroxylators

Table 3. **Data on Drug Metabolites in Sera of 27 Patients Receiving Amitriptyline Therapy**

	Concn, ng/mL	
	Mean	*Range*
AT	113	17–246
NT	102	25–258
cis-10-OH AT (U)	4.2	0–13
cis-10-OH AT (T)	10.4	4–22
trans-10-OH AT (U)	15.1	2.0–54
trans-10-OH AT (T)	143	30–281
cis-10-OH NT (U)	14.9	4.0–32
cis-10-OH NT (T)	31	15–64
trans-10-OH NT (U)	124	27–294
trans-10-OH NT (T)	393	177–766
Σpar	216	50–481
ΣOH(U)	158	39–392
ΣOH(T)	577	328–1098
Σall(U)	374	122–873
Ratios		
NT/AT	1.0	0.19–2.1
ΣOH(U)/Σpar	0.82	0.32–2.44
cis/*trans*(U)	0.16	0.05–0.36
cis/*trans*(T)	0.082	0.043–0.175
U/T	0.25	011–0.48

AT, amitriptyline; NT, nortriptyline; U, unconjugated; T, total. Adapted from Bock et al. *(41)*.

was excluded, this range was drastically reduced, to only fivefold. Ratios were much lower in patients receiving various antipsychotic drugs (see below). Only about 8.1% of the total plasma 2-OH-desipramine was unconjugated. Should 2-OH-desipramine concentrations be of clinical relevance, they can be measured with reasonable ease by HPLC.

The question remains of whether the hydroxylated metabolites are clinically active. In collaboration with Nelson *(85)* we elected to evaluate the more practical question of whether measurement of 2-OH-desipramine improved the clinical correlation with plasma drug concentrations over what was obtained with only the parent compound. Desipramine, having only one major hydroxylated metabolite, seemed a better choice than the tertiary amines as a model drug. By themselves, 2-OH-desipramine concentrations in plasma did not correlate with clinical response, nor did summing the concentrations of desipramine and its hydroxy-

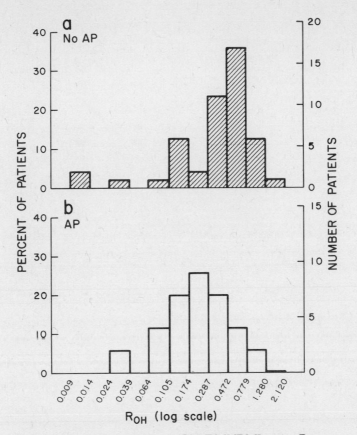

Fig. 2. Distribution of the 2-OH DMI/DMI ratio, R_{OH}, at steady-state in 45 patients on DMI alone *(top)*, and in 37 patients on DMI plus either a phenothiazine or haloperidol *(bottom)*

From Bock et al. *(42)*, used with permission. DMI, desipramine

metabolite improve the correlation achieved with desipramine alone (Table 4). Similarly, neither desipramine nor its sum with 2-OH-desipramine correlated with subjective scores for side effects or with major adverse reactions. Measurement of this metabolite may help to clarify the occasional patient who presents an unexpected or unusual clinical picture, but its routine measurement for clinical care appears to be unjustified at this time.

Regardless of the clinical activity of the hydroxylated metabolites, one reason to measure them might be to distinguish noncompliance from rapid metabolism in nonresponding patients with

Table 4. **Mean Concentrations of Desipramine (DMI) and Its Metabolites in Plasma from Responders and Nonresponders**

	n	Mean age, years	Mean dose, mg/kg	DMI	2-OH-DMI	DMI + 2-OH-DMI
				Plasma concn, mean $\pm$ SD, ng/mL		
Responders	10	45.8	2.77	200 ± 133	46 ± 17	246 ± 131
Nonresponders	18	48.2	2.50	73 ± 34	46 ± 27	119 ± 56
t-tests,[a] responders vs nonresponders			$t = 4.045$, $p < 0.001$	$t = 0.287$, n.s.	$t = 3.536$, $p = 0.002$	

[a] Because the variance for DMI concentrations differed in responders and nonresponders, $\log_e$ DMI concentrations, whose variance did not differ in the groups, were used to calculate t-values. Adapted from Nelson et al. (85).

low plasma concentrations of the parent drug. Individuals with rapid metabolism would be expected to show a *relatively* high concentration of metabolite or a low parent-to-metabolite ratio, whereas in noncompliers both compounds would be proportionately low. Analogously, rapid metabolizers of the antiepileptic drug phenytoin excrete relatively large amounts of the p-hydroxy-phenytoin in the urine, whereas relatively little is present in the urine of poor compliers.

Interaction between Tricyclic Antidepressants and Neuroleptic Drugs

In general, steady-state plasma concentrations of TCAs vary relatively little from day to day. In the absence of factors that might alter drug disposition, and with patient compliance, the constancy of steady-state concentrations is a good indication of assay reliability.

One variable that can abruptly and dramatically alter plasma concentrations of the TCAs is the co-administration of various neuroleptic drugs. Although not all drug interactions reported in the literature are of great clinical importance, the administration of some neuroleptics often is followed by a marked increase in total TCA concentrations. This effect is particularly striking with desipramine, for which our laboratory (86) and others (87) have demonstrated an approximate doubling of steady-state concentrations after treatment with neuroleptics. Table 5 illustrates the magnitude of this effect. Gram et al. (88–90) in single-dose studies reported that various neuroleptic drugs inhibit metabolism of the tricyclics, probably by inhibiting hydroxylation. Measuring con-

Group (n = 15 each)	Sex		Age, years		Dose, mg/kg		Plasma concn, ng/mL[a]	
	M	F	Mean	SD	Mean	SD	Mean	SD
Desipramine alone	5	10	38	13	2.55	0.18	110	81
Desipramine + antipsychotic	4	11	48	18	2.50	0.22	255	115

[a] $p < 0.002$, Mann–Whitney rank order test.
Adapted from Nelson and Jatlow (86).

centrations of 2-OH-desipramine before and after administration of perphenazine, we found that the increase in concentrations of desipramine was accompanied by a proportionate decrease in the relative concentration of 2-OH-desipramine (Figure 3) (42). Antipsychotic drugs are not infrequently administered with TCAs,

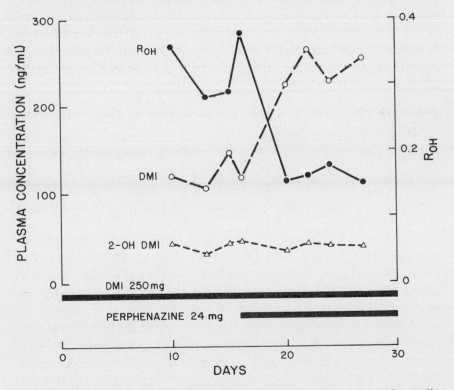
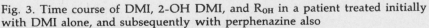

Fig. 3. Time course of DMI, 2-OH DMI, and R_{OH} in a patient treated initially with DMI alone, and subsequently with perphenazine also

From Bock et al. (42), used with permission. Abbreviations as in Fig. 2

and clinician and laboratory should be alerted to this particular interaction.

Antipsychotic Drugs

Interest in the measurement of plasma concentrations of the antipsychotic drugs has existed for at least as long as for the antidepressants (91); however, progress has been much slower. A wide range of dosages is used, with drugs of various potencies, yielding plasma mass concentrations that vary over almost two orders of magnitude. Thus, at least until recently, a single common methodology suitable for all antipsychotic agents has not been available. With the notable exception of haloperidol (92), antipsychotic drugs, especially the phenothiazines, have a vast number of metabolites, some of which are active. All metabolites, however, have not been well characterized, and measurement of the more polar metabolites, some of which are hydroxylated, is often technically difficult. Concentrations of active metabolites should somehow be taken into account, although exactly how is not clear. For example, relative concentrations of the active metabolite, 7-OH-chlorpromazine, reportedly correlate better with clinical measures than do concentrations of the parent compound (93).

Analytical Methodology

Radioreceptor assay. In theory, the development of radioreceptor assays for neuroleptic drugs overcomes the problem of active metabolites, and may have opened a new dimension in therapeutic monitoring of this class of drugs. Creese and Snyder (94) developed and first reported a competitive-binding radioassay in which a preparation of dopamine receptors, rather than antibody, was the binding agent. In brief: serum, a receptor preparation, and a radioligand, usually tritiated spiroperidol, are incubated together; after the receptor-bound fraction is separated, its radioactivity is counted. Appropriate controls for nonspecific binding are also included and, after correction, the percent bound is calculated and plotted against concentrations of a neuroleptic drug standard; binding of the labeled ligand is negatively correlated with concentration of neuroleptic drug. The attractiveness of this assay is its ability to normalize all circulating neuroactive compounds, parent compounds, and metabolites, regardless of potency, to a common unit of neuroleptic activity, based upon the ability to compete with the radiolabeled ligand for binding to dopamine receptors. The proposed clinical utility of this assay is based on the assumption, which has sound scientific documentation, that clinical activity of the neuroleptic correlates with the ability to block dopamine receptors (95).

One source of confusion in comparing various studies involving the dopamine radioreceptor assay relates to the definition of neuroleptic unit. In the original paper by Creese and Snyder (94), as well as in several subsequent studies (96, 97), chlorpromazine was the standard and plasma concentrations were reported as "chlorpromazine equivalents" or "CP-E" units. However, haloperidol has also been used as a standard, in which instance the absolute concentration units are not the same as with chlorpromazine. Furthermore, activity units are not likely to correlate well with mass units based on physical measurements (e.g., measurements with HPLC or gas chromatography), especially when drugs with multiple metabolites, some active, are studied. Comparison of data from studies based on the radioreceptor assay with those based on chromatography or radioimmunoassay is therefore difficult for most drugs.

Conceptually, the use of a radioreceptor assay seems highly appropriate when clinical correlation is the major issue. In such instances, total amounts of "active" circulating compound(s) may be more relevant than the separation of parent drugs from active metabolites. This logic assumes that binding to the receptor used in the assay correlates with the particular clinical manifestation of interest. On the other hand, a radioreceptor assay would generally be less suitable for pharmacokinetic or bioavailability studies, for which highly specific physical measurements are more appropriate. Many clinical studies with radioreceptor assays have apparently prepared their own receptor preparations in-house; however, a commercial kit (Burroughs Wellcome Co.) is now available that includes a receptor preparation from calf caudate.

Radioimmunoassay. Immunoassays, which are quite popular for therapeutic monitoring of many drugs, have also been used for the neuroleptics. However, for drugs with multiple metabolites, antibody specificity can be a significant factor. Figure 4 illustrates this problem as it relates to haloperidol, a drug thought not to have appreciable concentrations of circulating active metabolites.

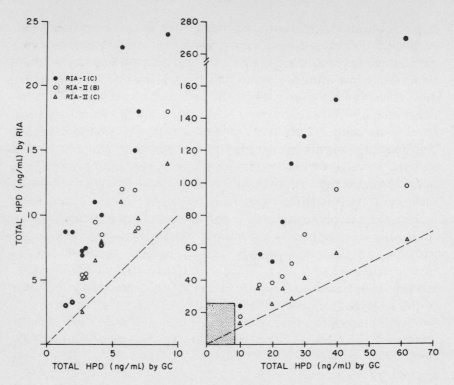

Fig. 4. Comparison of total haloperidol (HPD) concentrations as determined by three radioimmunoassays (RIA) systems (one with RIA-I antibody and two with RIA-II antibody) and by gas chromatography (GC)

RIAs were performed in California (C) and Belgium (B). *Left,* Magnification of shaded area on *right.* From Rubin et al. *(98),* used with permission (copyright 1980, American Medical Association)

In that study by Rubin et al. *(98),* haloperidol concentrations determined by radioimmunoassay were as much as threefold greater than those obtained by gas chromatography, the extent of the discrepancy varying with the antibody used: immunoassays, unlike radioreceptor assays, may also be affected by inactive metabolites.

Chromatography. Recent clinical correlation studies focusing on haloperidol have used physical (chromatographic) methods. Among the many antipsychotic drugs, haloperidol is a particularly attractive agent for therapeutic monitoring because it apparently produces no major active metabolites—although one biotransformation product, reduced haloperidol, is of undetermined significance. Concentrations and doses of haloperidol, as currently used, vary over a fairly wide range although, in general, steady-state concentrations tend to be less than 20 ng/mL after usual therapeutic doses. Most studies have used gas chromatography with the more sensitive electron-capture (99) and nitrogen detectors (100); more recently, HPLC has been used (101). In our laboratory we have been using HPLC with detection at low ultraviolet wavelengths; this permits measurement of concentrations as low as 2 ng/mL. Results for haloperidol by a chromatographic method might be expected to compare well with those by a radioreceptor assay, and such is the case in our experience.

Because haloperidol has a $t_{1/2}$ of about 16–24 h, steady-state concentrations are best assessed after approximately five to seven days on a constant dose. As with the TCAs, constancy of steady-state concentrations, in the absence of other factors that might modify drug clearance, represents a good quality-control monitor of the analytical procedure, laboratory performance, and (or) patient compliance (Figure 5).

As with TCAs, drug interactions may affect steady-state concentrations of neuroleptic drugs without any change in dosage of the primary drug. Lithium and anticholinergic medications reportedly lower the steady-state concentrations of chlorpromazine (103, 104), whereas haloperidol concentrations, according to most reports, are not significantly affected by anticholinergic medications. Because chlorpromazine is degraded by gut flora, changes in intestinal motility may affect this drug more than others.

Clinical Correlations

Numerous studies describe the relationship of plasma concentrations of neuroleptic drugs, especially chlorpromazine (105), to various measures of clinical response and (or) side effects. Many of the earlier studies that focused on the parent phenothiazines are contradictory, and will not be reviewed here, although they did yield new pharmacokinetic data as well as information on what plasma concentrations might be expected in patients receiving therapy with neuroleptic drugs. The data were not sufficiently conclusive, however, to justify measurement of neuroleptic drugs as a routine clinical tool.

More recent studies with radioreceptor assays or, in the case of haloperidol, chromatographic assays may have more relevance

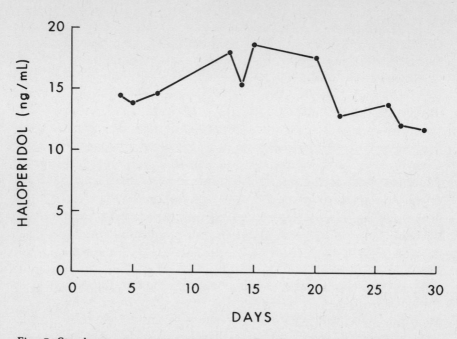

Fig. 5. Steady-state serum concentrations of haloperidol in a patient receiving 17 mg of drug per day

Values shown are morning trough concentrations, approximately 10 h after last dose. From Jatlow et al. *(101)*, used with permission

for eventual clinical monitoring of neuroleptic drugs. Using a radioreceptor assay to evaluate 30 patients receiving six different neuroleptics, Tune et al. *(97)* found that good clinical response was unlikely at concentrations less than 50 CP-E units/mL and suggested a tentative therapeutic range of 100–200 CP-E units/ mL; however, none of the patients in this study had concentrations above 200 CP-E units/mL. Correlation between dose and plasma concentrations was not very good, even when dosages were normalized for neuroleptic potency. Calil et al. *(96)*, also using a radioreceptor assay, evaluated a group of patients receiving a variety of antipsychotic drugs. The best clinical correlations were for haloperidol, for which plasma concentrations, expressed as CP-E units, correlated with improvement in thought disorder and paranoia. Drug concentrations did not, however, correlate with side effects, and the authors made no attempt to define a "therapeutic range."

Haloperidol has also been studied with more traditional methodology. Using a radioimmunoassay, Itoh et al. *(106)* found no correlation between plasma concentrations and treatment response. More recently, however, Magliozzi et al. *(107)*, using gas chromatography, suggested a therapeutic range of 8–17 ng/mL in a study of schizophrenic outpatients. Because subjects with higher concentrations of haloperidol showed a poorer response, the authors postulated a curvilinear relationship for plasma concentration and clinical response, analogous to the response to nortriptyline. In a subsequent report on chronic schizophrenics with a history of refractiveness to drug treatment, the same group *(108)* proposed an approximate therapeutic range of 20–50 ng/mL. They also suggested that patients who failed to respond to concentrations as high as 50 ng/mL were unlikely to benefit from additional increases in dosages. Several of the patients in their study were found to be noncompliant, which illustrates a benefit of plasma drug measurements that does not depend on establishment of a therapeutic range. In a study of hospital inpatients, Swigar et al.,[2] in collaboration with our laboratory, found that most patients with a good therapeutic response had haloperidol concentrations less than 20 ng/mL, and that a value below 10 ng/mL was often adequate. Most reported studies have not been constant-dose in design, which makes difficult a valid definition of the upper limit of a therapeutic range. In a more recent constant-dose study, Smith et al. *(109)*, using gas chromatography, reported a therapeutic window for erythrocyte haloperidol concentrations of about 2.5–5.0 ng/mL.

As with other drugs, interpretation of plasma concentrations may depend on the particular clinical entity under treatment. Morselli et al. *(110)* have reported that children with Tourette's syndrome showed drug-related side effects at haloperidol concentrations over 6 ng/mL, that tics responded to concentrations of 1 to 4 ng/mL, and that manifestations of psychoses showed no correlation with drug concentrations. The clinical significance of its concentration in plasma is not well enough established to recommend routine measurement of haloperidol concentrations in the clinical laboratory, but values below 2–3 ng/mL in nonresponders might favor an increase in dosage or investigation of compliance.

---

[2] Swigar M, Bowers M Jr, Julian W, et al. Haloperidol and prolactin levels and outcome. New Research Abstracts, Amer Psychiatric Assoc, 1982.

Measurement of serum prolactin by radioimmunoassay, already routine in many clinical laboratories for other purposes, has been used as a measure of dopamine-blocking activity and as an indirect reflection of neuroleptic concentration. Some data suggest that the increase in serum prolactin concentration after neuroleptic administration may correlate with plasma drug concentrations and (or) clinical response. The enormous literature on this complex topic has recently been critically reviewed by Meltzer et al. (111) and will not be further discussed here.

Methylphenidate

The sympathomimetic drug methylphenidate (MPH) is widely used to treat children with attention-deficit disorders. Until recently, little was known about the clinical pharmacology of this drug, but several studies now describe its pharmacokinetics (112–114), and some data are now available about plasma concentrations in children treated with it. Our data on the pharmacokinetics of MPH concur with those reported by others (Table 6, Figure 6).

The use and kinetics of MPH have several special aspects that need to be taken onto account in measuring its plasma concentra-

Table 6. **Pharmacokinetics of Methylphenidate in Children**

	Dose	
	0.34 mg/kg	*0.65 mg/kg*
T_{max}, observed (h)[a]	2.50 ± 0.65	1.90 ± 0.82
T_{max}, model (h)[b]	2.22 ± 0.49	1.81 ± 0.49
C_{max}, observed (ng/mL)[a]	11.2 ± 2.7	20.2 ± 9.1
k_e (h^{-1})[c]	0.288 ± 0.070	0.268 ± 0.031
$t_{1/2}$ (h)[c]	2.53 ± 0.59	2.61 ± 0.29
k_a (h)[b]	1.83 ± 1.5	2.07 ± 1.0
$t_{1/2a}$ (h)[b]	0.52 ± 0.23	0.38 ± 0.16
t_0 (h)[b]	0.78 ± 0.43	0.56 ± 0.25
$AUC_{0 \to \infty}$ (h × ng/mL)[c]	59.5 ± 13.9	103.7 ± 55.9

T_{max}, time to peak; C_{max}, peak concentration; k_e, elimination rate constant; $t_{1/2}$, elimination half-life ($0.693/k_e$); k_a, absorption rate constant; $t_{1/2a}$, absorption half-life ($0.693/k_a$); t_0, lag time for absorption; $AUC_{0 \to \infty}$, area under curve from $t = 0$ to ∞.
[a] Based on 14 studies at a dose of 0.34 mg/kg and five studies at a dose of 0.65 mg/kg.
[b] Based on seven studies (low dose) and three studies (high dose).
[c] Based on eight studies (low dose) and four studies (high dose) in whom sufficient samples were obtained to define these values.
Adapted from Shaywitz et al. (114).

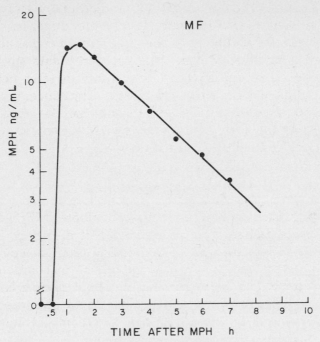

Fig. 6. Time course of plasma MPH concentration in a 10-year-old boy after a dose of 0.34 mg/kg

From Shaywitz et al. *(114)*, used with permission (copyright 1982, American Academy of Pediatrics)

tions. Traditionally, therapeutic monitoring of drugs involves monitoring steady-state trough concentrations in plasma. Less commonly, peak concentrations are sought. However, the usual manner of administration of MPH, as a single morning dose, sometimes repeated once, precludes achievement of a steady state. The $t_{1/2}$ of MPH being about 2 h, it is undetectable in the plasma well before the time of the next morning dose. Unlike many of the other compounds discussed, MPH does not appear to have important active metabolites in humans *(115)*; hydrolysis to ritalinic acid, which is inactive, is its major metabolic pathway. Moreover, MPH does not show interindividual differences in metabolism to the same extent as drugs dependent on microsomal oxidases for elimination. There are, however, considerable interindividual differences in "peak" plasma concentrations and "areas under curve" achieved on the same dose—perhaps in part due

337

to variations in bioavailability or, as has been suggested *(112)*, differences in volume of distribution.

After a lag phase of about 30 min, MPH is rapidly but variably absorbed and reaches its peak plasma concentration in about 1–2 h. Clinical studies therefore have had to rely on estimation of peak concentrations, usually derived from samples obtained 1 or 2 h after the dose. We have found that 2-h concentrations are reasonably reproducible, although Gaultieri et al. *(113)* comment on their variability. Peak concentrations after the usual therapeutic doses (0.3–0.6 mg/kg of body weight) generally range from about 5 to 20 ng/mL. These low concentrations have been measured by gas chromatography with nitrogen detection *(116)* and gas chromatography with mass spectrometry *(117)*. In general, these chromatographic procedures are very laborious. Increases in concentrations of serum growth hormone and decreases in prolactin coincide with increases in MPH *(114)*.

Some data relating MPH plasma concentrations to clinical effect have been published. Estimates of peak concentrations are bound to be less consistent than measurements at trough, but this appears to be the only practical option with MPH. Gaultieri at al. *(113)* found no differences in mean 1-h plasma concentrations between responders and nonresponders. Winsberg et al. *(118)* reported that MPH plasma concentrations correlated with improvement in behavior, but not in cognitive function; however, they noted that dosage correlated equally well with clinical improvement. Shaywitz et al. *(114)* found a correlation between peak plasma concentrations and response, as measured by the Connors Abbreviated Parent Teachers Rating Scale and by some measures of performance. Two of the three children who failed to respond showed barely detectable concentrations, and the third had only 6.6 ng/mL after a relatively large dose (0.68 ng/mL). Clinical monitoring of MPH would be inappropriate, given the present limited and preliminary data. However, a 2-h plasma concentration of less than 7 ng/mL might suggest that an increased dosage could be beneficial.

Conclusions

Data correlating plasma concentrations of psychotherapeutic drugs with clinical response are provocative and encouraging, albeit still inconclusive. Exact therapeutic ranges, if such really do exist, are less-well defined. Methodology for the accurate measurement of many psychotherapeutic agents exists, although in most instances it is too cumbersome and (or) expensive for large-scale clinical use. Criteria for optimal ordering and utilization of reported concentrations for psychotherapeutic drugs are still not established, nor is "routine" monitoring of all patients justified. The complexity of the assays probably has made us more critical in this regard than we are with more-simply performed laboratory tests. However, monitoring will probably benefit selected patients, especially patients who fail to respond to customary doses of usually successful therapies.

Considering the biological heterogeneity of various mental disorders treated with the same drugs, and differences in the severity of their manifestations among individuals, it may be unrealistic to postulate the existence of precisely defined, generally applicable, therapeutic ranges. Nonetheless, even if less emphasis is placed on exactly defined therapeutic ranges, useful clinical applications of psychotherapeutic drug measurements are still apparent, e.g., for evaluation of compliance—noncompliance being estimated in 20% or more of patients receiving antipsychotics and antidepressants (119, 120). The plasma concentrations at which individual patients respond might also be interpreted as customized therapeutic ranges: should a patient relapse or become toxic, a new measurement might help to determine whether plasma concentrations have changed (due to changes in compliance or kinetics), or if the nature or severity of the disease process has altered.

The clinical laboratory that plans to play a role in monitoring psychoactive drugs would probably do best to equip itself with versatile instrumentation and expertise, so as to cope with the large and apparently ever-changing variety of drugs. As analytical methodology becomes more efficient and economical, and perhaps as the biological basis for the classification of mental illness and selection of therapies is better understood, the indications for therapeutic drug monitoring of psychotherapeutic drugs will be better defined, as will its benefits.

Supported in part by National Institute of Mental Health grant 1 P50 MH30929 through the Yale Mental Health Clinical Research Center, New Haven, CT.

339

References

1. Maas JW. Biogenic amines and depression: Biochemical and pharmacological separation of two types of depression. *Arch Gen Psychiatry* **32**, 1357–1361 (1965).

2. Maas JW, Fawcett JA, Dekirmenjian H. Catecholamine metabolism, depressive illness, and drug response. *Arch Gen Psychiatry* **26**, 252–262 (1972).

3. Schildkraut JJ, Orsulak PJ, Schatzberg AF, et al. Toward a biochemical classification of depressive disorders I. Differences in urinary MHPG and other catecholamine metabolites in clinically defined subtypes of depression. *Arch Gen Psychiatry* **35**, 1427–1433 (1978).

4. Schatzberg AF, Rosenbaum AH, Orsulak PJ, et al. Toward a biochemical classification of depressive disorders III. Pretreatment urinary MHPG levels as predictors of response to treatment with maprotiline. *Psychopharmacology* **75**, 34–38 (1981).

5. Schatzberg AF, Orsulak PJ, Rosenbaum AH, et al. Toward a biochemical classification of depressive disorders IV. Pretreatment urinary MHPG levels as predictors of antidepressant response to imipramine. *Commun Psychopharmacol* **4**, 441–445 (1980–1981).

6. Carroll BJ, Feinberg M, Greden JF, et al. A specific laboratory test for the diagnosis of melancholia. *Arch Gen Psychiatry* **35**, 15–22 (1981).

7. Carroll BJ. The dexamethasone suppression test for depression. This volume, pp 69–84.

8. Prange AJ, Wilson IC, Breese GR, Lipton MA. Hormonal alteration of imipramine response: A review. In *Hormones, Behavior and Psychopathology*, EG Sachar, Ed., Raven Press, New York, NY, 1976, pp 41–67.

9. Prange AJ. The role of the thyroid axis in affective disorders. This volume, pp 85–99.

10. Baldessarini R. Status of psychotropic drug blood level assays and other biochemical measurements in clinical practice. *Am J Psychiatry* **136**, 1177–1180 (1979).

11. Hollister LE. Tricyclic antidepressants. *N Engl J Med* **299**, 1106–1109, 1168–1172 (1978).

12. Glassman AH, Perel JM. Tricyclic blood levels and clinical outcome: A review of the art. In *Psychopharmacology: A Generation of Progress*, MA Lipton, A Demascio, KF Killam, Eds., Raven Press, New York, NY, 1978, pp 917–922.

13. Risch SC, Hvey LY, Janowsky DS. Plasma levels of tricyclic antidepressants and clinical efficacy: Review of the literature. *J Clin Psychiatry* **40**, 4–16, 58–69 (1979).

14. Orsulak PJ, Schildkraut JJ. Guidelines for therapeutic monitoring of tricyclic antidepressant plasma levels. *Ther Drug Monit* **1**, 199–208 (1979).

15. Jatlow P. Therapeutic monitoring of tricyclic antidepressants from the perspective of the clinical laboratory. *Arch Pathol Lab Med* **104**, 341–344 (1980).

16. Scroggins BA, Maguire KP, Norman TR, et al. Measurement of tricyclic antidepressants. Part I. A review of methodology. Part II. Applications of methodology. *Clin Chem* **26**, 5–17, 805–815 (1980).

17. Gram LF, Pedersen OL, Kristenson LB. Drug level monitoring in psychopharmacology: Usefulness and clinical problems with special reference to tricyclic antidepressants. *Ther Drug Monit* **4**, 17–25 (1982).

18. Spector S, Spector NL, Almeida MP. Radioimmunoassay for desmethylimipramine. *Psychopharmacol Commun* **1**, 421–429 (1975).

19. Aherne GW, Piall EM, Marks V. The radioimmunoassay of tricyclic antidepressants. *Br J Clin Pharmacol* **3**, 561–565 (1976).

20. Robinson JD, Risby D, Reily G, Aherne GW. A radioimmunoassay for the determination of combined amitriptyline and nortriptyline concentrations in microliter samples of plasma. *J Pharmacol Exp Ther* **205**, 499–502 (1978).

21. Mould GP, Stout G, Aherne GW, Marks V. Radioimmunoassay of amitriptyline and nortriptyline in body fluids. *Ann Clin Biochem* **15**, 221–252 (1978).

22. Aherne GW, Marks V, Mould G, Stout G. Radioimmunoassay for nortriptyline and amitriptyline. *Lancet* **i**, 1215 (1977).

23. Robinson JD, Braithwaite RA, Dawling S. Measurement of plasma nortriptyline concentrations: Radioimmunoassay and gas chromatography compared. *Clin Chem* **24**, 2023–2025 (1978).

24. Midha KK, Loo JCK, Charette C, et al. Monitoring of therapeutic concentrations of psychotropic drugs in plasma by radioimmunoassays. *J Anal Toxicol* **2**, 185–192 (1978).

25. Brunswick DJ, Needelman B, Mendels J. Specific radioimmunoassay of amitriptyline and nortriptyline. *Br J Clin Pharmacol* **7**, 343–348 (1979).

26. Brunswick DJ, Needelman B, Mendels J. Radioimmunoassay of imipramine and desipramine. *Life Sci* **27**, 137–146 (1978).

27. Biggs JT, Holland WH, Chang SS, et al. The electron beam ionization mass fragmentographic analysis of tricyclic antidepressants in plasma. *J Pharm Sci* **65**, 261–268 (1976).

28. Claeys M, Muscettola G, Markey SP. Simultaneous measurement of imipramine and desipramine by selected ion recording with deuterated internal standards. *Biomed Mass Spectrom* **3**, 110–116 (1976).

341

29. Wilson JM, Williamson LJ, Raisys VA. Simultaneous measurement of secondary and tertiary tricyclic antidepressants by GC/MS chemical ionization mass fragmentography. *Clin Chem* **23**, 1012–1017 (1977).

30. Garland WA. Quantitative determination of amitriptyline and its principal metabolite, nortriptyline, by GLC-chemical ionization mass spectrometry. *J Pharm Sci* **66**, 77–81 (1977).

31. Garland WA, Mullino RR, Min BW, et al. A method for the determination of amitriptyline and its metabolites nortriptyline, 10-hydroxyamitriptyline and 10-hydroxynortriptyline in human plasma using stable isotope dilution and gas chromatography–chemical ionization mass spectrometry (GC-CIMS). *Clin Pharmacol Ther* **25**, 844–856 (1979).

32. Bailey D, Jatlow P. Gas chromatographic measurement of therapeutic concentrations of amitriptyline and nortriptyline with use of a nitrogen detector. *Clin Chem* **22**, 777–781 (1976).

33. Bailey D, Jatlow P. Gas chromatographic analysis for therapeutic concentrations of imipramine and desipramine with use of a nitrogen detector. *Clin Chem* **22**, 1697–1701 (1976).

34. Cooper TB, Allen D, Simpson GM. A sensitive method for the determination of amitriptyline and nortriptyline in human plasma. *Psychopharmacol Commun* **2**, 105 (1976).

35. Hucker HB, Stauffer SC. Rapid sensitive gas–liquid chromatographic method for the determination of amitriptyline and nortriptyline in plasma using a nitrogen-sensitive detector. *J Chromatogr* **138**, 437–442 (1977).

36. Wallace JE, Hamilton HE, Goggin LK, et al. Determination of amitriptyline at nanogram levels by electron capture gas-liquid chromatography. *Anal Chem* **47**, 1516–1519 (1975).

37. Proelss HF, Lohmann HJ, Miles DG. High performance liquid chromatographic simultaneous determination of commonly used antidepressants. *Clin Chem* **24**, 1948–1953 (1978).

38. Kraak JC, Bijster P. Determination of amitriptyline and some of its metabolites in blood by high pressure liquid chromatography. *J Chromatogr* **143**, 499–512 (1977).

39. Vandemark FL, Adams RF, Schmidt GJ. Liquid chromatographic procedure for tricyclic drugs and their metabolites in plasma. *Clin Chem* **24**, 87–91 (1978).

40. Mellstrom B, Braithwaite R. Ion-pair liquid chromatography of amitriptyline and metabolites in plasma. *J Chromatogr* **157**, 379–385 (1978).

41. Bock JL, Biller E, Gray S, Jatlow P. Steady-state plasma concentra-

tion of *cis* and *trans*-10-OH metabolites of amitriptyline. *Clin Pharmacol Ther* **31**, 609–616 (1982).

42. Bock J, Gray S, Nelson CN, Jatlow P. Desipramine hydroxylation: Variability and effect of antipsychotic drugs. *Clin Pharmacol Ther* **33**, 322–328 (1983).

43. Åsberg M, Cronholm B, Sjokvist F. Relationship between plasma levels and therapeutic effect of nortriptyline. *Br Med J* **iii**, 331–334 (1971).

44. Ziegler VE, Clayton PJ, Taylor JR, et al. Nortriptyline plasma levels and therapeutic response. *Clin Pharmacol Ther* **20**, 458–463 (1976).

45. Ziegler VE, Co BT, Taylor JR, et al. Amitriptyline blood levels and clinical response. *Clin Pharmacol Ther* **19**, 795–801 (1976).

46. Kupfer DJ, Hanin I, Spiker DG, et al. Amitriptyline plasma levels and clinical response in primary depression. *Clin Pharmacol Ther* **22**, 904–911 (1977).

47. Glassman AH, Perel JM, Shostak M, et al. Clinical implications of imipramine plasma levels for depressive illness. *Arch Gen Psychiatry* **34**, 197–204 (1977).

48. Gram LF, Reisby N, Ibsen I. Plasma levels and antidepressive effects of imipramine. *Clin Pharmacol Ther* **19**, 318–324 (1976).

49. Coppen A, Ghose K, Montgomery SA, et al. Amitriptyline plasma concentrations and clinical effect, a World Health Organisation collaborative study. *Lancet* **i**, 63–66 (1978).

50. Robinson DS, Cooper TB, Ravaris CL, et al. Plasma tricyclic drug levels in amitriptyline-treated depressed patients. *Psychopharmacology* **63**, 223–231 (1979).

51. Simpson GM, White KL, Boyd JL, et al. Relationship between plasma antidepressant levels and clinical outcome for in-patients receiving imipramine. *Am J Psychiatry* **139**, 358–360 (1982).

52. Nelson JC, Jatlow P, Quinlan DM, Bowers MB. Desipramine plasma concentrations and antidepressant response. *Arch Gen Psychiatry* **39**, 1419–1422 (1982).

53. Nelson JC, Jatlow PI, Bock J, et al. Serious adverse reactions during desipramine treatment. Relationship to drug plasma concentrations, antipsychotic treatment and patient characteristics. *Arch Gen Psychiatry* **39**, 1055–1061 (1982).

54. Friedel RO, Veith RC, Bloom V, et al. Desipramine plasma levels and clinical response in depressed outpatients. *Commun Psychopharmacol* **3**, 81–87 (1979).

55. Spiker DG, Weiss AN, Chang SS, et al. Tricyclic antidepressant overdose: Clinical presentation and plasma levels. *Clin Pharmacol Ther* **18**, 539–546 (1976).

343

56. Petit JM, Spiker DG, Ruwitch JF. Tricyclic antidepressant plasma levels and adverse effects after overdose. *Clin Pharmacol Ther* **21**, 47–50 (1977).
57. Åsberg M, Cronholm B, Sjoqvist F, et al. Correlation of subjective side effects with plasma concentrations of nortriptyline. *Br Med J* **iv**, 18–21 (1970).
58. Braithwaite RA, Goulding R, Theano G, et al. Plasma concentrations of amitriptyline and clinical response. *Lancet* **i**, 1297–1300 (1972).
59. Preskorn SH, Simpson S. Tricyclic-antidepressant-induced delirium and plasma concentration. *Am J Psychiatry* **139**, 822–823 (1982).
60. Veith RC, Friedel RO, Bloom V, et al. Electrocardiogram changes and plasma desipramine levels during treatment of depression. *Clin Pharmacol Ther* **27**, 796–802 (1980).
61. Rudorfer MV, Young RC. Anticholinergic effects and plasma desipramine levels. *Clin Pharmacol Ther* **27**, 703–706 (1980).
62. Glassman AH, Bigger JT Jr, Giardina EV, et al. Clinical characteristics of imipramine-induced orthostatic hypotension. *Lancet* **i**, 468–472 (1979).
63. Hollister LE. Monitoring of tricyclic antidepressant plasma concentrations. *J Am Med Assoc* **241**, 2530–2533 (1979).
64. Hollister LE, Pfefferbaum A, Davis KL. Monitoring nortriptyline plasma concentrations. *Am J Psychiatry* **137**, 485–486 (1980).
65. Cooper TB, Simpson GM. Prediction of individual dosage of nortriptyline. *Am J Psychiatry* **135**, 333–335 (1978).
66. Brunswick DJ, Amsterdam JD, Mendels J, et al. Prediction of steady-state imipramine and desmethylimipramine plasma concentrations from single-dose data. *Clin Pharmacol Ther* **25**, 605–610 (1979).
67. Potter WZ, Zavadil AP III, Kopin LJ, et al. Single-dose kinetics predict steady-state concentrations of imipramine and desipramine. *Arch Gen Psychiatry* **37**, 314–320 (1980).
68. Borga O, Azarnoff DL, Forshell GP. Plasma protein binding of tricyclic antidepressants in man. *Biochem Pharmacol* **18**, 2135–2143 (1969).
69. Glassman AH, Hurwic J, Perel JM. Plasma binding of imipramine and clinical outcome. *Am J Psychiatry* **130**, 1367–1369 (1973).
70. Alexanderson B, Borga O. Interindividual differences in plasma protein binding of nortriptyline in man—a twin study. *Eur J Clin Pharmacol* **4**, 196–200 (1972).
71. Potter WZ, Muscettola G, Goodwin FK. Binding of imipramine to plasma protein and to brain tissue: Relationship to CSF tricyclic levels in man. *Psychopharmacology* **63**, 187–192 (1979).

72. Bertilsson L, Braithwaite R, Tybering G, et al. Plasma protein binding of demethylchlorimipramine studied with various techniques. *Clin Pharmacol Ther* **26**, 265–271 (1979).
73. Piafsky KM, Borga O. Plasma protein binding of basic drugs. II. Importance of α_1-acid glycoprotein for individual variation. *Clin Pharmacol Ther* **22**, 545–549 (1977).
74. Rutledge PA, Shand DG, Barchowsky A. Relationship between α_1-acid glycoprotein and lidocaine disposition in myocardial infarction. *Clin Pharmacol Ther* **30**, 154–157 (1981).
75. Borga O, Piafsky KM, Nilsen OG. Plasma protein binding of basic drugs. I. Selective displacement from α_1-acid-glycoprotein by tris-(2-butoxyethyl) phosphate. *Clin Pharmacol Ther* **22**, 539–544 (1977).
76. Brunswick DJ, Mendels J. Reduced levels of tricyclic antidepressants in plasma from Vacutainers. *Commun Psychopharmacol* **1**, 131–134 (1977).
77. Perel JM, Stiller RC, Lin FC, et al. Effect of specimen collection in the analysis of haloperidol, a neuroleptic drug. *Clin Chem* **27**, 1102 (1981). Abstract.
78. Javaid JI, Perel JM, Davis JM. Inhibition of biogenic amines uptake by imipramine, desipramine, 2 OH-imipramine and 2 OH-desipramine in rat brain. *Life Sci* **24**, 21–28 (1979).
79. Potter WZ, Calil HM, Manian AA, et al. Hydroxylated metabolites of tricyclic antidepressants: Preclinical assessment of activity. *Biol Psychiatry* **14**, 601–613 (1979).
80. Bertilsson L, Mellstrom B, Sjoqvist F. Pronounced inhibition of noradrenaline uptake by 10-hydroxy-metabolites of nortriptyline. *Life Sci* **25**, 1285–1292 (1979).
81. Ziegler VE, Fuller TA, Biggs JT. Nortriptyline and 10-hydroxynortriptyline plasma concentrations. *J Pharm Pharmacol* **28**, 849–850 (1976).
82. Bertilsson L, Alexanderson B. Sterospecific hydroxylation of nortriptyline in man in relation to interindividual differences in its steady-state plasma level. *Eur J Clin Pharmacol* **4**, 201–205 (1972).
83. Mellstrom B, Bertilsson L, Sawe J, et al. E- and Z-10 hydroxylation of nortriptyline: Relationship to polymorphic debrisoquine hydroxylation. *Clin Pharmacol Ther* **30**, 189–193 (1981).
84. Potter WZ, Calil HM, Sutfin TA, et al. Active metabolites of imipramine and desipramine in man. *Clin Pharmacol Ther* **31**, 393–401 (1982).
85. Nelson JC, Bock J, Jatlow P. The clinical implications of 2-hydroxydesipramine in plasma. *Clin Pharmacol Ther* **33**, 183–189 (1983).
86. Nelson CN, Jatlow P. Neuroleptic effect on desipramine steady state concentrations. *Am J Psychiatry* **137**, 1232–1234 (1980).

87. Linnoila M, George L, Guthrie S. Interaction between antidepressants and perphenazine in psychiatric in-patients. *Am J Psychiatry* **130**, 1329–1331 (1982).

88. Gram LF, Overo KF. Drug interaction: Inhibitory effect of neuroleptics on metabolism of tricyclic antidepressants in man. *Br Med J* **i**, 463–465 (1972).

89. Gram LF, Overo KF, Kirk L. Influence of neuroleptics and benzodiazepines on metabolism of tricyclic antidepressants in man. *Am J Psychiatry* **131**, 863–866 (1974).

90. Gram LF. Effects of perphenazine on imipramine metabolism in man. *Psychopharmacol Commun* **1**, 165–175 (1975).

91. Cooper TB. Plasma level monitoring of antipsychotic drugs. *Clin Pharmacokinet* **3**, 14–38 (1978).

92. Forsman A, Larsson M. Metabolism of haloperidol. *Curr Ther Res* **24**, 567–568 (1978).

93. Mackay ANP, Healey AP, Baxter J. The relationship of plasma chlorpromazine to its 7-hydroxy and sulfoxide metabolites in a large population of chronic schizophrenics. *Br J Clin Pharmacol* **1**, 425–430 (1974).

94. Creese I, Snyder SH. A simple and sensitive radioreceptor assay for antischizophrenic drugs in blood. *Nature* **270**, 180–182 (1977).

95. Creese I, Burt DR, Snyder SH. Dopamine receptor binding predicts clinical and pharmacological potencies of antischizophrenic drugs. *Science* **192**, 481–483 (1976).

96. Calil HM, Avery DH, Hollister HE, et al. Serum levels on neuroleptics measured by dopamine radioreceptor assay and some clinical observations. *Psychiatry Res* **1**, 39–44 (1979).

97. Tune LE, Creese I, Depaulo JR, et al. Clinical state and serum neuroleptic levels measured by radioreceptor assay in schizophrenia. *Am J Psychiatry* **137**, 187–190 (1980).

98. Rubin RT, Forsman A, Heykarts J, et al. Serum haloperidol determinations in psychiatric patients. *Arch Gen Psychiatry* **37**, 1069–1074 (1980).

99. Forsman A, Martensson E, Myberg G, Ohman R. A gas-chromatographic method for determining haloperidol. *Naunyn-Schmiedebergs Arch Pharmacol* **286**, 113–124 (1974).

100. Bianchetti G, Morselli PL. Rapid and sensitive method for determination of haloperidol in human samples using nitrogen–phosphorus selective detection. *J Chromatogr* **153**, 202–209 (1978).

101. Jatlow PI, Miller R, Swigar M. Measurement of haloperidol in human plasma using reversed-phase high performance liquid chromatography. *J Chromatogr* **227**, 233–238 (1982).

102. Hornbeck CL, Griffiths JC, Neborsky RJ, Faulkner MA. A gas chro-

matographic mass spectrometric chemical ionization assay for haloperidol with selected ion monitoring. *Biomed Mass Spectrom* **6**, 427–430 (1979).

103. Rivera-Calimlin L, Kerzner B, Karch FE. Effect of lithium on plasma chlorpromazine levels. *Clin Pharmacol Ther* **23**, 452–455 (1978).
104. Rivera-Calimlin L, Nasrallah HA, Straus J, Lasagna L. Clinical response and plasma levels: Effect of dose, dosage schedules and drug interations on plasma chlorpromazine levels. *Am J Psychiatry* **133**, 646 (1976).
105. Rivera-Calimlin L. Problems in therapeutic blood monitoring of chlorpromazine. *Ther Drug Monit* **4**, 41–49 (1982).
106. Itoh H, Hagi G, Ohtsuka N, et al. Serum level of haloperidol and its clinical significance. *Prog Neuro-Psychopharmacol* **4**, 171–183 (1980).
107. Magliozzi JR, Hollister LE, Arnold KV, et al. Relationship of serum haloperidol levels to clinical response in schizophrenic patients. *Am J Psychiatry* **138**, 365–367 (1981).
108. Hollister LE, Kim DY. Intensive treatment with haloperidol of treatment-resistant chronic schizophrenic patients. *Am J Psychiatry* **139**, 1466–1468 (1982).
109. Smith RC, Vroulis G, Shuartsburg RA, et al. RBC and plasma levels of haloperidol and clinical response in schizophrenia. *Am J Psychiatry* **139**, 1054–1056 (1982).
110. Morselli PL, Zarifian E, Cuche H, et al. Haloperidol plasma levels monitoring in psychiatric patients. *Adv Biochem Psychopharmacol* **24**, 529–536 (1980).
111. Meltzer HY, Busch DA, Pang US. Effects of neuroleptics on serum prolactin levels in relationship to clinical response and neuroleptic blood levels. In *Clinical Pharmacology in Psychiatry*, E Usdin, Ed., Elsevier, New York, NY, 1981, pp 251–268.
112. Hungund BL, Perel JM, Hurwic MJ, et al. Pharmacokinetics of methylphenidate in hyperkinetic children. *Br J Clin Pharmacol* **8**, 571–576 (1979).
113. Gualtieri CT, Wargin W, Kanoy R, et al. Clinical studies of methylphenidate serum levels in children and adults. *J Am Acad Child Psychiatry* **21**, 19–26 (1982).
114. Shaywitz S, Hunt R, Jatlow P, et al. Psychopharmacology of attention deficit disorder: Pharmacokinetic, neuroendocrine and behavioral measures following acute and chronic treatment with methylphenidate. *Pediatrics* **69**, 688–694 (1982).
115. Faraj BA, Israili ZH, Perel JM, et al. Metabolism and disposition of methylphenidate-^{14}C: Studies in man and animals. *J Pharmacol Exp Ther* **191**, 535–547 (1974).
116. Hungund BL, Hanna M, Winsberg BG. A sensitive gas chromato-

graphic method for the determination of methylphenidate (ritalinic acid) in human plasma using nitrogen–phosphorus detector. *Commun Psychopharmacol* **2**, 203–208 (1978).

117. Gal J, Hodshon BJ, Pintauro C, et al. Pharmacokinetics of methylphenidate in the rat using single-ion monitoring GLC-mass spectrometry. *J Pharm Sci* **66**, 866–869 (1977).

118. Winsberg BG, Kupietz SS, Sverg JJ, et al. Methylphenidate oral dose plasma concentrations and behavioral response in children. *Psychopharmacology* **76**, 329–332 (1982).

119. Hollister LE. Plasma concentrations of tricyclics in clinical practice. *J Clin Psychiatry* **43**, 66–69 (1982).

120. Amdur MA. Medication compliance in outpatient psychotherapy. *Comp Psychiatry* **20**, 339–343 (1979).

Discussion—Session IV

QUESTION: When you speak of an increase or decrease of receptors, are you speaking of receptors to the particular drug used, or of the ability of a nerve to increase or decrease receptivity in general?

DR. MOLINOFF: In the experiments that I showed you with respect to the β-adrenergic receptor, we measured both kinds of properties. The experimental protocol is to take a homogenate of the tissue and measure the density of receptors in that tissue by using various concentrations of some radioactive ligand. We measure the density of binding sites by Scatchard analysis. In other aliquots of the same tissue homogenate we measure catecholamine-sensitive cyclase activity as a measure of the function of that particular receptor-mediated process. There is, in general, a very good agreement between changes in the density of receptors and changes in the maximum amount of catecholamine-stimulated adenylate cyclase activity. It's much harder to do these studies with dopamine receptors because, although we have a good biochemical measure for the D-1 receptor, many of the interesting phenomena we want to study apparently involve D-2 receptors, for which we don't have easily quantifiable biochemical responses.

Q: Is there any evidence that prolactin may be a neurotransmitter or a neuroregulator in the dopamine system?

DR. CREESE: That's actively under study by several groups. Treatment with neuroleptics might "up-regulate" dopamine receptors through a prolactin-mediated mechanism because, as some groups have shown, if you remove the pituitary, which removes the potential for the neuroleptics to increase prolactin, you can block the supersensitivity that develops after current treatment. Other groups have not replicated those studies, however. There's also interest in prolactin as a neuropeptide of the type that Dr. Karten was talking about.

Q: If an increase in the number of a certain subtype of dopamine receptor turns out to be significant in schizophrenia, do you think it would be possible to develop a selective neurotoxin

349

to abate some of these receptors rather than simply blocking them?

DR. CREESE: At first thought, the answer would be no, because the brain is a very homeostatic organ: if you start removing receptors, the brain will start producing them faster to replace them. Just recently, studies of receptor turnover are becoming feasible and we do know that receptor turnover is sensitive to pharmacological manipulation, changes with age, and so forth. Perhaps with the advent of receptor solubilization and purification, however, we will presumably produce antibodies to receptors, and these antibodies might well become a useful pharmacological agent. One could imagine a constant infusion of antibodies to that subtype of receptor to keep the receptors under control.

Q: In light of the evidence that behavior may be influenced at the transmitter/receptor level, what do you feel is the value of plasma, urine, or spinal fluid measurements of bioactive compounds and metabolites in behavioral studies? Should measurement in spinal fluid offer a particular advantage over other kinds of specimens?

DR. KARTEN: The person who asked this question has targeted one of the most difficult aspects of trying to correlate what's going on in the central nervous system with what is happening at the levels of the materials we measure. From many points of view, we are unable to measure the brain without the structural procedures. It's like looking under the lamp post for your keys—not because that's where you lost them, but because that's where you have the most light.

The issue of measuring spinal fluid, however, has become a more urgent matter, particularly in relation to peptides and peptide function. Again, the difficulty is that the risk to the patient when you sample spinal fluid is quite different from that for venipuncture. But components such as endorphins and various other peptides that we can measure in spinal fluid may have a very different and independent relationship from what we measure in blood. Also, what we measure in spinal fluid is more directly related to ongoing activity in the nervous system. The work on sleep peptides, for instance, has been very pertinent in this regard: none of these show up in the circulation at all, whereas some putative substances have been detected in CSF. I think we're going to see a tremendous amount of interest in the CSF over the next couple of years. Increasingly, we no longer think of the spinal fluid as merely some sort of a bathing medium that helps act as a shock absorber, but rather as an active transport mechanism. Just as we have come to think of axonal transport as a means of getting information from one neuron to the next or, e.g., that hormones are a means of getting substances in the vascular system from one area to the next, we are also increasingly starting to think of the CSF as a possible mechanism for carrying a peptide released from one area to the brain to be tracked globally over all areas of the brain. There are now several anatomically discrete areas of the brain that are likely candidates for major release sites for peptides into the CSF.

DR. MOLINOFF: Looking in the sewers of Moscow to find out what Andropov is thinking is probably a good analogy to measuring what comes out of the urine to find out what the affected tubercule is doing. On the other hand, if one is considering what may be genetically driven disorders, perhaps it's reasonable to think that a change in norepinephrine turnover or in dopamine release or in the density or properties of a given kind of receptor might be a general phenomenon, and one that would be expressed either in the periphery or the central nervous system. I don't think that measuring what comes out in the urine is going to tell you what's going on in a certain nucleus in the brain, but it may tell you what process is taking place, and a given process may be abnormal throughout the entire organism.

Q: Do some of the schizophrenic patients with normal numbers of receptors have tardive dyskinesia? The reverse might be, did patients with large numbers of receptors have tardive dyskinesia?

DR. CREESE: In the study that was done in England, unfortunately the clinical records weren't really satisfactory in determining whether the patients had tardive dyskinesia or not. That group of symptoms has to have a very standardized test for quantifying results in a research project. It wasn't done in that study. Other studies in England have looked at tardive dyskinesia and didn't find a relationship between the severity of tardive dyskinesia and the increase in D-2 receptors. That argues toward the increase in receptors being related to the schizophrenia and not to the drug-induced phenomena.

Q: When you stop neuroleptic drugs, tardive dyskinesia remains for a number of years, but the prolactin increase goes away very rapidly and dopamine is again able to inhibit prolactin. Therefore, are the receptors in the pituitary different from those in the brain?

DR. CREESE: Some studies in the rat suggest that the regulation of those receptors is different; this is supported by the data I showed indicating that some of the D-2 receptors in the brain may not be sensitive to guanine nucleotides. Dr. Molinoff's data also showed somewhat different pharmacological specificities; there might indeed be a difference between the majority of the receptors in the pituitary and those in the brain, even though they share a very general characteristic of being very sensitive to butyrophenones and ergot agonists.

Q: In the studies you discussed, in which patients were not receiving drugs for a month before death, did clinical signs and symptoms change in that last month?

DR. CREESE: The clinical records were not good enough to tell. The brains were actually collected in 1976 and the assays were all run in 1977. It isn't possible to go back now to answer those questions. One interesting study coming up involves a ward of schizophrenics who had never been treated with neuroleptic drugs because the psychiatrist didn't believe in the drugs. Those patients are old now and they're dying, and a researcher is collecting their brains; that should produce a very good set of data directly relevant to this question.

Q: Is there any demonstrable change in the affinity of dopamine receptors in schizophrenic patients?

DR. CREESE: No, there is a change in patients being treated with neuroleptic drugs but that seems to be related just to the presence of residual drug in the tissue. When a competitive drug is present, there is an apparent change, but if the neuroleptic is washed out, there is no change in the apparent affinity of the receptors.

Q: Can the concept of the use of a mild agonist to avoid the compensatory increase in receptors help reduce the rebound and supersensitivity to drug side effects?

DR. MOLINOFF: I think that potentially it can. We have a long way to go to understand what partial agonists are and how partial agonists act. However, we know several ways to avoid this rebound. Perhaps the simplest is to taper a drug over a period of days or weeks. Other alternatives are to use a very long-acting drug, which will taper itself during the course of stopping it, or to use a drug that has partial agonist activity. Use of a mild agonist may be a valuable technique.

Q: Could you comment on the recent suggestion that norepinephrine is involved in schizophrenia?

DR. CREESE: I am absolutely certain that not only will norepinephrine be involved in the final behavioral manifestations of schizophrenia, but also just about every other neurotransmitter/ neuromodulator. The question of course is, what is the *major* defect? What we'll probably see in the future is that, using pharmacological techniques, we will start subdividing schizophrenia into a number of different diseases. The clinical data already suggest that it's a mistake to consider schizophrenia as a single disease. The symptoms are similar, but the disease processes are probably different, and we'll probably find a different relative involvement of different neurotransmitters in each of the different forms of schizophrenia.

Q: Did your four alcoholics with the abnormal dexamethasone suppression test (DST) results at three weeks of abstinence have clinical depression or a family history of depression, or were you only measuring the degree of alcohol-induced liver damage?

DR. ROSENBAUM: Two of them met criteria for depression and responded; the other did not. So the results may still have something to do with the alcohol, though I think the test mainly showed that these were not patients with endogenous depression. In a group of alcoholics, about 10% are going to have endogenous depression. Some of them drink to feel better, and I think our studies fit that.

Q: Is there a correlation of the DST results in various depressives with their sleep history just before the test? Perhaps the patients who have abnormal sleep history have abnormal cyclical secretion of corticotropin and, therefore, of cortisol. Could this be related to the timing of the test?

DR. ROSENBAUM: There is one study showing positive correlation with decreased REM latency and DST results. No one has measured cortisol hypersecretion in connection with sleep abnormalities.

COMMENT BY DR. HOWARD L. MASCO: Dr. Jatlow, in covering the subject of neuroleptic monitoring, was obviously discussing blood concentration of neuroleptic drugs. It has been obvious, I think, throughout this entire program that it would be much more desirable to be measuring the pharmacologic effect of drugs, if, indeed, that is possible. Measuring the binding of the neuroleptics to receptor sites is obviously more desirable than measuring blood concentrations.

Another factor that needs to be looked at more closely is the often mentioned serum prolactin, which is a measure of the pharmacologic effect of these drugs. Sacher, a number of years ago, pointed out the increase in serum prolactin; but for one reason or another, he unfortunately reported that a maximum response occurs at low doses, and everybody seems to have accepted that as gospel, perhaps out of ignorance. I have for the past five to seven years routinely measured concentrations of serum prolactin in patients and monitored antipsychotic activity against serum prolactins, and I assure you that maximum response does not occur at low concentrations. I believe you will find that measuring serum prolactin to monitor neuroleptic effectiveness is a very useful clinical tool. In most patients an increase of serum prolactin to 100 μg/L ($\pm$ about 20 μg/L) is therapeutic. This presents a simple way of working without relying on the multiple chemical entities that we find in the antipsychotic area and the multiple metabolites that are possible with these drugs. If you will look at that in just a few patients, you will quickly realize that this is effective and useful.

Dr. Jatlow: There is abundant literature on prolactin and its possible relationship to clinical effects. Its omission was not an oversight; I simply didn't deal with it in the time available. This is a complicated area. Women, for example, differ from men in their prolactin response to neuroleptic drug treatment. We do have preliminary data suggesting that correcting the change in prolactin concentration for the haloperidol concentration gives a better correlation with clinical response.

Index

hypothalamus, 85–86, 231–232, 239, 246, 247, 258–259, 302
hysteroid dysphoria, 41–42, 132, 152

imipramine, 53–54, 86–91, 102–103, 112, 113, 116, 118, 137, 139, 141, 148–150, 180, 182, 183, 185, 186, 188, 209–214, 216, 217, 219, 313, 316–317, 321
immunoassays, 259, 313, 315, 323
incidence of mental disorders, 3–10, 13–14, 20, 23, 27
inpatient care, 5, 13–16, 101, 161, 175–177
iproniazid, 127, 150
isocarboxazid, 127, 137, 141, 146, 150, 159–161

Librium, *see* chlordiazepoxide
life-table probabilities and lithium treatment, 181, 184, 187, 189
limbic system, 72–73, 77, 100, 241, 247
lithium, 43, 56, 72, 106, 150, 157, 161, 170–200, 214, 224–228, 273, 304–306, 311–312, 333
    bromide, 170–171
    carbonate, 29, 38, 77, 172, 174, 178, 197, 224
    mechanism of action, 192–201, 224
    toxicity, 171, 177, 190–192, 198, 226–227, 304–305
loxapine, 209, 210
lymphocytes, β-adrenergic receptors on, 296–297

mania, 30, 33–34, 36–38, 49, 57, 65, 81, 85, 92, 102, 132, 171–174, 176, 178–181, 185, 189–190, 199, 211, 217, 225, 255, 301
manic depression, 29, 31–39, 43, 49, 54, 56, 65, 68, 102, 131, 153, 171, 173, 176–178, 180–183, 185, 187, 189–190, 198–201, 224–225
MAO, *see* monoamine oxidase
maprotiline, 53–54, 185, 188, 208, 211–212, 216, 217, 220
mebanazine, 127, 153

melancholia, 32, 35–37, 39, 69, 71–80, 100, 318; *see also* depression
melanotropin, 259, 265
mental disorders, incidence of, *see* incidence
mental hospitals, 3–4, 11–16, 23–25
meprobamate, 17, 71
metabolism, *see* drug metabolism
metanephrine, 55, 57
3-methoxy-4-hydroxyphenylglycol (MHPG), 31, 34, 43–44, 48–57, 66, 109, 110, 212, 229, 302–304, 306, 310–311
methylphenidate (MPH), 310, 311, 336–338
MHPG, *see* 3-methoxy-4-hydroxyphenylglycol
mianserin, 53, 185, 188, 208, 216–218
migraine headaches, 178, 216
Miltown, *see* meprobamate
monoamine oxidase (MAO), 48, 57, 154–155, 198, 228, 229
monoamine oxidase inhibitors, 29, 41, 71, 76, 80, 106, 125–162, 187, 190, 209, 214, 220, 224, 228–229, 306
mood disorders, *see* affective disorders
MPH, *see* methylphenidate

neuroleptics, 116, 210, 211, 243–245, 247, 250, 252, 256, 267, 271–275, 277–279, 328, 330–331, 333–334, 336, 349, 351–354
neurotic depression, *see* depression
Neurotic/Endogenous Rating Scale, 138, 144
neurotransmitters, 47, 54, 94, 127, 155, 193, 194, 199–201, 231–232, 240–241, 251, 255–257, 271, 273, 276, 294–295, 310, 349, 350, 353
nigrostriatal pathway, 245–247, 249, 256, 266, 270, 272
nomifensine, 208, 215–216
nonendogenous depression, *see* depression
nonhydrazine monoamine oxidase inhibitors, 126–128, 151–153

nonrapid-cyclers, 187, 189–190
noradrenergic, 47–48, 52, 54, 55, 110, 112
norepinephrine, 47–49, 55–57, 94, 107, 114–115, 126, 194, 199, 209, 211, 215, 217, 224, 239, 277, 291, 294–295, 302, 318, 324, 351, 353
normetanephrine, 55, 57
nortriptyline, 53, 105, 109, 114, 116–118, 209, 303, 313–314, 316–321, 325–326, 335

outpatient treatment, 4, 13–15, 20, 23, 71, 147, 162, 174–176, 180, 213–214, 300
oxaprotiline, 208, 212–213

panic disorder, see phobic anxiety
paranoia, 38, 39, 150, 178, 243, 334
parathyrin, 253, 279, 305
pargyline, 127, 128, 153, 157
Parkinsonism, 210, 246, 247, 249–250, 268, 271–273
peptide/transmitters, 232, 351
peroxidase, horseradish, nerve studies with, 232, 235–236
pharmacokinetics, 105, 107–118, 216, 312, 321, 331, 333, 336–338
phenelzine, 126–130, 133, 135–152, 156, 158–162, 229
phenothiazines, 12, 65, 156–157, 176, 178–179, 250, 252–254, 256, 259, 306, 328–330
phenylethylamine (PEA), 41, 125, 128, 154
phenytoin, 71, 328
phobic anxiety, 132–134, 142–144, 151, 219
pituitary, 85–86, 91–94, 100, 246, 249, 253, 254, 258–267, 278, 279, 302, 349, 352; see also hypothalamic-
placebo, response to, and placebo-controlled studies, 87–90, 102, 135–146, 148–153, 155–157, 160, 161, 178–185, 187–190, 209, 212–213, 215, 217–219, 300, 317

platelet MAO inhibition, 130, 158–159, 229
premenstrual depression syndrome, 178, 225
prolactin, 85, 94, 249, 259, 265, 302, 336, 338, 349, 351–352, 354
propranolol, 295, 296, 299
protein binding, 111, 322–324
pseudodementia, 40–41, 78–79
psychiatric
    chemistry, 47–58
    epidemiology, 5–8, 23, 27
    practitioners, 20, 22–23
psychomotor retardation, 38–39, 86–88, 106, 134, 173
psychosis/psychotic, 5, 15, 33, 35, 36, 67, 78, 131–132, 176, 179, 211, 243, 255, 274–276, 301, 335
psychosocial methods of therapy, 12, 23–24
psychotherapy, 3, 6, 9–11, 20–23, 25, 40, 43, 76, 80, 139
Purkinje cells, 295

radioimmunoassay, 70, 300, 301, 313, 331–332, 335, 336
radioligand binding, 243–245, 256–258, 260–279, 292–293, 295, 297
radioreceptor assay, 210, 268, 277–278, 292, 330–331, 333
rapid-cyclers, 43, 157, 174, 187, 189–190, 224, 228
receptor density, 274–275, 292, 295, 297, 349
receptors, 193, 200, 231–233, 236–239, 241, 292, 350–352, 354; see also dopamine receptors, adrenergic receptors
REM sleep, 31, 209, 211, 353
Research Diagnostic Criteria, 56, 74, 155, 156
reserpine, 243, 270, 299

schizoaffective disorder, 35, 37, 39, 40, 49–50, 178, 211

359